INTRODUCTION TO

CLINICAL

HYPNOSIS

THE BASICS AND BEYOND

GARY R. ELKINS

EDITOR

Introduction to Clinical Hypnosis: The Basics and Beyond
Gary R. Elkins, Ph.D., ABPP, ABPH, Editor
©2022 Individual Contributors

Published by:
Mountain Pine Publishing
Waco, TX

ISBN: 979-83560410-0-6

DEDICATION

In recognition of the Society for Clinical and Experimental Hypnosis, the American Society for Clinical Hypnosis, the Society for Psychological Hypnosis (American Psychological Association-Division 30) and the International Society of Hypnosis. The International Society of Hypnosis (ISH) was founded in 1959 paralleling the Society for Clinical and Experimental Hypnosis (SCEH). Each has had a world-wide influence on clinical hypnosis.

CONTENTS

ACKNOWLEDGMENTS

This book would not have been possible without the contributions of the many colleagues with specialized expertise who shared their knowledge for the content of the 21 chapters of this book. Each was invited based upon their areas of clinical teaching, knowledge of clinical hypnosis, research, and dedication to the field. I also want to thank Dr. Cameron Alldredge, Madison Messina and Scarlett Lin Latt for their reading of the chapters and suggested edits that have improved the quality. I also want to express appreciation to Elizabeth Beeton of B10 Mediaworx for her guidance and manuscript preparation. Most importantly, I am so very grateful for the love and support of my lovely wife, Guillerma throughout this process. This book was two years in the making and her support, reading manuscripts, suggestions, and help are things for which I am eternally grateful.

CONTRIBUTORS

Cameron Alldredge, Ph.D.
Post-Doctoral Fellow, Mind-Body Medicine Research Laboratory
Baylor University
Waco, Texas

Mattie Biggs, M.S.C.P.
V.A. Tennessee Valley Health Care System
Nashville, Tennessee

Ciara Christensen, Ph.D.
President, Society for Clinical and Experimental Hypnosis
Private Practice
Milwaukee, Wisconsin

Louis F. Damis, Ph.D., ABPP, FASCH
President-Elect, American Society of Clinical Hypnosis
Diplomate, American Board of Professional Psychology
Fellow, American Academy of Clinical Psychology
Director, Integrative Health Psychology, PA
Oviedo, Florida

Gary Elkins, Ph.D., ABPP, ABPH
Professor, Psychology and Neuroscience
Editor-in-Chief, *International Journal of Clinical and Experimental Hypnosis*
Director, Mind-Body Medicine Research Laboratory
Baylor University
Waco, Texas

Marie-Elisabeth Faymonville, Ph.D., M.D.
Arsène Burny Cancerology Institute, University Hospital of Liège,
and Sensation and Perception Research Group, GIGA Consciousness,
University of Liège, Belgium

Aaron Finley, M.S.C.P.
Research Assistant, Mind-Body Medicine Research Laboratory
Department of Psychology and Neuroscience
Baylor University
Waco, Texas

Olivia Gosseries, Ph.D.
Coma Science Group, GIGA Consciousness,
University of Liège; Centre du Cerveau[2], University Hospital of Liège, and
Sensation and Perception Research Group, GIGA Consciousness, University of
Liège, Belgium

Connor Kelley, M.S.C.P.
Research Assistant, Mind-Body Medicine Research Laboratory
Department of Psychology and Neuroscience
Baylor University
Waco, Texas

Cassie Kendrick, Psy.D.
Waco Psychological Associates
Waco, Texas

Dan Kohen, M.D.
Medical Director, Kohen Therapy Associates
Co-Director, National Pediatric Hypnosis Training Institute
Professor, Departments of Pediatrics and Family Medicine and Community
Health
Director, Developmental- Behavioral Pediatrics
Clinical Director, Developmental-Behavioral Pediatrics Program
Department of Pediatrics
University of Minnesota
Minneapolis, Minnesota

Nolwenn Marie, Ph.D. student
Coma Science Group, GIGA Consciousness, University of Liège,
and Sensation and Perception Research Group,
GIGA Consciousness, University of Liège, Belgium

Catherine McCall, M.D.
Assistant Professor, Psychiatry and Behavioral Sciences
University of Washington
Veterans Affairs Puget Sound Health Care System
Seattle, Washington

Barbara McCann, Ph.D.
Professor of Psychiatry and Behavioral Sciences
Mental Health Counseling and Hypnosis Endowed Chair
University of Washington
UW Medicine, Harborview Medical Center
Seattle, Washington

Don Moss, Ph.D.
Dean, College of Integrative Medicine and Health Sciences
Saybrook University
Oakland, California

Hyeji Na, Psy.D.
Clinical Psychologist
Veterans Administration North Texas Healthcare System
Dallas, Texas

Nicholas Olendzki, Psy.D.
Psychologist, Counseling & Student Development Center
University of Massachusetts – Dartmouth
Dartmouth, Massachusetts

Karen Olness, M.D., FAAP
Professor of Pediatrics, Global Health and Diseases
Case Western Reserve University
Board Certified in Developmental and Behavioral Pediatrics
Inaugural President of the National Pediatric Hypnosis Training Institute,
NPHTI Co-Director of Education (2010-2021), and Past President of the
American Society of Clinical Hypnosis, the Society for Clinical and
Experimental Hypnosis, the American Board of Hypnosis, the International
Society of Hypnosis and the Society for Developmental Behavioral Pediatrics
Cleveland, Ohio

Akira Otani, Ed.D., ABPH
Private Practice
Spectrum Behavioral Health, Arnold, Maryland
Faculty Associate, Johns Hopkins University School of Education
Baltimore, Maryland

David Patterson, Ph.D., ABPP
Professor of Medicine and Psychology
Adjunct Professor of Surgery
University of Washington
Harborview Medical Center Rehabilitation Consult Service
Seattle, Washington

David Reid, Psy.D.
College of Integrative Medicine and Health Sciences
Saybrook University, Oakland, California
Private Practice, Augusta Psychological Associates
Fishersville, Virginia

Joshua Rhodes, M.A.
Department of Psychology and Neuroscience
Baylor University
Waco, Texas

Lauren Simicich, M.S.C.P.
VA Salt Lake City Health Care System
Salt Lake City, Utah

Liz Slonena, Psy.D.
Director, Mindful Hypnosis Counseling & Consulting PLLC
Private Practice
Asheville, North Carolina

Morgan Snyder, M.A.
Department of Psychology and Neuroscience
Baylor University
Waco, Texas

Sam Stork, Psy.D.
Salt Lake City, Utah

Moshe Torem, M.D.
Professor, Department of Psychiatry
Northeast Ohio Medical University
Medical Director, Center for Mind-Body Medicine, Akron General Medical Center
Akron, Ohio

Audrey Vanhaudenhuyse, Ph.D.
Algology Interdisciplinary Center,
University Hospital of Liège, and Sensation
and Perception Research Group, GIGA Consciousness,
University of Liège, Belgium

Michael Vinson
Doctoral Student in Clinical Psychology
Baylor University
Mind-Body Medicine Research Laboratory
Student Representative to APA Division 30 Executive Committee
Washington, D.C.

Eric Willmarth, Ph.D.
Chair, Department of Psychophysiology
College of Integrative Medicine and Health Sciences
Saybrook University
Oakland, California

Ming Hwei Yek, Psy.D.
Assistant Professor in the Department of Psychiatry
Psychiatric Research Institute
University of Arkansas for Medical Sciences
Little Rock, Arkansas

CHAPTER 1
INTRODUCTION:
LEARNING CLINICAL HYPNOSIS

GARY ELKINS

Chapter Learning Objectives

1. Identify key domains of knowledge important in learning clinical hypnosis.

2. Review importance of both knowledge and experiential practice as a life-long learner.

3. Identify how to use this book.

Clinical hypnosis is practiced by a wide range of health care providers: psychologists, physicians, psychotherapists, clinical social workers, marriage and family therapists, mental health counselors, dentists, nurses, speech pathologists, physical therapists, chiropractors, acupuncturists, health coaches, and of course, hypnotherapists. Accordingly, clinical hypnosis has many uses, including: stress management, acute and chronic pain, irritable bowel syndrome, smoking cessation, sleep improvement, reduction of hot flashes among breast cancer survivors and post-menopause women, improving well-being, depression, emotional regulation, sports performance enhancement, management of anxieties in adults and children, increasing mindfulness, weight loss, and as an adjunct to treatment of post-traumatic stress disorder (PTSD). In fact, my companion book, *Handbook of Medical and Psychological Hypnosis* (Elkins, 2017), presents hypnotic inductions and research on over 70 disorders! However, learning clinical hypnosis takes time, knowledge, and development of skills. Each professional should use clinical hypnosis within their own discipline and expertise. Clinical hypnosis is a very powerful tool and learning the basics is essential to becoming a skilled clinical hypnosis practitioner.

My own journey in clinical hypnosis began in 1980. At that time, I was a clinical psychology resident at a major medical center that provided hypnotherapy for certain conditions such as pain management, smoking cessation, and for health conditions. I had the opportunity to observe an amazing demonstration of the power of hypnosis when used with skill and confidence. The case was a young woman who was to undergo a major surgical procedure and there was a desire to minimize the use of general anesthesia and narcotic medications. The patient was evaluated by one of my supervisors and a hypnotic induction was completed pre-surgery in which the patient demonstrated the ability to enter a deeply relaxed state and to respond to hypnotic suggestions. She did not want general anesthesia unless it was necessary. On the day of the surgery, a psychologist trained in clinical hypnosis completed a hypnotic induction and stayed with the patient, continuing positive suggestions for analgesia, comfort, calmness, and feeling well throughout the surgery. The surgery took over an hour and throughout the procedure the patient remained calm and very relaxed. Vital signs remained within normal limits as the surgery proceeded from incision to closure. She did not require any chemical anesthesia. Post-surgery she was alert and conversing with the surgeon and staff. Recovery went smoothly. I have left out a number of details in the interest of confidentiality. However, observing this patient undergo such a surgical procedure using clinical hypnosis and without pain or anxiety led me to several considerations:

1. *I decided I wanted to learn clinical hypnosis!* This experience was surely a demonstration of the most powerful psychological intervention I had (or ever have)

observed. I wanted to know more. I wanted to learn the basics and the applications of clinical hypnosis.

2. I wanted to understand exactly "what hypnosis is" and how it can be used to manage anxiety, control pain, stop smoking, and many other uses.

3. These decisions led me to a career of practice, teaching, and research of clinical hypnosis, that has included serving as Editor-in-Chief of the *International Journal of Clinical and Experimental Hypnosis*.

Hypnosis is generally understood as a state of consciousness which may occur through a hypnotic induction with a hypnotherapist or may occur spontaneously through self-hypnosis. This state of consciousness involves a focus of attention and is characterized by an enhanced capacity for response to therapeutic suggestions (Elkins et al., 2015). The hypnotic state is sometimes referred to as a "trance state", however, it is a state of consciousness that is normally experienced and reflects a capacity or ability to experience hypnosis. Chapters 2 (Drs. Hyeji Na and Elkins) and 3 (Mr. Joshua Rhodes, Dr. Gary Elkins, and Dr. Cameron Alldredge) of this book review the historical foundations and definition of hypnosis and hypnotherapy. This is essential knowledge to understand the historical context of hypnosis, how some misperceptions originated, and to clearly identify the terms "hypnosis," "hypnotic induction," "hypnotherapy," and "hypnotizability" as they relate to research and clinical practice.

Chapters 4 and 5 provide additional foundational knowledge of hypnosis. Theories of clinical hypnosis (Chapter 4 by Dr. Cassie Kendrick, Mr. Christopher Corlett, and Dr. Elkins) largely mirror some theories of psychotherapy but are more specific to the mechanisms of hypnosis. A solid theoretical understanding enhances being able to use hypnosis creatively and predicts applications and outcomes. Chapter 5 by Drs. Vanhaudenhuyse, Marie, Gosseries, and Faymonville, provides an excellent (and very readable!) explanation of the neurophysiology of hypnosis and research. Areas of the brain involved in the experience of hypnosis are identified. Further, brain function in response to specific suggestions (such as relaxation, pain reduction, etc.) are discussed. This may stimulate the reader to consider potential similarities and differences between hypnosis and other states of consciousness involving focused attention such as mindfulness and guided mental imagery.

Chapters 6, 7, 8, and 9 are written by some of the leading experts in clinical hypnosis (and highly sought teachers of clinical hypnosis workshops). A hypnotic induction generally involves a hypnotic induction followed by suggestions for deepening the hypnotic state and therapeutic suggestions before re-alerting. Chapter 6, by Dr. David Reid, provides an understanding of the process and key principles for completing hypnotic inductions. Chapter 7, by Dr. Moshe Torem, explains how to elicit and understand hypnotic phenomena. Response to hypnotic suggestions may involve experienced alterations in sensations, thoughts, or feelings. These alterations are referred to as "hypnotic phenomena" in clinical practice. Chapter 8, by Dr. Eric Willmarth and Mr. Michael Vinson, provides the fundamental knowledge for formulating hypnotic suggestions and therapeutic metaphors in clinical hypnosis. This is complemented by the chapter on *"Deepening and Intensification of the Hypnotic Experience"* by Dr. Barbara McCann (President-Elect of the Society for Clinical and Experimental Hypnosis), which provides guidance and skills in the process of deepening suggestions to enhance the response to hypnotic suggestions.

Chapters 10, 11, 12, and 13 cover the additional "basic" knowledge needed for practice of clinical hypnosis. A frequent use of hypnosis in clinical practice is to foster relaxation, feelings of confidence and well-being. This is addressed in Chapter 10 by Dr. Liz Slonena in which hypnotic induction and suggestions for ego-strengthening are covered. This is followed by an excellent chapter by Dr. Catherine McCall on teaching self-hypnosis. Chapter 12 by Dr. Akira Otani addresses how to manage resistance in hypnotherapy. Resistance refers to unconscious factors that may limit ability to experience response to hypnotic suggestions. Resistance can arise from many factors including some misunderstanding of hypnosis. Therefore, Chapter 13 by Dr. Louis Damis provides the essential knowledge needed for presenting clinical hypnosis to clients and patients, common myths and misconceptions, and conducting informed consent.

Additional knowledge essential to the practice of clinical hypnosis includes treatment planning and ethical principles. Chapter 14 by Dr. Donald Moss and Dr. Eric Willmarth explains how to assess and formulate a treatment plan using clinical hypnosis. Part of the skill in using clinical hypnosis is understanding the nature of the problem for which an individual seeks clinical hypnosis and how to best plan and adapt an overall treatment strategy. In some cases, hypnotherapy or self-hypnosis may be the primary treatment. In other cases, clinical hypnosis may be an adjunct to cognitive-behavioral therapy, interpersonal therapy, medications, or other procedures (Stewart, 2005). Chapter 15 by Ms. Lauren Simicich and Dr. Gary Elkins, presents foundational ethical considerations in practice of clinical hypnosis. Health care providers should adhere to the ethical and professional standards as dictated by their professional license or certification as well as ethical considerations specific to clinical hypnosis as identified by organizations such as the International Society of Hypnosis (ISH), American Society for Clinical Hypnosis (ASCH), and the Society for Clinical and Experimental Hypnosis (SCEH) as well as other organizations. Awareness of ethical principles and aspirational goals is essential to professional practice and for the welfare of those who seek clinical hypnosis services.

The second section of this book goes "***beyond the basics***" in regard to applications of clinical hypnosis. Chapter 16 by Dr. Ciara Christensen (President of the Society for Clinical and Experimental Hypnosis), Mr. Aaron Finley, and Mr. Connor Kelley provides an overview of the many applications of clinical hypnosis and supporting research. Guidance for integrating clinical hypnosis into practice is provided. Chapter 17 by Dr. David Patterson (world renowned expert on clinical hypnosis and pain management) and Mr. Joshua Rhodes provides a "deep dive" into the hypnotic inductions, therapeutic methods, and suggestions shown to be effective in chronic pain management. This is a major application of clinical hypnosis with much support.

Chapter 18 is written by two leading experts in child hypnosis and pediatric applications, Dr. Karen Olness (Past President of the American Society for Clinical and Experimental Hypnosis) and Dr. Daniel Kohen (co-founder of the National Pediatric Hypnosis Training Institute). Clinical hypnosis can be very effective in working with children due to imagination and high hypnotic abilities. However, specialized training and knowledge is needed for effectively using clinical hypnosis for problems such as anxiety, pain, stress, headaches, and habits in children.

Increasingly, the integration of mindfulness and clinical hypnosis has been recognized (Elkins & Olendzki, 2019). Mindfulness is similar to hypnosis in that both involve a focus of attention and non-judgmental awareness. However, there are also differences as mindfulness is generally directed toward *acceptance*, while clinical hypnosis is generally directed toward *change*. Mindful hypnotherapy draws upon Buddhist concepts and philosophy to combine aspects of mindfulness and hypnotherapy in a synergistic manner toward optimization. Chapter 19, *"Integration of Mindfulness and Clinical Hypnosis"* by Drs. Nicholas Olendzki, Liz Slonena, and Gary Elkins, provides a clear understanding of the integration and clinical practice of mindful hypnotherapy for problems such as stress as well as in clinician self-care.

Chapter 20, by Dr. Ming Hwei Yek, Mattie Biggs, Morgan Snyder, and Gary Elkins addresses the importance of clinicians having the skill and knowledge of how to assess the hypnotizability of their clients and patients. In this chapter, special emphasis is provided regarding the Elkins Hypnotizability Scale (Elkins, 2017) and the Elkins Hypnotizability Scale-Clinical Form (EHS-CF) is provided in the appendix. The EHS-CF takes about 15 minutes to administer and involves a hypnotic induction, deepening suggestions, and deter-mining response to several items such as arm heaviness, arm levitation, mental imagery, and dissociation. Research to date has shown the EHS to be a highly reliable and valid measure of hypnotizability. Clinicians can learn a great deal about hypnosis, hypnotic phenomena, and their patients and clients by integrating assessment of hypnotizability into their hypnotherapy practice. Also, research has shown the EHS to be an excellent way to introduce hypnosis to clients and that it can have therapeutic benefits when combined with self-hypnosis (Yek & Elkins, 2021).

The concluding chapter by Dr. Samuel Stork and Dr. Gary Elkins provides information about some avenues for certification in clinical hypnosis. There are a number of certifying bodies across the United States and in countries around the world. It would be beyond the scope of this book to cover all certifications; however, two recognized organizations that provide clinical hypnosis workshops and certification of training are the American Society of Clinical Hypnosis (ASCH) and the Society for Clinical and Experimental Hypnosis (SCEH). Both have certification programs, but only the Society for Clinical and Experimental Hypnosis has a track for certification in Academic/ Research Hypnosis. This is important as some researchers of hypnosis may not be clinicians or may be mainly engaged in research. Certification in clinical hypnosis can be a part of life-long learning as well as evidence of training and is encouraged.

The domains of knowledge covered in the chapters of this book are largely informed by a survey of clinicians regarding standards of training in clinical hypnosis (Elkins & Hammond, 1998) and material included in contemporary workshops on clinical hypnosis at the basic training level. In some regards, this book is a basic training resource for learning about clinical hypnosis. While hypnotherapy in various forms has existed for many years, it is only more recently that standards of training have been developed. I want to emphasize that skill in providing clinical hypnosis is developed through both reading and practice. I recommend that the reader attend workshop training or identify a mentor to review their hypnotic inductions and provide feedback for the refinement of skills. The Society for Clinical and Experimental Hypnosis has a network of clinicians for mutual learning and feedback regarding clinical hypnosis. Also, joining a professional organization and receiving relevant journal articles (such as from the *International Journal of Clinical and Experimental Hypnosis* or the *American Journal of Clinical Hypnosis*) can be very beneficial.

How to Use this Book

This book provides the basic foundational knowledge in clinical hypnosis. It is recommended that this book be read initially through in its entirety and only then returning to select chapters. How you use this book will depend on your level of existing knowledge of clinical hypnosis and your personal goals. The book is designed to be utilized as a reference guide and much-needed training manual for clinicians interested in hypnotic relaxation therapy.

Perhaps you are just beginning to learn clinical hypnosis and seeking essential knowledge that would be covered in a workshop or training, or you may be an experienced therapist and are reading this book as a refresher, or you may be an advanced clinical hypnosis practitioner and using this book in your workshops and teaching. In addition to a basic text, this book is also designed to serve as a reference for practicing clinicians.

Each chapter of this book begins with three learning objectives. This is a unique feature that is included to help focus and foster learning from the material. It is recommended that readers review the learning objectives before beginning a chapter and frequently refer back to them. It will be helpful to make notes to yourself and formulate your answers to each of the learning objectives to assure that you fully comprehend the material and are gaining the knowledge as intended.

At the end of each chapter are several "reflection questions." As you read the chapters it is likely that some ideas or questions occur to you as related to your own clinical work, interests and experiences. These reflection questions will help you "go beyond the basics" to more in-depth considerations and areas for further study.

This book is organized to first cover foundational knowledge in definitions, theories, and physiology of clinical hypnosis before going on to practical skills of completing hypnotic inductions and alerting, formulating hypnotic suggestions, and deepening. Understanding the basics is very important before moving beyond the basics into clinical applications. This book provides broad knowledge regarding the many applications of clinical hypnosis as well as interventions in particular areas such as stress management, ego-strengthening, teaching self-hypnosis, chronic pain, working with children, and integrating hypnosis and mindfulness. The fundamentals of treatment planning are discussed in Chapter 14 and throughout the book. The reader may use this book as a frequent reference for assessment and treatment planning as well as a resource for skill development. Clinical hypnosis is a specialized skill that integrates knowledge while at the same time recognizing that each client or patient is a unique individual. It is always important to convey respect for each client's values, religious beliefs, worldviews, goals, and preferences in introducing and utilizing clinical hypnosis.

In addition, material and information is provided that will allow the reader to learn how to assess hypnotizability using the *Elkins Hypnotizability Scale-Clinical Form* (EHS-CF). Clinicians reading this book are encouraged to practice with the EHS-CF to refine skills and to develop comfort with assessment of hypnotizability. It is generally recommended that clinicians conduct at least twelve competent administrations of the EHS-CF to become adequately skilled. Attending a workshop on the EHS-CF or seeking supervision is also encouraged.

This book also includes chapters on professional ethics and certification. Each profession that uses clinical hypnosis has its own standards of practice and there are differing laws and regulations for clinical hypnosis practitioners. It is important to become familiar with the regulations in the state, province, or country where you practice as well as existing ethical guidelines for practice. I believe clinical hypnosis has great use in relieving suffering and increasing well-being. These goals are best achieved when one is knowledgeable, follows respective ethical standards, and is committed to life-long learning.

CHAPTER 1
REFLECTION QUESTIONS

1. Why are standards of training in clinical hypnosis important?

2. How can I gain experiential practice in clinical hypnosis?

3. What is the best way for me to use this book along with seeking mentorship or workshops?

REFERENCES

Elkins, G. (2017). *Handbook of medical and psychological hypnosis: Foundations, applications, and professional issues.* Springer Publishing Co.

Elkins, G., Barabasz, A., Council, J., & Speigel, D. (2015). Advancing research and practice: The Revised APA Division 30 Definition of Hypnosis. *International Journal of Clinical and Experimental Hypnosis, 63*(1), 1-9. doi:10.1080/00207144. 2014.961870

Elkins, G. & Hammond, D. (1998). Standards of training in clinical hypnosis: Preparing professionals for the 21st century. *American Journal of Clinical Hypnosis, 41*(1), 55-64.

Elkins, G. & Olendzki, N. (2019). *Mindful hypnotherapy: The basics for clinical practice.* Springer Publishing Co.

Stewart, J. (2005). Hypnosis in contemporary medicine, *Mayo Clinic Proceedings, 80*(4), 511-524.

Yek, M. W., & Elkins, G. (2021). Therapeutic use of the Elkins Hypnotizability Scale: A feasibility study. *International Journal of Clinical and Experimental Hypnosis, 69*(1), 124-141. doi:10.1080/00207144.2021.1831390

CHAPTER 2
HISTORICAL FOUNDATIONS
OF CLINICAL HYPNOSIS

HYEJI NA AND GARY ELKINS

Chapter Learning Objectives

1. Describe major historical figures and events relevant to the history of hypnosis.

2. Review the evolution of methods and theories associated with hypnosis at different points in history.

3. Identify the various terms to which hypnosis has been referred.

In this chapter we will review the major historical events, individuals, and terms in the evolution of understanding clinical hypnosis. Reviewing the historical foundations of clinical hypnosis is instrumental to understanding the current perspectives of hypnosis. It provides a backdrop for today's public opinion of hypnosis and may embolden its practitioners and researchers to continue its innovation in the 21st century. This chapter will provide summative material of key individuals and developments throughout the history of hypnosis.

ANCIENT CIVILIZATION: DEEP ANCESTRY OF HYPNOSIS

While the contemporary understanding of hypnosis is that it involves: a state of consciousness involving focused attention and increased capacity for response to suggestion (Elkins et al., 2015), the meaning of *clinical hypnosis* (or hypnotherapy) is much broader as it refers to the application of hypnosis in treatment involving a very wide range of methods, techniques, and approaches. With our modern understanding of *clinical hypnosis*, the deep ancestry of hypnosis or hypnosis-like practices can be traced back to the rituals of healing performed in ancient civilizations. Found in nearly all ancient civilizations, various methods—including chanting, singing, dancing, drumming, and visualization—have been used to focus attention in order to produce trance states that actuate healing. The ancient Egyptians used rhythmic chants and magnetized objects, thousands of years before Mesmer became infamously associated with magnetism. Ailing Egyptians would visit sleep temples, dedicated to the god of Imhotep, where they would be put into a sleep-like trance and given suggestions to elicit hallucinations or dreams that were then interpreted by the priest to invoke healing (Edmonston, 1986). Similarly, in the sleep temples in ancient Greece and Rome, dedicated to the physician god of Asclepiades, priests would use chanting and "magical spells" to put sick individuals into a somnambulistic trance state known as incubation. During incubation, the sick person would receive visions from the healing god. Hypnosis-like rituals have also been documented in ancient India, China, Africa, and Native America. The use of fixation of attention, suggestions, imagination, and expectancies for the purpose of healing appear to be as old as … well, ancient history.

THE LATE 18th CENTURY:
THE ORIGINS OF ANIMAL MAGNETISM
AND MESMERISM

Franz Anton Mesmer (1734 – 1815)

Notwithstanding ancient healing rituals that are comparable to hypnosis, it is generally accepted that the dawn of modern hypnosis began in the late 18th century with Austrian physician, Franz Anton Mesmer (Gauld, 1992; Green et al., 2014; Elkins, 2014; Pintar, 2010; Pintar & Lynn, 2008). In 1773, Mesmer started to treat Franziska Oesterline, a young woman who was afflicted with a myriad of symptoms including toothaches, convulsions, and vomiting. Frustrated with his failures to cure her with traditional medical treatments, he turned to magnetic treatments—first introduced by Paracelsus, a Swiss physician and alchemist who claimed that "the human body was endowed with a double magnetism" (Weir, 1894, p. 921) and that health and disease could be acted upon like magnets (Edmonston, 1986; Pattie, 1994; Weir, 1894).

After making Oesterline ingest a libation containing iron, Mesmer attached magnets to her body which he had borrowed from a Jesuit priest and astronomer named Maximilian Hell. Eventually, Oesterline experienced a sensation of a fluid being expelled out of her body and she was ostensibly cured of her malady by Mesmer (Pintar & Lynn, 2008). In 1774, The dramatic cure of Oesterline made an indelible impression on Mesmer and thus set the stage for the practice of *animal magnetism*, the precursor to hypnosis. In 1779, Mesmer published his theory of animal magnetism, a healing system based on the belief of a universal magnetic fluid—its imbalance and equilibrium having impacts on illness and health, respectively. According to Mesmer, the true sign of having been magnetized was a *crisis* that often included dramatic symptoms such as convulsions and was a sign the illness was being purged; crisis was both the evidence of disease and the means to its cure (Pintar, 2010; Ellenberger, 1970). Further along in his work, Mesmer abandoned the use of magnets when he discovered that he could achieve therapeutic effects through other methods. He believed that his personal animal magnetism was powerful enough to produce healing. As Mesmer's own animal magnetism captivated the public, his practice and techniques became synonymous with his name—*mesmerism.*

In lockstep with the Enlightenment period, animal magnetism marked a shift in the understanding of illness from a religious perspective and theories of demonic possession to a more scientifically inclined one (Ellenberger, 1970). When Johann Joseph Gassner (1727-1779), a German priest, obtained celebrity for his sensational exorcisms and astonishing healings during a period where enlightened tendencies were gaining traction, a number of inquiries were ordered to investigate his procedures. In 1775, Mesmer, aware of Gassner's prowess, was invited to participate in an inquiry made by the Bavarian Academy of Sciences and effectively demonstrated that Gassner's exorcisms were de facto animal magnetism. Interestingly, it has been argued that Gassner's procedure, what was later recognized to be hypnotic phenomena, was a form of hypnotic training in self-control, and ultimately the real predecessor to modern hypnosis (Peter, 2005).

Mesmer's animal magnetism and extraordinary cures brought him a prodigious reputation, but not without controversy. Contemporary critics lambasted Mesmer's theory of animal magnetism and accused him of fraud, particularly after Mesmer claimed to have restored sight to Maria-Theresia Paradis, a blind musician from a wealthy family (Ellenberger, 1970). Fallen into considerable disfavor, Mesmer left Vienna and eventually moved to Paris in 1778, where his discoveries were rapidly accepted especially among the wealthy and influential. Mesmer partnered with a well-respected private physician, Charles d'Elson, and together they attempted to convince the medical and scientific community of the legitimacy of animal magnetism without much success. Nevertheless, Mesmer's practice became quite lucrative as he accepted patients from the aristocracy and magnetized them for large fees. To keep up with the demand for his services, he facilitated group sessions with a *baquet*, or wooden tub, presented with the theatrics for which he had become known. "The patients were arranged in several rows around the *baquet*, connected with each other by cords passed round their bodies, and by a second chord, formed by joining hands. As they waited a melodious air was heard, proceeding from a pianoforte, or harmonicon, placed in the adjoining room ... Mesmer, wearing a coat of lilac silk, walked up and down amid this palpitating crowd ... [He] carried a long iron wand, with which he touched the bodies of the patients, and especially those parts which were diseased" (Binet & Féré, 1887, pp. 8-10).

The Royal Commission in 1784

Eager to earn scientific validation for animal magnetism, either Mesmer or d'Elson—it is unclear under whose influence—effectively secured an official investigation of animal magnetism (Hammond, 2013; Donaldson, 2014; Gauld, 1992). In 1784, King Louis XVI of France ordered an inquiry and two commissions were formed to investigate animal magnetism. Benjamin Franklin, the American ambassador to France at that time, was appointed to lead the first commission, typically referred to as the Franklin Commission. The Franklin Commission was comprised of four physicians from the Paris Faculty of Medicine and five scientists from the Royal Academy of Sciences, including chemist Antoine Lavoisier, astronomer Jean-Sylvain Bailly, and physician Joseph Ignace Guillotin, eponym of the mechanized execution device. The second commission, typically referred to as the Society Commission, was comprised of five phy-sicians from the Royal Society of Medicine. For reasons not entirely clear, both commissions were tasked with investigating d'Elson and the existence of a physical magnetic fluid; neither commission exam-ined Mesmer's practices.

The commissioners devised a series of experiments that were conceivably the first placebo-controlled, single-blind studies. In one experiment, a boy was asked to hug several trees, ignorant of which ones had been magnetized. In other experiments, d'Elson's patients were blindfolded and made to believe that d'Elson was performing animal magnetism, when in fact he was not even present. Conversely, patients, unbeknownst to them, were magnetized behind a paper partition. In another cleverly designed experiment, a patient was provided with cups of magnetized water, which were in fact not magnetized. When the patient experienced a crisis by the fourth cup, she was given actual magnetized water but told it was regular water. The observations from these experiments are the first demonstrations of the role of expectancy in the procedure from which modern hypnosis evolved.

In their 1784 report, the Franklin Commission condemned animal magnetism as the existence of a physical magnetic fluid thar was not substantiated and instead concluded that therapeutic effects were promoted through "touch, imagination, and imitation" (Franklin Commission, 1784/2014, p. 64; Ellenberger, 1970). Though less comprehensive, the Society Commission's report essentially reached the same conclusion. Less known, there was a secret report that outlined the more risqué observations and potential risk of sexual exploitation as magnetism typically involved touching, often erotic, which "in the case of vivacious and sensitive women, the final effect, the end of the sweetest of emotions, is often a convulsion" (Bailly, 1784/2014, p. 69). Because the theoretical base for animal magnetism was discredited, Mesmer was disgraced and soon moved to Switzerland, where he lived in relative obscurity. Despite the Franklin Commission's castigation of animal magnetism and the shameful exit of its originator, the practice of mesmerism continued to be adopted and modified by many followers.

The Marquis de Puységur (1751 – 1825)

One such follower, The Marquis de Puységur started to question the requirement of a crisis to the mesmeric process, after having successfully treated a patient named Victor Race without the dramatic hallmark. Instead, Race entered a sleep-like state and Puységur gave him suggestions to focus on pleasant imagery and song, which prefigured the later methods of hypnotism. Puységur later found that he was able to induce this sleep-like state in several other patients with good results and believed that it was this languorous condition, which he coined *artificial somnambulism*, rather than a cathartic crisis which was the indication that a patient was mesmerized (Pintar & Lynn,

2008). Followers of Puységur focused on artificial somnambulism and believed that mesmeric phenomena were a product of psychological factors and the mesmerist's will, whereas orthodox mesmerists held to the original doctrine of crisis and fluid theory (Ellenberger, 1970). Puységur was agnostic about magnetic fluid, being much more interested in the clinical effectiveness of mesmerism than the mechanism of action. Despite the differences between the *fluidists*, those who believed in the existence of magnetic fluid, and *animists*, those who believed that mesmeric phenomena were a product of psychological factors, both shared the foundation that the role of the mesmerist was essential; fluidists believed the mesmerist was the medium for healthy magnetic fluid and animists believed it was the mesmerist's will and suggestions (Waterfield, 2013).

THE FIRST HALF OF THE 19th CENTURY: FROM MESMERISM TO HYPNOTISM

Abbé Faria (1753 – 1816)

A student of Puységur, Jose Custodio di Faria, better known as Abbé Faria, was a Portuguese priest who criticized the theory of a physical magnetic fluid and hypothesized that the therapeutic effects of mesmerism were activated within the patient's own mind and body, rather than externally by the mesmerist. In other words, the therapeutic effects were induced by suggestion. Abbé Faria was the first to propagate the idea that suggestion was central to the theory of mesmerism (Waterfield, 2013). With Abbé Faria's line of thinking, mesmerism further evolved from the power being within the mesmerist to within the subject. Abbé Faria would seat his patients in comfortable chairs, have them fixate on his hand, and then instruct them to sleep in a commanding tone. During the time that patients were experiencing artificial somnambulism, Abbé Faria would suggest visions and posthypnotic suggestions (Ellenberger, 1970).

John Elliotson (1791 – 1868)

John Elliotson, a British physician, was a passionate advocate of mesmerism and a fluidist, a position that was becoming increasingly untenable. In 1838, Thomas Wakely, an outspoken detractor and founding editor of the medical journal *The Lancet*, publicly debunked magnetism and embarrassed Elliotson—which led to Elliotson's resignation from University College Hospital and, eventually, from all his academic appointments (Pintar & Lynn, 2008). Despite his professional alienation, Elliotson remained zealous about promoting mesmerism and its therapeutic effectiveness. Because *The Lancet* refused to publish his work with mesmerism, he established *The Zoist: A Journal of Cerebral Psychology and Mesmerism and Their Applications to Human Welfare*, which highlighted the clinical applications of mesmerism (Hammond, 2013). He was particularly fascinated with mesmerism's effect on pain and regularly utilized and published about mesmeric-induced anesthesia (Elliotson, 1843).

James Esdaile (1808 – 1859)

The Zoist highlighted the work of James Esdaile, a Scottish surgeon, who practiced mesmerism in India. Esdaile performed hundreds of procedures with mesmeric analgesia, including limb amputations, tumor removal, and cataract excision (Pintar & Lynn, 2008). Despite the introduction of ether and chloroform in the 1840s, Esdaile preferred mesmerism, believing it produced fewer side-effects and was less dangerous than the chemical anesthetics (Pintar & Lynn, 2008). Even with the dwindling support of the fluidists, Esdaile's (1852) writings described a series of examples that he believed were "sufficient to give the coup de grace to the theory of suggestion and imagination as explanatory of the results obtained in [his] practice of Mesmerism" (p. 226). Interestingly, he goes on to describe the "electro-magnetic fluid" (p. 234), for he believed the vital energy was composed of both forms, could be "thought-modified" (p. 267) or "will-impelled" (p. 234) by the mesmerist and then transmitted to the mesmerized person, a process similar to how an electrical telegraph sends and receives messages (Esdaile, 1852).

James Braid (1795 – 1860)

James Braid, like Elliotson and Esdaile, was fascinated with mesmeric analgesia, but unlike Elliotson and Esdaile, he spurned the idea of magnetic fluid and believed that mesmerism was a special state of consciousness that was elicited through relaxation, controlled breathing, and eye fixation (Braid, 1843, as cited in Pintar, 2010), techniques that are homologous to modern-day hypnosis. He believed that this special state of consciousness, induced by eye fixation, was due to psychological and physiological processes within the subject, as opposed to any external magnetized force—whether from the mesmerist's will, the passing of hands, or a magnetized object (Pintar & Lynn, 2008). Braid's theory, while reminiscent of Abbé Faria's view that healing was activated within the patient, was distinct in its emphasis on the physiology of mesmeric phenomena (Pintar & Lynn, 2008). Braid claimed hypnosis was induced in discrete physiological stages, including "torpor," "catalepsy," and "anesthenia" (Braid, 1843, as cited in Pintar & Lynn, 2008).

Because of his observation that this special state of consciousness was sleep-like, in his 1843 article *Neurypnology, or the Rationale of Nervous Sleep*, Braid introduced the terms *hypnotism* and *hypnotize*, derived from the Greek word for sleep, *hypnos*, to distinguish his own theory and practice of mesmerism from previous iterations (Pintar, 2010). Therefore, Braid is considered by many as the father of hypnosis (e.g., Dell, 2017) and the first true hypnotist, as opposed to the magnetists and mesmerists who preceded him. Braid later preferred the term *monoideism* over hypnotism because the term more accurately captured the hypnotic state as focused attention and prolonged absorption, rather than a state of sleep (Spiegel et al., 2005). Yet, destiny positioned the misnomer squarely in the evolving nomenclature, with *hypnosis* persisting as the lexical terminus of the modern-day clinical practice.

THE LATE 19th CENTURY:
THE NANCY SCHOOL TRIUMPHS

Jean-Martin Charcot (1825 – 1893)

A different theoretical debate emerged in the late 19th century, with French neurologist, Jean-Martin Charcot playing a key role. Starting in the late 1870s at the Salpêtrière women's asylum in Paris, Charcot hypnotically treated female patients diagnosed with hysteria. No longer recognized as a legitimate medical diagnosis today, female hysteria, as understood in the 19th century, was thought to be a neurological disorder with an eclectic symptomatology that could include practically anything. Prevailing symptoms of hysteria included hallucinations, convulsions, paralysis, or delirium. From the observations of the hysterical women he hypnotized, Charcot ascertained that the similarities between the symptoms of hysteria and hypnotic behavior meant that the ability to be hypnotized was a manifestation of hysteria (Pintar, 2010). Charcot observed discrete stages of hypnosis in his hysterical patients: catalepsy, lethargy, and somnambulism.

In 1882, Charcot presented his theory of *grand hypnotisme*, that hypnosis was a pathological sign of hysteria, to the French Academy of Sciences. Having been censured by the Academy within the past century under "magnetism," Charcot's acceptance into the Academy granted hypnosis the scientific respectability that Mesmer coveted but never achieved (Ellenberger, 1970; Pintar & Lynn, 2008). In a somewhat ironic twist, Charcot's conviction in grand hypnotisme, the doctrine that brought Charcot and hypnosis academic recognition, would soon be revealed to be his tragic flaw. Charcot and his followers at the Salpêtrière School would soon gain the attention of two hypnotists in the city of Nancy, France, provoking an intellectual debate between the Salpêtrière School and the Nancy School.

Ambroise-Auguste Liébault (1823 – 1904)
Hippolyte Bernheim (1840 – 1919)

Ambroise-Auguste Liébault was introduced to animal magnetism as a medical student in 1848 and then later used Braid's hypnotic techniques with focus of attention and suggestions for relaxation in his clinic in the city of Nancy. Liébault's hypnotic induction involved direct eye contact with the patient and suggestions for sleep (Ellenberger, 1970). In 1866, he published a book that described his theory on the hypnotic state being produced by suggestion. After hearing of Liébault's reputation and reading his book, fellow Nancy doctor, Hippolyte Bernheim, visited Liébault and quickly became an advocate of hypnosis.

Together, Liébault and Bernheim founded the Nancy School, a school of thought that conceptualized hypnosis as state facilitated by and not due to pathology. Diametrically opposed to Charcot's grand hypnotisme, Bernheim and other supporters of the Nancy School rejected the theory that hypnosis was a pathological state associated with hysteria and instead demonstrated that the three stages of grand hypnotisme were simply a product of suggestion (Pintar & Lynn, 2008). Bernheim later concluded that suggestion alone, without the use of hypnosis, was sufficient to induce therapeutic effects and championed what he labeled *suggestive therapy* (Green et al., 2014). By the 1890s the theoretical debate between the two schools was decidedly won by the Nancy School with the Salpêtrière sympathizers admitting that they had been wrong.

Pierre Janet (1859 – 1947)

Working with psychiatric patients at the Salpêtrière, Pierre Janet initially agreed with Charcot's theory that hypnosis could be characterized as hysterical somnambulism. However, he eventually agreed with the Nancy School position that normal, psychologically healthy people could also be hypnotized. In a documented critique of grand hypnotisme, Janet (1925) concluded that the three stages of grand hypnotisme were a result of demands made explicit by Charcot's students and that Charcot ignored the effects of context when explaining hypnotic phenomena (Green et al., 2014; Ellenberger, 1970). Essentially, Charcot's conviction ultimately blinded him to evidence or a line of inquiry that would have otherwise challenged his darling theory. Influenced by Charcot's work and ideas on dissociation and a dynamic unconscious, Janet also developed additional theories that emphasized dissociation as a mechanism of hypnosis (Pintar & Lynn, 2008).

THE FIRST HALF OF THE 20th CENTURY:
THE LULL

While the Nancy School's position on hypnosis gained acceptance across Europe and the United States, other developments were in motion that may have contributed to the general decline of hypnosis in mainstream medicine during the first half of the 20th century (Pintar & Lynn, 2008; Gauld, 1992). Somewhat ironically, Bernheim's eventual theoretical position that there was no difference in suggestibility between regular waking consciousness and hypnosis likely bolstered the skepticism around hypnosis; himself declaring at a conference in 1897 that "there is no such thing as hypnotism" (Pintar, 2010, p. 35) because he believed every hypnotic behavior was a product of suggestion, including hypnosis itself. In addition to the question of the existence of hypnosis as a special state, there was an additional concern that hypnosis posed a moral danger of relinquishing autonomy and causing an unhealthy dependence on the hypnotist (Gauld, 1992; Janet, 1925). During a time when individualism was valued and hypnosis was largely misunderstood as a passive treatment, other psychotherapeutic methods were embraced and hypnosis was relegated as an alternative approach, a position still apparent today.

The rise of psychoanalytic techniques, developed by Sigmund Freud (1856 – 1939), coincided with the fall of hypnosis (Pintar & Lynn, 2008). Freud studied with both Charcot and Bernheim in the late 19th century and frequently utilized hypnosis in his own clinical work. Freud even attended the First International Congress for Experimental and Therapeutic Hypnotism held in Paris in 1889; other notable attendees included Charcot, Liébault, and Bernheim. However, when Freud introduced psychoanalysis in the early 1890s, he eventually discarded hypnosis in favor of his own psychoanalytic techniques. Nonetheless, methods and ideas associated with hypnosis, such as rapport, the use of suggestions, the role of the unconscious, and dissociation were still present in Freud's psychoanalytic work which eventually contributed to the historical roots of psychotherapy (Green et al., 2014). As Freud's influence and psychoanalysis flourished, the clinical use of hypnosis diminished.

Though there is a relative lull in the history and research of hypnosis spanning the first half of the 20th century, a notable exception was the contributions made by Clark Hull (1884 – 1952). Hull established a rigorous scientific method for the study of hypnosis, published in his book *Hypnosis and Suggestibility: An Experimental Approach*, stating that establishing the scientific principles of hypnosis in a laboratory, rather than a clinical setting, was long overdue (Pintar & Lynn, 2008).

THE SECOND HALF OF THE 20th CENTURY: THE GOLDEN AGE OF HYPNOSIS

Milton Erickson (1902 – 1980)

Importantly, there is some evidence that the successful use of hypnosis to treat pain and traumatic stress during both World Wars contributed to the renewed interest in clinical hypnosis. Milton Erickson, a psychiatrist and prominent hypnotherapist, has justifiably been given the credit for such interest. (Pintar & Lynn, 2008). Even though most of his work was established prior to the 1950s, Erickson's mature professional work had an indelible influence on the "golden age" of hypnosis (Gauld, 1992, p. 579). Erickson's innovative approach, which influenced the field beyond hypnosis, was characterized by taking a nonpathological stance, conceptualizing symptoms as positive and individualistic, regarding the unconscious as a repository of positive resources, use of indirect suggestions and metaphors, and accepting and utilizing the patient's behavior and perceptions for therapeutic change (Lankton, 2008; Lankton & Matthews, 2010).

Establishment of Professional Organizations

The resurgence of interest in hypnosis was evident in the establishment of professional organizations dedicated to the promotion of clinical and experimental hypnosis. The Society for Clinical and Experimental Hypnosis was founded in the United States in 1949. A few years later in 1957, the American Society of Clinical Hypnosis was founded by Erickson. In 1959, the International Society of Hypnosis was founded. In 1969, the American Psychological Association (APA) formed a division dedicated to hypnosis (referred to as Division 30 of the APA).

The Rise of the Scientific Study of Hypnosis

While Erickson contributed to the renewed interest in the clinical practice of hypnosis, the golden age of hypnosis was particularly recognized for its advancements in the scientific study of hypnosis. In the 1950s, Ernest Hilgard developed the Laboratory of Hypnosis Research at Stanford University. With his colleague, Andre Weitzenhoffer, Hilgard developed the Stanford Hypnotic Susceptibility Scales (SHSS; Weitzenhoffer et al., 1959) because they believed that a standard measure of hypnosis was necessary to properly study hypnosis. In 1959, Martin Orne formed the Hypnosis Research Project at the Massachusetts Mental Health Center. Orne and his colleagues also studied hypnotizability and developed the Harvard Group Scale of Hypnotic Susceptibility (HGSHS:A; Shor & Orne, 1962). The study and development of hypnotizability scales not only provided a reliable and valid method to measure hypnotizability, but it also made it possible to examine the relationship between individual responsiveness and clinical outcomes.

THE 21st CENTURY: THE EVIDENCE-BASED ERA

The rapid expansion of scientific research during the last half of the 20th century acted as a natural catalyst for the synergy between clinical practice and empirical study (Elkins, 2014), defining the 21st century as an evidence-based era in the history of hypnosis. In this evidence-based era, hypnotherapists integrate their clinical expertise, best scientific evidence, and patient values and preferences in order to provide high quality care (Alladin et al., 2007).

Scientifically rigorous studies have established the value of clinical hypnosis in addressing a wide variety of medical and psychological concerns. Comprehensive reviews conclude that hypnosis can alleviate many types of pain and meets the criteria for a well-established treatment (Patterson & Jensen, 2003; Elkins et al., 2007). Clinical hypnosis has also been found to be effective in addressing irritable bowel syndrome, even in refractory cases (Palsson et al., 2006; Schaefert et al., 2014). Additionally, there is empirical support for the use of hypnosis in the treatment of hot flashes, with studies reporting a 68% to 80% reduction in hot flash scores (Elkins et al., 2008; Elkins et al., 2013).

Regarding psychological concerns, the evolving research literature on clinical hypnosis supports the use of hypnosis for stress and anxiety in a wide range of clinical and non-clinical populations (Hammond, 2010) as well as improving depressive symptoms (Alladin & Alibhai, 2007; Shih et al., 2009). Furthermore, there is evidence of the efficacy of hypnotic interventions for the treatment of post-traumatic stress disorder (PTSD) as a meta-analysis of six studies found that hypnosis had a positive effect on PTSD symptoms in all six studies (O'Toole et al., 2016).

CONCLUSION

With evidence-based practice in vogue, the growing empirical support for clinical hypnosis will only continue to flourish. Musing over a vibrant history spanning over nearly 250 years, with colorful characters and controversies aplenty, the future of clinical hypnosis looks bright. Reflected in this prescient quote from a book on artificial somnambulism over 150 years ago, the hope for scientific legitimacy has come to pass and the promise for a rewarding and curious future is optimistically anticipated: "I am fully persuaded that [hypnosis] will stand the utmost scrutiny, and like virgin gold, the oftener it is smelted the purer it will come forth from the furnace of its examination. It is now barely sifted from the dross, and in the mantle of unblushing truth presented to the world. Let it but have that justice which is due, and time will show whether it shall be denied the title of a Science" (Fahnestock, 1869, p. 328).

CHAPTER 2
REFLECTION QUESTIONS

1. When did hypnotic practices originate?

2. What historical events have contributed misconceptions about hypnosis?

3. How has the emphasis on scientific research during the late 20th century been impactful on contemporary knowledge about hypnosis?

REFERENCES

Alladin, A., & Alibhai, A. (2007). Cognitive hypnotherapy for depression: An empirical investigation. *International Journal of Clinical and Experimental Hypnosis, 55*(2), 147-166. https://doi.org/10.1080/00207140 601177897

Alladin, A., Sabatini, L., & Amundson, J. K. (2007). What should we mean by empirical validation in hypnotherapy: Evidence-based practice in clinical hypnosis? *International Journal of Clinical and Experimental Hypnosis, 55*(2), 115-130. https://doi.org/10.1080/00207140601177871

Bailly, J. S. (2014). Secret report on mesmerism or animal magnetism (I. M. L. Donaldson, Trans.). *The reports of the royal commission of 1784 on Mesmer's system of animal magnetism and other contemporary documents: New English translations and an introduction.* 68-71. (Original work published 1784)

Binet, A,. & Féré, C. (1887). *Animal magnetism.* Kagan Paul, Trench & Co. https://www.woodlibrarymuseum.org/wp-content/uploads/rare-books/S_ACJF-2.pdf

Dell, P. F. (2017). What is the essence of hypnosis? *International Journal of Clinical and Experimental Hypnosis, 65*(2), 162-168.

Donaldson, I. M. L. (2014). *The reports of the royal commission of 1784 on Mesmer's system of animal magnetism and other contemporary documents: New English translations and an introduction.* Royal College of Physicians of Edinburgh. https://www.rcpe.ac.uk/sites/default/files/files/the_royal_commission_on_an imal_-_translated_by_iml_donaldson_1.pdf

Edmonston, W. E. (1986). *The induction of hypnosis.* John Wiley & Sons.

Elkins, G. (2014). *Hypnotic relaxation therapy: Principles and applications.* Springer Publishing Company.

Elkins, G., Barabasz, A., Council, J., & Speigel, D. (2015). Advancing research and practice: The Revised APA Division 30 Definition of Hypnosis. *International Journal of Clinical and Experimental Hypnosis, 63*(1), 1-9. doi:10.1080/002071 44.2014.961870

Elkins, G. R., Fisher, W. I., Johnson, A. K., Carpenter, J. S., & Keith, T. Z. (2013). Clinical hypnosis in the treatment of post-menopausal hot flashes: A randomized controlled trial. *Menopause, 20*(3). https://doi.org/10.1097/GME.0b013e 31826 ce3ed

Elkins, G., Jensen, M. P., & Patterson, D. R. (2007). Hypnotherapy for the management of chronic pain. *International Journal of Clinical and Experimental Hypnosis, 55*(3), 275-287. https://doi.org/10.1080/00207140701338621

Elkins, G., Marcus, J., Stearns, V., Perfect, M., Rajab, M. H., Ruud, C., Palamara, L., & Keith, T. (2008). Randomized trial of a hypnosis intervention for treatment of hot flashes among breast cancer survivors. *Journal of Clinical Oncology, 26*(31), 5022-5026. https://doi.org/10.1200/JCO.2008.16.6389

Ellenberger, H. F. (1970). *The discovery of the unconscious: The history and evolution of dynamic psychiatry*. Basic Books.

Elliotson, J. (1843). *Numerous cases of surgical operations without pain in the mesmeric state: with remarks upon the opposition of many members of the Royal Medical and Chirurgical Society and others to the reception of the inestimable blessings of mesmerism*. Lea and Blanchard.

Esdaile, J. (1852). *Natural and mesmeric clairvoyance, with the practical application of mesmerism in surgery and medicine*. Schulze and Co.

Fahnestock, W. B. (1869). *Artificial somnambulism, hitherto called mesmerism, or animal magnetism*. Barclay and Co.

Franklin Commission (2014). Report of the commissioners charged by the King with the examination of animal magnetism (I. M. L. Donaldson, Trans.). *The reports of the royal commission of 1784 on Mesmer's system of animal magnetism and other contemporary documents: New English translations and an introduction*, 39-67. (Original work published 1784)

Gauld, A. (1992). *A history of hypnotism*. Cambridge University Press. https://doi.org/10.1080/00029157.1993.10403044

Green, J. P., Laurence, J. R., & Lynn, S. J. (2014). Hypnosis and psychotherapy: From Mesmer to mindfulness. *Psychology of Consciousness: Theory, Research, and Practice, 1*(2), 199-212. https://psycnet.apa.org/doi/10.1037/cns0000015

Hammond, D. C. (2010). Hypnosis in the treatment of anxiety-and stress-related disorders. *Expert Review of Neurotherapeutics, 10*(2), 263-273. https://doi.org/10.1586/ern.09.140

Hammond, D. C. (2013). A review of the history of hypnosis through the late 19th century. *American Journal of Clinical Hypnosis, 56*(2), 174-191. https://doi.org/10.1080/00029157.2013.826172

Janet, P. (1925). *Principles of psychotherapy* (H. M. Guthrie & E. R. Guthrie, Trans.). Macmillan.

Lankton, S. (2008). An Ericksonian approach to clinical hypnosis. In M. R. Nash & A. J. Barnier (Eds.), *The Oxford handbook of hypnosis: Theory, research and practice* (pp. 467-485). Oxford University Press. https://doi.org/10.1093/oxfordhb/9780198570097.013.0018

Lankton, S. R., & Matthews, W. J. (2010). An Ericksonian model of clinical hypnosis. In S. J. Lynn, J. W. Rhue, & I. Kirsch (Eds.), *Handbook of clinical hypnosis* (pp. 209-237). American Psychological Association. https://psycnet.apa.org/doi/10.2307/j.ctv1chs5qj.12

O'Toole, S. K., Solomon, S. L., & Bergdahl, S. A. (2016). A meta-analysis of hypnotherapeutic techniques in the treatment of PTSD symptoms. *Journal of Traumatic Stress, 29*(1), 97-100. https://pubmed.ncbi.nlm.nih.gov/26855228/

Palsson, O. S., Turner, M. J., & Whitehead, W. E. (2006). Hypnosis home treatment for irritable bowel syndrome: A pilot study. *International Journal of Clinical and Experimental Hypnosis, 54*(1), 85-99. https://doi.org/10.1080/002071 40500328666

Patterson, D. R., & Jensen, M. P. (2003). Hypnosis and clinical pain. *Psychological Bulletin, 129*(4), 495-521. https://doi.org/10.1037/0033-2909.129.4.495

Pattie, F. A. (1994). *Mesmer and animal magnetism: A chapter in the history of medicine.* Edmonston Publishing. https://doi.org/10.1080/00029157. 1994.10403115

Peter, B. (2005). Gassner's exorcism-not Mesmer's magnetism-is the real predecessor of modern hypnosis. *International Journal of Clinical and Experimental Hypnosis, 53*(1), 1-12. https://doi.org/10.1080/00207140 490914207

Pintar, J. (2010). Il n'y a pas d'hypnotisme: A history of hypnosis. In S. J. Lynn, J. W. Rhue, & I. Kirsch (Eds.), *Handbook of clinical hypnosis* (pp. 19-46). American Psychological Association. https://psycnet.apa.org/doi/10.2307/j.ctv1chs5qj.6

Pintar, J., & Lynn, S. J. (2008). *Hypnosis: A brief history.* John Wiley & Sons Ltd. http://dx.doi.org/10.1002/9781444305296

Schaefert, R., Klose, P., Moser, G., & Häuser, W. (2014). Efficacy, tolerability, and safety of hypnosis in adult irritable bowel syndrome: Systematic review and meta-analysis. *Psychosomatic Medicine, 76*(5), 389-398. https://doi.org/10.1097/psy.0000000000000039

Shih, M., Yang, Y. H., & Koo, M. (2009). A meta-analysis of hypnosis in the treatment of depressive symptoms: A brief communication. *International Journal of Clinical and Experimental Hypnosis, 57*(4), 431-442. https://doi.org/10.1080/00207140903099039

Shor, R. E., & Orne, E. C. (1962). Harvard Group Scale of Hypnotic Susceptibility, Form A. Consulting Psychologists Press. https://doi.org/10.1080/00207148008409827

Spiegel, H., Greenleaf, M., & Spiegel, D. (2005). Hypnosis: An adjunct for psychotherapy. In B. J. Sadock & V. A. Sadock (Eds.), *Kaplan & Sadock's Comprehensive Textbook of Psychiatry* (8th ed.); (pp. 2548-2568). Lippincott, Williams, & Wilkins.

Waterfield, R. (2013). *Hidden depths: The story of hypnosis.* Routledge. https://doi.org/10.4324/9780203955314

Weir, J., (1894). The psychology of hypnotism. *The American Naturalist, 28*(335), 921-928. https://www.journals.uchicago.edu/doi/10.1086/276041

Weitzenhoffer, A. M., Hilgard, E. R., Cooper, L. M., Lauer, L. W., & Morgan, A. H. (1959). *Revised Stanford profile scales of hypnotic susceptibility forms I and II: To provide measures of differential susceptibility to a variety of suggestions within the induced hypnotic state: With revised standardization data. Stanford hypnotic susceptibility scale: Forms A and B: For use in research investigations in the field of hypnotic phenomena.* Consulting Psychologists Press.

CHAPTER 3
DEFINITION OF HYPNOSIS
AND HYPNOTHERAPY

JOSHUA RHODES, GARY ELKINS,
AND CAMERON ALLDREDGE

Chapter Learning Objectives

1. Describe the origin of the term *hypnosis* as it relates to the original understanding of the practice.

2. Identify the most relevant attempts at a consensus definition within the past 30 years.

3. Summarize the shortcomings of previous definitions of hypnosis.

4. Articulate the current definition of the following terms: hypnosis, hypnotherapy, hypnotic induction, and hypnotizability.

Hypnosis, and similar states have a deep historical context which have an active influence on perceptions and clinical applications. The origin of the term *hypnosis* can be traced to James Braid (1785-1860) who implemented an adaption of mesmerism in his own medical practice. Originally understood as a sleep-like state, the term *hypnotism* was derived from the Greek word for sleep, *hypnos* (Braid, 1853). Further research helped to correct and clarify that during the process of hypnosis, individuals are not asleep; instead, the process involves concentrated attention and prolonged absorption (Spiegel & Spiegel, 2004; Tellegan & Atkinson, 1974). While the term *hypnosis* may be a slight misnomer for describing the actual process of the practice, it has historically remained the term of preference for clinicians and researchers around the globe. Despite widespread agreement on terminology, a concise and agreed upon definition of hypnosis, until recently, has historically eluded the field of research and clinical practice.

This chapter will first discuss the reasons why disagreements upon the definition of hypnosis are to be expected. This will be followed by an outline of why a singular definition is important for both clinical and experimental contexts. The chapter will then review previous definitions of hypnosis including various attempts by Division 30 of the American Psychological Association (APA) to bring clarity to the field. Critiques of these previous definitions will be examined and finally, a summary of the status of the field regarding a definition will be provided.

DISAGREEMENT ON DEFINITION IS EXPECTED

The use of the term *hypnosis* has varied throughout time and across individuals, and thus clarity of the definition is essential. It has been used to describe many different things including a therapy, a process, and a state of consciousness. Some individuals have defined hypnosis as the product of a procedure, while others have defined it as the procedure itself (Nash, 2005). Disagreement on the overall definition leads to increased uncertainty regarding the understanding of various related terms such as hypnotizability, hypnotic induction, and hypnotherapy (Elkins et al., 2015).

Elkins and colleagues (2015) identify two reasons why this disagreement on a definition is to be expected. First, the mechanisms responsible for the effects of hypnosis are not yet fully identified. This lack of identification is a driving force behind the difficulty of consensus on a definition. There have been multiple attempts to provide models of the mechanisms, but most have excluded various aspects of hypnosis in order to focus on yet other specific aspects (Hammond, 2005). In 2015, Jensen and colleagues brought attention to the previous models and concluded that the field lacked an overall framework to organize the various factors contributing to hypnotic responding. In an attempt to provide such organization, a biopsycho-social model of hypnosis was proposed (Jensen et al., 2015).

A second reason why disagreement can be expected is that arguments about the accuracy of a definition will almost certainly occur when definitions involve a theoretical bias (Elkins et al., 2015). Theories of hypnosis include, but are not limited to, Hilgard's (1973) neodissociation interpretation, Spanos' (1991) sociocognitive approach, Kirsch's (1985) theory of response-expectancy, and Woody and Bowers' (1994) dissociated control theory. The complexity and nuances of these competing theories and their arguments over the state or non-state aspect of hypnosis add even further room for disagreement as to what hypnosis truly is. While engaging in dialogue regarding competing theoretical frameworks is both necessary and informative, we must be reminded that theoretical analysis is the last step in the process of providing understanding to the field (Killeen & Nash, 2003). The first step, where it all begins, is a concise definition.

THE IMPORTANCE OF A CONCISE, UNIVERSAL DEFINITION

Without a standardized definition, it is nearly impossible to accurately identify the occurrence of any phenomenon. This is true for hypnosis both clinically and experimentally. A concurrence of what hypnosis is creates a channel for common language which allows both research-ers and clinicians to discuss it effectively. This, in turn, hopefully leads to key advancements in how we examine and use hypnosis.

Elkins and colleagues (2015) indicated that defining hypnosis is "fundamental to scientific inquiry" (p. 2) and should simplify its identification. Equipped with a standard definition, researchers can produce novel or replicated methodologies to study hypnosis and disseminate findings in ways that can be widely understood. At the same time, it is also important that the definition be general enough to allow for different theories to drive additional research. It will be important for future research to elaborate on how hypnosis is operationalized within the context of the definition outlined in this chapter.

A uniform definition of hypnosis is also essential in clinical practice when presenting hypnosis to patients and in contexts of training and supervision. The stigmatic and dramatized picture often painted of hypnosis creates difficulty for the general public to navigate what hypnosis is, what it is not, how it is experienced, and how it can help. Consensus among professionals (even if they do not actively practice hypnosis themselves) will help guide patients and practitioners to an accurate understanding and lay the foundation for productive communication. Chapter 13 provides additional information on presenting clinical hypnosis to patients.

PREVIOUS DEFINITIONS OF HYPNOSIS

In 1993, the Division 30 of the APA approved a definition of hypnosis that accounted for different theoretical perspectives in an attempt to generate "a statement on which people holding divergent views of hypnosis could agree and which the members of Division 30 would find useful as something that could be given to lay persons (e.g., clients) interested in hypnosis" (Kirsch, 1994, p. 160). Hypnosis was thus defined as a procedure "during which a health professional or researcher suggests that a client, patient, or subject experience changes in sensations, perceptions, thoughts, or behavior" (Kirsch, 1994, p. 143). The definition received much criticism and ultimately was determined unsatisfactory. Critiques of the definition cited its excessive length and significant theoretical limitations, specifically its lacking mention of the "state" concept which was perceived as bias towards opposing theoretical frameworks (Elkins et al., 2015). Additionally, the proposed definition later outlines certain applications of hypnosis such as pain, depression, anxiety, stress, and habit disorders (Kirsch, 1994) which may be misinterpreted as the only applications for which hypnosis is beneficial.

As a response to the critiques of this definition, the APA Division 30 spent the next decade forming several subcommittees. Ultimately, a final committee was tasked with the goal of shortening the definition, eliminating the list of its potential uses, and incorporating the critiques received (Elkins et al., 2015). These efforts resulted in a lengthy definition of hypnosis that states:

> *Hypnosis typically involves an introduction to the procedure during which the subject is told that suggestions for imaginative experiences will be presented. The hypnotic induction is an extended initial suggestion for using one's imagination, and may contain further elaborations of the introduction. A hypnotic procedure is used to encourage and evaluate responses to suggestions. When using hypnosis, one person (the subject) is guided by another (the hypnotist) to respond to suggestions for changes in subjective experience, alterations in perception, sensation, emotion, thought, or behavior. Persons can also learn self-hypnosis, which is the act of administering hypnotic procedures on one's own. If the subject responds to hypnotic suggestions, it is generally inferred that hypnosis has been induced. Many believe that hypnotic responses and experiences are characteristic of a hypnotic state. While some think that it is not necessary to use the word "hypnosis" as part of the hypnotic induction, others view it as essential. Details of hypnotic procedures and suggestions will differ depending on the goals of the practitioner and the purposes of the clinical or research endeavor. Procedures traditionally involve suggestions to relax, though relaxation is not necessary for hypnosis and a wide variety of suggestions can be used including those to become more alert. Suggestions that permit the extent of*

hypnosis to be assessed by comparing responses to standardized scales can be used in both clinical and research settings. While the majority of individuals are responsive to at least some suggestions, scores on standardized scales range from high to negligible. Traditionally, scores are grouped into low, medium, and high categories. As is the case with other positively scaled measures of psychological constructs such as attention and awareness, the salience of evidence for having achieved hypnosis increases with the individual's score. (Green et al., 2005, pp. 262-263).

This updated definition provided some level of clarity but evidently missed the mark in regard to its length and might be considered more of a discussion than definition. Critiques of the definition, beyond its excessive length (Heap, 2005), included its contradictions within the definition (McConkey, 2005), narrow view and restrictions of alternate theories (Rossi, 2005), and its lack of clear distinction between hypnotic procedures and hypnosis itself (Nash, 2005).

Distinction Between Procedure and Product

To some, the distinction between hypnotic procedures and hypnosis itself may seem to be of little relevance. However, this distinction is critical to the eventual development of a consensus definition. If hypnosis is a state, then the procedures to induce this state should be distinct from the resulting state itself. It is important to determine where these procedures end and where the state of hypnosis begins. The procedure of hypnosis has occurred once a hypnotic induction (to be defined later) and a single suggestion have been given, however this does not guarantee that the product of hypnosis has resulted from this procedure (Barnier & Nash, 2008). Differing factors can influence this resulting state of hypnosis including attitude (i.e., willingness) and hypnotizability (Spanos et al., 1987) which do not necessarily bolster the effect of hypnosis, but instead ensure that there are at least the components present to achieve a hypnotic state.

CURRENT DEFINITION OF HYPNOSIS AND HYPNOTHERAPY

The current and only contemporary consensus definition of hypnosis is a result of the APA Division 30's Hypnosis Definition Committee (HDC) established in 2013. The committee outlined two guidelines to aid in the creation of the revised definition: (1) the definition should be a concise description that identifies the object of interest and its characteristics, and (2) the definition should be heuristic and allow for alternative theories of the mechanisms (Elkins et al., 2015). Taking previous critiques into consideration, the committee provided a consensus definition for the term *hypnosis*, but also its associated terms (*hypnotic induction, hypnotizability*, and *hypnotherapy*).

Hypnosis

The provided, and current, definition states that hypnosis is "***a state of consciousness involving focused attention and reduced peripheral awareness characterized by an enhanced capacity for response to suggestion***" (Elkins et al., 2015, p. 6).

Although much has been written about whether hypnosis should be defined as a "state of consciousness," an "altered state," or something of a sociocognitive construct, the debate tends to focus less on whether a unique state of consciousness is experienced and more on whether a certain state defines the essence of hypnotic phenomena (Wickramaskera, 2015). The committee's choice of using *state of consciousness* seems to achieve the goal of "theoretical neutrality" (Sanchez-Armass, 2015, p. 445) while also highlighting the importance of consciousness in the pursuit of understanding the essence and nature of hypnosis (Pekala, 2015). The idea of focused attention and reduced peripheral awareness has been likened to looking through a camera using a telephoto lens rather than a wide-angle lens (Spiegel, 2015). In looking through a telephoto lens, great detail is observed on a single point while the greater context is out of frame. Relating to hypnosis, this illustrates the idea that mental energy is allocated to select stimuli (whether real or imagined) which facilitates reduced awareness of the greater context—the mental and physical environment. It is also important to note the language around an enhanced capacity for response to suggestion. This verbiage denotes the individual differences observed in responding to suggestions and emphasizes that it is, in fact, the capacity that changes and not necessarily a concept of "suggestibility" itself. The suggestion referred to can come from another individual (the person facilitating the hypnosis) or delivered to the self through means of self-hypnosis.

Hypnotherapy

Hypnotherapy, (or clinical hypnosis), is defined as "*the use of hypnosis in the treatment of a medical or psychological disorder or concern*" (p. 7). The provided definition of *hypnotherapy* is of importance as there can often exist a strong preference regarding the terminology used which has been coupled with some level of confusion due to a lack of clarity regarding the difference between *hypnosis* and *hypnotherapy*. Previous definitions continually received critiques for their lack of distinction between hypnosis itself and the process associated with it. In response to these concerns, the HDC included the specific definition of *hypnotherapy* that avoids the limitations of a list of applications and is broad enough to apply to all health care disciplines (Elkins et al., 2015). This distinction between hypnosis and its process of implementation is critical to our understanding of the practice and its advancement.

Associated Terminology

Further, **Hypnotic Induction** was defined as "*a procedure designed to induce hypnosis*" (Elkins et al., 2015, p. 6), and **Hypnotizability** as "*an individual's ability to experience suggested alterations in physiology, sensations, emotions, thoughts, or behavior during hypnosis*" (Elkins et al., 2015, p. 6).

The general nature of the definition of hypnotic induction allows for a variety of procedures characterized as inductions. These procedures can involve, but are not limited to, both self-hypnosis procedures and interactions between therapists and clients (Elkins et al., 2015). The terminology used for an individual's ability to experience hypnosis often varies, so the term *hypnotizability* was specifically chosen based on data discerning terminology preference (Christensen, 2005).

CONSENSUS DEFINITION

The field of hypnosis has seen multiple attempts at a consensus definition, and while most have been unsuccessful, the most recent definition (Elkins et al., 2015) has provided a much-needed foundation for clinical practice and research. Beyond understanding within the field, this definition provides a simplified understanding of the practice in alignment with APA Division 30's 1993 goal of providing something that can be given to individuals interested in hypnosis but who are unfamiliar with the practice and its associated research.

CONCLUSION

With this foundational definition, the field can continue to move in unison towards building a strong structure of research. Future research should continue to seek to clearly identify the mechanisms of hypnosis, its clinical applications, and its efficacy as compared to conventional treatment models. Recent increases in the amount of randomized controlled trials examining hypnosis and its efficacy are evidence that the field is not only still healthy, but continually growing.

CHAPTER 3
REFLECTION QUESTIONS

1. Why is it so important for clinicians, clients, and the public to have a clear understanding of the definition of hypnosis?

2. How do the clear and concise definitions of hypnosis, hypnotic induction, and hypnotizability, advance research and practice?

REFERENCES

Barnier, A. J., & Nash, M. R. (2008). Introduction: A roadmap for explanation, a working definition. In M. R. Nash & A. J. Barnier (Eds.), *The oxford handbook of hypnosis: Theory, research, and practice* (pp. 1-18). Oxford University Press.

Braid, J. (1853). *The rationale of nervous sleep considered in relation with animal magnetism.* London, United Kingdom: Churchill.

Christensen, C. C. (2005). Preferences for descriptors of hypnosis: A brief communication. *International Journal of Clinical and Experimental Hypnosis, 53,* 281-289.

Elkins, G. R., Barabasz, A. F., Council, J. R., & Speigel, D. (2015). Advancing research and practice: The revised APA Division 30 definition of hypnosis. *International Journal of Clinical and Experimental Hypnosis, 63*(1), 1-9. doi: 10.1080/00207144.2014.961870

Green, J. P., Barabasz, A. F., Barrett, D., & Montgomery, G. H. (2005). Forging ahead: The 2003 Division 30 definition of hypnosis. *International Journal of Clinical and Experimental Hypnosis, 53*, 259-264.

Hammond, D. C. (2005). An integrative, multi-factor conceptualization of hypnosis. *American Journal of Clinical Hypnosis, 48*(2-3), 131-135.

Heap, M. (2005). Defining hypnosis: The UK experience. *American Journal of Clinical Hypnosis, 48*, 117-122.

Hilgard, E. R. (1973). A neodissociation interpretation of pain reduction in hypnosis. *Psychological Review, 80*(5), 396-411.

Jensen, M. P., Adachi, T., Tomé-Pires, C., Lee, J., Osman, Z. J., & Miró, J. (2015). Mechanisms of hypnosis: Toward the development of a biopsychosocial model. *International Journal of Clinical and Experimental Hypnosis, 63*(1), 34-75.

Killeen, P. R., & Nash, M. R. (2003). The four cases of hypnosis. *International Journal of Clinical and Experimental Hypnosis, 51*, 195-231.

Kirsch, I. (1985). Response expectancy as a determinant of experience and behavior. *American Psychologist, 40*(11), 1189-1202.

Kirsch, I. (1994). Defining hypnosis for the public. *Contemporary Hypnosis, 11*, 142-143.

McConkey, K. M. (2005). On finding the balanced path of hypnosis definition. *American Journal of Clinical Hypnosis, 48*, 137-139.

Nash, M. R. (2005). The importance of being earnest when crafting definitions: Science and scientism are not the same thing. *International Journal of Clinical and Experimental Hypnosis, 53*(3), 265-280.

Pekala, R. J. (2015). Hypnosis as a "state of consciousness": How quantifying the mind can help us better understand hypnosis. *American Journal of Clinical Hypnosis, 57*(4), 402-424. https://doi.org/10.1080/00029157.2015.1011480

Rossi, E. L. (2005). Let's be honest with ourselves and transparent with the public. *American Journal of Clinical Hypnosis, 48*, 127-129.

Sanchez-Armass, O. (2015). A defining moment: Commentary on the revised APA Division 30 definition of hypnosis. *American Journal of Clinical Hypnosis, 57*(4), 445-447. https://doi.org/10.1080/00029157.2015.1011497

Spanos, N. P. (1991). A sociocognitive approach to hypnosis. In S. J. Lynn & J. W. Rhue (Eds.), *Theories of hypnosis: Current models and perspectives* (pp. 324-361), The Guilford Press.

Spiegel, D. (2015). Hypnosis and pain control. In T. R. Deer, M. S. Leong, & A. L. Ray (Eds.), *Treatment of chronic pain by integrative approaches: The American Academy of Pain Medicine textbook on patient management* (pp. 115–122). Springer Science + Business Media. https://doi.org/10.1007/978-1-4939-1821-8_9

Spiegel, H., & Spiegel, D. (2004). *Trance and Treatment* (2nd ed.). Arlington, VA: American Psychiatric Publishing.

Tellegen, A., & Atkinson, G. (1974). Openness to absorbing and self-altering experiences ("absorption"), a trait related to hypnotic susceptibility. *Journal of Abnormal Psychology*, *83*(3), 268-277.

Woody, E., & Bowers, K. (1994). A frontal assault on dissociated control. In S. J. Lynn and J. W. Rhue (Eds.), *Dissociation: Clinical and theoretical perspectives* (pp. 52-79), The Guilford Press.

CHAPTER 4
THEORIES OF CLINICAL HYPNOSIS

CASSIE KENDRICK AND CHRIS CORLETT

Chapter Learning Objectives

1. Identify major theoretical bases for hypnotic response.

2. Discuss factors comprising theoretical foundations of hypnosis.

3. Understand how theoretical foundations influence clinical application of hypnosis.

This chapter is meant to offer a practical guide—rather than exhaustive reference—for all possible theories of hypnotic response. In keeping with this practicality, the chapter will outline the following theoretical understandings of hypnosis and hypnotic responding:

- Psychoanalytic
- Neodissociation
- Adaptive dissociation theory
- Social cognitive
- Multidimensional
- Integrative

OVERVIEW

Since its origins, hypnosis has provoked numerous theoretical suppositions in an effort to better understand and explain hypnotic phenomenon. These theories are generally classified as either state or non-state theories. State theories are rooted in the idea that hypnosis produces an altered or dissociated state of consciousness and that this altered state of consciousness allows for a response to suggestion and is therefore responsible for hypnotic phenomenon. Generally speaking, state theories assume two points. Firstly, humans possess the capacity to differentiate between internal and external stimuli. Secondly, hypnotic responding involves an alteration in the process of differentiating internal and external events such that the actions taken under suggestion are perceived as involuntary (Elkins, 2014).

Nonstate theories do not necessarily deny that persons participating in hypnosis may experience a hypnotic state. However, dissociation is not perceived as a requirement of hypnotic responding. Further, nonstate theories posit that certain cognitive factors or innate abilities may exert their effect in conjunction with situation-specific attitudes, personal interpretations of task demands, and subjects' motivations to align their experiences and behavior in terms of those demands (Braffman & Kirsch, 1999; Kirsch & Lynn, 1998). Moreover, response to suggestion is seen as the aggregate effect of influences from factors such as motivation (Everett, Patterson, Burns, Montgomery, & Heinbach, 1993; Kirsch, 2005; Lynn, 2000), demand characteristics (Spanos & Hewitt, 1980), variation in suggestion (Spanos, Gwynn, & Stam, 1983; Spanos, Radtke, & Bertrand, 1985), situation-specific attitudes (Kirsch, 1991; White, 1941), personal interpretations of task demands (Kirsch & Lynn, 1998; Spanos & Hewitt, 1980), subjects' motivations to align their experiences and behavior in terms of those demands (Braffman & Kirsch, 1999), the influence of cultural norms (Kirsch, 1985; Kirsch & Lynn, 1998; Lynn, 1997), and expectancy (Kirsch & Lynn, 1998; Wickless & Kirsch, 1989; Hylands-White & Derbyshire, 2007; Kirsch, Silva, Carone, Johnston, & Simon, 1989).

The chapter will begin with three state theories: (1) psychoanalytic, (2) neodissociation, and (3) adaptive dissociation. The second part of the chapter will then examine nonstate theories: 1) social cognitive and 2) multifactor/multidimensional, after which it will offer information on an integrative approach.

STATE THEORIES

Psychoanalytic Theory

- Transition to hypnotic state is not a regression but a transitional phase.

- Hypnotic state involves a shift from secondary to primary process thinking via topographic regression.

- Hypnotic state is time-limited and occurs when patient feels safe.

Well-known as one of the most significant figures in the history of psychology, Sigmund Freud was a strong proponent of hypnotherapy, especially early in his career. As a young medical doctor, he reported utilizing hypnotherapy as a "principal instrument" in his practice (Freud, 1925/1959, p. 17). As Freud's career progressed, he emphasized the importance and influence of the unconscious mind by focusing his attention on practicing psychoanalysis and developing a psychoanalytic theory. He did suggest, however, that psychoanalysis could potentially be combined with hypnotherapy for a quicker but less effective result than psychoanalysis alone (Freud, 1955).

Psychological regression, which Freud (1966) first proposed as early as 1895, is the process in which a mature individual descends from logical, rational secondary thinking such as problem solving and *systematic thinking* to primary process thinking, characterized by pleasurable fantasies, illogicality, and magical thinking. Freud later developed this idea into two different phenomena known as temporal regression and topographic regression. He proposed that, in temporal regression, the individual is reverted to a childlike state and that their mental processes are as well (Freud, 1957). Research has since disproven the existence of such a state (Nash, 2008). Topographic regression, however, represents a similar shift from secondary process thinking to primary process thinking seen in psychological regression. Freud posited that such a shift is made possible via a shortcut that bypasses tedious and effortful secondary process thinking and allows the individual to rely on sensory perceptions and visual imagery to guide their decision making (Freud, 1963; Nash, 2008). Freud's early contributions to understanding a psychoanalytic theory of hypnosis would allow later practitioners and researchers to develop current understanding of a psychoanalytic theory of hypnosis.

In one of the most recent contributions to psychoanalytic theory of hypnosis, Michael Nash (2008) suggested a clinically-informed approach to understanding hypnotic response. Nash proposed that Freud's psychoanalytic concept of topographic regression—in contrast to psychological regression- can explain the established similarity of various phenomena seen in both hypnosis and psychopathology. From this understanding, Nash (2008) proposed that hypnosis represents a topographic regression that, unlike the complete and permanent regression seen in psychopathology, is "incomplete, transient, contained and reversible."

Nash was not the first to make this connection. Gill and Brenman (1961) proposed that the hypnotic induction is a transitional phase, similar to the hypnogogic state prior to sleep, that leads to the established regression of the hypnotic state. They saw the development and establishment of a transference between the therapist and the client as evidence of regression, and also classified hypnotic regression as a regression in service of the ego rather than regression proper. This parallels Nash's later analysis. Regression in service of the ego is time-limited and occurs only when the participant feels safe. Regression, like what happens in psychopathology, is outside the individual's control and takes place when the behavior is inappropriate (Gill & Brenman, 1961).

To make an argument against his position that the hypnotic state is a regression, Nash proposes that aspects of a hypnotic state provide evidence for five conditions of a regression. These conditions are: 1) changes toward primary process thinking; 2) greater access to emotional content; 3) changes in how one experiences their body; 4) transference with the therapist; and 5) a disruption in one's relationship with personal agency. Nash concludes that the evidence is sufficient to claim that the hypnotic state is a psychoanalytic regression. However, he also acknowledges that his findings do not invalidate other theories of hypnosis like social, dissociative, or cognitive (Nash, 2012).

Neodissociation Theory

- Hypnosis is dissociative and reflects a divided consciousness.

- During hypnosis, executive function is suspended and can be influenced by the hypnotist.

- The hypnotic state allows for separation of executive monitoring from behavioral execution.

In order to describe the involuntary nature of hypnotic response and the disconnect between monitoring and executing one's behavior, Ernest Hilgard (1973) posited "neodissociation" theory. Hilgard (1977, 1991) theorized that, during hypnosis, executive control of cognitive subsystems is briefly suspended and executive function can therefore be influenced by the hypnotist. Further, he noted that "If dissociation is conceived broadly to imply an interference with or a loss of familiar associative processes, most phenomena of hypnosis could be conceived as dissociative" (1991, p. 84). That is, hypnotic response, per Hilgard, could be understood as reflecting a divided consciousness.

Hilgard found empirical support for neodissociation theory in the nonvolition of subjects' responses to suggestion and a phenomenon he deemed the "hidden observer," which he discovered during a series of experiments on hypnotic-induced pain analgesia and deafness (Hilgard, 1991). Highly hypnotizable persons were told that they had a hidden part or "hidden observer" that could be accessed by a predetermined prompt from the hypnotist and could experience pain (or other sensation) while the individual experienced an absence of such sensation. For example, following hypnotic suggestion for pain analgesia, highly responsive subjects inserted their hand and forearm into ice water. Some subjects reported no overt pain, and others reported great pain via automatic key pressing, thus giving Hilgard evidence for dissociation between the conscious and unconscious (Hilgard, Morgan, & Macdonald, 1975).

Hilgard (1977; 1994) later posited the coexistence of corresponding streams of consciousness in which a "cloak of amnesia" creates division among coexisting channels of experience and separates executive monitoring from behavioral execution. With this concept and his experiments demonstrating the hidden observer phenomenon, Hilgard then devised a theory of hierarchical levels of open, independent, yet interrelated subsystems that create functionality within the organism. From Hilgard's perspective, the hypnotist directly affects executive function through suggestion, causing change in these hierarchical workings and thereby altering perceptual, memory, and motor function (Hilgard, 1991).

Adaptive Dissociation Theory of Hypnosis

- The hypnotic state involves a shift in thinking toward the unconscious/experiential system.

- The hypnotic state is a function of dissociation.

- Hypnotic dissociation is beneficial and therefore adaptive.

In a similar manner to Freud's description of primary process and secondary process thinking, Seymour Epstein proposed a paradigm of systems of thinking as a part of Cognitive-Experiential Self Theory (CEST). Epstein posited these systems of thinking as consisting of two separate and distinct cognitive modes; that is unconscious/experiential thinking and rational/conscious thinking (Epstein, 1973).

Per Epstein, the unconscious/experiential system is driven by emotion, and thus works quickly and without purposeful cognitive effort on the part of the individual. Communication within the unconscious/experiential system occurs via imagery, metaphor, and narrative. In contrast, Epstein proposed that the rational/conscious system was a system of logistical thinking that operates and communicates primarily through language. Epstein posited that both of these cognitive modes are always active to a certain degree; however, the relative workload of each changes according to situational demands (Epstein, 1994). For example, in a conscious, alert adult, it is anticipated that the rational/conscious system is primary, and the actions of the unconscious/experiential system would be secondary (Elkins, 2014).

Regarding the concept of dissociation, theoretical perspectives that emphasize dissociation as a primary factor in hypnotic responding assume that humans readily differentiate between internal and external stimuli. Furthermore, that during hypnosis, the ability to differentiate between internal and external events is altered such that actions taken under suggestion are perceived as involuntary (Elkins, 2014). Janet (1907) first proposed the idea of dissociation as a state during which some mental processes are no longer accessible and an individual is more open to suggestion. As a part of his neodissociation theory of hypnotic responding, Hilgard (1973) proposed that the hypnotic state involves a brief dissociation and suspension of the individual's executive control, during which certain behaviors were experienced as involuntary. Dissociated control theory (Singer & Bowers, 1990) proposed that, during hypnosis, dissociation results in a decrease of executive control and perception of effort, therefore providing a heightened sensation of involuntariness.

Building upon these ideas, Elkins (2014) developed the Adaptive Dissociation Theory of hypnosis to further explain hypnotic responding. Per Elkins, the hypnotic state is characterized by a cognitive shift in which there is more access to the unconscious/experiential system rather than the rational/conscious system, and that shift is achieved through dissociation. While often perceived negatively because of its association with pathology, dissociation can also be beneficial as a defense mechanism, or, in the case of hypnotherapy, as a temporary state during which significant progress can be made in the treatment of mental health problems (Elkins, 2014). In this manner, dissociation is not synonymous with pathology; nor does it indicate malfunctioning cognitive processes. Rather, in the hypnotic state, dissociation is adaptive and is therefore both functional and beneficial.

In this state of adaptive dissociation associated with hypnosis, the rational/conscious system is less dominant than it would normally be therefore allowing for greater executive control by the experiential/unconscious system. The degree of dissociation an individual experiences during hypnosis is determined by their ability to experience feelings and images and to perform suggested behaviors. The stronger the dissociative experience, the more likely the individual is to experience his or her actions within a hypnotic state as involuntary. More difficult suggestions are generally only possible in those with a stronger capacity for dissociation. Thus, the achievement of the hypnotic state is considered an adaptive form of dissociation because it allows for greater hypnotic responding, which is associated with more benefits from hypnotic treatment (Elkins, 2014).

NONSTATE THEORIES

Social Cognitive or Social Psychological Theories of Hypnotic Response

- Hypnosis does not require an altered state of consciousness.

- Response to hypnosis is influenced by multiple factors, including environmental and social factors.

- An altered state of consciousness may occur as a result of hypnosis but is not the cause of other hypnotic effects.

While dissociative theories have remained popular amongst practitioners, such theories have not gone without challenge as researchers and practitioners have sought to explain hypnotic response. According to Lynn, Kirsch, and Hallquist (2008), dissociative theories were initially challenged in 1933 by Clark Hull, who did not dismiss the potential influence of a trance state, but demonstrated—through comparing the effects of suggestion in hypnotic and waking states— only negligible effects from a hypnotic induction. Hull cited suggestibility (both hypnotic and nonhypnotic) as an explanatory factor in behavioral response to hypnosis. Hull's work marked the beginning of what today are termed "nonstate theories" (Hull, 1933). Some of the most prominent nonstate theories fall into the social cognitive domain, a theoretical approach that attributes hypnotic response to social, psychological, and cognitive factors and has been praised for demonstrating "the most successful approach to documenting correlates of hypnotizability" (Spiegel, 2008, p. 245). Lynn, Kirsch, and Hallquist (2008) point out that the beginnings of this theoretical approach can also be found in the works of Harvard researcher Robert White, who studied the effects of social variables such as motivation and attitude in hypnotic response (White, 1941). From the social cognitive perspective, hypnosis and hypnotic responding becomes a creation of the procedure instead of an entity being appraised by such processes (Spanos, 1986).

One of the earliest social cognitive theories was Theodore Sarbin's role theory. In 1950, he began his work in an effort to describe hypnotic behavior within the larger social-psychological realm of "role-taking." Sarbin was the first theorist to completely reject "state" theories of hypnosis (Lynn, Kirsch, & Hallquist, 2008) and argued that theory should account for the influence of interpersonal factors that are a dominant part of the hypnotic experience, as well as the objective phenomena associated with hypnosis. He postulated that the degree to which an individual involved him- or herself in the hypnotic "role" had the greatest determination upon response to suggestion (Sarbin, 1950). He also proposed that the success of role-taking behavior depended on the ability attend to environmental contextual cues for reciprocal role information, the degree of congruence between role requirements and personal characteristics, perceived expectations of a particular role, role-taking aptitude, and role demands (Sarbin & Coe, 1972, p. 94). Further, he noted that hypnotic subjects enact their role within the hypnotic environment even if that requires that they deceive themselves—not in a disingenuous manner, but in one likened to that of certain theologies, where belief depends upon the subconscious "suspension of the law of non-contradiction, the rule that something cannot be both A and not A at the same time." In so doing, persons receiving hypnosis are able to resolve their doubt and simultaneous belief in hypnotic happenings (Sarbin, 1989, p. 413). Thus, role theory does not equate hypnotic experiences with make-believe, but instead explains such occurrences as a result of an individual's unique response to contextual clues, rather than the product of an induction procedure (Sarbin, 1950; Sarbin, & Coe, 1972).

Following the work of Sarbin, Theodore X. Barber (1969) set out to understand hypnosis by conducting a series of experiments investigating factors influencing hypnotic responsiveness (e.g., Barber & Calverley, 1965, 1966). These experiments showed that behaviors characteristic of hypnotic responding—in particular, passing typical items of suggestion—were achieved by 45% of a nonhypnotized sample instructed that their level of response would be determined by how hard they "imagine" and "try" to produce behavior in a comparable manner to those who underwent a hypnotic induction. In another experiment, Barber and Calverley (1963) experimentation demonstrated that "task motivated instructions," in which subjects' cooperation with the hypnotist was highly encouraged and subjects were provided with information that their capacity to imagine suggestions was being tested, had essentially the same impact as hypnosis carried out through an induction. Later, Barber and Calverley (1964) demonstrated that subjects' responsiveness could be altered according to labeling a procedure "hypnosis" or "control" and by varying labels of suggested items as "easy" or "difficult." Barber's research eventually led him to attribute hypnotic responding to eight variables: "attitudes, expectancies, the wording and tone of suggestions, motivation, the definition of the situation as 'hypnosis,' suggestions for relaxation, the wording of the inquiry with which the response is assessed, and the behavior of the experimenter" (Lynn, Kirsch, & Hallquist, 2008, p. 117). More recently, Barber (1999) suggested that three aspects of hypnosis—fantasy-proneness, proneness to amnesia, and positive social psychological characteristics—as well as other influential factors (e.g., demand characteristics, the role of the hypnotist, and reaction to the variation of suggestions), were influential in hypnotic responding. Barber concluded that suggestibility is not dependent upon dissociation (Lynn, Kirsch, & Hallquist, 2008).

Multifactorial Theory

- Hypnosis does not indicate a state of altered consciousness.

- Response to hypnosis is influenced by multiple, varied environmental, personal, and social factors.

- Contextual factors, such as the influence of perceived roles and goal-directed fantasy, create a perceived feeling of involuntariness; however, voluntary control of behavior remains intact.

Following Sarbin and Barber, Nicholas Spanos expanded the work in social cognitive theories in more than 250 studies. Spanos proposed his multifactorial theory, which would be considered "one of the most influential contemporary theoretical approaches to the understanding of hypnotic behavior" (Lynn, Kirsch, & Hallquist, 2008, p. 118). Like others, he cited social cognitive factors such as environmental influences, expectancy, attitudes, perceptions, ascription of meaning, wording of suggestion, information designed to alter attitudes and interpretations of the hypnotic situation, and strategic, goal-directed responding meant to meet testing demands (Spanos, 1986, 1991) as influential in hypnotic response. For example, by comparing subjects' responses to a posthypnotic cue word in formal (within the experimental context) and informal (outside the experimental context) settings, Spanos and his colleagues demonstrated that the effects of the experimental context, expectancy, and the goal-directed nature of responding affect hypnotic response when subjects are unaware of experimentation and observation (Spanos, Menary, Brett, Cross, & Ahmed, 1987).

Spanos (1991) conceptualized hypnosis as an "interaction that proceeds through mutually negotiated self-presentations and reciprocal role validation" (p. 326). He saw this role enactment as being directed by situational norms, unspoken understanding between involved parties and situational implications related to how the endeavor is understood, and what is deemed suitable behavior according to this understanding. Thus, in Spanos' view—like that of Sarbin—hypnosis involves endeavors of "role enactment" (p. 326). Spanos did not suggest persons undergoing hypnosis imitate responses, but rather indicated they put forth purposeful effort to generate expected response to suggestion. Thus, in this context, hypnosis does not indicate a state or condition of altered consciousness but instead is influenced by social interaction and relates to participants' perception of what constitutes hypnosis or "the historically rooted conceptions of hypnotic responding that are held by the participants in the minidrama that is labeled hypnosis" (p. 326) and is—like that of most other responses—determined in many ways from a social interaction.

The hypnotic role offers legitimacy for the behavioral demands of the hypnotic situation. But what makes hypnosis unusual is the behavioral demands suggested and legitimated by the hypnotic role. Within this understanding, hypnotic responding becomes the product of attentiveness and organization of contextual cues to guide action and interaction that usually progresses with little effort due to common situational understanding—a via cultural understanding with well-formed ideas that hypnotized persons respond involuntarily to suggestion (Spanos, 1991). In many ways, one part of "becoming hypnotized" involves acting out goal-directed, culturally driven behaviors while construing such behaviors as involuntary (Spanos, 1982).

Spanos suggested that goal-directed fantasy or "imaginings that are congruent with the aims of the suggestion" (Spanos, 1971) could produce feelings of involuntariness (Spanos & Gorassini, 1984) and that, while the hypnotic context is filled with direct and indirect suggestion that subjects' behavior is supposed to be involuntary, which encourages and justifies subjective involuntariness, subjects retain voluntary control. (e.g., Spanos, Cobbs, & Gorassini, 1985; Spanos & Gorassini, 1984). He also discovered factors such as passive voice in suggestion (Spanos & Katsanis, 1989), and relative disparity between internal feedback and proposed suggestion influenced an individual's experience of involuntary responding (Spanos & Gorassini, 1984; Spanos, 1991).

In a number of studies, Spanos suggested that, despite attributions, hypnotic subjects retain voluntary control. However, he noted that the hypnotic context is filled with direct and indirect suggestion that subjects' behavior is supposed to be involuntary, which encourages and justifies subjective involuntariness (e.g., Spanos, Cobbs, & Gorassini, 1985; Spanos & Gorassini, 1984). Spanos and his colleagues also correlated subjective involuntariness with the wording of suggestions in passive voice versus directives (e.g., Spanos & deGroh, 1983). In one such study, which assigned subjects to either actively or passively worded "hypnotic analgesia" or "waking analgesia," pain reduction was equivalent in high hypnotizables in all conditions, but reports of nonvolition were only seen in those groups that received passive instructions (Spanos & Katsanis, 1989). Moreover, Spanos and his colleagues demonstrated variability in hypnotic responsiveness related to the disparity between internal feedback and proposed suggestion. For example, suggestions for an outstretched hand to become heavier (acted upon by gravity) were more likely to be experienced as "involuntary" than suggestions that an outstretched arm and hand would become lighter and begin to rise (Spanos & Gorassini, 1984). Spanos (1991) noted that "suggestions invite subjects to adopt and temporarily treat as veridical an imaginary or counterfactual definition of the situation—namely that their own actions are no longer self-initiated or goal-directed" (p. 327). Moreover, in a series of studies, Spanos demonstrated that, through appropriate training, subjects could alter their hypnotizability ratings, which are generally considered a stable, trait-like influence upon hypnotic responsiveness (see Gorassini & Spanos, 1999). Further, Spanos and his cohorts demonstrated that response to hypnosis as a social situation can be altered with changing demand characteristics, subjects' response to suggestion (e.g., Spanos, 1990; Spanos, Flynn, & Gabora, 1989; Spanos & McLean 1986; Spanos, 1990), and, as previously mentioned, training (Spanos, 1991).

AN INTEGRATED MODEL

- Valid, but incomplete, theories suggest the need for an integrated model of hypnotic response.

- Evidence provides support for multiple contributing factors in response to hypnotherapy

In response to a review by Kirsch and Lynn (1998) of dissociative theories of hypnotic responding, Woody and Sadler (1998) suggested that the field would benefit from integrating a number of theories of hypnosis. They proposed that theories should be viewed as provisional because of the need to constantly revise them according to the latest research findings. Further, they noted that Bowers' (1990, 1992) theories of dissociated experience and dissociated control and social cognitive theories could be interrelated and were not unreasonably inconsistent. Thus, they proposed a model of hypnotic response that integrated Bowers' aforementioned dissociation theories with socio-cognitive theories of hypnotic responding according to a dual systems model (e.g., Norman & Shallice, 1986, as cited in Woody & Sadler, 1998), in which complementary systems manage various aspects of behavior. According to Woody and Sadler's integrative model, then, hypnotic responding, such as subjective reports of nonvolition, could be viewed as the combined result of social cognitive factors, as well as changes in conscious control of behavior, and alterations in control of behavior by executive functions.

Taking into account the aforementioned, Elkins (2014) proposed revised definitions of hypnosis and hypnotherapy. He offered that hypnosis can be defined as, "...a state of consciousness involving focused attention and reduced peripheral awareness characterized by an enhanced capacity for response to suggestion" (Elkins et al., 2014, pg. 6). He additionally defined hypnotherapy as, "the use of hypnosis in the treatment of a medical or psychological disorder or concern" (Elkins et al., 2014, pg. 7). This concise, yet flexible framework can provide the basis for an integrated model of hypnotherapy that can account for factors that evidence has shown to be relevant in understanding response to hypnotherapy.

This integrated approach to understanding hypnotic response— like the previously discussed dissociative and social cognitive theories—developed out of a history of hypnosis in which researchers and clinicians sought to understand its nature and evaluate its effects and clinical utility. Understanding and utilization of an integrative theoretical approach should be informed by examining evidence of influence of factors from biological, psychological, and social domains as well as the influence of factors as proposed by multiple theoretical viewpoints, such as hypnotizability, expectancy, and rapport.

Hypnotizability, or an individual's ability to experience hypnotic suggestions in sensation, emotion, or thought (Elkins et al., 2014) is valued less within social cognitive theories but is critical within a dissociation model of hypnotic response. Dissociative models consider hypnotizability to be the result of biological based factors in an individual, while socio-cognitive theorists consider hypnotic response, or hypnotizability, to be the outcome of psychological influence. Notwithstanding the origins of hypnotizability, many differences have been found between highly hypnotizable individuals and those with low hypnotizability (Jensen et al., 2015). For example, individuals who are highly hypnotizable show more theta brainwave activity following hypnosis than low hypnotizable participants (Freeman et al., 2000; Galbraith et al., 1970). They additionally show more frontal cortex activity when given suggestions for motor imagery (Müller et al., 2013) and pain analgesia (Crawford et al., 1993) than their low hypnotizability counterparts. Additionally, examination of structural differences of the brains of individuals who are highly hypnotizable show greater connectivity between the prefrontal cortex and the anterior cingulate cortex when in a resting state than is seen in individuals with low hypnotizability (Hoeft et al., 2012).

In addition to hypnotizability, expectancy, or the degree to which a participant believes they will experience the desired result following hypnotic therapy, is another psychological factor central to numerous theories of hypnotic responding. It is thought that expectancies are related to automatic processes that are influenced by past and present experience as well as participant-therapist interactions, and evidence supports the role of expectancy in response to hypnotic suggestion.

For example, larger expectancy effects are seen when the suggestions are complicated, and the effect of expectancy is greater in highly hypnotizable than low hypnotizable individuals (Kirsch et al., 1995). The results of most relevant studies point to expectancies as a partial mediator in hypnotic response, the effects of which are moderated by differences in factors between individuals and the symptom being treated (Jensen et al., 2015).

Patient-therapist rapport is another psychosocial factor that has been shown to affect response to hypnotic therapy. Like expectancy, rapport has been more greatly emphasized in nonstate theories and less so within state or dissociative models of hypnotic response (Jensen et al., 2015). Sheehan (1980) demonstrated that poor rapport between a patient and hypnosis practitioner may negatively affect hypnotic responsiveness. Similarly, rapport has been associated with hypnotic responding and moderately correlated with post-training hypnotizability (Gfeller, Lynn, & Pribble, 1987). Additionally, hypnotizability may moderate the effects of rapport and has been shown to have a greater effect on low hypnotizable persons than individuals with high hypnotizability (Lynn et al., 1991).

Collectively, examination of evidence evaluating the varied influence of factors involved in hypnotic response supports comprehensive, biopsychosocial theoretical approaches in understanding hypnosis and response to suggestion. Future collaborative research efforts further examining the interaction of influences upon hypnotic response may be indicated.

CONSIDERATION FOR TEACHING AND SUPERVISION

In teaching, supervising, or presenting, emphasis on understanding of basic underpinnings of hypnotic response is critical. Not only does such information help the clinician develop well informed, user friendly answers to questions regarding how hypnosis works, but such knowledge also allows the skilled practitioner to develop, deliver, and deepen effective hypnotic interventions. When teaching or supervising, more time can be devoted to theory. However, even when presenting in conferences, offering the main, basic highlights of state, nonstate, and integrative theoretical models will provide a foundation for understanding and utilizing techniques. It may be additionally important that value of state and nonstate perspectives are highlighted despite personal bias. Even the strongest proponent of state theories will likely benefit from enhancing social-cognitive factors. Further, the advocate of nonstate theories will be most effective in delivering hypnotic intervention when he or she understands and appreciates the proponents of state theories. Finally, offering conference participants, students, or supervisees the tenets of integrative perspectives will provide the practitioner with additional freedom to practice in such a way as to maximize hypnotherapeutic response.

CONCLUSION

The components of state and nonstate theories highlight that it is crucial to provide clinicians with a practical understanding of the theoretical basis of hypnotic response. Understanding all of these foundational principles will allow the practitioner to better utilize hypnosis in clinical practice as well as effectively communicate underpinnings of hypnotic response in teaching and supervision.

CHAPTER 4
REFLECTION QUESTIONS

1. What are the main tenets of state and nonstate theories of hypnotic response?

2. What factors might a provider consider enhancing given socio-cognitive perspectives of hypnosis?

3. In what ways might a provider utilize the ideas presented in this chapter to inform hypnotic intervention?

REFERENCES

Barber, T. X., & Calverley, D. S. (1963). The relative effectiveness of task-motivating instructions and trance-induction procedure in the production of "hypnotic-like" behaviors. *Journal of Nervous and Mental Disease, 137,* 107-116.

Barber, T. X. (1969). *Hypnosis: A scientific approach.* New York: Van Nostrand Reinhold.

Barber, T. X. (1999). A comprehensive three-dimensional theory of hypnosis. In I. Kirsch, E. Cardena, & S. Amigo (Eds.), *Clinical hypnosis and self-regulation: Cognitive-behavioral perspectives* (pp. 21-48). Washington, DC: American Psychological Association.

Barber, T. X., & Calverley, D. S. (1965). Empirical evidence for a theory of hypnotic behavior: Effects on suggestibility of five variables typically included in hypnotic induction procedures. *Journal of Consulting Psychology, 29,* 98-107.

Barber, T. X., & Calverley, D. S. (1966). Toward a theory of "hypnotic" behavior: Experimental analyses of suggested amnesia. *Journal of Abnormal Psychology, 71,* 95-107.

Barber, T. X., & Calverley, D. S. (1964). Toward a theory of hypnotic behavior: Effects on suggestibility of defining the situation as hypnosis and defining response to suggestions as easy. *Journal of Abnormal and Social Psychology, 68,* 585-592.

Bowers, K. S. (1992). Imagination and dissociation in hypnotic responding. *International Journal of Clinical and Experimental Hypnosis, 40*(4), 253-275.

Crawford, H. J., Gur, R. C., Skolnick, B., Gur, R. E., & Benson, D. M. (1993). Effects of hypnosis on regional cerebral blood flow during ischemic pain with and without suggested hypnotic analgesia. *International Journal of Psychophysiology, 15*(3), 181-195.

Elkins, G. (2014). *Hypnotic relaxation therapy: Principles and applications.* New York: Springer.

Elkins, G. R., Barabasz, A. F., Council, J. R., & Spiegel, D. (2014). Advancing research and practice: The revised APA Division 30 definition of hypnosis. *International Journal of Clinical and Experimental Hypnosis, 63*(1), 1-9.

Epstein, S. (1973). The self-concept revisited: Or a theory of a theory. *American Psychologist, 28*(5), 404-416.

Epstein, S. (1994). Integration of the cognitive and the psychodynamic unconscious. *American Psychologist, 49*(8), 709-724.

Everett, J., Patterson, D., Burns, G., Montgomery, B., & Heinbach, D. (1993). Adjunctive interventions for burn pain control: comparison of hypnosis and Adavan: The 1993 clinical research award. *Journal of Burn Care and Rehabilitation, 14,* 676-683.

Freeman, R., Barabasz, A., Barabasz, M., & Warner, D. (2000). Hypnosis and distraction differ in their effects on cold pressor pain. *American Journal of Clinical Hypnosis, 43*(2), 137-148.

Freud, S. (1955). Lines of advance in psychoanalytic therapy. In L. Strachey (Ed. & Trans.), *The standard edition of the complete psychological works of Sigmund Freud* (Vol. 17, pp. 157-168). London: Hogarth Press. (1919)

Freud, S. (1957). *Thoughts for the times on war and death (1917)* (Vol. 14). London: Hogarth Press.

Freud, S. (1963). *Introductory lectures on psychoanalysis (Part III) (1916-1917)* (Vol. 16). London: Hogarth Press.

Freud, S. (1966). *Pre-psychoanalytic publications and unpublished drafts.* London: Hogarth Press.

Galbraith, G. C., London, P., Leibovitz, M. P., Cooper, L. M., & Hart, J. T. (1970). EEG and hypnotic susceptibility. *Journal of Comparative and Physiological Psychology, 72*(1), 125-131.

Gfeller, J. D., Lynn, S. J., & Pribble, W. E. (1987). Enhancing hypnotic susceptibility: Interpersonal and rapport factors. *Journal of Personality and Social Psychology, 52*(3), 586-595.

Gill, M. M., & Brenman, M. (1961). *Hypnosis and related states: Psychoanalytic studies in regression.* Madison, CT: International Universities Press.

Gorassini, D. R., & Spanos, N. P. (1999). The Carleton Skill Training Program. In I. Kirsch, A. Capafons, E. Cardena, & S. Amigo (Eds.), *Clinical hypnosis and self-regulation: Cognitive-behavioral perspectives* (pp. 141-177). Washington, DC: American Psychological Association.

Hilgard, E. R. (1973). A neodissociation interpretation of pain reduction in hypnosis. *Psychological Review, 80,* 391-398.

Hilgard, E. R. (1977). *Divided consciousness: Multiple controls in human thought and action.* New York: Wiley.

Hilgard, E. R. (1991). A neodissociation interpretation of hypnosis. In S. J. Lynn, & J. W. Rhue (Eds.), *Theories of hypnosis: Current models and perspectives* (pp. 83-104). New York: Guilford Press.

Hilgard, E. R. (1994). Neodissociation theory. In S. J. Lynn & J. W. Rhe (Eds.), *Disassociation: Clinical and theoretical perspectives* (pp. 32-51). New York: Guilford.

Hilgard, E. R., Morgan, A. H., & MacDonald, H. (1975). Pain and dissociation in the cold pressor test: A study of hypnotic analgesia with "hidden reports" through automatic key-pressing and automatic talking. *Journal of Abnormal Psychology, 84,* 280-289.

Hoeft, F., Gabrieli, J. D., Whitfield-Gabrieli, S., Haas, B. W., Bammer, R., Menon, V., & Spiegel, D. (2012). Functional brain basis of hypnotizability. *Archives of General Psychiatry, 69*(10), 1064.

Hull, C. L. (1933). *Hypnosis and suggestibility: An experimental approach.* New York: Appleton.

Hylands-White, N., & Derbyshire, S. W. G. (2007). Modifying pain perception: Is it better to be hypnotizable or feel that you are hypnotized? *Contemporary Hypnosis, 24*(4), 143-153.

Janet, P. (1907). *The major symptoms of hysteria.* New York: Macmillan.

Jensen, M. P., Adachi, T., Tomé-Pires, C., Lee, J., Osman, Z. J., & Miró, J. (2014). Mechanisms of hypnosis: Toward the development of a biopsychosocial model. *International Journal of Clinical and Experimental Hypnosis, 63*(1), 34-75.

Kahneman, D. (2013). *Thinking, fast and slow.* New York: Farrar, Straus and Giroux.

Kirsch, I. (1985). Response expectancy as a determinant of experience and behavior. *American Psychologist, 40,* 1189-1202.

Kirsch, I. (1991). The social learning theory of hypnosis: Current models and perspectives. In S. J. Lynn, & J. W. Rhue (Eds.), *Theories of hypnosis: Current models and perspectives* (p. 439-465). New York: Guilford Press.

Kirsch, I. (2005). The flexible observer an [*sic*] neodissociation theory. *Contemporary Hypnosis, 22,* 152-153.

Kirsch, I., & Lynn, S. J. (1998). Dissociation theories of hypnosis. *Psychological Bulletin, 123*(1), 100-115.

Kirsch, I., Silva, C. E., Carone, J. E., Johnston, D. J., & Simon, B. (1989). The surreptitious observation design: An experimental paradigm for distinguishing artifact from essence in hypnosis. *Journal of Abnormal Psychology, 98*(2), 132-136.

Kirsch, I., Silva, C. E., Comey, G., & Reed, S. (1995). A spectral analysis of cognitive and personality variables in hypnosis: Empirical disconfirmation of the two-factor model of hypnotic responding. *Journal of Personality and Social Psychology, 69*(1), 167-175.

Lynn, S. J. (1997). Automaticity and hypnosis: A socio-cognitive account. *International Journal of Clinical and Experimental Hypnosis, 45,* 239-250.

Lynn, S. J. (2000). Hypnosis as an empirically supported clinical intervention: The state of the evidence and a look to the future. *International Journal of Clinical and Experimental Hypnosis, 48*(2), 239-259.

Lynn, S. J., Kirsch, I., & Hallquist, M. N. (2008). Social cognitive theories of hypnosis. In S. J. Lynn & A. J. Barnier (Eds.), *The Oxford Handbook of Clinical Hypnosis* (pp. 111-139). Oxford, UK: Oxford University Press.

Lynn, S. J., Weekes, J. R., Neufeld, V., Zivney, O., (1991). Interpersonal climate and hypnotizability level: Effects on hypnotic performance, Rapport, and archaic involvement. *Journal of Personality and Social Psychology, 60*(5), 739-743.

Müller, K., Bacht, K., Prochnow, D., Schramm, S., & Seitz, R. J. (2013). Activation of thalamus in motor imagery results from gating by hypnosis. *NeuroImage, 66,* 361-367.

Nash, M. R., & Barnier, A. J. (2008). A psychoanalytic theory of hypnosis: A clinically informed approach. In *The Oxford Handbook of Hypnosis: Theory, Research and Practice* (pp. 201-222). Oxford, UK: Oxford University Press.

Norman, D. A., & Shallice, T. (1986). Attention to Action. In R. J Davidson, G.E., Schwartz, & D. Shapiro (Eds) *Consciousness and Self-Regulation*, Boston, MA; Springer

Sarbin, T. (1989). The construction and reconstruction of hypnosis. In N. P. Spanos & J. S. Chaves (Eds.), *Hypnosis: The cognitive-behavioral perspective* (pp. 400-416). Buffalo, NY: Prometheus.

Sarbin, T. R. (1950). Contributions to role-taking theory: Hypnotic behavior. *Psychological Review, 57*, 255-269.

Sarbin, T. R., & Coe, W. C. (1972). *Hypnosis: A social psychological analysis of influence communication.* New York: Holt, Rinehart, and Winston.

Sheehan, P. W. (1980). Factors influencing rapport in hypnosis. *Journal of Abnormal Psychology, 89*(2), 263-281.

Singer, J. L., & Bowers, K. S. (1990). Unconscious influences and hypnosis. In *Repression and dissociation: Implications for personality theory, psychopathology, and health* (pp. 143-179). Chicago: University of Chicago Press.

Spanos, N. P. (1971). Goal-directed fantasy and the performance of hypnotic test suggestions. *Psychiatry, 34*, 86-96.

Spanos, N. P. (1982). Hypnotic behavior: A cognitive, social psychological perspective. *Research Communications in Psychology, Psychiatry & Behavior, 7*(2), 199-213.

Spanos, N. P. (1986). Hypnotic behavior: A social-psychological interpretation of amnesia, analgesia, and "trance logic." *The Behavioral and Brain Sciences, 9*, 449-502.

Spanos, N. P. (1991). A socio-cognitive approach to hypnosis. In S. J. Lynn, & J. W. Rhue (Eds.), *Theories of Hypnosis* (pp. 324-361). New York: Guilford Press.

Spanos, N. P., & DeGroh, M. (1983). Structure of communication and reports of involuntariness by hypnotic and nonhypnotic subjects. *Perceptual and Motor Skills, 57*(3, part 2), 1179-1186.

Spanos, N. P., & Gorassini, D. R. (1984). Structure of hypnotic test suggestions and attributions of responding involuntarily. *Journal of Personality and Social Psychology, 46*, 688-696.

Spanos, N. P., & Katsanis, J. (1989). Effects of instructional set on attributions of nonvolition during hypnotic and nonhypnotic analgesia. *Journal of Personality and Social Psychology, 56*, 183-188.

Spanos, N. P., & McLean, J. (1986). Hypnotically created pseudomemories: Memory distortions or reporting biases? *British Journal of Experimental & Clinical Hypnosis, 3*, 155-159.

Spanos, N. P., Cobbs, P. C., & Gorassini, D. R. (1985). Failing to resist hypnotic test suggestions: A strategy for self-presenting as deeply hypnotized. *Psychiatry: Journal for the Study of Interpersonal Processes, 48*, 282-292.

Spanos, N. P., Flynn, D. M., & Gabora, N. J. (1989). Suggested negative visual hallucinations in hypnotic subjects: When no means yes. *British Journal of Experimental & Clinical Hypnosis, 6*, 63-67.

Spanos, N. P., Gwynn, M. I., & Stam, H. J. (1983). Instructional demands and ratings of overt and hidden pain during hypnotic analgesia. *Journal of Abnormal Psychology, 92*(4), 479-488.

Spanos, N. P., Menary, E., Brett, P. J., Cross, W., & Ahmed, Q. (1987). Failure of posthypnotic responding to occur outside the experimental setting. *Journal of Abnormal Psychology, 96*(1), 52-57.

Spanos, N. P., Perlini, A. H., Patrick, L., Bell, S., et al. (1990). The role of compliance in hypnotic and nonhypnotic analgesia. *Journal of Research in Personality, 24*, 433-453.

Spanos, N. P., Radtke, L. H., & Bertrand, L. D. (1985). Hypnotic amnesia as a strategic enactment: Breaching amnesia in highly susceptible subjects. *Journal of Personality and Social Psychology*, 1155-1169.

Spanos, N., & Hewitt, E. C. (1980). The hidden observer in hypnotic analgesia: Discovery or experimental creation. *Journal of Personality and Social Psychology, 39*(6), 1201-1214.

Spiegel, D. (2008). Intelligent design or designed intelligence? Hypnotizability as neurobiological adaptation. In M. R. Nash & A. J. Barnier (Eds.), *The Oxford handbook of hypnosis: Theory, research, practice* (pp 179-200). Oxford, UK: Oxford University Press.

White, R. W. (1941). An analysis of motivation in hypnosis. *Journal of General Psychology, 24,* 145-162.

Wickless, C., & Kirsch, I. (1989). Effects of verbal and experiential expectancy manipulations on hypnotic susceptibility. *Journal of Personality and Social Psychology,* 762-768.

Woody, E., & Sadler, P. (1998). On reintegrating dissociated theories: Comment on Kirsch and Lynn (1998). *Psychological Bulletin, 123*(2), 192-197.

CHAPTER 5
NEUROPHYSIOLOGY OF HYPNOSIS

AUDREY VANHAUDENHUYSE, NOLWENN MARIE, OLIVIA GOSSERIES, AND MARIE-ELISABETH FAYMONVILLE

Chapter Learning Objectives

1. Understand the modulation of brain networks (pain and consciousness networks) during hypnosis.

2. Examine the contribution of neuroimaging to our understanding of hypnosis sensitivity (i.e., hypnotizability).

3. Discuss how the neurophysiological processes of hypnosis can have implications for clinical practice.

Although hypnosis has been proven to be an effective tool in clinical practice (Vanhaudenhuyse et al., 2020), its underlying mechanisms remain unclear in the scientific literature (Landry et al., 2017). One way to improve our understanding of hypnosis processes is by looking at neuroimaging results. In this chapter, we first review the brain mechanisms of hypnosis in healthy volunteers, without stimulation (i.e., resting state studies) and with stimulation (e.g., pain, auditory stimuli), in high versus low hypnotizable individuals. We then focus on studies that investigate the benefits of hypnosis in a clinical population using functional Magnetic Resonance Imaging (fMRI), Positron Emission Tomography (PET), and electroencephalography

(EEG). Finally, the combination of hypnosis with virtual reality is proposed as a new technique to help patients in the management of acute pain. The details of studies are found in Table 5-1 at the end of this chapter (see Table 5-1: Neuroimaging clinical trials investigating the effects of hypnosis on brain functioning).

HYPNOSIS IN HEALTHY VOLUNTEERS UNDER THE MICROSCOPE OF NEUROIMAGING

Modulation of Consciousness Networks during Hypnosis

In 1987, one of the first neuroimaging studies showed a global increase (up to 16%) of cerebral blood flow during hypnosis, with specific increases in the occipital and right temporal regions (Ulrich et al., 1987). A few years later, increased activation of the left-sided occipital, parietal, precentral, premotor, and ventrolateral prefrontal cortices, and right-sided occipital lobe and anterior cingulate cortex, combined with an activity decreased in the precuneus, bilateral temporal, medial prefrontal, and right premotor cortices were observed during hypnosis (Maquet et al., 1999). In addition, increased theta power in posterior brain areas, combined with a global increase in alpha activity over the whole brain and possible changes in gamma activity were reported in patients in a hypnotic state (for reviews, see Hiltunen et al., 2021; Jensen et al., 2015). However, most of the EEG studies conducted to date have focused on differences based on the hypnotizability of subjects. We will therefore elaborate on this point below. These pioneer studies allowed the first objectivation of hypnosis processing by showing that hypnosis is a particular cerebral waking state where the subject experiences vivid, multimodal, coherent, and memory-based mental imagery (Maquet et al., 1999).

In addition, during hypnosis compared to a normal eyes-closed waking state, the functional connectivity of the external (awareness of the environment) and internal (self-awareness) consciousness networks was modified (Demertzi et al., 2011), simultaneous with a modification of the internal and external awareness level as subjectively evaluated by volunteers (i.e., higher for self-awareness and lower for external awareness; Demertzi et al., 2015). While studies have yielded substantially divergent results, we can still draw a consensus that the activity of Default Mode Network (DMN) is significantly disrupted during hypnosis (for a review, see Vanhaudenhuyse et al., 2020), with a greater decrease in its anterior part correlated to the hypnotic depth (McGeown et al., 2015). These changes in DMN activity may reflect a decrease in the retrieval of information from the external world relating to the self (e.g., visuospatial orientation, episodic memory retrieval, social cognition, visuospatial perspective taking, agency), and a decrease in spontaneous thinking; while the decrease in connectivity observed in the external consciousness network is a consequence of the sensory systems being blocked from receiving stimuli following entry into hypnosis (Demertzi et al., 2011; McGeown et al., 2015). The lack of consensus on fMRI data can be explained by the use of hypnotic instructions that differ between studies. For example, hypnosis will not be the same if the subject is asked to recall a pleasant autobiographical memory as opposed to performing neutral hypnosis, or by using a different experimental design (e.g., block-design or a continuous eyes-closed resting state). However, it appears that hypnosis influences neural connectivity as well as the subjective perception of internal and external consciousness.

Individual Differences regarding Hypnotizability

Even if the hypnosis phenomenon cannot be reduced to a unique variable related to individual ability, but rather involves complex variables (e.g., motivation, context, patient-professional relationship, abilities), we cannot hide the importance of the hypnotizability question in the scientific literature on hypnosis. In addition, a recurring question about hypnosis in clinical practice is the relevance of proposing hypnosis without knowing the patients' ability to enter into this non-ordinary state of consciousness. Hypnotizability is the 'individual's ability to experience suggested alterations in physiology, sensations, emotions, thoughts, or behavior during hypnosis' (Elkins et al., 2015). Hypnotizability can be measured with standardized scales, consisting of the observation of subjects' responses to hypnotic suggestion. These scales incorporate a classification system in which subjects' scores are grouped into ranges such as high, medium, and low hypnotizability. Recently, faster assessments of hypnotizability were proposed by either using a self-rated score of dissociation (0-10 scale; Vanhaudenhuyse et al., 2019), or with an online screening of hypnotic response (Palfi et al., 2020). Highly hypnotizable subjects have the ability to enter more easily into a subjective experience following the suggestion of the interlocutor with visual, auditory, and kinesthetic alterations in perception leading to pleasant sensations. Subjects with low hypnotizability have a feeling of relaxation during hypnosis, combined with a less vivid mental imagery experience (Rousseaux et al., 2020b). Furthermore, hypnotizability is not immutable and depends on the recruitment of attentional processes (Cojan et al., 2015). Training in self-hypnosis, relaxation, or neurofeedback can improve the level of hypnotizability (Batty et al., 2006). Interestingly, the application of low-frequency repetitive transcranial magnetic stimulation (rTMS) to the left dorsolateral prefrontal cortex improved the subjective response to hypnotic suggestion and thus the level of hypnotizability (Dienes & Hutton, 2013). Nowadays, only a small proportion of the population (20 – 30%, for a review, see Landry et al., 2017) is considered to have high or low suggestibility. In addition, we know that that patients with medium suggestibility may achieve as much pain relief as patients with high suggestibility (for a review, see Milling, 2008), suggesting that it is not necessary to have high hypnotizability to benefit from these interventions. Finally, in our clinical experience, we never test hypnotizability before practicing hypnosis in either surgical contexts or the management of chronic diseases. Thus, we consider that all patients (including low hypnotizable) can benefit from hypnosis (Vanhaudenhuyse et al., 2020).

MRI studies have revealed *anatomical differences* between people with low and high hypnotizability, especially in the left temporal-occipital cortex frontal areas (McGeown et al., 2015), the superior and medial frontal gyri, the insula (Huber et al., 2014), the corpus callosum (larger in high—) (Horton et al., 2004) and in the left cerebellar lobules and right inferior temporal gyrus (smaller in high—) (Picerni et al., 2019). These anatomical differences suggest a modification in the mechanisms of attention, inhibition, transfer of information, sensorimotor integration, and emotional processing, as well as a more efficient control and inhibition of undesirable stimuli from consciousness in high hypnotizable subjects (Horton et al., 2004; Picerni et al., 2019). *Functional differences* were also reported: highly hypnotizable individuals seem to be characterized by a better recruitment of the anterior cingulate cortex (ACC; Cojan et al., 2015; Egner et al., 2005), an increased connectivity between the posterior cingulate cortex (PCC)/precuneus and the bilateral visual and the left frontoparietal networks (Huber et al., 2014), between the left dorsolateral cortex and the salience network (Hoeft et al., 2012) and a lower connectivity within the DMN (McGeown et al., 2015). A study also showed a positive correlation between GABA concentration in the ACC and hypnotizability (DeSouza et al., 2020). These results shed light on the specificity of the executive control processing, the detection/integration of somatic and emotional information, and thus a global attentional system modulation in highly hypnotizable subjects.

Studies have also reported changes in all EEG bands. *Delta rhythms* (<4 Hz, involved in deep meditative states) seem to decrease in highly hypnotizable individuals (Fingelkurts et al., 2007), with a modulation of the synchronization mostly in the frontal lobe (Baghdadi & Nasrabadi, 2012). *Theta activity* (4-8 Hz, involved in learning and memory consolidation) was reported to be increased in occipital (Fingelkurts et al., 2007; Freeman et al., 2000), central, temporal areas (Graffin et al., 1995; Kihlstrom, 2013; Oakley & Halligan, 2013) as well as in the left parietal cortex (Freeman et al., 2000) in highly hypnotizable subjects. These results should be considered with caution since increased theta activity was also found in both high and low hypnotizable subjects in frontal, central, and occipital/posterior areas of the brain (Graffin et al., 1995; Sabourin et al., 1990). An increase in *alpha rhythms* (8-12 Hz, involved in vigilance and meditative states) was reported in the occipital lobe of high hypnotizable subjects (Fingelkurts et al., 2007), but also of the whole brain in both low and high hypnotizable individuals (Graffin et al., 1995), while a decrease was observed in high hypnotizable only in motor and visual brain areas (Lipari et al., 2012). In addition, a greater functional connectivity of alpha rhythms was observed in the parietal regions in high hypnotizable subjects (Keshmiri et al., 2020), while a diminished frontal-parietal phase synchrony of the alpha waves was also noted (Terhune et al., 2011). Finally, high hypnotizable subjects were also characterized by higher distributed brain region coherence within alpha bands in a resting state condition, compared to low hypnotizable individuals (Kirenskaya et al., 2011). Results focused on the *beta rhythms* (15-30 Hz, involved in cognitive engaged tasks) are controversial since some authors reported a decrease in high hypnotizable subjects (Fingelkurts et al., 2007; Kirenskaya et al., 2011), while other research has reported an increase in high hypnotizable individuals (De Pascalis, 1999). Finally, both an increase (De Pascalis, 1999; Schnyer & Allen, 1995) and a reduction in *gamma rhythms* (>35 Hz, involved in deep attentional state) were reported in high hypnotizable subjects (De Pascalis, 1999; Fingelkurts et al., 2007; Kirenskaya et al., 2011).

In summary, the theta activity modulation observed in high hypnotizable subjects suggests an intensification of attentional processes as well as being related to a potentially more intense relaxation state, while the alpha modulation could indicate the relaxed state of the subjects, whatever their level of hypnotizability, with potentially better flexibility of attentional processes in high hypnotizable subjects that allows them to be more sensitive to hypnotic induction. Finally, for the moment, a clear conclusion cannot be drawn concerning the implication of gamma rhythms to distinguish high and low hypnotizable subjects.

Event-related potential (ERP) studies have also been used to characterize hypnotic states in high versus low hypnotizable subjects. The mismatch negativity (MMN; i.e., negative component of ERP caused by any change in the sequence of monotonic auditory stimuli in inattentive subjects) was found to be weaker in the baseline condition than in hypnosis, potentially reflecting an improved pre-attentive treatment related to the hypnotic state (Jamieson et al., 2005; Kallio et al., 1999), notably in high hypnotizable subjects (Facco et al., 2014). Nevertheless, the increase in MMN has also been found in low hypnotizable subjects, which suggests that it is not attributable to distinctive hypnotic processes per se, although it could be related to the hypnosis condition (Jamieson et al., 2005). However, no difference in MMN amplitude during hypnosis was reported in high hypnotizable subjects (Hiltunen et al., 2019). An increase of P300 amplitude in frontal areas was found in high hypnotizable subjects (compared to low), suggesting that these subjects have more effective frontal attentional systems with better detection, integration, and filtering processes (Kirenskaya et al., 2019).

Altogether, structural and functional neuroimaging and neurophysiological data showed that high and low hypnotizable subjects are characterized by distinct mechanisms, specifically in terms of their information processing and attentional systems. High hypnotizable subjects seem to recruit different brain areas involved in attentional, integration, and filtering processes. We should note that studies are conducted on small samples and that the protocols used by the research teams for hypnotic induction and suggestion are not homogeneous. Future studies should include bigger samples and could also investigate if different types of suggestion used to induce the hypnotic state result in different brain modulation in low and high hypnotizable subjects.

HYPNOSIS AND NEUROIMAGING
IN CLINICAL POPULATIONS

Hypnosis to Modulate Acute Pain

Hypnosedation (i.e., combination of hypnosis, conscious sedation, and local anaesthesia; Faymonville et al., 1999) is a relevant illustration of the interest in using hypnosis in the context of acute pain management. Compared to general anaesthesia, hypnosedation has been shown to improve peri- and post-operative comfort and conditions during the performance of surgery; to reduce anxiety, emotional distress, pain, and nausea; diminish intraoperative requirements for anxiolytic and analgesic drugs; allow faster recovery with a significant decrease in the delay before restarting professional activity (for reviews and meta-analysis see Montgomery et al., 2000; Tefikow et al., 2013; Thompson et al., 2019; Vanhaudenhuyse et al., 2020). Studying brain modulation of acute pain perception during hypnosis will allow a better understanding of these positive effects reported in the management of acute pain.

Pain is a complex phenomenon that combines sensory, emotional, and cognitive processes (Raja et al., 2020; Turk et al., 2011) and generates the activation of a large brain network, namely the 'pain neuromatrix, encompassing the primary somatosensory (S1) and secondary cortex (S2), the insular cortex (IC), the ACC, prefrontal cortex (PFC), thalamus, cerebellum, and the periaqueductal grey matter; in addition to part of the reward circuit (i.e., hippocampus, nucleus accumbens, amygdala; for a review, see Bicego et al., 2021b). This pain network is divided into two distinct networks, namely the sensory component (i.e., S1 and S2—duration and location of the stimulus) and the emotional/motivational component (i.e., PFC, ACC, insula—unpleasantness of the stimulus) Bushnell et al., 2013. Hypnosis is currently well known to reduce both sensory and emotional components of noxious stimuli by modulating the whole pain matrix, with specific mediation of the ACC (involved in the emotional component of pain, (Faymonville et al., 2000; Rainville et al., 1997; Vanhaudenhuyse et al., 2009). Analgesic suggestion during hypnosis was associated specifically with an increase in the activation of right lateralization in the ACC and insula and a decrease in the midline thalamic nuclei (Del Casale et al., 2015). In addition, the sensory aspect of pain was more reduced than the affective aspect during hypnosis (Casiglia et al., 2020). Interestingly, it would also be possible to activate the pain brain network with hypnosis in the absence of actual pain stimulation (Derbyshire et al., 2004; Raij et al., 2005).

EEG and ERP studies have also shown a modulation of brain electrical responses to pain stimulation during hypnosis, i.e., a decrease in activity of the early (N20-reflecting sensory processing) and late (P100, P150, P250 - reflecting affective integration processing) components (Perri et al., 2019; Ray et al., 2002). An increase in amplitude induced by hyperalgesic suggestion was also reported for both N140 (mainly in left frontal and frontocentral areas) and P200 (left frontocentral, central, and bilateral centroparietal and parietal areas) waves (De Pascalis et al., 2015). We can thus assume that hypnotic suggestion increases subjects' capacity to focus their attention to form the mental images designed to reduce/amplify pain sensations.

Hypnosis to Improve the Global Quality of Life with Chronic Pain

Acute pain can evolve into chronic pain when it is persistent and prolonged, lasting at least 3 months (Turk et al., 2011). This major societal health problem encompasses biological, psychological, and socio-professional factors that significantly impair patients' everyday life (Turk et al., 2011). In 2006, a large European survey revealed that approximately 20% of Europeans suffer from chronic pain and 64% report that pharmacological treatments are insufficient (Breivik et al., 2006). Various non-pharmacological treatments are therefore proposed to patients, and hypnosis has been shown to be an effective complementary approach to help chronic pain patients regain a better quality of (Bicego et al., 2021b; Elkins et al., 2012; Vanhaudenhuyse et al., 2015; Vanhaudenhuyse et al., 2018). We will here summarize the clinical benefits reported in the literature regarding chronic pain and link these with neuroimaging studies focused on hypnosis used in chronic pain management. Details of each study cited can be read in Table 5-1.

Six sessions of self-hypnosis combined with self-care activities may benefit chronic pain patients, in terms of decreased pain intensity, pain interference, anxiety and depression, improved quality of life, and modifications in coping strategies (Bicego et al., 2021a; Vanhaudenhuyse et al., 2015; Vanhaudenhuyse et al., 2018). A meta-analysis (6 studies; 239 patients) focusing on fibromyalgia concluded that hypnosis allows improvements in pain sensation and sleep problems (Bernardy et al., 2011). Hypnosis was also shown to reduce headaches in migraine sufferers (Flynn, 2018). Finally, a meta-analysis (12 studies; 669 patients) comparing hypnosis to standard care or psychological intervention revealed a moderately more efficacious effect of hypnosis in chronic pain patients (Adachi et al., 2014).

Emotional and cognitive dimensions are involved in the development and modulation of chronic pain. Brain areas involved in the affective and cognitive aspects of chronic pain were impaired in patients, including the medial PFC, amygdala, nucleus accumbens, hippocampus, ACC, and insula (Simons et al., 2014; Taylor, 2018; Zhuo, 2008). Currently, PET and fMRI studies can elucidate the neural mechanisms of hypnosis in chronic pain (for a review, see Bicego et al., 2021b). In a Laser-Evoked Potentials study, hypnosis induced a change in N2-P2 amplitude, compared to an attentional distraction condition (text listening), which was hypothesized to reflect an inhibition of the afferent nociceptive transmission related to a possible modulation of the ACC (Squintani et al., 2017). A PET study with fibromyalgia patients showed that pain reduction was correlated with increased activity in the bilateral subcallosal cingulate cortex, left inferior parietal cortex, and right thalamus, and decreased bilateral PCC and ACC activity during hypnosis as compared with an ordinary state of consciousness (Wik et al., 1999). An fMRI study investigated the effect of hypo- and hyperalgesia hypnotic suggestion, compared to an ordinary state of consciousness, in chronic temporomandibular pain (Abrahamsen et al., 2010). Results showed that hypnotic hypoalgesia was associated with a large suppression of cortical activity, with only the right insula remaining activated during painful stimulation, combined with a significant decrease of self-reported pain and unpleasantness scores. Inversely, hyperalgesia suggestion related to the posterior insula, inferior parietal lobule, and precentral gyrus activation (Abrahamsen et al., 2010). In a PET study with chronic low back pain patients divided into two groups: one receiving direct suggestion of analgesia (targeting the sensory-discriminative pain experience); one receiving indirect suggestion focused on well-being (no mention of pain, targeting the motivational-affective pain experience), in two conditions (ordinary state of consciousness and hypnosis), both types of suggestion decreased subjectively-reported pain perception during hypnosis while only direct suggestion decreased subjective pain perception during the ordinary state of consciousness (Nusbaum et al., 2010).

These results combined with results in healthy volunteers during pain stimulation highlight the fact that hypnotic suggestion acts in a dynamic, multidirectional way rather than in a linear and unidirectional way (De Benedittis, 2015; De Benedittis, 2020). Furthermore, other studies conducted with fibromyalgia patients show that hypnosis modifies the cortico-limbic system involved in the emotional processing of pain in patients suffering from chronic pain, notably through the activation of the cerebellum, anterior medial cingulate cortex, posterior and anterior insula, inferior parietal cortex, and right PFC (Derbyshire et al., 2009; Derbyshire et al., 2017).

Hypnosis in Oncology

Cancer is a pathology that affects all spheres of daily life. Symptoms such as pain (Ewertz & Jensen, 2011), sleep difficulties (Die Trill,

2013), fatigue (Donovan et al., 2013; Fransson, 2010), anxiety (Die Trill, 2013), or emotional distress (Dauchy et al., 2013; Hernández Blázquez & Cruzado, 2016) are negative side-effects that are now well documented in the literature. These consequences are under-diagnosed and pharmacological treatments also seem to have little effect (Grégoire et al., 2017b). Thus, there is a growing interest in complementary therapies and in particular hypnosis (Grégoire et al., 2017; Grégoire et al., 2020). In recent years, several systematic reviews have demonstrated the effectiveness of hypnosis in reducing pain, anxiety, fatigue, and emotional distress in cancer patients (Carlson et al., 2018; Cramer et al., 2015; Schnur et al., 2008; Sine et al., 2021). Pediatric application of hypnosis was also recently reported (Grégoire et al., 2019). Finally, the prevalence of severe chronic post-surgical pain following breast cancer surgery is estimated to be 5-10%, and results in a Hypnosis is an effective approach in this context, decreasing the incidence of post-surgical chronic pain (Lacroix et al., 2019), by targeting coping significant reduction in daily functioning, work capability, and quality of life (Andersen & Kehlet, 2011). strategies and outcome expectancies after the surgery and thus allowing prevention of chronic post-surgical pain in women with breast cancer.

A case study conducted with a 57-year-old female undergoing breast cancer surgery has captured the effects of hypnosedation on electrical brain activity (Prinsloo et al., 2019). Increased activity in occipital regions (as the patient utilized visual imagery), decreased activity in the sensorimotor area (related to pain perception), increased activity in the retrosplenial cortex (known to mediate between perceptual and memory functions and to play a role in episodic memory), and decreased activity in the dorsal and ventral ACC (involved in the affective component of pain perception) was recorded in this patient during hypnosis. In addition, while the following results are not strictly related to neuroimaging observations, we consider it interesting to better understand the mechanisms of hypnosis in the oncological context. Respiration rate modulations during radiotherapy sessions were recorded in two conditions in patients with lung cancer: ordinary state of consciousness, and during 25 minutes of hypnosis (Li et al., 2013). Hypnosis was shown to effectively stabilize respiration motion, as patients were able to relax and felt comfortable during the radiotherapy session. A fMRI study conducted with healthy volunteers offers initial insight into the neural mechanisms of hypnosis for respiration control (Liu et al., 2020): results showed that 30 minutes of hypnosis, compared to a resting state condition, related to increased neural activity in the right calcarine cortex, bilateral fusiform gyrus, and left middle temporal gyrus, and decreased activity in the left cerebellum posterior lobe. This suggests the involvement of emotional processing and regulation of perceptual consciousness during breathing in hypnosis.

Neural Correlates of Smoking Craving Diminished with Hypnosis

Hypnosis is a widely used technique in smoking cessation (Li et al., 2020) and would even appear to be more effective than nicotine sub-stitutes (Hasan et al., 2014). Nevertheless, two meta-analyses (Barnes et al., 2019; Tahiri et al., 2012) have reported divergent results regarding the effectiveness of hypnosis in smoking cessation. Barnes et al. (2019) reported no evidence in favor of hypnosis over a control condition/placebo or over brief behavioral therapies, while Tahiri et al. (2012) demonstrated the effectiveness of hypnosis in the long term for smoking cessation.

As primary observations, EEG recordings have shown increased theta and delta coherence and decreased alpha and beta coherence during hypnosis (using aversion suggestion) compared to the baseline. In addition, delta coherence between the right frontal region and the left posterior region predicted a decrease in the desire to smoke after hypnotic induction (Li et al., 2017). The reduction of cravings following hypnotic aversion suggestion was then proposed to work through a prefrontal-insula network in a top-down direction. More specifically, increased activation in the dorsolateral prefrontal, medial frontal (related to attentional control processes), and insular (related to feelings of disgust) cortices was observed with fMRI during hypnosis, when pictures of smoking and aversion suggestion were presented to subjects. In addition, increased functional connectivity between these two brain regions was identified after hypnotic aversion suggestion. Further EEG source analysis indicated that the dorsolateral prefrontal cortex (DLPFC) was activated first, followed by activation of the insula, suggesting top-down regulation of these two brain areas in the hypnotic aversion process (Li et al., 2019). Finally, an additional study went further in understanding the neuronal basis of the short- and long-term effects of hypnotic aversion suggestion (Li et al., 2020). The activation of the right middle frontal gyrus was positively related to hypnotic depth as well as to the number of cigarettes smoked at one week and one month. The right middle frontal gyrus would therefore appear to be involved in the mechanisms of smoking control. In addition, in the resting-to-normal scan, the number of cigarettes smoked at one week and one-month was positively correlated with functional connectivity between the insula and rDLPFC, suggesting that the greater the number of cigarettes smoked, the greater the functional connectivity required to control the urge to smoke. Altogether, these results highlight the modulating role of the insula-right and DLPFC connectivity in the urge to smoke via the suggestion of hypnotic aversion.

Hypnosis to Treat Phobia

Phobia is an irrational and persistent fear of an object, animal, or situation leading to avoidance behavio, resulting in a severe anxiety reaction, and characterized by significant physiological and behavioral manifestations that cannot be voluntarily controlled (American Psychiatric Association, 2013; Curtis et al., 1998). Phobia, like severe anxiety disorders, has a serious impact on professional, private, social, and intimate relationships (Kessler et al., 2005). Moreover, anxiety and phobic disorders characteristically couple mental/psychic stress with body/physical stress; this makes the hypnosis technique interesting as it allows patients to regain control over the mind through a change in the body experience. Furthermore, phobias could be described as having a hypnotic component, i.e., the person focuses their attention on a specific object, which is the source of anxiety, and thus react to the fearful object (Spiegel, 2013). In recent years there has been an increase in the use of complementary techniques such as hypnosis in the management of anxiety disorders and phobias, such as dental phobia (Abdeshahi et al., 2013; Glaesmer et al., 2015; Halsband & Wolf, 2015), MRI claustrophobia (Napp et al., 2021), needle phobia (Birnie et a., 2018), airplane phobia (Spiegel, 2013), etc. (for a complete review, see Vanhaudenhuyse & Faymonville, 2020).

One study suggested that the degree of hypnotizability can modulate brain responses recorded by EEG in patients with animal phobias (Gemignani et al., 2006). More specifically, both high and low hypnotizable phobic patients showed an increase in gamma waves, indicating activation of the attentional and emotional system, while only the high hypnotizable patients showed a decrease in alpha and theta rhythms. These EEG results were combined with an increase in heart and respiratory rates and a decrease in skin responses that were less pronounced in high hypnotizable phobic patients, compared to low hypnotizable patients. It would therefore seem that the brain mechanisms and reactions of the autonomic system respond differently according to the level of hypnotizability of patients suffering from phobia (Gemignani et al., 2006).

Hypnosis can also be used to reduce both pain and severe anxiety during dental surgery. Several case studies and controlled trials have shown beneficial effects of hypnosis in dentistry, such as reduction of anxiety (Abdeshahi et al., 2013; Glaesmer et al., 2015), extreme fear (Hammarstrand et al., 1995), pain (Abdeshahi et al., 2013), blood loss during tooth removal (Abdeshahi et al., 2013), as well as increased speed of recovery (Abdeshahi et al., 2013; Montgomery et al., 2000;

Montgomery et al., 2002). Significant changes in alpha and theta EEG rhythms were observed during maxillofacial surgical interventions conducted with hypnosis, with a peak of activation in the posterior part of the brain and a shifting laterality from the left to the right hemisphere (Heckmann et al., 2006). Finally, the application of hypnosis (suggestion of mental and physical relaxation) in fMRI showed a decrease in activation in the left amygdala, ACC, insula, and hippocampus (involved in anxiety processes) in both dental phobia patients and healthy volunteers visualizing unpleasant dental stimuli (Halsband & Wolf, 2015). These results suggest that hypnosis is an effective method for inhibiting the brain regions involved in the perception of anxiety-provoking stimuli in this clinical population (Halsband & Wolf, 2015).

Hypnosis to Understand Conversion Disorders

Conversion disorder refers to what was formerly called 'hysteria' and is defined as a neurological dysfunction (such as paralysis of one or more limbs, tremor or involuntary movement, anaesthesia, blindness, deafness) occurring in the absence of an organic neurological lesion but during psychological stress or conflict (American Psychiatric Association, 1994). The hypothesis that hypnosis and hysteria share similar processes was put forward since the activity of sensory or motor pathways could be affected by dysfunctional (non-damaging) processes within the central nervous system and could explain hysterical seizures, which could also be induced by particular ideas, suggestion, or psychological states (Vuilleumier, 2005). A few studies have tested the effectiveness of hypnosis in this disorder and the results are divergent, with some in favour of hypnosis and others not showing any positive effect of this technique to treat conversion disorders (for a review see Vanhaudenhuyse et al., 2014). Nevertheless, a recent review of 894 participants showed a lack of current evidence regarding the effectiveness of interventions such as hypnosis for this disorder (Ganslev et al., 2020). However, hypnosis can be used to induce symptoms similar to those observed in conversion disorders, allowing a better understanding of the underlying neural processes. Different authors have pointed to similar brain activity patterns between motor inhibition suggested during hypnosis and conversion disorders, involving the frontal regions (Bell et al., 2011; Oakley, 1999), prefrontal cortex (Cojan et al., 2013; Ward et al., 2003), and ACC (Oakley, 1999). Finally, greater hypnotic susceptibility was reported in patients with conversion disorder, by determining the activation of similar brain areas during hypnotic suggestion of paralysis compared with conversion disorder (Srzich et al., 2016).

Urinary Incontinence

Urinary incontinence can lead to various psychological consequences including anxiety and depression (Coyne et al., 2009) as well as social consequences such as loss of independence and employment (Sexton et al., 2009). According to some authors, urinary incontinence is not only a somatic disorder but a functional disorder requiring management focused on the mental faculties (Komesu et al., 2020). In this respect, very few studies have explored the effects of hypnosis in the context of this pathology, although positive clinical effects, even superior to behavioral therapies, have been reported in a series of studies (Freeman & Baxby, 1982; Y. Komesu et a., 2011; Komesu et al., 2020).

Recent studies have demonstrated a relationship between dysfunctional perceptual awareness and urinary incontinence using fMRI (Griffiths et al., 2015). People suffering from this pathology present an abnormal activation of the regions that modulate the perception and interpretation of physiological stimuli, i.e., interoception (Ketai et al., 2021). While both hypnosis and medication (oxybutynin or tolterodine) intervention patients showed an improvement in incontinence episodes, the hypnosis group showed greater functional connectivity between the ACC and the left DLPFC cortex, associated with the attentional network (Ketai et al., 2021). In summary, we can conclude from these studies combining clinical observations and brain process recordings that the modulation of attentional, self-awareness, and emotional networks induced by hypnosis is a first step to understanding the mechanisms underlying the clinical changes observed when hypnosis is integrated into the treatment of these patients.

FUTURE PERSPECTIVE:
VIRTUAL REALITY COMBINED WITH HYPNOSIS

Broader clinical applications are emerging today in order to combine hypnosis with new emerging technologies. Hypnosis can sometimes be difficult to organize in a clinic context given the number of clinicians needed and the time required (Ganry et al., 2018). Thus, support from virtual reality (VR) technology in the clinic and research can make sense and offer new opportunities (Rousseaux et al., 2020a). While VR is a well-documented technology in the field of entertainment and science, VR combined with hypnosis (VRH) in clinical applications is an emerging field, particularly in the area of pain (Rousseaux et al., 2020a).

Short term improvement of quality of life has been reported in patients with chronic neuropathic pain (Oneal et al., 2008) and orthopaedic injuries (Teeley et al., 2012) when VRH was used. Furthermore, while hypnotizability appears to influence hypnotic induction, this does not appear to be the case for VR and VRH (Enea et al., 2014; Patterson et al., 2006). Nevertheless, these studies suffer from limitations due to the procedures used, making it difficult to compare them; hypnosis is either administered alone and then VR is used, or vice versa, or both. A recent literature review (8 VRH studies, 262 participants) has highlighted that we cannot affirm that VR brings superior benefits to hypnosis when they are combined (Rousseaux et al., 2020a). A prospective randomized study conducted with patients in cardiac surgery has shown no significant differences among patients benefitting from hypnosis, VR, or VRH for anxiety, pain, fatigue, or relaxation (even if relaxation increases and anxiety decreases in all groups) and none of the techniques was better than another, nor better than the control group receiving no treatment (Rousseaux et al., 2022), which does not affirm the superiority of one technique over another. In view of these different results, it appears necessary to develop effective tools and to continue studies in randomized controlled trials on a larger population.

One first study analyzed VR from a neurophysiological perspective and was conducted with 30 healthy volunteers divided into 3 groups (control group, passive VR (no interaction with virtual world), and active VR (interactive virtual environment)) during which participants received painful electrical stimuli at random intervals. The results indicate that active VR reduced pain by allowing a decrease in the amplitude of N1 and P3 amplitudes; namely, a decrease in the EEG signature of pain (Lier et al., 2020). These results were confirmed in our recent study with 18 volunteers who received painful electrical stimulation in resting state eyes-open and VRH conditions: VRH induced a decrease in the amplitude of the early (N100) and late (P200) ERP components (Rousseaux et al., under review). Furthermore, at the physiological level, VRH increased heart rate while reducing EMG response and respiratory rate (Rousseaux et al., under review). These initial results indicate that VRH is an approach to be explored in pain reduction.

CONCLUSION

Throughout this chapter, we have reviewed the various neurophysiological studies to learn more about the mechanisms of hypnosis and its implications for clinical practice. Hypnosis is a useful approach in the clinical routine for treatment of patients suffering from diverse health problems (e.g., acute/chronic pain, oncology, phobias). Some studies have focused on the potential brain modulation caused by hypnosis in these clinical contexts. The current results are not consensual and highlight the need for similar protocols between studies, with large sample of patients, in order to be able to compare them with each other. Nevertheless, all these results indicate the relevance of hypnosis to modulate interconnected networks of cortical and subcortical regions. By acting through both sensorimotor and affective/motivational brain networks, hypnosis actively participates in the reduction of symptoms caused by both somatic and psychiatric pathologies. Hypnosis is also a valuable tool to better understand the functioning of human consciousness and to open new perspectives for understanding other states of consciousness, such as near-death experiences (Martial et al., 2019) and self-induced cognitive trance (Gosseries et al., 2020; Grégoire et al., 2021, 2022). Please refer to **Table 5-1: Neuroimaging clinical trials investigating the effects of hypnosis on brain functioning** for a summary of neuroimaging studies in clinical trials.

CHAPTER 5
REFLECTION QUESTIONS

1. How does hypnosis affect consciousness networks in healthy volunteers?

2. What are the structural and functional neurophysiological differences between high and low hypnotizable subjects?

3. How does hypnosis benefit the clinical population— including chronic pain, oncology, phobia, conversion disorders, and urea incontinence?

TABLE 5-1: NEUROIMAGING CLINICAL TRIALS INVESTIGATING THE EFFECTS OF HYPNOSIS ON BRAIN FUNCTIONING

Abbreviations: LEPS : laser-evoked potentials, **Min** : minutes, **PET** : Positron Emission Tomography scanner, **EEG** : electroencephalography, **fMRI** : functional Magnetic Resonance Imaging, **ERP** : Event-related potential, **ECG** : electrocardiogram, **EOC** : electro-oculogram, **EMG** : electromyogram, **VR** : virtual reality, **VRH** : VR combined with hypnosis, **SHSS** : Stanford Hypnotic Susceptibility Scale, **R**: Right, **L**: Left, **rDLPFC** : right dorsal lateral prefrontal cortex, **PFC**: Prefrontal Cortex, **ACC**: Anterior Cingulate Cortex, **HH** : Highly hypnotizable, **LH** : Low hypnotizable, **NA** : not applicable

AUTHORS, YEAR	DESIGN	TECH-NIQUE	CONDITIONS	STIM-ULUS	NUMBER OF PATIENTS	DIAGNOSIS	LEVEL OF HYPNO-TIZABILITY	LIMITATIONS	RESULTS
CHRONIC PAIN									
Wik et al., 1999	Prospective non-randomized	PET	Ordinary consciousness Hypnosis, analgesia suggestions	NA	8	Fibromyalgia	High	* Small sample size * Only women * No use of experimental pain	* Hypnosis: ↑ activation in bilateral cingulate gyrus, R thalamus, L inferior parietal cortex ↓ activation in bilateral posterior cingulate cortex, posterior anterior cingulate gyrus ↓ pain perception
Derbyshire et al., 2009	Prospective randomized	fMRI	Hypo- and hyper-algesia suggestions in 2 conditions: * Ordinary consciousness * Hypnosis	NA	13	Fibromyalgia	High	* Sample heterogeneity: some patients taking medication * Small sample size * Wide range of non-specific symptoms	* Ordinary consciousness: ↑ activation R thalamus, L mid ACC, bilateral S1 and L prefrontal cortex * Hypnosis: ↑ activation in cerebellum, ACC, anterior/posterior insula, inferior parietal cortex, R prefrontal cortex à correlated with changes in pain perception
Abrahamsen et al., 2010	Prospective randomized (except control condition always first)	fMRI	Ordinary consciousness Hypnosis with hypo-algesia suggestions during hypnosis Hypnosis with hyper-algesia suggestions	Pin-prick stimuli	19	Temporo-mandibular disorders	High	* Much larger proportion of women * "Ceiling" effect of the painful pin-prick stimulation due to the general effect of hypnosis	* Ordinary consciousness: activation R posterior insula, S1. * Hypnotic hypo-algesia: activation in the posterior insula * Hypnotic hyper-algesia: activation in the R posterior insula, middle frontal gyrus, L supramarginal gyrus

CHRONIC PAIN

AUTHORS, YEAR	DESIGN	TECHNIQUE	CONDITIONS	STIMULUS	NUMBER OF PATIENTS	DIAGNOSIS	LEVEL OF HYPNO-TIZABILITY	LIMITATIONS	RESULTS
Nusbaum et al., 2010	Prospective randomized	PET	Ordinary consciousness Hypnosis: - Direct suggestions of analgesia - Indirect suggestions, mention of well-being, no mention of pain itself	NA	14	Chronic low-back pain	Medium, High	* No use of experimental pain * Lack of randomization	* Hypnosis: ↑ activation of anterior insula, left nucleus, accumbens, bilateral lenticular and caudate nuclei, ACC ↓ activation in L precuneus, R posterior cingulate gyrus. * Direct suggestion during hypnosis: ↑ activation L medial and lateral PFC, bilateral orbitofrontal cortex ↓ activation posterior cingulate cortex, R middle temporal cortex, L parahippocampal gyrus, L precentral gyrus. * Indirect suggestion during hypnosis: ↑ activation bilateral anterior insula and precentral gyrus, L inferior parietal lobule, L lenticular nucleus, R ACC ↓ activation L precuneus, L cuneus, R superior parietal lobule
Derbyshire et al., 2017	Prospective non randomized	fMRI	Ordinary consciousness Hypnosis, hypoalgesia/hyperalgesia suggestions	Thermal hot stimuli	28	13 Fibromyalgia 15 Healthy subjects	High	* Lack of behavioral data * Pain more intense at baseline for control group	* Patients: Hypnosis ↑ activation with pain reports in brainstem, thalamus, mid-cingulate cortex, insula, prefrontal cortex, sensory cortices * Control: Hypnosis ↓ activation with pain reports
Squintani et al., 2017	Prospective non-randomized	LEPs	Ordinary consciousness Hypnosis, suggestions of changes subjective experience and perception of pain Distraction of attention	Laser stimuli	10	Chronic pain (various aetiologies)	NA	* Subjects were familiar with hypnosis * Lack of homogeneity in aetiologies * Small sample size	* Ordinary consciousness: No change * Hypnosis: ↓ N2- P2 amplitude, correlated with ↓ in pain intensity and unpleasantness. * Distraction attention: No change

AUTHORS, YEAR	DESIGN	TECHNIQUE	CONDITIONS	STIMULUS	NUMBER OF PATIENTS	DIAGNOSIS	LEVEL OF HYPNOTIZABILITY	LIMITATIONS	RESULTS
ONCOLOGY									
Prinsloo et al., 2019	Case study	EEG	Hypnosedation	Surgery	1	Breast cancer surgery	NA	* Case study	* Hypnosis: visual cortex is active while sensorimotor areas ↓ in activity ↑ retrosplenial cortex ↓ dorsal and ventral ACC
SMOKING CRAVING									
Li et al., 2017	Prospective	EEG	Ordinary consciousness Hypnosis, smoking disgust suggestion	NA	42	Smokers	High	* EEG spatial resolution is limited * Self-reported tool to measure cigarette * Only male * Oscillation power and coherence may not be independent	* Hypnosis: ↑ delta and theta frequency ↓ alpha and beta frequency Delta coherence between the R frontal region and the L posterior region predicted cigarette craving reduction
Li et al., 2019	Prospective	fMRI and EEG	2 conditions in fMRI and EEG: Ordinary consciousness Hypnosis, smoking disgust suggestion	Neutral images/ smoking-related images	45	Smokers	High	* More pictures included in EEG group than fMRI group * Higher proportion of men * Short period of abstinence before hypnosis * Analysis of short-term effects only	* Hypnosis: ↓ craving ↑ R dorsal lateral prefrontal cortex (rDLPFC) and L insula ↑ functional connectivity between the rDLPFC and L insula Activation in the R DLPFC preceded L insula
Li et al., 2020	Prospective pseudo-randomized	fMRI	Ordinary consciousness Hypnosis with aversion suggestions	neutral and smoking-related images	24	Smokers	High	* Higher proportion of men * Only high hypnotizable * Only one session of hypnotic aversion suggestion on craving to smoke	* Hypnosis: ↓ craving ↑ R DLPFC, L insula, R middle frontal gyrus ↑ functional connectivity between the R DLPFC and L insula R middle frontal gyrus positively related to hypnotic depth Number of cigarettes smoked at 1 week and 1 month positively correlated with functional connectivity between the insula and R DLPFC

PHOBIA

AUTHORS, YEAR	DESIGN	TECHNIQUE	CONDITIONS	STIMULUS	NUMBER OF PATIENTS	DIAGNOSIS	LEVEL OF HYPNO-TIZABILITY	LIMITATIONS	RESULTS
Gemignagni et al., 2006	Prospective randomized	EEG EOC EMG	2 groups (low vs high): * Relaxation * Description of a neutral situation * Relaxation before phobic stimulation * Description of an aversive situation	Phobic stimulus (spider)	14	Right-hand female students	7 low 7 high	* Small sample size * Only women	* Both groups: ↑ heart and respiratory frequency ↓ skin resistance less pronounced in Highs than in Lows during phobic stimulation ↑ gamma activity * High: ↓ alpha and theta activity
Heckman et al., 2006	Prospective	EEG, ECG and physiological measurements (e.g. heart rate, blood, respiratory rate,)	4 groups: Control without treatment Control with hypnosis Control with surgical intervention without hypnosis Study group with surgical intervention and hypnosis	Dental surgical intervention	45	Patients with or without surgical intervention	NA	* Therapist changes at the last session	* Hypnosis: ↓ systolic, diastolic blood pressure, respiration rate, heart rate ↑ alpha, theta activity with a peak of activation in the posterior part of the brain Brain activity shifting from the L to the R hemisphere, from anterior to posterior segments
Halsband & Wolf, 2015	Prospective pseudo-randomized	fMRI	2 conditions for all participants: Experimental condition: dental videos Control condition: videos of electronic household instruments	Audio-visual stimuli	24	12 dental phobic patients 12 healthy controls	NA	* High hypnotizable only * Small sample size	* Hypnosis: ↓ in the L amygdala and bilaterally in the ACC, insula and hipocampus

AUTHORS, YEAR	DESIGN	TECH-NIQUE	CONDITIONS	STIM-ULUS	NUMBER OF PATIENTS	DIAGNOSIS	LEVEL OF HYPNO-TIZABILITY	LIMITATIONS	RESULTS
URINARY INCONTINENCE									
Ketai et al., 2021	Prospective randomized	fMRI	Hypnotherapy (8 weekly, 1-hour) Medication	NA	64	Women with urgency urinary incontinence	NA	* Manual fluid infusion in this study vs use of an infusion pump in other protocols * No exploration of altered activation and connectivity of the attentional network in the longer term * Widespread clinical improvement in both treatment groups	* Both groups: ↑ improvement in incontinence episodes * Hypnosis: ↑ functional connectivity between the ACC and the L dorsolateral prefrontal cortex, a component of the dorsal attentional network

REFERENCES

Abdeshahi, S. K., Hashemipour, M. A., Mesgarzadeh, V., Shahidi Payam, A., & Halaj Monfared, A. (2013). Effect of hypnosis on induction of local anaesthesia, pain perception, control of haemorrhage and anxiety during extraction of third molars: A case—control study. *Journal of Cranio-Maxillofacial Surgery*, *41*(4), 310-315. https://doi.org/10.1016/j.jcms.2012.10.009

Abrahamsen, R., Dietz, M., Lodahl, S., Roepstorff, A., Zachariae, R., Østergaard, L., & Svensson, P. (2010). Effect of hypnotic pain modulation on brain activity in patients with temporomandibular disorder pain. *PAIN®*, *151*(3), 825-833. https://doi.org/10.1016/j.pain.2010.09.020

Adachi, T., Fujino, H., Nakae, A., Mashimo, T., & Sasaki1, J. (2014). A meta-analysis of hypnosis for chronic pain problems: A comparison between hypnosis, standard care, and other psychological interventions. *International Journal of Clinical and Experimental Hypnosis*, *62*(1), 1-28. https://doi.org/10.1080/00207144.2013.841471

American Psychiatric Association. (2013). *Diagnostic and statistical manual of mental disorders: DSM-5* (5th ed). American Psychiatric Association.

American Psychiatric Association, C. C. (1994). DSM-IV: Diagnostic and Statistical Manual of Mental Disorders. *JAMA*, *272*(10), 828-829. https://doi.org/10.1001/ jama.1994.03520100096046

Andersen, K. G., & Kehlet, H. (2011). Persistent pain after breast cancer treatment: A critical review of risk factors and strategies for prevention. *Journal of Pain*, *12*(7), 725-746. https://doi.org/10.1016/j.jpain.2010.12.005

Baghdadi, G., & Nasrabadi, A. M. (2012). EEG phase synchronization during hypnosis induction. *Journal of Medical Engineering & Technology*, *36*(4), 222-229. https://doi.org/10.3109/03091902.2012.668262

Barnes, J., McRobbie, H., Dong, C. Y., Walker, N., & Hartmann-Boyce, J. (2019). Hypnotherapy for smoking cessation. *Cochrane Database of Systematic Reviews*, *6*. https://doi.org/10.1002/14651858.CD001008.pub3

Batty, M. J., Bonnington, S., Tang, B.-K., Hawken, M. B., & Gruzelier, J. H. (2006). Relaxation strategies and enhancement of hypnotic susceptibility: EEG neurofeedback, progressive muscle relaxation and self-hypnosis. *Brain Research Bulletin*, *71*(1), 83-90. https://doi.org/10.1016/j.brainresbull. 2006.08.005

Bell, V., Oakley, D. A., Halligan, P. W., & Deeley, Q. (2011). Dissociation in hysteria and hypnosis: Evidence from cognitive neuroscience. *Journal of Neurology, Neurosurgery & Psychiatry*, *82*(3), 332-339. https://doi.org/10.1136/ jnnp.2009.199158

Bernardy, K., Füber, N., Klose, P., & Häuser, W. (2011). Efficacy of hypnosis/guided imagery in fibromyalgia syndrome—A systematic review and meta-analysis of controlled trials. *BMC Musculoskeletal Disorders*, *12*(1), 133. https://doi.org/ 10.1186/1471-2474-12-133

Bicego, A., Monseur, J., Collinet, A., Donneau, A.-F., Fontaine, R., Libbrecht, D., Malaise, N., Nyssen, A.-S., Raaf, M., Rousseaux, F., Salamun, I., Staquet, C., Teuwis, S., Tomasella, M., Faymonville, M.-E., & Vanhaudenhuyse, A. (2021a). Complementary treatment comparison for chronic pain management: A randomized longitudinal study. *PLOS ONE*, *16*(8), e0256001. https://doi.org/10.1371/journal.pone.0256001

Bicego, A., Rousseaux, F., Faymonville, M.-E., Nyssen, A.-S., & Vanhaudenhuyse, A. (2021b) Neurophysiology of hypnosis in chronic pain: A review of recent literature. *American Journal of Clinical Hypnosis*, *64*(1), 62-80. https://doi.org/ 10.1080/00029157.2020.1869517

Birnie, K. A., Noel, M., Chambers, C. T., Uman, L. S., & Parker, J. A. (2018). Psychological interventions for needle-related procedural pain and distress in children and adolescents. *Cochrane Database of Systematic Reviews*, *10*. https://doi.org/10.1002/14651858.CD005179.pub4

Breivik, H., Collett, B., Ventafridda, V., Cohen, R., & Gallacher, D. (2006). Survey of chronic pain in Europe: Prevalence, impact on daily life, and treatment. *European Journal of Pain*, *10*(4), 287-333. https://doi.org/10.1016/j.ejpain. 2005.06.009

Bushnell, M. C., Čeko, M., & Low, L. A. (2013). Cognitive and emotional control of pain and its disruption in chronic pain. *Nature Reviews Neuroscience*, *14*(7), 502-511. https://doi.org/10.1038/nrn3516

Carlson, L. E., Toivonen, K., Flynn, M., Deleemans, J., Piedalue, K.-A., Tolsdorf, E., & Subnis, U. (2018). The role of hypnosis in cancer care. *Current Oncology Reports, 20*(12), 93. https://doi.org/10.1007/s11912-018-0739-1

Casiglia, E., Finatti, F., Tikhonoff, V., Stabile, M. R., Mitolo, M., Albertini, F., Gasparotti, F., Facco, E., Lapenta, A. M., & Venneri, A. (2020). Mechanisms of hypnotic analgesia explained by functional magnetic resonance (fMRI). *International Journal of Clinical and Experimental Hypnosis, 68*(1), 1-15. https://doi.org/10.1080/00207144.2020.1685331

Cojan, Y., Archimi, A., Cheseaux, N., Waber, L., & Vuilleumier, P. (2013). Time-course of motor inhibition during hypnotic paralysis: EEG topographical and source analysis. *Cortex, 49*(2), 423-436. https://doi.org/10.1016/j.cortex.2012.09.013

Cojan, Y., Piguet, C., & Vuilleumier, P. (2015). What makes your brain suggestible? Hypnotizability is associated with differential brain activity during attention outside hypnosis. *NeuroImage, 117*, 367-374. https://doi.org/10.1016/j.neuroimage.2015.05.076

Coyne, K., Wein, A., Tubaro, A., Sexton, C., Thompson, C., Kopp, Z., & Aiyer, L. (2009). The burden of lower urinary tract symptoms: Evaluating the effect of LUTS on health-related quality of life, anxiety and depression: EpiLUTS. *BJU International Supplemental 3*, 4-11. https://doi.org/10.1111/j.1464-410X.2009.08371.x

Cramer, H., Lauche, R., Paul, A., Langhorst, J., Kümmel, S., & Dobos, G. J. (2015). Hypnosis in breast cancer care: A systematic review of randomized controlled trials. *Integrative Cancer Therapies, 14*(1), 5-15. https://doi.org/10.1177/1534735414550035

Curtis, G., Magee, W. J., Eaton, W. W., Wittchen, H.-U., & Kessler, R. C. (1998). Specific fears and phobias: Epidemiology and classification. *The British Journal of Psychiatry, 173*(3), 212-217. https://doi.org/10.1192/bjp.173.3.212

Dauchy, S., Dolbeault, S., & Reich, M. (2013). Depression in cancer patients. *EJC Supplements, 11*(2), 205-215. https://doi.org/10.1016/j.ejcsup.2013.07.006

De Benedittis, G. (2015). Neural mechanisms of hypnosis and meditation. *Journal of Physiology-Paris, 109*(4), 152-164. https://doi.org/10.1016/j.jphysparis.2015.11.001

De Benedittis, G. (2020). Hypnosis: From neural mechanisms to clinical practice. *OBM Integrative and Complementary Medicine, 5*(3), 1-7. https://doi.org/10.21926/obm.icm.2003039

de Pascalis, V. (1999). Psychophysiological correlates of hypnosis and hypnotic susceptibility. *International Journal of Clinical and Experimental Hypnosis*, *47*(2), 117-143. https://doi.org/10.1080/00207149908410026

de Pascalis, V. Varriale, V., & Cacace, I. (2015). Pain modulation in waking and hypnosis in women: Event-Related potentials and sources of cortical activity. *PLOS ONE*, *10*(6), e0128474. https://doi.org/10.1371/journal.pone.0128474

Del Casale, A., Ferracuti, S., Rapinesi, C., De Rossi, P., Angeletti, G., Sani, G., Kotzalidis, G. D., & Girardi, P. (2015). Hypnosis and pain perception: An Activation Likelihood Estimation (ALE) meta-analysis of functional neuroimaging studies. *Journal of Physiology-Paris*, *109*(4), 165-172. https://doi.org/10.1016/j.jphys paris. 2016.01.001

Demertzi, A., Soddu, A., Faymonville, M.-E., Bahri, M. A., Gosseries, O., Vanhaudenhuyse, A., Phillips, C., Maquet, P., Noirhomme, Q., Luxen, A., & Laureys, S. (2011). Hypnotic modulation of resting state fMRI default mode and extrinsic network connectivity. In E. J. W. Van Someren, Y. D. Van Der Werf, P. R. Roelfsema, H. D. Mansvelder, & F. H. Lopes Da Silva (Eds.), *Progress in Brain Research* (Vol. 193, p. 309-322). Elsevier. https://doi.org/10.1016/ B978-0-444-53839-0.00020-X

Demertzi, A., Vanhaudenhuyse, A., Noirhomme, Q., Faymonville, M.-E., & Laureys, S. (2015). Hypnosis modulates behavioural measures and subjective ratings about external and internal awareness. *Journal of Physiology-Paris*, *109*(4), 173-179. https://doi.org/10.1016/j.jphysparis.2015.11.002

Derbyshire, S. W. G., Whalley, M. G., & Oakley, D. A. (2009). Fibromyalgia pain and its modulation by hypnotic and non-hypnotic suggestion: An fMRI analysis. *European Journal of Pain*, *13*(5), 542-550. https://doi.org/10.1016/ j.ejpain.2008.06.010

Derbyshire, S. W. G., Whalley, M. G., Seah, S. T. H., & Oakley, D. A. (2017). Suggestions to reduce clinical fibromyalgia pain and experimentally induced pain produce parallel effects on perceived pain but divergent functional MRI-based brain activity. *Psychosomatic Medicine*, *79*(2), 189-200. https://doi.org/10.1097/ PSY.0000000000000370

Derbyshire, S. W. G., Whalley, M. G., Stenger, V. A., & Oakley, D. A. (2004). Cerebral activation during hypnotically induced and imagined pain. *NeuroImage*, *23*(1), 392-401. https://doi.org/10.1016/j.neuroimage.2004.04.033

DeSouza, D. D., Stimpson, K. H., Baltusis, L., Sacchet, M. D., Gu, M., Hurd, R., Wu, H., Yeomans, D. C., Willliams, N., & Spiegel, D. (2020). Association between anterior cingulate neurochemical concentration and individual differences in hypnotizability. *Cerebral Cortex, 30*(6), 3644-3654. https://doi.org/10.1093/cercor/bhz332

Die Trill, M. (2013). Anxiety and sleep disorders in cancer patients. *EJC Supplements, 11*(2), 216-224. https://doi.org/10.1016/j.ejcsup.2013.07.009

Dienes, Z., & Hutton, S. (2013). Understanding hypnosis metacognitively: RTMS applied to left DLPFC increases hypnotic suggestibility. *Cortex, 49*(2), 386-392. https://doi.org/10.1016/j.cortex.2012.07.009

Donovan, K. A., McGinty, H. L., & Jacobsen, P. B. (2013). A systematic review of research using the diagnostic criteria for cancer-related fatigue. *Psycho-Oncology, 22*(4), 737-744. https://doi.org/10.1002/pon.3085

Egner, T., Jamieson, G., & Gruzelier, J. (2005). Hypnosis decouples cognitive control from conflict monitoring processes of the frontal lobe. *NeuroImage, 27*(4), 969-978. https://doi.org/10.1016/j.neuroimage.2005.05.002

Elkins, G., Johnson, A., & Fisher, W. (2012). Cognitive hypnotherapy for pain management. *American Journal of Clinical Hypnosis, 54*(4), 294-310. https://doi.org/10.1080/00029157.2011.654284

Elkins, G., Barabasz, A., Council, J. & Speigel, D. (2015) Advancing research and practice: The Revised APA Division 30 Definition of Hypnosis. *International Journal of Clinical and Experimental Hypnosis, 63*(1), 1-9. doi:10.1080/0020 7144.2014.961870

Enea, V., Dafinoiu, I., Opriş, D., & David, D. (2014). Effects of hypnotic analgesia and virtual reality on the reduction of experimental pain among high and low hypnotizables. *International Journal of Clinical and Experimental Hypnosis, 62*(3), 360-377. https://doi.org/10.1080/00207144.2014.901087

Ewertz, M., & Jensen, A. B. (2011). Late effects of breast cancer treatment and potentials for rehabilitation. *Acta Oncologica, 50*(2), 187-193. https://doi.org/10.3109/0284186X.2010.533190

Facco, E., Ermani, M., Rampazzo, P., Tikhonoff, V., Saladini, M., Zanette, G., Casiglia, E., & Spiegel, D. (2014). Top-Down regulation of left temporal cortex by hypnotic amusia for rhythm: A pilot study on mismatch negativity. *International Journal of Clinical and Experimental Hypnosis, 62*(2), 129-144. https://doi.org/10. 1080/ 00207144.2014.869124

Faymonville, M. E., Laureys, S., Degueldre, C., DelFiore, G., Luxen, A., Franck, G., Lamy, M., & Maquet, P. (2000). Neural mechanisms of antinociceptive effects of hypnosis. *Anesthesiology, 92*(5), 1257-1267. https://doi.org/10.1097/ 00000542-200005000-00013

Faymonville, M. E., Meurisse, M., & Fissette, J. (1999). Hypnosedation: A valuable alternative to traditional anaesthetic techniques. *Acta Chirurgica Belgica, 99*(4), 141-146. https://doi.org/10.1080/00015458.1999.12098466

Fingelkurts, A. A., Fingelkurts, A. A., Kallio, S., & Revonsuo, A. (2007). Cortex functional connectivity as a neurophysiological correlate of hypnosis: An EEG case study. *Neuropsychologia, 45*(7), 1452-1462. https://doi.org/10.1016/ j.neuropsychologia.2006.11.018

Flynn, N. (2018). Systematic review of the effectiveness of hypnosis for the management of headache. *International Journal of Clinical and Experimental Hypnosis, 66*(4), 343-352. https://doi.org/10.1080/00207144.2018.1494432

Fransson. (2010). Fatigue in prostate cancer patients treated with external beam radiotherapy: A prospective 5-year long-term patient-reported evaluation. *Journal of Cancer Research and Therapeutics, 6*(4) 516-520. doi: 10.4103/0973-1482.77076.

Freeman, R., Barabasz, A., Barabasz, M., & Warner, D. (2000). Hypnosis and distraction differ in their effects on cold pressor pain. *American Journal of Clinical Hypnosis, 43*(2), 137-148. https://doi.org/10.1080/00029157.2000. 10404266

Freeman, R. M., & Baxby, K. (1982). Hypnotherapy for incontinence caused by the unstable detrusor. *British Journal of Medicine (Clin Res Ed), 284*(6332), 1831-1834. https://doi.org/10.1136/bmj.284.6332.1831

Ganry, L., Hersant, B., Sidahmed-Mezi, M., Dhonneur, G., & Meningaud, J. P. (2018). Using virtual reality to control preoperative anxiety in ambulatory surgery patients: A pilot study in maxillofacial and plastic surgery. *Journal of Stomatology, Oral and Maxillofacial Surgery, 119*(4), 257-261. https://doi.org/ 10.1016/j.jormas.2017.12.010

Ganslev, C. A., Storebø, O. J., Callesen, H. E., Ruddy, R., & Søgaard, U. (2020). Psychosocial interventions for conversion and dissociative disorders in adults.

Cochrane Database of Systematic Reviews, 7. https://doi.org/10.1002/1465 1858. CD005331.pub3

Gemignani, A., Sebastiani, L., Simoni, A., Santarcangelo, E. L., & Ghelarducci, B. (2006). Hypnotic trait and specific phobia: EEG and autonomic output during phobic stimulation. *Brain Research Bulletin*, *69*(2), 197-203. https://doi.org/ 10.1016/j.brainresbull.2005.12.003

Glaesmer, H., Geupel, H., & Haak, R. (2015). A controlled trial on the effect of hypnosis on dental anxiety in tooth removal patients. *Patient Education and Counseling*, *98*(9), 1112-1115. https://doi.org/10.1016/j.pec.2015.05.007

Gosseries, O., Fecchio, M., Wolff, A., Sanz, L. R. D., Sombrun, C., Vanhaudenhuyse, A., & Laureys, S. (2020). Behavioural and brain responses in cognitive trance: A TMS-EEG case study. *Clinical Neurophysiology*, *131*(2), 586-588. https://doi. org/ 10.1016/j.clinph.2019.11.011

Graffin, N. F., Ray, W. J., & Lundy, R. (1995). EEG concomitants of hypnosis and hypnotic susceptibility. *Journal of Abnormal Psychology*, *104*(1), 123-131. https://doi.org/10.1037//0021-843x.104.1.123

Grégoire, C., Bragard, I., Jerusalem, G., Etienne, A.-M., Coucke, P., Dupuis, G., Lanctôt, D., & Faymonville, M.-E. (2017a) Group interventions to reduce emotional distress and fatigue in breast cancer patients: A 9-month follow-up pragmatic trial. *British Journal of Cancer*, *117*(10), 1442-1449. https://doi.org/10.1038/ bjc.2017.326

Grégoire, C., Chantrain, C., Faymonville, M.-E., Marini, J., & Bragard, I. (2019). A Hypnosis-Based Group Intervention to Improve Quality of Life in Children with Cancer and Their Parents. *International Journal of Clinical and Experimental Hypnosis*, *67*(2), 117-135. https://doi.org/10.1080/ 00207144.2019.1580965

Grégoire, C., Faymonville, M.-É., Jerusalem, G., Bragard, I., Charland-Verville, V., & Vanhaudenhuyse, A. (2017b) Intérêt et utilisation de l'hypnose pour améliorer le bien-être physique et psychologique en oncologie. *Hegel*, *4*(4), 267-275.

Grégoire, C., Faymonville, M.-E., Vanhaudenhuyse, A., Charland-Verville, V., Jerusalem, G., Willems, S., & Bragard, I. (2020). Effects of an intervention combining self-care and self-hypnosis on fatigue and associated symptoms in post-treatment cancer patients: A randomized-controlled trial. *Psycho-Oncology*, *29*(7), 1165-1173. https://doi.org/10.1002/pon.5395

Grégoire, C., Marie, N., Sombrun, C., Faymonville, M.-E., Kotsou, I., van Nitsen, V., de Ribaucourt, S., Jerusalem, G., Laureys, S., Vanhaudenhuyse, A., & Gosseries, O. (2022). Hypnosis, meditation, and self-induced cognitive trance to improve post-treatment oncological patients' quality of life: Study protocol. *Frontiers in Psychology, 13.* https://www.frontiersin.org/article/10.3389/fpsyg. 2022.807741

Grégoire, C., Sombrun, C., Gosseries, O., & Vanhaudenhuyse, A. (2021). La transe cognitive auto-induite: Caractéristiques et applications thérapeutiques potentielles. *Hegel, 2*(2), 192-201.

Griffiths, D., Clarkson, B., Tadic, S. D., & Resnick, N. M. (2015). Brain mechanisms underlying urge incontinence and its response to pelvic floor muscle training. *Journal of Urology, 194*(3), 708-715. https://doi.org/10.1016/j.juro.2015. 03.102

Halsband, U., & Wolf, T. G. (2015). Functional changes in brain activity after hypnosis in patients with dental phobia. *Journal of Physiology-Paris, 109*(4), 131-142. https://doi.org/10.1016/j.jphysparis.2016.10.001

Hammarstrand, G., Berggren, U., & Hakeberg, M. (1995). Psychophysiological therapy vs. hypnotherapy in the treatment of patients with dental phobia. *European Journal of Oral Sciences, 103*(6), 399-404. https://doi.org/10.1111/ j.1600-0722.1995.tb01864.x

Hasan, F. M., Zagarins, S. E., Pischke, K. M., Saiyed, S., Bettencourt, A. M., Beal, L., Macys, D., Aurora, S., & McCleary, N. (2014). Hypnotherapy is more effective than nicotine replacement therapy for smoking cessation: Results of a randomized controlled trial. *Complementary Therapies in Medicine, 22*(1), 1-8. https://doi.org/10.1016/j.ctim.2013.12.012

Heckmann, J., Eitner, S., Wichmann, M., Schultze- Mosgau, S., Schlegel, A., Leher, A., Heckmann, S., & Holst, S. (2006). Neurophysiologic and long-term effects of clinical hypnosis in oral and maxillofacial treatment: A comparative interdisciplinary clinical study. *International Journal of Clinical and Experimental Hypnosis, 54*(4), 457-479. https://doi.org/10.1080/ 00207140600856897

Hernández Blázquez, M., & Cruzado, J. A. (2016). A longitudinal study on anxiety, depressive and adjustment disorder, suicide ideation and symptoms of emotional distress in patients with cancer undergoing radiotherapy. *Journal of*

Psychosomatic Research, *87*, 14-21. https://doi.org/10.1016/j.jpsychores.
2016.05.010

Hiltunen, S., Karevaara, M., Virta, M., Makkonen, T., Kallio, S., & Paavilainen, P.
(2021). No evidence for theta power as a marker of hypnotic state in highly
hypnotizable subjects. *Heliyon*, *7*(4), e06871. https://doi.org/10.1016/
j.heliyon.2021.e06871

Hiltunen, S., Virta, M., Kallio, S., & Paavilainen, P. (2019). The effects of hypnosis and
hypnotic suggestions on the mismatch negativity in highly hypnotizable
subjects. *International Journal of Clinical and Experimental Hypnosis*, *67*(2),
192-216. https://doi.org/10.1080/00207144.2019.1580966

Hoeft, F., Gabrieli, J. D. E., Whitfield-Gabrieli, S., Haas, B. W., Bammer, R., Menon, V., &
Spiegel, D. (2012). Functional brain basis of hypnotizability. *Archives of
General Psychiatry*, *69*(10), 1064-1072. https://doi.org/10.1001/
archgenpsychiatry.2011.2190

Horton, J. E., Crawford, H. J., Harrington, G., & Downs, J. H., III. (2004). Increased
anterior corpus callosum size associated positively with hypnotizability and
the ability to control pain. *Brain*, *127*(8), 1741-1747. https://doi.org/
10.1093/brain/awh196

Huber, A., Lui, F., Duzzi, D., Pagnoni, G., & Porro, C. A. (2014). Structural and
functional cerebral correlates of hypnotic suggestibility. *PLOS ONE*, *9*(3),
e93187. https://doi.org/10.1371/journal.pone.0093187

Jamieson, G. A., Dwivedi, P., & Gruzelier, J. H. (2005). Changes in mismatch negativity
across pre-hypnosis, hypnosis and post-hypnosis conditions distinguish high
from low hypnotic susceptibility groups. *Brain Research Bulletin*, *67*(4),
298-303. https://doi.org/10.1016/j.brainresbull.2005.06.033

Jensen, M. P., Adachi, T., & Hakimian, S. (2015). Brain oscillations, hypnosis, and
hypnotizability. *American Journal of Clinical Hypnosis*, *57*(3), 230-253.
https://doi.org/10.1080/00029157.2014.976786

Kallio, S., Revonsuo, A., Lauerma, H., Hämäläinen, H., & Lang, H. (1999). The MMN
amplitude increases in hypnosis: A case study. *NeuroReport*, *10*(17),
3579-3582.

Keshmiri, S., Alimardani, M., Shiomi, M., Sumioka, H., Ishiguro, H., & Hiraki, K. (2020).
Higher hypnotic suggestibility is associated with the lower EEG signal

variability in theta, alpha, and beta frequency bands. *PLOS ONE*, *15*(4), e0230853. https://doi.org/10.1371/journal.pone.0230853

Kessler, R. C., Chiu, W. T., Demler, O., & Walters, E. E. (2005). Prevalence, severity, and comorbidity of 12-Month DSM-IV Disorders in the National Comorbidity Survey Replication. *Archives of General Psychiatry*, *62*(6), 617-627. https://doi.org/10.1001/archpsyc.62.6.617

Ketai, L. H., Komesu, Y. M., Schrader, R. M., Rogers, R. G., Sapien, R. E., Dodd, A. B., & Mayer, A. R. (2021). Mind-body (hypnotherapy) treatment of women with urgency urinary incontinence: Changes in brain attentional networks. *American Journal of Obstetrics and Gynecology*, *224*(5), 498.e1-498.e10. https://doi.org/10.1016/j.ajog.2020.10.041

Kihlstrom, J. F. (2013). Neuro-hypnotism: Prospects for hypnosis and neuroscience. *Cortex*, *49*(2), 365-374. https://doi.org/10.1016/j.cortex.2012.05.016

Kirenskaya, A. V., Novototsky-Vlasov, V. Y., & Zvonikov, V. M. (2011). Waking EEG spectral power and coherence differences between high and low hypnotizable subjects. *International Journal of Clinical and Experimental Hypnosis*, *59*(4), 441-453. https://doi.org/10.1080/00207144.2011.594744

Kirenskaya, A. V., Storozheva, Z. I., Solntseva, S. V., Novototsky-Vlasov, V. Y., & Gordeev, M. N. (2019). Auditory evoked potentials evidence for differences in information processing between high and low hypnotizable subjects. *International Journal of Clinical and Experimental Hypnosis*, *67*(1), 81-103. https://doi.org/10.1080/00207144.2019.1553764

Komesu, Y. M., Schrader, R. M., Rogers, R. G., Sapien, R. E., Mayer, A. R., & Ketai, L. H. (2020). Hypnotherapy or medications: A randomized noninferiority trial in urgency urinary incontinent women. *American Journal of Obstetrics and Gynecology*, *222*(2), 159.e1-159.e16. https://doi.org/10.1016/j.ajog.2019.08.025

Komesu, Y., Sapien, R., Rogers, R., & Ketai, L. (2011). Hypnotherapy for treatment of overactive bladder: An RCT pilot study. *Female Pelvic Medicine & Reconstructive Surgery*, *17*(6), 308-313. https://doi.org/10.1097/SPV.0b013e31823a08d9

Lacroix, C., Duhoux, F. P., Bettendorff, J., Watremez, C., Roelants, F., Docquier, M.-A., Potié, A., Coyette, M., Gerday, A., Samartzi, V., Piette, P., Piette, N., & Berliere, M. (2019). Impact of perioperative hypnosedation on postmastectomy chronic pain: Preliminary results. *Integrative Cancer Therapies, 18*, 1-8. https://doi.org/10.1177/1534735419869494

Landry, M., Lifshitz, M., & Raz, A. (2017). Brain correlates of hypnosis: A systematic review and meta-analytic exploration. *Neuroscience & Biobehavioral Reviews, 81*, 75-98. https://doi.org/10.1016/j.neubiorev.2017.02.020

Li, R., Deng, J., & Xie, Y. (2013). Control of respiratory motion by hypnosis intervention during radiotherapy of lung cancer. *BioMed Research International, 2013*, e574934. https://doi.org/10.1155/2013/574934

Li, X., Chen, L., Ma, R., Wang, H., Wan, L., Bu, J., Hong, W., Lv, W., Yang, Y., Rao, H., & Zhang, X. (2020). The neural mechanisms of immediate and follow-up of the treatment effect of hypnosis on smoking craving. *Brain Imaging and Behavior, 14*(5), 1487-1497. https://doi.org/10.1007/s11682-019-00072-0

Li, X., Chen, L., Ma, R., Wang, H., Wan, L., Wang, Y., Bu, J., Hong, W., Lv, W., Vollstädt-Klein, S., Yang, Y., & Zhang, X. (2019). The top-down regulation from the prefrontal cortex to insula via hypnotic aversion suggestions reduces smoking craving. *Human Brain Mapping, 40*(6), 1718-1728. https://doi.org/10.1002/hbm.24483

Li, X., Ma, R., Pang, L., Lv, W., Xie, Y., Chen, Y., Zhang, P., Chen, J., Wu, Q., Cui, G., Zhang, P., Zhou, Y., & Zhang, X. (2017). Delta coherence in resting-state EEG predicts the reduction in cigarette craving after hypnotic aversion suggestions. *Scientific Reports, 7*(1), 2430. https://doi.org/10.1038/s41598-017-01373-4

Lier, E. J., Oosterman, J. M., Assmann, R., de Vries, M., & Van Goor, H. (2020). The effect of Virtual Reality on evoked potentials following painful electrical stimuli and subjective pain. *Scientific Reports, 10*(1), 9067. https://doi.org/10.1038/s41598-020-66035-4

Lipari, S., Baglio, F., Griffanti, L., Mendozzi, L., Garegnani, M., Motta, A., Cecconi, P., & Pugnetti, L. (2012). Altered and asymmetric default mode network activity in a "hypnotic virtuoso": An fMRI and EEG study. *Consciousness and Cognition, 21*(1), 393-400. https://doi.org/10.1016/j.concog.2011.11.006

Liu, Y., He, Y., Li, R., Yu, S., Xu, J., & Xie, Y. (2020). Coupled temporal fluctuation and global signal synchronization of spontaneous brain activity in hypnosis for respiration control: An fMRI study. *Neuroscience, 429*, 56-67. https://doi.org/10.1016/j.neuroscience.2019.12.032

Maquet, P., Faymonville, M. E., Degueldre, C., Delfiore, G., Franck, G., Luxen, A., & Lamy, M. (1999). Functional neuroanatomy of hypnotic state. *Biological Psychiatry*, *45*(3), 327-333. https://doi.org/10.1016/S0006-3223(97)00546-5

Martial, C., Mensen, A., Charland-Verville, V., Vanhaudenhuyse, A., Rentmeister, D., Bahri, M. A., Cassol, H., Englebert, J., Gosseries, O., Laureys, S., & Faymonville, M.-E. (2019). Neurophenomenology of near-death experience memory in hypnotic recall: A within-subject EEG study. *Scientific Reports*, *9*(1), 14047. https://doi.org/10.1038/s41598-019-50601-6

McGeown, W. J., Mazzoni, G., Vannucci, M., & Venneri, A. (2015). Structural and functional correlates of hypnotic depth and suggestibility. *Psychiatry Research: Neuroimaging*, *231*(2), 151-159. https://doi.org/10.1016/j.pscychresns.2014.11.015

Milling, L. S. (2008). Is high hypnotic suggestibility necessary for successful hypnotic pain intervention? *Current Pain and Headache Reports*, *12*(2), 98. https://doi.org/10.1007/s11916-008-0019-0

Montgomery, G. H., David, D., Winkel, G., Silverstein, J. H., & Bovbjerg, D. H. (2002). The effectiveness of adjunctive hypnosis with surgical patients: A meta-analysis. *Anesthesia & Analgesia*, *94*(6), 1639-1645. https://doi.org/10.1213/00000539-200206000-00052

Montgomery, G. H., Duhamel, K. N., & Redd, W. H. (2000). A meta-analysis of hypnotically induced analgesia: How effective is hypnosis? *International Journal of Clinical and Experimental Hypnosis*, *48*(2), 138-153. https://doi.org/10.1080/00207140008410045

Napp, A. E., Diekhoff, T., Stoiber, O., Enders, J., Diederichs, G., Martus, P., & Dewey, M. (2021). Audio-guided self-hypnosis for reduction of claustrophobia during MR imaging: Results of an observational 2-group study. *European Radiology*, *31*(7), 4483-4491. https://doi.org/10.1007/s00330-021-07887-w

Nusbaum, F., Redouté, J., Le Bars, D., Volckmann, P., Simon, F., Hannoun, S., Ribes, G., Gaucher, J., Laurent, B., & Sappey-Marinier, D. (2010). Chronic low-back pain modulation is enhanced by hypnotic analgesic suggestion by recruiting an emotional network: A PET imaging study. *International Journal of Clinical and Experimental Hypnosis*, *59*(1), 27-44. https://doi.org/10.1080/00207144.2011.522874

Oakley, D. A. (1999). Hypnosis and conversion hysteria: A unifying model. *Cognitive Neuropsychiatry*, *4*(3), 243-265. https://doi.org/10.1080/135468099395954

Oakley, D. A., & Halligan, P. W. (2013). Hypnotic suggestion: Opportunities for cognitive neuroscience. *Nature Reviews Neuroscience*, *14*(8), 565-576. https://doi.org/10.1038/nrn3538

Oneal, B. J., Patterson, D. R., Soltani, M., Teeley, A., & Jensen, M. P. (2008). Virtual reality hypnosis in the treatment of chronic neuropathic pain: A case report. *International Journal of Clinical and Experimental Hypnosis*, *56*(4), 451-462. https://doi.org/10.1080/00207140802255534

Palfi, B., Moga, G., Lush, P., Scott, R. B., & Dienes, Z. (2020). Can hypnotic suggestibility be measured online? *Psychological Research*, *84*(5), 1460-1471. https://doi.org/10.1007/s00426-019-01162-w

Patterson, D. R., Hoffman, H. G., Palacios, A. G., & Jensen, M. J. (2006). Analgesic effects of posthypnotic suggestions and virtual reality distraction on thermal pain. *Journal of Abnormal Psychology*, *115*(4), 834-841. https://doi.org/10.1037/0021-843X.115.4.834

Perri, R. L., Rossani, F., & Di Russo, F. (2019). Neuroelectric evidence of top-down hypnotic modulation associated with somatosensory processing of sensory and limbic regions. *NeuroImage*, *202*, 116104. https://doi.org/10.1016/j.neuroimage.2019.116104

Picerni, E., Santarcangelo, E., Laricchiuta, D., Cutuli, D., Petrosini, L., Spalletta, G., & Piras, F. (2019). Cerebellar structural variations in subjects with different hypnotizability. *The Cerebellum*, *18*(1), 109-118. https://doi.org/10.1007/s12311-018-0965-y

Prinsloo, S., Rebello, E., Cata, J. P., Black, D., DeSnyder, S. M., & Cohen, L. (2019). Electroencephalographic correlates of hypnosedation during breast cancer surgery. *Breast Journal*, *25*(4), 786-787. https://doi.org/10.1111/tbj.13328

Raij, T. T., Numminen, J., Närvänen, S., Hiltunen, J., & Hari, R. (2005). Brain correlates of subjective reality of physically and psychologically induced pain. *Proceedings of the National Academy of Sciences*, *102*(6), 2147-2151. https://doi.org/10.1073/pnas.0409542102

Rainville, P., Duncan, G. H., Price, D. D., Carrier, B., & Bushnell, M. C. (1997). Pain affect encoded in human anterior cingulate but not somatosensory cortex. *Science*. https://doi.org/10.1126/science.277.5328.968

Raja, S. N., Carr, D. B., Cohen, M., Finnerup, N. B., Flor, H., Gibson, S., Keefe, F. J., Mogil, J. S., Ringkamp, M., Sluka, K. A., Song, X.-J., Stevens, B., Sullivan, M. D., Tutelman, P. R., Ushida, T., & Vader, K. (2020). The revised International Association for the Study of Pain definition of pain: Concepts, challenges, and compromises. *PAIN*, *161*(9), 1976-1982. https://doi.org/10.1097/j.pain.0000000000001939

Ray, W. J., Keil, A., Mikuteit, A., Bongartz, W., & Elbert, T. (2002). High resolution EEG indicators of pain responses in relation to hypnotic susceptibility and suggestion. *Biological Psychology*, *60*(1), 17-36. https://doi.org/10.1016/S0301-0511(02)00029-7

Rousseaux, F., Bicego, A., Ledoux, D., Massion, P., Nyssen, A.-S., Faymonville, M.-E., Laureys, S., & Vanhaudenhuyse, A. (2020a). Hypnosis associated with 3D immersive virtual reality technology in the management of pain: A review of the literature. *Journal of Pain Research*, *13*, 1129-1138. https://doi.org/10.2147/JPR.S231737

Rousseaux, F., Bicego, A., Malengreaux, C., Faymonville, M.-E., Ledoux, D., Massion, P., Nyssen, A.-S., & Vanhaudenhuyse, A. (2020b) L'hypnose a-t-elle sa place en réanimation? *Médecine Intensive Réanimation*. https://doi.org/10.37051/mir-00012

Rousseaux, F., Dardenne, N., Massion, P. B., Ledoux, D., Bicego, A., Donneau, A.-F., Faymonville, M.-E., Nyssen, A.-S., & Vanhaudenhuyse, A. (2022). Virtual reality and hypnosis for anxiety and pain management in intensive care units: A prospective randomised trial among cardiac surgery patients. *European Journal of Anaesthesiology*, *39*(1), 58-66. https://doi.org/10.1097/EJA.0000000000001633

Rousseaux, F., Panda, R., Toussaint, C., Bicego, A., Niimi, M., Faymonville, M. E., Nyssen, A.-S., Laureys, S., Gosseries, O., & Vanhaudenhuyse, A. (Under review). *Virtual reality hypnosis modifies cerebral pain processing and reduces subjective pain: A prospective cross-over randomized-study (under review).*

Sabourin, M. E., Cutcomb, S. D., Crawford, H. J., & Pribram, K. (1990). EEG correlates of hypnotic susceptibility and hypnotic trance: Spectral analysis and coherence. *International Journal of Psychophysiology*, *10*(2), 125-142. https://doi.org/10.1016/0167-8760(90)90027-B

Schnur, J. B., Kafer, I., Marcus, C., & Montgomery, G. H. (2008). Hypnosis to manage distress related to medical procedures: A meta-analysis. *Contemporary Hypnosis*, *25*(3-4), 114-128. https://doi.org/10.1002/ch.364

Schnyer, D. M., & Allen, J. J. (1995). Attention-related electroencephalographic and event-related potential predictors of responsiveness to suggested posthypnotic amnesia. *International Journal of Clinical and Experimental Hypnosis, 43*(3), 295-315. https://doi.org/10.1080/00207149508409972

Sexton, C. C., Coyne, K. S., Vats, V., Kopp, Z. S., Irwin, D. E., & Wagner, T. H. (2009). Impact of overactive bladder on work productivity in the United States: Results from EpiLUTS. *American Journal of Managed Care, 15*(4 Suppl), S98-S107.

Simons, L. E., Elman, I., & Borsook, D. (2014). Psychological processing in chronic pain: A neural systems approach. *Neuroscience & Biobehavioral Reviews, 39*, 61-78. https://doi.org/10.1016/j.neubiorev.2013.12.006

Sine, H., Achbani, A., & Filali, K. (2021). The effect of hypnosis on the intensity of pain and anxiety in cancer patients: A systematic review of controlled experimental trials. *Cancer Investigation,* 40(15), 1-45. https://doi.org/10.1080/07357907.2021.1998520

Spiegel, D. (2013). Transformations: Hypnosis in brain and body. *Depression and Anxiety, 30*(4), 342-352. https://doi.org/10.1002/da.22046

Squintani, G., Brugnoli, M., Pasin, E., Segatti, A., Concon, E., Polati, E., Bonetti, B., & Matinella, A. (2017). Changes in laser-evoked potentials during hypnotic analgesia for chronic pain: A pilot study. *Annals of Palliative Medicine, 6*, 1004-1004. https://doi.org/10.21037/apm.2017.10.04

Srzich, A. J., Byblow, W. D., Stinear, J. W., Cirillo, J., & Anson, J. G. (2016). Can motor imagery and hypnotic susceptibility explain Conversion Disorder with motor symptoms? *Neuropsychologia, 89*, 287-298. https://doi.org/10.1016/j.neuropsychologia.2016.06.030

Tahiri, M., Mottillo, S., Joseph, L., Pilote, L., & Eisenberg, M. J. (2012). Alternative smoking cessation aids: A meta-analysis of randomized controlled trials. *American Journal of Medicine, 125*(6), 576-584. https://doi.org/10.1016/j.amjmed.2011.09.028

Taylor, A. M. W. (2018). Corticolimbic circuitry in the modulation of chronic pain and substance abuse. *Progress in Neuro-Psychopharmacology and Biological Psychiatry, 87*, 263-268. https://doi.org/10.1016/j.pnpbp.2017.05.009

Teeley, A. M., Soltani, M., Wiechman, S. A., Jensen, M. P., Sharar, S. R., & Patterson, D. R. (2012). Virtual reality hypnosis pain control in the treatment of multiple fractures: A case series. *American Journal of Clinical Hypnosis*, *54*(3), 184-194. https://doi.org/10.1080/00029157.2011.619593

Tefikow, S., Barth, J., Maichrowitz, S., Beelmann, A., Strauss, B., & Rosendahl, J. (2013). Efficacy of hypnosis in adults undergoing surgery or medical procedures: A meta-analysis of randomized controlled trials. *Clinical Psychology Review*, *33*(5), 623-636. https://doi.org/10.1016/j.cpr.2013.03.005

Terhune, D. B., Cardeña, E., & Lindgren, M. (2011). Differential frontal-parietal phase synchrony during hypnosis as a function of hypnotic suggestibility. *Psychophysiology*, *48*(10), 1444-1447. https://doi.org/10.1111/j.1469-8986.2011.01211.x

Thompson, T., Terhune, D. B., Oram, C., Sharangparni, J., Rouf, R., Solmi, M., Veronese, N., & Stubbs, B. (2019). The effectiveness of hypnosis for pain relief: A systematic review and meta-analysis of 85 controlled experimental trials. *Neuroscience & Biobehavioral Reviews*, *99*, 298-310. https://doi.org/10.1016/j.neubiorev.2019.02.013

Turk, D. C., Wilson, H. D., & Cahana, A. (2011). Treatment of chronic non-cancer pain. *The Lancet*, *377*(9784), 2226-2235. https://doi.org/10.1016/S0140-6736(11)60402-9

Ulrich, P., Meyer, H.-J., Diehl, B., & Meinig, G. (1987). Cerebral blood flow in autogenic training and hypnosis. *Neurosurgical Review*, *10*(4), 305-307. https://doi.org/10.1007/BF01781956

Vanhaudenhuyse, A., Boly, M., Balteau, E., Schnakers, C., Moonen, G., Luxen, A., Lamy, M., Degueldre, C., Brichant, J. F., Maquet, P., Laureys, S., & Faymonville, M. E. (2009). Pain and non-pain processing during hypnosis: A thulium-YAG event-related fMRI study. *NeuroImage*, *47*(3), 1047-1054. https://doi.org/10.1016/j.neuroimage.2009.05.031

Vanhaudenhuyse, A., & Faymonville, M. E. (2020). L'hypnose, un outil de gestion des phobies: Que nous apprend la recherche? *Hypnose & Thérapies brèves, Hors-série n°15 "Peurs et phobies"*.

Vanhaudenhuyse, A., Gillet, A., Malaise, N., Salamun, I., Barsics, C., Grosdent, S., Maquet, D., Nyssen, A.-S., & Faymonville, M.-E. (2015). Efficacy and cost-effectiveness: A study of different treatment approaches in a tertiary pain centre. *European Journal of Pain*, *19*(10), 1437-1446. https://doi.org/10.1002/ejp.674

Vanhaudenhuyse, A., Gillet, A., Malaise, N., Salamun, I., Grosdent, S., Maquet, D., Nyssen, A.-S., & Faymonville, M.-E. (2018). Psychological interventions influence patients' attitudes and beliefs about their chronic pain. *Journal of Traditional and Complementary Medicine*, *8*(2), 296-302. https://doi.org/ 10.1016/ j.jtcme.2016.09.001

Vanhaudenhuyse, A., Laureys, S., & Faymonville, M.-E. (2014). Neurophysiology of hypnosis. *Neurophysiologie Clinique/Clinical Neurophysiology*, *44*(4), 343-353. https://doi.org/10.1016/j.neucli.2013.09.006

Vanhaudenhuyse, A., ledoux, D., Gosseries, O., Demertzi, A., Laureys, S., & Faymonville, M.-E. (2019). Can subjective ratings of absorption, dissociation, and time perception during neutral hypnosis predict hypnotizability?: An exploratory study. *International Journal of Clinical and Experimental Hypnosis*, *67*(1), 28-38. https://doi.org/10.1080/00207144.2019.1553765

Vanhaudenhuyse, Nyssen, A.-S., & Faymonville, M.-E. (2020). Recent insight on how the neuroscientific approach helps clinicians. *OBM Integrative and Complementary Medicine*, *5*(3), 1-7. https://doi.org/10.21926/obm.icm.2003039

Vuilleumier, P. (2005). Hysterical conversion and brain function. In S. Laureys (Éd.), *Progress in Brain Research* (Vol. 150, p. 309-329). Elsevier. https://doi.org/10.1016/S0079-6123(05)50023-2

Ward, N. S., Oakley, D. A., Frackowiak, R. S. J., & Halligan, P. W. (2003). Differential brain activations during intentionally simulated and subjectively experienced paralysis. *Cognitive Neuropsychiatry*, *8*(4), 295-312. https://doi.org/10.1080/13546800344000200

Wik, G., Fischer, H., Bragée, B., Finer, B., & Fredrikson, M. (1999). Functional anatomy of hypnotic analgesia: A PET study of patients with fibromyalgia. *European Journal of Pain*, *3*(1), 7-12. https://doi.org/10.1016/S1090-3801(99)90183-0

Zhuo, M. (2008). Cortical excitation and chronic pain. *Trends in Neurosciences*, *31*(4), 199-207. https://doi.org/10.1016/j.tins.2008.01.003

CHAPTER 6
PRINCIPLES AND PROCESS OF HYPNOTIC INDUCTION, DEEPENING, AND RE-ALERTING

DAVID REID

Chapter Learning Objectives:

1. Identify and describe three hypnotic induction techniques.

2. Identify the pros and cons of using more permissive hypnotic induction techniques.

3. Identify and describe three deepening interventions to enhance the hypnotic experience.

If there is a "trinity" of clinical hypnosis, I suppose it would include hypnotic induction, deepening, and re-alerting. Intended interventions that denote the beginning, middle, and conclusion of a formal hypnosis intervention, respectively. This chapter is dedicated to three elements of hypnosis that some consider crucial for clinical efficacy while others, perhaps with the exception of re-alerting, question the necessity and even the clinical utility of formal inductions and deepening interventions. More on that later.

   In a recent revision of their Level I (Basic) Standards of Training, the American Society of Clinical Hypnosis (ASCH) updated the number of hours dedicated to didactic and experiential training in addition to renaming the terms that have historically served as pinnacles of hypnosis. ASCH's new standards require 120 minutes for learning induction (elicitation) techniques and re-alerting (reorienting) interventions, and 60 minutes for the review and demonstration of deepening (intensification) applications for facilitating trance (ASCH, 2019). Furthermore, a series of group experiences including demonstrations of a hypnotic encounter that reviews and identifies the characteristics of the "trance state," and four small group practice opportunities totaling 435 minutes over a 21-hour continuing education workshop provide additional exposure and reinforcement of the importance of inductions, deepening techniques, and re-alerting interventions.

Before delving into the detailed aspects of the varied and common induction, deepening, and re-alerting techniques, and the definition of hypnosis will be reviewed. The American Psychological Association (APA), Division 30 (Society of Clinical Hypnosis) defined hypnosis as, "A state of consciousness involving focused attention and reduced peripheral awareness characterized by an enhanced capacity for response to suggestion." (Elkins, Barabasz, Council, & Spiegel, 2015, p. 6). While this was a welcomed revision to the 2003 HDC definition of hypnosis (Green, Barabasz, Barrett, & Montgomery, 2003) it was not wholeheartedly embraced by the clinical hypnosis community. Lankton (2015), for instance opined, "It seems that we are still using the same card deck of terminology and just arranging the cards in a different order" (p. 367). Others maintained that the definition conflated the terms "hypnosis" and "trance," thereby promoting the notion that hypnosis is not only a *state of mind,* but something someone *does* to another (Hope & Sugarman, 2015; Reid, 2016; Sugarman, Linden, & Brooks, 2020).

When considering hypnotic techniques and interventions, one might ask, "When does hypnosis begin?" Or for that matter, "When does trance begin?" Some maintain that trance and hypnosis begin when the clinician introduces an induction technique. Others (Hope & Sugarman, 2015; Sugarman, Linden, & Brooks, 2020) including myself

(Reid, 2016) propose that trance begins well before the hypnosis. Perhaps trance begins the moment an individual awakens. Some moments throughout the day involve deeper levels of absorption (e.g., reading a captivating book, watching a suspenseful movie, considering the hypnosis experience before arriving at the clinician's office) that involve trance. Some trance experiences are future focused (i.e., age progression or when dysfunctional promote anxiety). Absorption in one's past (i.e., age regression) can also involve challenging experiences if there are issues associated with regret and resentment (i.e., depression). Hypnosis, in contrast, begins when the clinician deliberately initiates it, whether through a formal induction, or more indirectly through conversation.

It should be noted that not all clinicians and hypnosis researchers consider trance to be an important component of hypnosis. Instead they adhere to a socio-cognitive model which emphasizes an individual's expectations, beliefs, attitudes, and other cognitive processes which influence social responsiveness as related to hypnosis (Green & Lynn, 2011; Lynn, Kirsch, & Hallquist, 2008; Lynn, Green, & Maxwell, 2017; Lynn & Sherman, 2000).

HYPNOTIC INDUCTION

Since 1950, the terms "induction" and/or "induce" have appeared in the titles of 87 articles published in the *American Journal of Clinical Hypnosis* and 97 articles published in the *International Journal of Clinical and Experimental Hypnosis*. It is apparent that the term induction has been, and continues to be, embraced and promoted as an essential component of hypnosis. Trance is elicited, and to some extent, facilitated by hypnotic inductions (Reid, 2016; Zeig, 2014). In 2019, ASCH formally replaced the term "induction" with "elicitation" in their revised training language though "induction" continues to be understood and used by most clinicians and researchers, including this author for this chapter.

Pragmatic techniques that vivify hypnotic induction continue to be part of the core curriculum of workshops sponsored by clinical hypnosis societies. More specifically, there is the eye-roll technique (Spiegel & Spiegel, 1978), arm and hand levitation induction (Erickson, 1958), eye fixation technique (Spiegel & Spiegel, 1978; Weitzenhoffer, 2000), Chiasson's induction (Hammond, 1990), conscious/unconscious dissociation induction (Lankton & Lankton, 1983/2008), progressive relaxation induction (Kirsch, Lynn, & Rhue, 1993), and alert hypnosis induction (Bányai, 2018; Wark, 2006, 2015; Wark & Reid, 2018), and many other techniques that are only limited by the constraints of a creative mind.

Following the establishment of rapport, hypnotic induction has generally been considered the second in a series of sequential hypnosis rituals (ASCH, 2019; Hammond & Elkins, 2005). Formal inductions are intentional and essentially "declare" that hypnosis has begun. Contextual or subtle *cues* (e.g., dimming lights, closing window shades, changing voice tone and intonation) can precede and reinforce the notion that hypnosis is under way. Given that formal inductions are part of linear and stepwise interventions, they have been considered to be a component of a "legacy model" (see Alter & Sugarman, 2017) in contrast to more informal, conversational interventions. Formal inductions also comprise the lion's share of induction techniques taught at beginning (Level I) and intermediate (Level II) hypnosis workshops. Three of the more commonly used induction techniques are reviewed below.

For the uninitiated, the hypnotic induction can be a particularly curious, interesting, and engaging subject matter at workshops. Faculty demonstrations of hypnotic inductions eliciting seemingly involuntary responses (e.g., arm and hand levitation) and what appears to be the opening of a portal into the unconscious mind can be compelling, if not entertaining. For most clinicians attending their first clinical hypnosis workshop, it is during their first small group practice that they readily appreciate that inductions are easier *seen* than *done*. But like many things in life, with practice comes proficiency and mastery of induction techniques.

A plethora of hypnotic induction techniques are available to the clinician (see Chapter 9). Some inductions involve direct, perhaps authoritarian, suggestions (e.g., *"Close your eyes and go into trance"*) while others can be characterized as "permissive." Permissive suggestions, as the term implies, essentially provide the client with permission to control and manage their trance experience in ways that are comfortable for them. Including the terms like, "it's up to you," "if you like," "whatever seems right for you," "allow your unconscious mind to decide" during an induction can promote a greater sense of control for clients.

SPECIFIC HYPNOTIC INDUCTION (ELICITATION) TECHNIQUES

Eye Fixation

Eye fixation is one of the simplest, less threatening, and more rapid hypnosis induction techniques that has been popularized by the movie industry. After inviting the client to be as comfortable as they can be, the clinician directs them to fixate their vision on some spot in the room or upon some object (e.g., a pendulum, tip of a pen, clinician's thumb). Some clinicians prefer to encourage the client to focus on a spot on the ceiling, taking advantage of eventual eyestrain that promotes eventual eye closure. Another strategy is to encourage the person to focus their eyes anywhere they like then while keeping their eyes fixated on a particular spot, they are encouraged to gently lower their head without moving their eyes. This too will generate eventual strain. At the same time, if the client does not close their eyes, they can simply be invited to "keep them open." This is a strategy referred to as utilization. Essentially, the clinician utilizes and accepts whatever the person gives them during the session. A sample script that employs eye fixation is provided below:

I invite you to be as comfortable as you can be and when you are ready, allow your eyes to focus on a spot somewhere in the distance. As you focus on that spot, take in a comfortable breath and gently release it. Notice with each exhale how much more focused you can become. Perhaps noticing that spot moves a bit, becomes a little blurry. Those eyelids (dissociative terminology—those eyes vs. your eyes) may become heavier, fluttering just a little. As you continue to focus on that spot realize that there is a part of you that can hear my words and another part of you ... some refer to it as the unconscious or subconscious mind ... can allow for a very different experience. And as those eyes continue to focus on that spot, perhaps even blurrier now, you can also see something different. You can hear my voice, understand my words, but see yourself somewhere else ... someplace pleasant and comfortable. It could be a place that you are very familiar with or perhaps a place you have never been but would like to visit. And those eyes can close at any time (this can be suggested at any time it seems the eyelids are getting heavier). And as those eyes close, notice how much clearer things are for you. Things you can see ... hear ... and feel.

Notice the word "imagine" is not utilized. Rather than encourage someone to *imagine* an experience, it is likely more beneficial for them to experience it being as *real* as it can be. The term "imagine" also tends to conjure up more a more active, conscious experience, which ultimately may impede the utilization of unconscious resources.

Counting Inductions

Counting methods blend inductions with deepening techniques. Counting typically involves counting downward, with the implication of "going down" and deeper into trance. Between numbers the clinician offers suggestions for relaxation and comfort. The process is usually drawn out so that the mention of each descending number corresponds with a deepening trance experience. Counting techniques can also involve the client counting out loud as the clinician intersperses deepening suggestions. Variations also include having the client keep their head still and roll their eyes up on even numbers and drop their eyes on odd numbers as they slowly count downward from 100. Eventually, the clinician invites eye closure and transitions into another phase of hypnosis.

Counting is popular at hypnosis workshops due to its simplicity as evidenced in the following sample script:

> As you allow yourself to become as comfortable as you can, I am going to begin slowly counting downward from the number 10 to 1. As I count down you can continue to be comfortable and relax even more. When I finally get to the number 1, you can be very comfortable and relaxed in a way that allows your unconscious mind to be more available for you ... available to help you. I will begin now with the number 10 ... comfortable ... relaxed ... 9 even more comfortable ... noticing how you become even more relaxed with each breath you release ... 8 that's right now even more comfortable ... 7 just noticing how your breathing has slowed down just a little already ... 6 even more relaxed ... and how much more relaxed than you were moments ago ... 5 and even deeper relaxed and knowing you will go even deeper as I continue to count down 4, 3, 2, 1 ...

Another counting intervention variation involves progressive muscle relaxation. Rather than counting, the clinician can encourage and suggest relaxation of different muscle groups, starting from the top of the head and ending at the bottom of the feet. It has been my experience that while progressive muscle relaxation inductions can be productive, they tend to be prolonged, and in the end are moot and unnecessary. While some clients prefer direct suggestions for eliciting trance and find counting inductions to be very effective, others will experience the intervention as superficial, perhaps authoritarian, akin to what they may have witnessed with stage hypnosis.

Arm and hand levitation

Arm and hand levitation is a hypnotic phenomenon that can be used to help facilitate trance, deepen trance, or link trance experiences to productive change. The process itself is actually quite simple although it does require some practice to master the timing of your suggestions with your client's breathing. Some refer to this induction as "arm levitation" excluding the term "hand." Realize there may be times that clients may only raise a few fingers or slightly lift their wrist while their arm remains flaccid and unmoving. Consequently, suggestions can be specified for hand levitation, having no need to mention the client's arm if it has not responded to suggestions. The clinician should focus attention on the client's hand and if there is little to no response, then the fingers garner attention and suggestions for movement. Once a finger or hand moves slightly an appropriate response would be: "That's right. Just like that it can begin to feel even lighter" (ensuring that the word "lighter" is said on the client's inhalation as inhaling mimics a lifting sensation).

Finding one's "hypnotic voice" is essential for enhancing a client's experience. *How* you say something can sometimes be more impor-tant than *what* you say. The clinician's voice becomes a contextual cue, distinguishing between what is and is not the hypnosis work. In their evaluation of nearly 200 hypnosis trainees, Montgomery et al., (2019) found that "paraverbal errors" (i.e., tone, pacing, phrasing) were common during the induction, deepening, and re-alerting components, underscoring the importance of including training opportunities that focus on encouraging trainees to be mindful of using a more hypnotic voice tone.

Below is an example of an arm and hand levitation induction.

*As you sit there in your chair with both your hands on your lap, eyes closed, feet on the floor, your head gently resting against the back of the chair just listen to my words and continue to be as comfortable as you can be. That's right ... just like that. And as you take this time to go into trance, if you'd like (permissiveness) ... notice those hands there. Focus on both of them and notice they feel right now. Maybe they are warm, or cold, maybe heavy or even feel a little light. It doesn't matter, just notice them. And as you continue to go into trance you can have an experience where one of your hands ... maybe even both of them ... become **lighter**. I'm not even certain which hand will feel **lighter** first, or if both of them will feel **lighter**. You can even let your unconscious mind decide. So as you go deeper into trance as your unconscious mind becomes available and helps make a choice, perhaps you can then see which one will become **lighter** as if the gravity beneath your fingers and thumb just get **lighter**. The less you try, the easier it becomes. In fact, there is no need to try anything. Maybe you will notice one hand becoming **lighter** right now and maybe that other hand seems heavier as the other is just **lighter**. I wonder which hand will **lift** now. Maybe it will be both. I don't know. Let your unconscious mind decide that as it goes into trance. And when it does, it can **lift**. That gravity beneath it just getting **lighter** now. (When movement is observed the clinician should tend to it and reinforce it.) That's right. Just like that as it's **lifting** ... higher ... and high (if both hands lift respond to both). And your unconscious mind has made up its mind and can keep **lifting** even higher. I'm not sure how high it will lift your hand and arm. Maybe it will lift all the way to your face or just **float right there**.*

An alternative arm and hand levitation takes advantage of physiological mechanics and is first demonstrated by the clinician. The clinician starts of by simultaneously taking in a slow deep breath while gradually raising both hands off their lap until they extend above their head. This is followed by a slow exhale as the arms, with bent, limp wrists, slowly find their way back to the lap, fingertips just barely grazing the lap. This positioning is ideal for facilitating a "floatation feeling" in both hands and arms. As the hands gently lower to the lap the clinician could say, "And notice just how they begin to *float. Floating* down to the lap and just hovering there." Embedding the word "float" seeds an expectation for some kind of levitation experience. The clinician can then use the verbiage provided above to enhance arm and hand levitation.

To the best extent possible, arm and hand levitation should be experienced by the client as involuntary; as if the arm and hand lifted without conscious intention or control. Encouraging brief eye opening for an individual to "spy" how high their arms have lifted serves as an opportunity to ratify (i.e., validate) the trance experience. Many times, during a debriefing following the hypnosis session, individuals are surprised to see that their arms were in a different place and position than they expected before opening their eyes. Suggestions involving ideomotor responses also afford the clinician with an opportunity to observe an individual's level and rate of responsiveness to suggestions.

Final thought on inductions

Induction techniques eventually become simplified after working repeatedly with the same client. Typically, for instance, there is no clinical need to continue with arm and hand levitation after several sessions. In some cases, I have observed spontaneous arm and hand levitation as if the client was simultaneously using their own self-hypnosis in the midst of a hetero-hypnosis session. After a few sessions, eye fixation, focused breathing, or simply an invitation to "be as comfortable as you can be and allow yourself to go into a pleasant trance that can be as deep as you like, with every breath you take in ... and release" will suffice as a successful induction technique.

DEEPENING TECHNIQUES

Deepening, or intensifying interventions have traditionally been utilized immediately after, or interspersed within, a formal induction in an effort to intensify the client's experience (Gibbons & Lynn, 2021, Yapko, 2019). But how deep is deep enough? Perhaps it's a cop-out, but the answer to this question is, "It depends."

According to Yapko (2019) a deeper hypnotic experience is not necessarily a clinically more successful one. When working with athletes, deep, relaxing trance experiences facilitated by multiple deepening techniques can be contraindicated (Reid, 2012). Professional hypnosis societies continue to dedicate hours reviewing and teaching deepening techniques in their curricula for Level I and Level II training despite limited empirical research touting any benefits for enhancing a hypnosis experience or clinical outcome (Page & Handley, 1992). Nevertheless, establishing deeper levels of trance promotes opportunities for certain experiences (dissociation, more involuntary responses, time distortion) that can promote the ratification of hypnosis.

As with induction techniques, there are many deepening interventions that a clinician may choose from in an attempt to enhance the impact of the hypnosis intervention. Generally, deepening techniques fall into two primary categories: fantasy/imagery techniques and somatosensory-attentional suggestions. The former tends to be more directive suggestions and involve "guided imagery" experiences, while the latter operate on more naturalistic experiences elicited from the client.

Fantasy/Imagery Techniques

Descending stairs/elevator/escalator

The obvious metaphor here involves a variation of themes involving imagined descension (*down ... down ... deeper and deeper*). The further one imagines (hearing, seeing, feeling) him or herself going down a "special" flight of stairs, escalator or elevator, the "deeper" one can go into trance (Barabasz & Watkins, 2005). The clinician suggests that the client imaging "going down the stairs, one step at a time, and going deeper, and deeper into trance." Alternatively, if an elevator is employed clients can "go deeper and deeper with each floor that passes" until reaching the bottom floor. Here is a brief sample script for using this technique (italics spoken on the exhale also indicate a bit more prolonged, softened tone of voice).

> *Take a moment as I am talking to you to see yourself standing at the top of a special stairway ... each stair offers you an opportunity to become even more relaxed ... see and feel yourself there now ... getting ready to take your first step ... going even deeper into trance ... as you take your first step ... and another ... feeling even more absorbed ... relaxed and comfortable with that next step ... taking your time ... and another step into even more relaxation and comfort ... knowing that with one ... two ... three or more steps ... you can become more comfortable ... that's right ... even deeper ...*

It is important to be aware beforehand that the client does not have any issues or concerns with going down a set of stairs (like being stuck in a basement) or escalator or being in an elevator which can be a claustrophobic experience for some).

Deeper into water

As mentioned before in this chapter, deepening techniques do not always follow an induction. At times, they are intertwined. Here is an example of a guided intervention that utilizes the metaphor of a pool with interspersed suggestions (also known as "interspersal") to go even deeper into trance:

> *As you become more comfortable now, you can close those eyes ... take a slow comfortable breath in and gently release as you see yourself now sitting near a swimming pool ... you are just observing ... as you sit there, you notice someone walking up to pool ... they are taking their time ... feet in the pool ... waiting a moment ... walking in slowly, step-by-step ... just a little deeper ... and they stop and wait ... getting used to the water before going any deeper ... and eventually, they go all the way in ... And you notice another person sitting on the side of the pool ... their feet are dangling in the water ... so they are all the way in ... but they are partly in ... and just like that, you can go into trance ... maybe not all the way in ... part of your conscious mind can hear what I am saying ... and another part of you can go into trance. And you know there are people that can walk up to the side of the pool and just dive all the way in ... I work with a number of people who can sit down in a chair ... take a slow deep breath in ... gently release it ... and go into trance just like that.*

Of course, this induction/deepening technique is not suitable for everyone, especially if the client has fears surrounding pools and water. Realize the person in this experience does not go into the pool and instead is a passive observer.

Somatosensory/Attentional Techniques

Some deepening interventions rely on the resources of the client and the situation. It requires the clinician to monitor and observe the client and respond through suggestions as if operating much like a biofeedback machine. These deepening interventions also enhance and promote the client's ability to control (and maintain a sense of responsibility and credit for) their experience.

Breathing

Something that a clinician can always be available to is to utilize and respond to is the client's breathing. As mentioned elsewhere in this chapter, suggestions with the intention of helping the client go "deeper" and experience feelings of heaviness, should be spoken on the client's exhale. Floating sensations, intentions for facilitating arm and hand levitation, and lightness suggestions should be provided on the client's exhale or out-breath. A sample script relying on a person's breathing for deepening could go like this:

> *I don't know if you have noticed or not, but your breathing*
> *has slowed down just a bit. With each breath you take in*
> *and release, notice how much more comfortable you can be*
> *... I wonder how much deeper you can go into trance ... with*
> *each breath you release ... just like that (spoken on the*
> *client's exhale) ... maybe you wonder how much more*
> *comfortable and absorbed you can be and will be in the next*
> *two ... three ... four or more breaths you release ... and how*
> *much clearer your experience be ... maybe noticing colors*
> *becoming clear and more vivid ... noticing things you can*
> *see up close and even in the distance ... how much clearer*
> *that all becomes for you with each breath you release ...*
> *textures ... shapes ... things you can feel ... and hear ... as real*
> *as the sound of my voice ... and even deeper if you want*
> *(permissive suggestion) with that next breath ...*

Progressive Heaviness/Lightness

An effective somatosensory deepening technique involves offering clients the opportunity to experience sensations of body parts becoming heavier or lighter. Hands, feet, and legs offer wonderful targets for these interventions. Again, pairing suggestive words with the client's breathing can enhance their experience. An intervention could go something like this:

> Take a moment now to just notice those hands (dissociative language) resting there on your lap. How they feel right now ... how each finger on each hand feels as it rests there ... how still they are ... and I wonder if you can feel how much heavier they can begin to feel ... maybe warmer ... and heavier ... and with each breath you exhale how they become even heavier ... and heavier ... it's as if gravity beneath those hands got a little stronger ... and heavier still ... and even though part of your mind knows those hands (dissociative language) could move and even lift if they needed to ... a part of your mind can allow you to have an experience and feeling that they are so heavy they can't move ... the more you try the harder it is ... the heavier they become. And that feeling of heaviness can spread anywhere else in the body ... allowing it to feel more comfortable ... more relaxed ...

Whether heaviness or lightness is suggested, it is important to ensure that the intervention makes sense and is aligned with the client's goal. For instance, utilizing suggestion for heaviness would not be recommended when working with individuals who desire to lose weight.

Silence

Silence is truly golden. Clinicians can use it to their advantage to regroup when somewhat "lost" in the session, to brainstorm alternative interventions, and to facilitate a deepening experience for the client. It is also a good idea to provide the client with an estimated time period that silence will persist (i.e., two-minutes of clock time) since they could be experiencing a sense of time distortion. Here is a sample script for introducing silence as a deepening technique:

> *Just continue to be comfortable as you can be. That's right.*
> *Maybe you can become even more comfortable. To help you*
> *with that, I'm going to give you a couple of minutes of clock*
> *(or real) time to see how much more comfortable you can*
> *be. Notice how much deeper an experience you can have in*
> *this silence. Taking time now ... to take care of you. I will be*
> *quiet for two minutes and when I start talking again, you*
> *can just continue to be comfortable in your trance ...*

Fractionation

This deepening technique can be particularly helpful for individuals whose attention span is limited or challenged. Individuals who are very depressed, highly anxious, in pain, or just have difficulties focusing their attention could benefit from fractionation.

The intervention involves a stepwise process of deepening, gently re-alerting, more deepening, another gentle re-alerting, and some more deepening. In fact, attendees at hypnosis workshops experience fractionation throughout a long weekend as they go in and out of trance through small group practice experiences. Fractionation goes something like this:

> *Allow those eyes to close now as you become more focused*
> *and absorbed ... going into a deeper trance as those eyes*
> *close ... and notice how much deeper you could go with each*

*breath you release ... that's right ... even deeper ... taking
just the time you need to be even more absorbed ... and in a
moment I am going to invite you to open those eyes ... and as
you open those eyes in a moment, you can continue to be in
a comfortable trance ... opening those eyes and seeing what
you can see ... as you remain in trance ... that's right, so just
let them open a bit ... and notice how your breathing has
slowed ... allowing you to stay in trance ... and maybe
noticing how heavy those eyelids are ... and they can close
when they want ... and going even deeper ... just as those
eyes close ... deeper.*

Linking

An intervention referred to as "linking" can also be beneficial for enhancing deepening experiences for any of the above techniques. Linking involves the use of conjunctions like the word "and." For instance the clinician could say, "*With each breath you release, notice how much deeper you can go into trance and the deeper you go into trance the more comfortable you can be.*" This suggestion could be linked yet again: "*And the more comfortable you feel, the clear things can be that you can see, feel, and hear.*"

RE-ORIENTATION AND RE-ALERTING

As an induction serves as a formal initiation of the hypnosis session, the re-alerting intervention concludes it. Traditionally, the termination of hypnosis has been referred to as "awakening." This outdated, and inaccurate, term that presumes the client is asleep during hypnosis has been replaced by a more suitable term, "re-alerting." In their recent SOT revision, ASCH replaced the term "re-alerting" with "re-orientation" though I am not certain this term is as an improved substitute since many, if not most individuals, are not "disoriented" during the hypnosis session. Nevertheless, the conclusion of a hypnosis session warrants careful attention and assessment of the client to ensure that they are adequately re-alerted.

The clinician establishes when hypnosis begins as well as when, but not necessarily *how*, trance concludes. Surely, in deciding when closure and disengagement is appropriate, the clinician will also determine the manner of the re-alert. Remaining consistent with the style of the induction, goals for the session, and overall treatment plan usually informs the re-alerting process. For instance, a session that has been more directive and authoritarian may involve counting (with a subtle increase in the clinician's volume for effect) for facilitating closure. It could go something like this:

> *And now I am going to begin counting from 5 down to 1 and you will become more alert and aware of everything going on around you with each number I say ... more aware of the sound of my voice ... sounds outside this office ... 5 beginning to be more alert ... 4 more aware now ... more alert 3 moving your hands and other body parts, coming back now ... 2 now about to open your eyes ... and 1 fully alert and aware!*

As with inductions, counting for the re-alert is a common re-alerting intervention taught at many hypnosis workshops. It is a rare occasion, however, that an individual is as fully alert and aware as suggested by the time the clinician concludes the countdown. It also tends to be an abrupt termination to what was likely a very pleasant and comfortable experience. In some ways, taking control of the re-alert in this manner takes control from the client. If one ultimate goal of hypnosis is to enhance self-care it seems that concluding a hypnosis session with an authoritative countdown runs contrary to this intention.

Alternatively, a more permissive session that reinforces the utilization of a client's internal resources can likewise conclude with a more permissive and unhurried approach like this one:

*In a moment I will invite you to be more alert and aware of
your surroundings. For now, take a moment and realize that
you have created this experience (ego strengthening, see
Chapter 9) ... your unconscious mind has become more
available to help and assist ... and when you feel very
confident that you have internalized this experience in a
way that it remains with you and is available for you, allow
yourself to become more alert ... eventually as alert as you
were before you walked into my office, but perhaps more
comfortable and relaxed. So when you are ready, take the
time you need in the time we have left (and not "take all the
time you need") to begin to become more alert ... moving
around, stretching if you like ... being here in this present
moment ... when you are ready.*

An approach that fosters personal control and management of a
trance experience is likely to align with treatment goals and objects
than one that is predominantly managed by the clinician. It also allows
the clinician to intersperse an opportunity for ego strengthening by
reinforcing the client for taking time to take care of themselves.

A more permissive approach does require some planning and also
an ample amount of time to permit the client to be adequately re-
alerted. It is therefore suggested that the hypnosis session begin with
the end in mind. That is, allowing for at least 10-15 minutes at the end
of the treatment session for the re-alert and, if necessary, debriefing
following the hypnosis. It is also important to establish boundaries at
the conclusion of the session if the re-alert is going to be more
permissive. Saying "take all the time you need" without including
"with the time we have left" can serve as a very welcoming suggestion
to just hang out in trance as long as they like!

Some words of caution for re-alerting

Without question, as reported by hypnosis expert and psychiatrist, Richard Kluft, M.D. "The vast majority of trances begin and end uneventfully" (2012, p. 142). There are unlikely and infrequent instances when a re-alert derails and the client does not re-alert as expected. Kluft referred to these instances as "rogue trances" which he defined as "a trance that persists and takes on a 'life of its own' despite re-alerting efforts" (2012, p. 143). In his 2012 paper in the *American Journal of Clinical Hypnosis*, Kluft (2012) provided over a dozen interventions when someone fails to fully re-alert as expected. It behooves the reader to review Kluft's recommendations despite the infrequency of these occurrences.

Regardless of the re-alerting intervention that is employed, it is very important that clinicians ensure that their clients are fully alert and reoriented (if necessary) before dismissing them either from an office or a virtual hypnosis session. Some clinicians utilize the Howard Alertness Scale (Howard, 2017), a pre- and post-hypnosis measure of level of alertness that alerts a clinician to potential concerns associated with possible rogue trances.

CONCLUSION

As this textbook serves as an introduction to clinical hypnosis, this chapter has focused on an overview of the basic elements associated with hypnotic induction, deepening, and re-alerting. However, an overview of each of these hypnotic interventions could easily serve as stand-alone chapters, and in some cases (e.g., hypnotic induction) could even be the singular focus of entire textbooks (see Jensen, 2017; Kumar & Lankton, 2018; Zeig, 2014). Nevertheless, the individualization of hypnotic induction is crucial not only for establishing and maintaining rapport treatment outcomes, but also for ensuring the comfortability of the patient.

CHAPTER 6
REFLECTION QUESTIONS

1. What are the basic elements of hypnotic induction, deepening, and re-alerting?

2. How do direct and indirect approaches differ for specific hypnotic induction techniques?

3. What are the two main deepening techniques? Describe each of them.

4. What are the pros and cons of a more direct counting re-alerting vs a more permissive re-alerting approach?

REFERENCES

Alter, D. S., & Sugarman, L. I. (2017). Reorienting hypnosis education. *American Journal of Clinical Hypnosis, 59*(3), 235-259. https://doi.org/10.1080/00029157.2016.1231657.

American Society of Clinical Hypnosis (2019). *Standards of training, 2019. Level I: Fundamentals of Clinical Hypnosis Workshop* [Unpublished Manuscript].

Bányai, É. I. (2018). Active-alert hypnosis: History, research, and applications. *American Journal of Clinical Hypnosis, 61*(2), 88-107. doi/pdf/10.1080/00029157.2018.1496318

Barabasz, A. & Watkins, J. (2005). *Hypnotherapeutic techniques* (2nd ed.). New York: Brunner-Routledge.

Erickson, M. (1958). Naturalistic techniques of hypnosis. *American Journal of Clinical Hypnosis, 1*, 3-8. doi:10.1080/00029157.1958.10401766

Gibbons, D. & Lynn, S. (2010). Hypnotic inductions: A primer. In S. Lynn, J. Rhue, & I. Kirsch (Eds.), *Handbook of clinical hypnosis* (2nd ed., pp. 267-291). American Psychological Association.

Green, J. P., Barabasz, A. F., Barrett, D., & Montgomery, G. H. (2003). Forging ahead: The 2003 APA division 30 definition of hypnosis. *International Journal of Clinical and Experimental Hypnosis, 53*, 259-264. doi:10.1080/00207140590961321

Green, J. & Lynn, S. (2011). Hypnotic responsiveness: Expectancy, attitudes, fantasy prone-ness, absorption, and gender. *International Journal of Clinical and Experimental Hypnosis, 59*(1), 103-121.

Hammond, D. C. (1990). *Handbook of hypnotic inductions and metaphors.* W. W. Norton.

Hammond, D. C., & Elkins, G. R. (2005). *Standards of training in clinical hypnosis.* American Society of Clinical Hypnosis-Education and Research Foundation.

Hope, A. E., & Sugarman, L. I. (2015). Orienting hypnosis. *American Journal of Clinical Hypnosis, 57*, 212-229.

Howard, H. (2017). Promoting safety in hypnosis: A clinical instrument for the assessment of alertness. *American Journal of Clinical Hypnosis, 59*(4), 344-362.

Jensen, M. P. (Ed.). (2017). *The art and practice of hypnotic induction: Favorite methods of master clinicians (1), Voices of experience.* Denny Creek Press.

Kirsch, I., Lynn, S., & Rhue, J. (1993). Introduction to clinical hypnosis. In J. Rhue, S. Lynn, & I. Kirsch (Eds.), *Handbook of clinical hypnosis* (pp. 3-22). American Psychological Association.

Kluft, R. (2012). Approaches to difficulties in re-alerting subjects from hypnosis. *American Journal of Clinical Hypnosis, 55*(2), 140-159.

Kumar, V. K., and Lankton, S. R. (Eds.). (2019). *Hypnotic induction: Perspectives, strategies, and concerns.* Routledge/Taylor and Francis.

Lankton, S., & Lankton, C. (2008). *The answer within: A clinical framework of Ericksonian hypnotherapy.* Crown House Publishers, Inc. (Original work published 1983).

Lynn, S. J., Kirsch, I., & Hallquist, M. (2008). Social cognitive theories of hypnosis. In M. Nash & A. Barnier (Eds.), *The Oxford Handbook of Hypnosis* (pp. 111-139). Oxford University Press.

Lynn, S. J., Maxwell, R., & Green, J. P. (2017). The hypnotic induction in the broad scheme of hypnosis: A sociocognitive perspective. *American Journal of Clinical Hypnosis, 59*(4), 363-384.

Lynn, S. J. & Sherman, S. (2000). The clinical importance of socio-cognitive models of hypnosis: Response set theory and Milton Erickson's strategic interventions. *American Journal of Clinical Hypnosis, 42*(3-4), 294-315.

Montgomery, G. H., Green, J. P., Erblich, J., Force, J., & Schnur, J. B. (2021). Common paraverbal errors during hypnosis intervention training. *American Journal of Clinical Hypnosis, 63*(3), 252-268.

Page, R. A., & Handley, G. W. (1992). Effects of "deepening" techniques on hypnotic depth and responding. *International Journal of Clinical and Experimental Hypnosis, 40*(3), 157-168.

Reid, D. B. (2012). *Hypnosis for behavioral health: A guide to expanding your professional practice.* Springer Publishing Company.

Reid, D. B. (2016). Hypnotic induction: Enhancing trance or mostly myth? *American Journal of Clinical Hypnosis, 59*(2), 128-137. doi:10.1080/00029157.2016.1190310

Spiegel, H., & Spiegel, D. (1978). *Trance and treatment: Clinical uses of hypnosis.* Basic.

Sugarman, L. I. (2021). Leaving hypnosis behind? *American Journal of Clinical Hypnosis, 64*(2), 139-156.

Sugarman, L. I., Linden, J. H., & Brooks, L. W. (2020). *Changing minds with clinical hypnosis: Narratives and discourse for a new health care paradigm.* Routledge/Taylor and Francis.

Wark, D. M. (2006). Alert hypnosis: A review and case report. *American Journal of Clinical Hypnosis, 48*(4), 291-300. doi:10.1080/00029157.2006.10401536

Wark, D. M. & Reid, D. B. (2018). Looking at alert, conversational hypnosis. *American Journal of Clinical Hypnosis, 61*(2), 85-87.

Yapko, M. D. (2019). *Trancework: An introduction to the practice of hypnosis.* (5th ed.). Routledge/Taylor and Francis.

Zeig, J. K. (2014). *The induction of hypnosis: An Ericksonian elicitation approach.* Milton Erickson Foundation Press.

CHAPTER 7
HYPNOTIC PHENOMENA

MOSHE TOREM

Chapter Learning Objectives

1. List at least three hypnotic phenomena.

2. Describe use of at least one hypnotic phenomenon.

3. Describe at least one therapeutic benefit of activating a hypnotic phenomenon in clinical work.

Hypnotic phenomena are fundamental ingredients for all healthcare professionals using hypnosis in their clinical work. Clients need to experience at least one hypnotic phenomenon to improve their chances of responding well to a variety of suggestions and other therapeutic interventions aimed at achieving the best possible hypnotically mediated treatment outcome. In general, there are two models for understanding and eliciting hypnotic phenomena. The traditional model views hypnosis as a unique state referred to as 'hypnotic trance' that can be activated by a procedure called 'hypnotic induction'. In this model hypnotic phenomena are elicited with the client in a state of hypnotic trance. The very fact that the hypnotic phenomenon was elicited becomes confirmation that the client was hypnotized into a trance state. (Janet, 1907; Bowers, 1976; Spiegel & Spiegel, 1978; Spiegel & Spiegel, 2004). The alternative model referred by some as the 'naturalistic utilization' model views hypnotic phenomena as clinically structured amplifications of common life experiences. (Erickson, 1958). In other words, hypnotic phenomena are distilled concentrated forms of everyday life occurrences (Yapko, 2019). The following is a list of common hypnotic phenomena: Age progression; Age regression; Alteration in the subjective sense of time (Time distortion); Amnesia & Hypermnesia; Analgesia; Anesthesia & Hyperesthesia; Automatic writing & drawing; Catalepsy; Dissociation; Hallucinations (negative & positive); Ideodynamic responses (ideoaffective, ideocognitive, ideomotor, ideosensory); Sensory alterations and Trance logic. In this chapter I will focus on selected hypnotic phenomena that are easier to elicit with most clients and are easier to learn and incorporate into clinical practice.

AGE PROGRESSION

Age Progression is a hypnotic phenomenon that involves experiencing the future as if as if it is happening in the present, (Torem 1992, Bonshtein & Torem 2017). Ideally this experience involves all our senses (visual, auditory, tactile, olfactory, and gustatory). A person's thoughts, and fantasies about one's own future influence the actual outcome of the future, this was described by Watzlawick (1984) as a form of self-fulfilling prophecies. Later, Watzlawick (1993) stated that it is the future not the past that affects our life in the present. This is compatible with Erickson's view that people come for therapy to change their future not to change the past. Havens (1985) devoted a whole book to report on the creative therapeutic techniques of Milton Erickson, when he addressed the issue of time he wrote "Erickson's primary focus of attention was on the future adjustments of his patients rather than upon their past failures" (Havens, 1985, p. 400). Later, Havens (1986), reported on his own successful clinical adoption of this strategy. According to Erickson (1954, 1980), therapeutic techniques associated with age progression are designed to act as an antidote to the patient's sense of futurelessness (Erickson, 1954). He described age progression as a technique facilitated by hypnosis, which he termed "pseudo-orientation in time". Erickson would guide the patient into a hypnotic state and then have the patient travel forward to the future into a time and space in which the patient has achieved a resolution of the current problem. Erickson would then suggest that the patient accept the future time as the present, and he would inquire what the patient learned that helped to solve the problem. When Erickson obtained this information, he would facilitate amnesia for having done so and may then use this information as a therapeutic strategy.

Clinical Application of Age Progression

In the "Back from the Future" technique, the focus is on suggestions of positive thinking and pleasant feelings of joy and satisfaction in reaching a solution to a specific problem. This is also accompanied by suggestions for a sense of health, strength, accomplishment, resilience, and a sense of inner resourcefulness and creativity in coping with life's stresses. The patient is then instructed to store the above experiences, sensations, positive feelings, images, and sense of accomplishment, which are then internalized and encoded consciously and subconsciously as the patient is hypnotically guided back from the future into the present. The patients are told that these positive images, sensations, feelings, and experiences are special gifts that they bring back with them on their mental time trip "back from the future" into the present and that these gifts will guide them on a conscious and subconscious level in their journey of healing and recovery. When the patient is out of the formal hypnotic state, a brief discussion is conducted about the patient's experience; the therapist actively listens to the patients' report on their experience. This is followed by a homework assignment in which the patient is asked to write about the experience and to describe what it was like to take such a voyage into the future and to experience a solution to the problem. This written assignment may be requested while the patient is still in a state of hypnotic trance and may be given as a gentle suggestion. The patient is asked to bring the written assignment to the following session and to read it out loud to the therapist. It is not uncommon that the initial patient's verbal narrative about the future-focused experience includes verbs that are grammatically past based. For example, a patient verbally describing the experience of a future not-yet-happened event, when her currently 10-year-old son is participating in the ceremony of graduating from high school at the age of 18, may say the following "I saw my son all dressed up in cap and gown as he was walking to receive his high school diploma, I felt so proud when they called his name, later he gave me a hug and a kiss and I could smell the scent of his after-shave lotion." In my clinical experience, individuals who spontaneously describe their time being back from the future experience and use past tense verbs usually have better outcomes with this type of future-focused intervention. The symptoms of futurelessness, helplessness, and hopelessness are significantly reduced and are replaced by a sense of new hope, strength, inner resourcefulness, self-mastery, and belief in one's recovery. The suggestions for age progression are used after the patient has learned self-hypnosis and is guided into a state of self-hypnotic trance. This can be followed by a discussion of the patient's experience and an assignment to have the experience put in written form to be reviewed in the following session. Since 1990, I have reported on the use of this "Back from the Future" technique in the treatment of depression (Torem, 2006, 2017b), the treatment of eating disorders (Torem, 1991, 2001, 2017c), the control of self-inflicted violence (Torem, 1995, 1997), for enhancing ego-strengthening (Torem, 1990), for enhancing internal integration of separate ego states (Torem & Gainer, 1995), for the treatment of hyperemesis gravidarum (Torem, 1994), and the treatment of autoimmune disorders (Torem, 2007, 2017c). Moreover, the successful utilization of the "Back from the Future" technique was also reported by Stanton (1994) in his application of sports imagery with hypnosis. Jensen (2011, 2017) reported on the value of using the "Back from the Future" technique in the treatment of patients who suffer from chronic pain. More recently, Bonshtein and Torem (2017) reported on using a modified version of this technique as a "forward affect bridge" in the practice of psychotherapy. According to Yapko (2019), age progression can be utilized in two general strategies. The first is activated as a therapeutic intervention and the second is used to examine the benefit & value of the current clinical work. Using age progression as a therapeutic intervention is based on the foundation of the concept of expectancy as described by Kirsch (1990a, 1990b, 2000, 2001, 2006). Age progression can be activated in a highly structured way very focused on a specific event jointly chosen by the clinician and the patient (Torem, 1992, 2006, 2007, 2017a, 2017b, 2019). Age progression may also be used in a non-structured way to explore the clients' hidden negative expectations that may turn into self-fulfilling prophecies. Such hidden expectations require to be changed with further therapeutic work. The second strategy utilizes age progression to explore the actual value and benefit of the current clinical work by looking at the actual results in the future. This method provides vital information for both clinician & client to see what worked, what has not, and what needs to be changed to get better results.

Eliciting Age Progression

The "Back from the Future" technique was first described more than 30 years ago (Torem, 1989, 1990) and then was published in the American Journal of Clinical Hypnosis (Torem, 1992a). This technique is based on the utilization of age-progression interventions enhanced by hypnosis. Age progression can be elicited by very direct hypnotic suggestions such as a magical time machine to fly into the future (Torem, 1992, 2007, 2017a, 2019). Indirect ways may invite clients to use their imagination and describe in detail what life is like having achieved their goal of symptom relief, recovery from a medical procedure, graduation from a challenging educational program, etc. An important caveat for clinicians using age progression is utilize future projection that have plausible chance of being realized based on the client's personality, intelligence, and the context of life circumstances. Clinicians should be careful not to be using age progression as a magical intervention to achieve unrealistic goals. (Torem, 2006, 2017a, 2019).

AGE REGRESSION

Kroger, (1963, 2008) defined age regression as a hypnotic phenomenon whereby the subject plays a role in a simulated pattern of acting out past events in the framework of the present. Weitzenhoffer (2000), defined age regression as a hypnotic phenomenon whereby the subject relives past events cognitively, emotionally, and behaviorally. Yapko (2019), defines age regression as an intensified absorption in an experiential utilization of memory. Yapko describes two forms of age regression: "revivification" and "hypermnesia". In revivification, the client is guided back in time to re-experience a specific past event as if it were happening in the here and now. The client feels, thinks and behaves as if he/she is in that past event. In hypermnesia, the person remains consciously in the present and recalls vividly details of a specific past event. Age regressions may be experienced by some people without any formal induction of hypnosis. This is reported as being engrossed in memories and actual experiences of past events triggered by looking at pictures, listening to certain songs, or experiencing the smell and taste of certain foods. Some people find it comforting especially when such memories activate positive feeling of being loved and appreciated for others. This relieves a source of pain stemming from wounds that never healed and continue to produce symptoms and dysfunctional behaviors affecting their daily life in the present. Such people may benefit from the potential therapeutic effects of age regression.

Clinical Applications of Age Regression

According to Yapko (2019), there are two general strategies in the clinical use of age regression. The first strategy activates age regression to remember in detail a negative experience even if it were to be traumatic in nature. This is provided that the mature adult ego state is co-present and participates as an observer in the experience in order to work it through and develop a new understanding the provides a new perspective that has a healing effect on present day to day functioning, (Lynn & Kirsch, 2006; Spiegel, 2010). The second strategy is to remember positive events and experiences from the past. Specifically—remembering times when learning something new or acquiring a new skill was not easy and persistence with patience and determination helped in achieving the desired goal. This allows clients to connect to hard times from the past and the skills and strengths the were used to eventually be successful. It may also be utilized to connect with positive loving experiences with family members or childhood friends when a client felt unconditional love and acceptance. This allows the client to reconnect with such positive childhood experiences and memories that are now consciously internalized and brought into the present-day life of the client.

Eliciting age regression

There are a variety of methods to elicit age regression for example, Suggesting the use of a special machine to time travel in the past, sitting at home in one's safe comfortable chair with a special remote control to play a video of special to be explored events of one's childhood. This provides double safety for the client who may use the remote-control device to activate a variety of different functions such as: forward play, review, zoom in, zoom out, pause, etc. This allows the present-day adult client to watch and carefully review specific events of one's childhood in a safe environment protecting the client from being retraumatized by watching on the TV screen specific painful events of one's childhood. Watkins, (1971), described a hypnotically mediated technique he called 'affect bridge' to guide a client to a specific childhood event using an imaginary bridge guided by one's affect that originated from a significant past event.

Some important caveats for clinicians using age regression

It is very important to note that using age regression with hypnosis does not and will not provide a procedure to uncover the true memories of what really happened in one's childhood. Memory is not some hidden event that was recorded in the subconscious mind of the client and can be uncovered with hypnosis and age regression. Memory is to be understood as a process based on subjective perception and is modified and changed throughout one's life to serve certain dynamic functions to help with a positive perception of oneself and best optimal functioning with the activities of daily living. (Kandel, 2007; Squire & Kandel, 2008; Yapko, 2019). According to Loftus (2017, memories can be influenced intentionally or unintentionally because of their suggestible nature, this is supported by Sheehan (1988, 1995). Some individuals may spontaneously age regress in response to an external trigger connected to some traumatic event from their childhood. Some of these individuals are stuck in this child like state of mind and end up in the emergency room of the hospital diagnosed as being in a psychotic state not responsive to antipsychotic medication. Clinicians who are well trained in hypnosis can recognize this as trance like age regression and with their hypnotic skills are able to dehypnotize such patients out of this age regressed state back into their regular adult state of consciousness. This can sometimes be very dramatic in its quick results demonstrating the benefit and value of being knowledgeable and skillful in the use of hypnosis in the clinical setting.

HYPNOTIC AMNESIA

Edmonston (1986) points out that prior to the twentieth century spontaneous amnesia was once considered to be specific to hypnosis and served as confirmation that the subject was truly hypnotized. According to Kroger (1963, 2008), the phenomenon of amnesia occurs as a daily experience without any formal hypnosis. As a hypnotic phenomenon it is most often observed through posthypnotic suggestions. Nance, Orne and Hammer (1974), concluded from their research that hypnotic amnesia is different from common forgetting in day to day living. Zeig (1985) described hypnotic amnesia as a process whereby "a subject responds without full awareness of the response or of the stimulus that effected it" (p. 320). Weitzenhoffer (2000) classified hypnotic amnesias as either a spontaneous type or a suggested type. He pointed out that the suggested type was studied much more while the spontaneous type less so. According to Cox & Bryant (2008) hypnotic amnesia involves the inability to recall items suggested to be unavailable for conscious recall and the ability to later recall when the suggestion is reversed. Barber (2000) described a particular hypnotic responder he called the "amnesia prone" individual as a person who becomes very absorbed in the hypnotic experience and becomes disconnected from the immediate surrounding reality. Such a person typically develops spontaneous amnesia to the hypnotic experience.

Clinical Applications of Amnesia

Edgette and Edgette (1995) described two types of therapeutic use of hypnotic amnesia, first as the primary intervention and second as a supportive intervention. As a primary intervention, amnesia has a therapeutic value by erasing from conscious memory any past experiences of severe pain or failure. Edgette and Edgette (1995), provide some relevant examples for using amnesia as a therapeutic tool, such as, a client suffering from chronic pain who is obsessed with ruminating thoughts and memories of helplessness and suffering. An athlete can use amnesia to remove memories of failure and falls as he or she train for their future performances. A client engaged in efforts to stop smoking may benefit from developing amnesia to any pleasure experienced with the habit of smoking. Zeig (1985) mentioned the use of posthypnotic amnesia as tool to convince clients that they were in fact hypnotized. Amnesia may also be used therapeutically as a supportive intervention to a primary intervention method. Erickson (1954) used suggested hypnotic amnesia as way for some patients to have no conscious memory of the suggestions given under hypnosis. This allowed many of his clients to experience their behavioral changes as coming from within them and take greater ownership of such changes. This method is especially effective for clients resisting to change as a result of hypnotic suggestions. This general strategy was also reported by Gilligan (1987).

Methods to elicit Hypnotic Amnesia

Yapko (2019) lists several ways of eliciting hypnotic amnesia. Direct suggestion to forget what was said in the hypnotic state works best when the client is invited to make his/her choice to forget certain parts of the hypnotic experience since it does not serve a relevant or important part in day to living. Indirect suggestions to elicit hypnotic amnesia invite the client to consider the option of remembering only the important and relevant issues and details of what was discussed and experienced in the hypnotic state. 'Forgetting' is not mentioned in such indirect suggestions. Attentional shift is a common phenomenon in daily living contributing to the experience of not remembering a name or a thought, and then dismissing it by saying to oneself "it must not be that important otherwise I would remember it". Clinicians may choose this method in the hypnotic communication by abruptly shifting the client's attention to another issue after spending some time on it, as typically the client does not remember what was said or discussed prior to the attentional shift. It is important to point out to all clinicians who want to elicit hypnotic amnesia as part of the therapeutic process to avoid asking the client after he/she was guided out of trance to describe what was their experience being in a hypnotic state or what they remember of what happened since this may undo the desired amnesia. In general, the deliberate use of amnesia as a therapeutic tool should be avoided by beginning clinicians not yet experienced with hypnosis

HYPNOTIC ANALGESIA AND ANESTHESIA

Analgesia refers to the elimination of pain sensations without the loss of consciousness or other sensations. Anesthesia refers to the loss of all physical sensations with or without the loss of consciousness.

Clinical Applications of Analgesia and Anesthesia

There are two general groups for using hypnotic analgesia and anesthesia. These are: 1.) Performing medical, dental and surgical procedures without using any drugs. 2.) Chronic pain and other indications. The goal of eliciting hypnotic analgesia is to allow for a medical dental or surgical procedures to be done without the need to use a specific drug or chemical to achieve a significant reduction to complete elimination of pain sensations during the procedure. The use of hypnotic analgesia and anesthesia go back to reports from James Esdaile (1846) who was a Scottish surgeon serving in India. Esdaile documented performing many major surgeries utilizing hypnosis as the sole anesthetic with good outcomes and with fewer post-surgical complications. Since then, there has been significant research on using hypnosis for pain relief (Kroger, 1951; August, 1960; Hilgard, & Hilgard, 1975; Jensen, & Barber, 2000; Lang, 2017a; 2017b). Many published clinical reports document the use of hypnosis for achieving a state of anesthesia for medical, dental and surgical procedures without any anesthetic chemicals, or with a significant reduction in the dose of anesthetic drugs. (Rosen, 1959; Ruiz & Fernandez, 1960; Gravitz, 1988; Crabtree, 1993; Faymonville et al., 1995; Thompson, 2004; Elkins et al., 2007; Montgomery et al., 2017; Spiegel, 2007; Hammond, 2008; Rosenfeld, 2008; Goodman & Filo, 2017). Hypnosis for pain control in Obstetrical procedures including Cesarian sections without the need for chemical anesthetic drugs was documented and reported by many clinicians. (Kroger, 1951; August, 1959, 1960, 1961; Chiasson, 1992; Goldman, 1992; Cyna et al., 2007; Werner, 2017).

Using Hypnotic Analgesia & Anesthesia for Treating Chronic Pain and Other Conditions

There are people who suffer from chronic pain for whom hypnotic analgesia may also be very helpful as documented and reported by many clinicians. (Kirsch & Lynn, 1995; Patterson, 2010; Jensen, 2011; Elkins, Johnson & Fisher, 2012; Jenson & Patterson, 2014). Moreover, some clinicians have developed a detailed structured program including self-hypnosis in the treatment of chronic pain. (Jensen, Barber, Romano, Hanley et al., 2009; Jensen, 2011; Jensen et al., 2011; Jensen, 2017). Edgette and Edgette (1995), pointed out that hypnotic analgesia and anesthesia can also be used metaphorically to better deal with emotional pain, clients can learn to develop what was termed 'focal psychological numbing' for a past trauma that is too overwhelming with mental pain to handled directly. Some clients can learn to use hypnotic analgesia to numb down their severe anxiety, thus preventing a full-blown panic attack. Clients suffering from addiction to alcohol and drugs may learn to effectively use hypnotic analgesia and anesthesia to numb down the intensity of their agitation and craving instead of relapsing to the alcohol or the drug of abuse.

Eliciting Hypnotic Analgesia or Anesthesia

There are many ways to elicit hypnotic analgesia or anesthesia. The 'glove anesthesia' technique is a classical example for hypnotic sensory alteration.

The client in the hypnotic state is given suggestions to experience full numbness in one or both hands as a result of putting on a special glove that produces this numbness through the sensation of heat or coldness. (Danziger et al., 1998; Faymonville et al., 1995, 2003; Faymonville, Boly, & Laureys, 2006; Fidanza et al., 2017; Virot & Bernard, 2018).

HYPNOTIC CATALEPSY

Kroger (1963) defined catalepsy as an "involuntary tonicity of muscles" together with an inhibition of voluntary movement. Erickson (Erickson & Rossi, 1981) understood catalepsy as a sign that the subject is in hypnotic trance especially when catalepsy appears spontaneously without any direct suggestion to produce it. For example, a subject is guided into a state of trance with suggestions to focus on breathing and in this process the subject's head spontaneously drops down forward resting on the chest and stays in this position without any movement for the rest of the trance session. Catalepsy may frequently be associated with sensations of numbness and anesthesia when for example one arm has levitated upwards like floating in the air without any further movement (Spiegel, 1977).

Clinical Applications of Catalepsy

Erickson (Erickson & Rossi, 1981) believed that spontaneous hypnotic catalepsy reflects a heightened receptivity to suggestions and readiness for change that may be needed in therapeutic work. The suspended physical movement of the body is viewed as reflecting an internal mental suspension of awareness ready to quickly internalize new ideas, perspectives or experiences (Edgette & Edgette, 1995). Yapko (2019) conceptualized two separate ways of therapeutic catalepsy. First, catalepsy can be used to facilitate deepening of the hypnotic state by helping the client recognize his or her state of involuntary body movement. Second, catalepsy may be actively suggested (if it does not happen spontaneously) in order let the client experience a state of calm, restful non-movement that can also be a pleasant healing experience. This applies especially for clients who get in trouble by acting on impulses of the moment without the opportunity to wait and reflect on the consequences of one's actions. Learning to experience the capacity to inhibit impulsive action, helps clients to acquire a new adaptive skill. The skill of learning and practicing comfortable stillness and pleasant effortless immobility has adaptive value for clients when an injection is given or the moment for venipuncture to draw blood from a vein for testing, or when there is a need to start an intravenous line. Moreover, temporary immobility is also required during an MRI, when an eye procedure is performed by an ophthalmologist requesting complete stillness, or when splinters of broken glass must be removed from an injured arm (Edgette & Edgette, 1995). Hypnotic catalepsy may be unhelpful for clients who suffer from extreme fatigue and daytime sleepiness due to depression associated with psychomotor retardation. In addition, clinicians should be aware that for some clients with obsessive ruminations and fear of action hypnotic catalepsy may be countertherapeutic.

Eliciting Therapeutic Catalepsy

One way I found helpful is share with clients the adaptive natural biological phenomenon of freezing all movements. Most people are familiar with the fight or flight response in the face danger. I point out to them the third response of 'freeze' and tell them about the example from nature how the American Opossum behaves when it senses danger or the hibernation response of certain mammals during winters when no food or shelter are available. These examples make it easier for some clients to accept catalepsy as a skill that has adaptive value with clear benefits in certain situations. One simple and easy way to elicit catalepsy is with suggestions for arm levitation and adding the suggestion; "your arm floats upwards bending at the elbow and stays there comfortably when you open your eyes you see your floating effortlessly and you are amazed how it stays that way and it does not concern you at all, we have been focusing on the successful resolution of the smoking habit". The client is the taught self-hypnosis using the arm levitation to enter a trance state with natural induced catalepsy and then to get reoriented coming back to the regular state of consciousness. This is described in detail by Spiegel (1977).

DISSOCIATION

Pierre Janet (1889) was first to define and formulate the concept of dissociation. Janet's original definition of the term dissociation is found in his book *L'automatisme psychologique*, (Janet, 1889). In French it appears as, *desagregation*, it was translated to English as *dissociation*, it first appears in the book *Principles of psychology* by William James (1890). The English term *dissociation* was accepted by Janet himself as evident in 1907 during his Harvard lectures on *The Major Symptoms of Hysteria*. English & English (1958) provide an English translation of Janet's definition of dissociation as: "A process whereby a group of psychological activities processing a certain unity among themselves lose most of their relationship with the rest of the personality and function more or less independently". Kroger (1963) believed that dissociation may happen naturally with or without formal hypnotic trance. Hilgard (1977, 1992) conceptualized dissociation as a basic mechanism of the hypnotic experience. In his opinion there is no hypnosis without dissociation. Hilgard called his formulation the neodissociation theory of hypnosis. As dissociation takes place, certain parts of an individual's mental functions become separated from central conscious awareness. These parts may function separately with some degree of independence from each other and without awareness of the individual's central state of consciousness. Elkins (2017 p. 85) believes that "the concept of dissociation may explain a shift to a state of consciousness in which critical thinking is decreased and internal imagery becomes a primary reality for the patient in a hypnotic state".

Elkins introduced the concept of *adaptive dissociation* to distinguish it from dissociation occurring as part of psychopathological states such as in dissociative disorders. According to Elkins *adaptive dissociation* is central to hypnotic relaxation therapy (HRT). Adaptive dissociation contributes to healthy functioning with the activities of daily living. Yapko (2019 p. 322) defined dissociation as *"the ability to break a global experience into its component parts,* setting the stage to amplify awareness for one part while diminishing awareness for the others." Yapko later points out correctly that what differentiates adaptive dissociation from pathological dissociation is not the process but rather the outcome it generates. Yapko later clarifies (2019 p. 323) that "hypnosis is by its very nature a dissociative experience and dissociation may be regarded as the defining characteristic of hypnosis".

Clinical Applications of Dissociation

All clinicians should learn to understand and identify what dissociative states look like in clinical settings and learn how to best help patients who present in such states (Torem 1989). One of the best ways to understand and utilize dissociative phenomena in clinical practice is learn and understand the concept and origins of ego state theory and how to use ego state therapy in managing therapeutically dissociated ego states. (Watkins, J.G. & Watkins, H.H. 1979, 1991, 1997; Torem 1993, 1994,1995; Torem & Gainer 1995; Gainer & Torem 1993; Abramowitz & Torem 2018). Dissociation may be used adaptively in learning to separate oneself from unresolved problems at work and separate from these issues when arriving at home after work and be able to feel, behave and act appropriately as a spouse or parent. Some clients who are chronic worriers may also benefit from learning to use this hypnotic phenomenon adaptively. Some people have a hard time falling asleep due to chronic worries about unresolved issue that from daily life, teaching such a person the skill adaptive dissociation helps them to successfully get a full and healthy sleep habit. Some individuals with chronic depression continue to stay pessimistic about their life and these feelings of hopelessness with self-deprecation continue to add to their chronic depressed state. Clinicians may apply adaptive dissociation to identify and separate an ego state the is optimistic about life and use such positivity to be expressed in certain situations and then affect the of the client's ego states.

Eliciting Hypnotic Dissociation

Since dissociation is so much part of the hypnotic experience it is rather easy to elicit this phenomenon from the first hypnotic induction. For example a clinician may say: *"As you are sitting here in this chair in my office you may take an imaginary trip to your favorite Florida beach it is a sunny comfortable warm day, the sun is shining the skies are clear and blue take a look at ocean do you see the waves braking and receding describe to me what do you see, do you notice the sea gulls floating up and down with currents of the air."* This continues reviewing the beach experience with all five senses. Then the clinician may say: *"Is this interesting a part of you was enjoying itself on your favorite Florida beach and another part of you was sitting here in this chair in my office, it is like being here and being there and you can learn to your focus based on what serves your needs best."* Edgette and Edgette (1995 p. 151) propose using evocative language in the hypnotic session to elicit dissociation such phrases as: *"divide up, get some distance, that part of you can become independent, disconnected from, apart from, you can put that aside."* In preparing a patient for a medical or dental procedure on may say: *"While I am working on your arm removing all these sutures you are going to be on your favorite ocean beach sitting in your comfortable chair and listening to seagulls."* A dentist may use a similar technique in doing his dental work. Lankton and Lankton (1983) provide a useful example of seeding for eliciting dissociation: *"You can wonder with your conscious mind what kind of trance you'll develop today as your unconscious mind simply goes about the business of doing it."*

HYPNOTIC TIME DISTORTION

Cooper (1948) was the first to document the hypnotic phenomenon of time distortion. Time distortion is defined as a change in one's subjective experience of time becoming dissociated from the standard measures of time by the clock or watch. Erickson and Erickson (1958), provide further clarification on subjective time condensation as distinct from time expansion. We are familiar with the saying, *"Time flies when you're having fun"* which is a good example of time contraction. Other times in a boring lecture time may be experienced as passing slower than what the watch shows, and five minutes are experience as an hour, which is a good example of time expansion. The subjective experience of time can also be altered by hypnotic suggestions as documented several authors (Cooper, 1952; Cooper & Erickson, 1954; Gilligan, 1987; Edgette & Edgette, 1995).

Clinical Applications of Time Distortion

There many clients with severe chronic pain using hypnotic time contraction as a very helpful intervention (Patterson, 2010; Jensen, 2011). Women in labor feel some comfort between contractions, this time of comfort can be expanded with hypnotic suggestion and comfort to a woman in labor (Kroger, 1976, 2008).

Eliciting Hypnotic Time Distortion

Time distortion happens frequently during hypnotic induction, most individuals are surprised to discover the discrepancy between their subjective experience of time and actual recorded clock time. There also a way to elicit time distortion with direct suggestions. For example you may say to a client while in hypnosis,

> *"as you are sitting here, your mind may experience all the pleasant and joyful sensations on this slow comfortable walk*

on your favorite ocean beach ... and time passes so much quicker as you are having fun, that a day may feel just like a couple of minutes to you ... and yet these memories can remain so fresh and pleasant in your subconscious mind for a much longer time." Another example: *"As you go forward in time enjoying your 80th birthday party notice that your visit may stretch out for many hours giving you time to enjoy this very special event to the fullest so that minutes may feel to you like many hours staying with you with a special positive enjoyable effect."*

AUTOMATIC WRITING AND DRAWING

This is a very interesting hypnotic phenomenon referring to an individual's expression of feelings, thoughts, ideas, opinions, in written words, numbers, figures or symbols in a trance state or as part of a post hypnotic suggestion. This expression occurs due to a suspension of a cognitive self-evaluation, or critical examination of the written material and frequently there is amnesia to the phenomenon or to the content of what was communicated without conscious awareness (Hilgard, 1992; Edgette & Edgette, 1995). Apparently, it is reported that Erickson used this hypnotic phenomenon in the successful treatment of a young man with acute obsessional depression. (Erickson & Kubie, 1938, 1980 pp. 158-176).

Clinical Applications of Automatic Writing

Automatic writing can be used to help clients in the process of better understanding unconscious drives and motivation to behaviors that are at times self-defeating and puzzling. It may also be used to facilitate more helpful communication with hidden ego-states in ego-state therapy. It can also be utilized in the therapeutic interpretation of dreams (Weitzenhoffer, 2000). In the therapeutic resolution of amnesia, the sexual abuse and trauma (Dolan, 1991). Moreover, it has also been successfully used in the treatment of authors with 'blocked writers' syndrome and students who feel blocked on written comprehensive exams.

Eliciting Hypnotic Automatic Writing

Automatic writing can be elicited with direct suggestion during hypnotic trance or post hypnotic suggestion saying for example, *"later when you get the signal from me have eye lids open any important communication from your subconscious may express itself by using this pen on note pad."* It is prudent for the safe and therapeutic benefits of the client to verify that the communicated material may be shared and discussed in the post hypnotic state of mind.

HYPNOTIC IDEODYNAMIC RESPONSES

Ideodynamic responses are defined as conversion of an idea into a dynamic response (Erickson & Rossi, 1981). Many functions in our daily living are carried out automatically, this frees up our brain to become involved in activities of higher function such as planning, analyzing options and selecting the best one, assessing risk reward analysis, inhibition of impulses and effective use of time with the activities of daily living. Automatic functions exist on four different levels: affective, cognitive, motoric and sensory (Yapko, 2019). The ideodynamic responses are named accordingly, ideoaffective, ideocognitive, ideomotoric, and ideosensory.

Clinical Applications of Ideodynamic Phenomena

The most commonly clinical used is the hypnotic ideomotor response, which is the body's unconscious physical movement expression of thoughts. Ideomotor response can be clinically applied for diagnostic or therapeutic uses. Diagnostically, clinicians may set up in the hypnotic state an upward movement of the index finger in the non-dominant hand as a 'yes' response, a downward movement as a 'no' response and a no movement as a 'I don't know response. Sometimes no movement may communicate a conflictual response indicating a sometimes 'yes' and sometimes 'no' depending on the situation, this requires further exploration using verbal communication. (Cheek & LeCron, 1968; Ewin & Eimer, 2006; Ewin, 2009; Shenefelt, 2011; Yapko, 2019). Therapeutically, ideomotor responses can be used to deepen the hypnotic state, to obtain confirmation before deciding on a specific treatment strategy, or to obtain additional details of a specific issue to be explored. Hypnotic ideomotor response requires training and practice however, it should not be relied on as the tool to obtain the ultimate truth and direction but rather as additional aid to many other tools and approaches in the overall therapeutic hypnotic interventions. Ideocognitive responses refer to automatic thoughts or responses hypnotically activated through cognitive behavior therapy interventions. Ideocognitive techniques help to identify cognitive distortions, unrealistic expectations, or irrational beliefs, that contribute to the client's symptoms and dysfunctional behaviors requiring corrections and repair (Alladin, 2008, 2012, 2016, 2017; Yapko, 2001a, 2001b; Zarren & Eimer, 2001). Ideoaffective responses are emotional automatic responses to certain questions, stimuli, or thoughts. These responses can be set up with the client in the hypnotic state and serve as a diagnostic or therapeutic aid. Ideosensory responses are automatic experiences in the arena of sensations in response to certain thoughts, questions, verbal statements, or in response to hypnotic suggestions. Such sensory sensations may include any or all the following: cold, warm, itching, pain, smell, taste, touch, pinch, burning sensation, pleasant touch etc. These experiences can be utilized for further exploration and therapeutic change.

Eliciting Ideodynamic Responses

Ideodynamic responses are part of the hypnotic experience. It is up to the clinician together with the client to decide when and how to clinically utilize them to obtain the best benefits.

Additional Hypnotic Phenomena

Whether hypnotic hallucinations are negative or positive, they may be valuable in clinical work to reduce symptoms in patients with dissociative disorders, posttraumatic stress disorders and atypical psychosis not otherwise specified. In these conditions the potential use of hypnosis may modify or eliminate the hallucinations and thus serve as important diagnostic and therapeutic tool.

Trance logic is a term was originally coined by Orne (1959). Trance logic refers to the hypnotic phenomenon whereby a client in a hypnotic state can tolerate without any apparent distress the coexistence of two or more logically inconsistent perceptions or ideas. Orne identified this hypnotic phenomenon in his creative set up to distinguish between clients who attempt to fake hypnosis for some secondary gain and clients who experience real hypnosis.

CONCLUSION

Experiencing hypnotic phenomena is a crucial aspect of responding well to suggestions in clinical hypnosis. Among different types of hypnotic phenomena includes age progression, whereby the client experiences the present as if it is the future which offers therapeutic benefit by inducing positive expectancy. Age regression is another hypnotic phenomenon which is used for either remembering details of negative events in the past or restoring positive memories of the past to present-day life. Knowledge of age regression hypnosis could help clinicians dehypnotize patients who spontaneously age regress in response to an external trigger as well. Other types of hypnotic phenomena include amnesia which can act as a clinical tool toward removing memories of severe pain or memories that induce helplessness and suffering. In addition, hypnotic analgesia and aesthesia can be used toward pain control for chronic pain, as well as medical, dental, or surgical procedures too.

Additional occurrences of hypnotic phenomena happen in hypnotic catalepsy, whereby the subject experiences involuntary inhibition of movement which can be useful toward deepening the hypnotic trance as well as inhibiting impulsive actions in clients. Moreover, hypnotic phenomenon could occur with adaptative dissociation which can contribute to healthy activities of daily living as the individual learns to diminish awareness of worries and unresolved issues. Time distortion is also another hypnotic phenomenon which can be used toward either reducing or extending the patient's subjective length of time. Lastly, automatic writing and drawing which can be used to better understand unconscious drives, as well as ideodynamic responses, which are automatic responses toward diagnosing or confirming therapeutic effect are also useful hypnotic phenomena which are described in this chapter.

CHAPTER 7
REFLECTION QUESTIONS

1. What are some examples of common hypnotic phenomena?

2. Describe each of the hypnotic phenomena that could be experienced even without formal hypnosis.

3. What are the clinical applications of hypnotic phenomena—including age progression, age regression, amnesia, analgesia and anesthesia, hypnotic catalepsy, adaptative dissociation, time distortion, automatic writing, and ideodynamic response?

REFERENCES

Faymonville, M., Roediger, L., Del Fiore, G., Delgueldre, C., Phillips, C., Lamy, M., & Laureys, S. (2003). Increased cerebral functional connectivity underlying the antinociceptive effects of hypnosis. *Cognitive Brain Research, 17*(2), 255-262.

Fidanza, F., Varanini, M., Ciaramella, A., Carli, G., & Santarcangelo, E. L. (2017). Pain modulation as a function of hypnotizability: Diffuse noxious inhibitory control induced by cold pressor test vs explicit suggestions of analgesia. *Physiology & Behavior, 171,* 135-141.

Fine, C. G. (2012). Cognitive behavioral hypnotherapy for dissociative disorders. *American Journal of Clinical Hypnosis, 54*(4), 331-352.

Gilligan, S. (1987). *Therapeutic trances: The cooperation principle in Ericksonian hypnotherapy.* New York: Brunner and Mazel.

Goldman, L. (1992). The use of hypnosis in obstetrics. Psychiatric Medicine, 10(4), 59-67.

Goodman, A., & Filo, G. (2017). Dental applications. In G. Elkins (Ed.), *Handbook of medical and psychological hypnosis: Foundations, applications, and professional issues,* (pp. 205-212). New York: Springer.

Gravitz, M. (1988). Early uses of hypnosis in surgical anesthesia. *American Journal of Clinical Hypnosis, 30*(3), 201-208.

Hammond, D. (2008). Hypnosis as sole anesthesia for major surgeries: Historical & contemporary perspectives. *American Journal of Clinical Hypnosis, 51*(2), 101-121.

Havens, R. (2003). *The Wisdom of Milton H. Erickson: The Complete Volume.* Williston, VT: Crown House Publishing Ltd.

Hilgard, E., & Hilgard, J. (1975). *Hypnosis in the relief of pain.* New York: Wm. Kaufman.

Hilgard, E. (1974). Toward a neo-dissociation theory: Multiple cognitive controls in human functioning. *Perspectives in Biology and Medicine, 17,* 301-316.

Hilgard, E. (1977). *Divided consciousness: Multiple controls in human thought and action.* New York: John Wiley.

Hilgard, E. (1982). Hypnotic susceptibility and implications for measurement. *International Journal of Clinical and Experimental Hypnosis, 30*, 394-403.

Hilgard, E. (1991). A neodissociation interpretation of hypnosis. In S. Lynn & J. Rhue (Eds.), *Theories of hypnosis: Current models and perspectives* (pp. 83-104). New York: Guilford.

Hilgard, E. (1992). Dissociation and theories of hypnosis. In E. Fromm & M. Nash (Eds.), *Contemporary Hypnosis Research* (pp. 69-101). New York: Guilford.

Hilgard, E. (1994). Neodissociation theory. In S. Lynn & J. Rhue (Eds.), *Dissociation: Clinical, theoretical and research perspectives* (pp. 32-51). New York: Guilford.

James, W. (1890). *The Principles of Psychology*, New York, Holt.

Janet, P. (1889). *L'automatismme psychologique*. Paris, Alcan.

Janet, P. (1907). *The major symptoms of hysteria*. New York, Macmillan.

Jensen, M. P. (2011). *Hypnosis for chronic pain management: Therapist Guide*. New York: Oxford University Pres.

Jensen, M. P. (2017). Pain management-chronic pain. In G. Elkins (Ed.), *Handbook of medical and psychological hypnosis: Foundations, applications, and professional issues* (pp. 341-360). New York: Springer.

Jensen, M.P., & Barber, J. (2000). Hypnotic analgesia of spinal cord injury pain. *Australian Journal of Clinical and Experimental Hypnosis, 28*(2), *150-168.*

Jensen, M. P., & Patterson, D. (2014). Hypnotic approaches for chronic pain management: Clinical implications of recent research findings. *American Psychologist, 69*(2), 167-177.

Kandel, E. (2007). *In search of memory: The emergence of a new Science of mind.* New York: Norton., W. (1970). *Childbirth with hypnosis*. Los Angeles: Wilshire Book Co.

Kirsch, I., & Lynn, S. (1995). The altered state of hypnosis. *American Psychologist, 50*, 846-858.

Kirsch, I. (1990a). *Changing expectations: A key to effective psychotherapy*. Pacific Grove, CA: Brooks and Cole.

Kirsch, I. (1990b). *How expectancies shape experience*. Washington, DC: American Psycho- logical Association.

Kirsch, I. (2000). The response set theory of hypnosis. *American Journal of Clinical Hypnosis, 42*(3-4), 274-293.

Kirsch, I. (2001). The response set theory of hypnosis: Expectancy and physiology. *American Journal of Clinical Hypnosis, 44*(1), 69-73.

Kirsch, I. (2006). Medication and suggestion in the treatment of depression. In M. Yapko (Ed.), *Hypnosis and treating depression: Applications in clinical practice* (pp. 271-280). New York: Routledge.

Kroger, W., & Esdaile, J. (1957). *Hypnosis in medicine and surgery*. Chicago: Institute for Research in Hypnosis.

Kroger, W., & Fezler, W. (1976). *Hypnosis and behavior modification: Imagery Conditioning*. Philadelphia: J.B. Lippincott.

Kroger, W,. & Freed, S. (1951). *Psychosomatic gynecology: Including problems of obstetrical care*. Philadelphia: Saunders

Kroger, W. (1963, 2008). *Clinical and experimental hypnosis in medicine, dentistry and psychology* (Revised 2nd ed.). Philadelphia, PA: Lippincott, Williams & Wilkins.

Lang, E. (2011). *Patient sedation without medication: Rapid rapport and quick hypnotic techniques: A resource guide for doctors, nurses, and technologists*. CreateSpace.

Lang, E. (2017a). Pain control: Acute and procedural. In G. Elkins (Ed.), *Handbook of medical and psychological hypnosis: Foundations, applications, and professional issues* (pp. 333-340). New York: Springer.

Lang, E. (2017b). No pain no gain: A neuroethical place for hypnosis in invasive intervention. In J. Illes (Ed.), *Neuroethics: Anticipating the future* (eBook Chapter 11). Oxford: Oxford University Press.

Lang, E., Benotsch, E., Fick, L., Lutgendorf, S., Berbaum, M., Berbaum, K., Logan, H., & Spiegel, D. (2000). Adjunctive nonpharmacological analgesia for invasive medical procedures: A randomized trial. *The Lancet, 355*(9214), 1486-1490.

Lang, E., Joyce, J., Spiegel, D., Hamilton, D., & Lee, K. (1996). Self-hypnotic relaxation during interventional radiological procedures: Effects on pain perception and intra- venous drug use. *International Journal of Clinical and Experimental Hypnosis*, *44*, 106-119.

Lankton, S. R., & Lankton, C. H. (1983). *The answer within: A clinical framework of Erickson hypnotherapy*. New York, Brunner/Mazel.

Loftus, E., & Hoffman, H. (1989). Misinformation and memory: The creation of new memories. *Journal of Experimental Psychology: General*, *118*, 100-104.

Loftus, E. (2017). Eavesdropping on memory. *Annual Review of Psychology*, *68*, 1-18.

Lynn, S. J,. & Kirsch, I. (2006). *Essentials of clinical hypnosis: An evidence-based approach*. Washington, DC: American Psychological Association.

Melges, F.T. (1972). Future oriented psychotherapy. *American Journal of Psychotherapy*, *26*, 22-33.

Melges, F.T. (1982). *Time and the inner future*. New York, John Wiley & Sons.

Montenegro, G., Alves, L., Zaninotto, A. L., Pinheiro Falcãco, D., & Batista de Amorim, R. (2017). Hypnosis as a valuable tool for surgical procedures in the oral and maxillofacial area. *American Journal of Clinical Hypnosis*, *59*(4), 414-421.

Nance, E.P., Orne, M.T. & Hammer, A.G. (1974). Posthypnotic amnesias as an active psychic process. Archives of General Psychiatry, *31,* 257-260.

Orne, M. (1959). The nature of hypnosis: Artifact and essence. *Journal of Abnormal and Social Psychology*, *58*, 277-99.

Patterson, D. (2010). *Clinical hypnosis for pain control*. Washington, DC: American Psychological Association.

Rosen, G. (1959). History of medical hypnosis. In J. Schneck (Ed.), *Hypnosis in modern medicine* (2nd ed., pp. 3-27). Springfield, IL: Charles C. Thomas Publisher, Ltd.

Rosenfeld, S. (2008). *A critical history of hypnotism: The unauthorized story*. Available from the author at https://www.historyofhypnotism.com/.

Ruiz, O. R. G. and Fernandez, A. (1960). Hypnosis as an anesthetic in ophthalmology. *American Journal of Ophthalmology*, *50*(163); 132-142.

Sheehan, P. (1988). Memory distortion in hypnosis. *International Journal of Clinical and Experimental Hypnosis, 36,* 296-311.

Sheehan, P. (1995). The effects of asking leading questions in hypnosis. In G. Burrows & R. Stanley (Eds.), *Contemporary International Hypnosis* (pp. 55-62). Chichester, UK: Wiley.

Shenefelt, P. (2017). Skin disorders. In G. Elkins (Ed.), *Handbook of medical and psychological hypnosis: Foundations, applications, and professional issues* (pp. 409-418). New York: Springer.

Spiegel, D. (2010). Hypnosis in the treatment of posttraumatic stress disorders. In S. Lynn, J. Rhue, & I. Kirsch (Eds.), *Handbook of clinical hypnosis* (2nd ed., pp. 415-432). Washington, DC: American Psychological Association.

Spiegel, H., & Spiegel, D. (1978, 2004). *Trance and treatment: Clinical uses of hypnosis.* Washington, DC: American Psychiatric Association.

Spiegel, H. (1972, 2010). An eye-roll test for hypnotizability. *American Journal of Clinical Hypnosis, 53*(1), 15-18.

Spiegel, H. (1977). The Hypnotic Induction Profile: A review of its development. In *Conceptual and investigative approaches to hypnosis and hypnotic phenomena.* Annals of the New York Academy of Sciences, 296, pp. 129-142.

Spiegel, H. (2007). Comment: Remembrance of hypnosis past. *American Journal of Clinical Hypnosis, 49*(3), 179-180.

Squire, L. & Kandel, E. (2008). *Memory: From mind to molecules.* Greenwood Village, CO: Roberts and Company Publishers.

Thompson, K. (2004). Hypnosis in dentistry. In S. Kane & K. Olness (Eds.), *The art of therapeutic communication: The collected works of Kay F. Thompson* (pp. 345-364), Crown House Publishing Ltd.

Torem, M. (1987). Hypnosis in the treatment of depression. In W. Wester (Ed.), *Clinical hypnosis: A case management approach* (pp. 288-201). Cincinnati, OH: Behavioral Science Center, Inc. Publications.

Torem, M. (1989). Recognition and management of dissociative regressions. *Hypnos: Swedish Journal of Hypnosis in Psychotherapy & Psychosomatic Medicine, 16,* 197-213.

Torem, M. (1992a). "Back from the future": A powerful age-progression technique. *American Journal of Clinical Hypnosis, 35*, 81-88.

Torem, M. (1992b). The use of hypnosis with eating disorders. *Psychiatric Medicine, 10*, 105-118.

Torem, M. (2001). Eating disorders: Anorexia and bulimia. In G. Burrows, R. Stanley, & P. Bloom (Eds.), *International Handbook of Clinical Hypnosis* (pp. 205-219). New York: John Wiley & Sons.

Torem, M. (2006). Treating depression: A remedy from the future. In M. Yapko (Ed.), *Hypnosis and treating depression: Applications in clinical practice* (pp. 97-119). New York: Routledge.

Torem, M. (2007). Mind-body hypnotic imagery in the treatment of auto-immune disorders. *American Journal of Clinical Hypnosis, 50*, 157-170.

Torem, M. (2017a). Future-focused therapeutic strategies for integrative health. *International Journal of Clinical and Experimental Hypnosis, 65*(3), 353-378.

Torem, M. (2017b). Depression. In G. Elkins (Ed.), *Handbook of medical and psychological hypnosis: Foundations, applications, and professional issues* (pp. 505-522). New York: Springer.

Torem, M. (2017c). Eating disorders. In G. Elkins (Ed.), *Handbook of medical and psychological hypnosis: Foundations, applications, and professional issues* (pp. 523-534). New York: Springer.

Torem, M. (2017d). Autoimmune disorders. In G. Elkins (Ed.), *Handbook of medical and psychological hypnosis: Foundations, Applications, and professional issues* (pp. 169-178). New York: Springer.

Torem, M. (2019). Age progression as a therapeutic modality. In M. P. Jensen (Ed.) *Handbook of hypnotic techniques, favorite methods of master clinicians.* (pp. 11-28). Kirkland, Washington, Denny Creek Press.

Virot, C., & Bernard, F. (2018). *Hypnosis, acute pain and anesthesia.* Arnette, Paris.

Voit, R., & Delaney, M. (2004). *Hypnosis in clinical practice: Steps for mastering hypnotherapy.* New York: Brunner and Routledge.

Watkins, J. G. (1971). The affect bridge: A hypnoanalytic technique. *International Journal of Clinical and Experimental Hypnosis, 19*(1), 21-27.

Watzlawick, P. (1978). *The language of change: Elements of therapeutic communication.* New York: Basic Books.

Watzlawick, P. (1984). Self-fulfilling prophecies. In P. Watzlawick (Ed.), *The invented reality* (pp. 95-116). New York: W. W. Norton & Company.

Watzlawick, P. (1985). Hypnotherapy without trance. In J. Zeig (Ed.), *Ericksonian Psychotherapy, Vol. 1: Structures* (pp. 5-14). New York: Brunner and Mazel.

Watzlawick, P. (1993). If you desire to see learn how to act. In G. Nardone and P. Watzlawick (Eds.), *The Art of Change.* San Francisco: Jossey-Bass.

Watzlawick, P., Weakland, J., & Fisch, R. (1974). *Change: Principles of problem formation & problem resolution.* New York, W. W. Norton & Company.

Weitzenhoffer, A. M. (2000). *The practice of hypnotism* (2nd ed.). New York: John Wiley & Sons.

Werner, A. (2017). Labor and delivery. In G. Elkins (Ed.), *Handbook of medical and psychological hypnosis: Foundations, applications, and professional issues* (pp. 295-306). New York: Springer.

Yapko, M. (2001a). *Treating depression with hypnosis: Integrating cognitive behavioral and strategic approaches.* Philadelphia, PA: Brunner-Routledge.

Yapko, M. (2001b). Hypnosis in treating symptoms and risk factors of major depression. *American Journal of Clinical Hypnosis, 44,* 97-108.

Yapko, M. (2006). *Hypnosis and treating depression: Application in clinical practice.* New York, NY: Routledge.

Yapko, M. (2019). *Trancework: An introduction to the practice of clinical hypnosis* (5th ed.). New York: Routledge.

Yapko, M. (2021). *Process-oriented hypnosis: Focusing on the forest, not the trees.* New York, W. W. Norton & Company.

Zarren, J., & Eimer, B. (2001). *Brief cognitive hypnosis: Facilitating the change of dysfunctional behavior.* New York: Springer.

Zeig, J. (1985). The clinical use of amnesia: Ericksonian methods. In J. Zeig (Ed.), *Ericksonian Psychotherapy, Vol. 1: Structures* (pp. 317-337). New York: Brunner/Mazel.

CHAPTER 8
FUNDAMENTALS OF HYPNOTIC COMMUNICATION AND FORMULATION OF HYPNOTIC SUGGESTIONS AND METAPHORS

ERIC K. WILLMARTH
AND MICHAEL VINSON

Chapter Learning Objectives

1. Explain the purpose and importance of effective hypnotic communication.

2. Describe laws and principles underlying the formulation of effective suggestions and metaphors.

3. Examine the different considerations involved in individualizing effective hypnotic suggestions and metaphors.

In this chapter, we will review the purpose and basic components of hypnotic communication. Hypnotic communication is a style of communication that harnesses the psychology of the subconscious mind in order to create positive expectancy and guide patients to successful therapeutic outcomes. It is most often used within a hypnotic induction but can be used effectively in daily conversation as well, as it is fundamentally a style of communication that is respectful and empowering. Being aware of your words, using them intentionally, and avoiding unintended messages is the ambition of this chapter. In the following pages, we will teach you the principles of effective hypnotic communication so that by the end of this chapter you will be, if not fluent in hypnotic language, at least able to ask for directions.

The Story of Sue

It seems fitting to begin a chapter related to communication and metaphors with a story from the first author. A few years ago (or once upon a time) I (the first author) had the opportunity to teach a beginning hypnosis workshop to a group of nurses who worked in a pain management setting. The workshop was largely organized by Sue, who had attended one hypnosis study group in the past and felt that all nurses could benefit from learning more about communication and suggestion for their daily work. Sue let it be known that when it came to demonstrations, she wanted to be the first volunteer since she had enjoyed her earlier experience. On the first day of the workshop, the entire morning was spent in talking about the importance of words, language and communication at multiple levels. The workshop was held on a college campus very close to a mall, and the group decided to walk the short distance to the mall Food Court for lunch. In spite of a light rain, we began to head for lunch in several groups. Once I got outside I heard my name being called and looked over to see someone lying on the side of a hill with others around them, calling me. My first suspicion was that a prank or hoax was about to occur, however when I got to the group I found that it was Sue on the ground with a broken ankle, her foot twisted in the wrong direction.

As someone called an ambulance, I performed my first demonstration of the day with the full class standing in the rain and Sue, who was in fact my first volunteer, lying in the mud in extreme pain. Fortunately, Sue had significant hypnotic ability, only enhanced by the situation, and very quickly was able to dissociate and alter the perception of her pain as she imagined her foot in a "cool blue box". What I remember most about that day was the long wait for the ambulance and the first words of the driver when she got to Sue: "This is going to hurt a lot". Since Sue was already in trance, I assured her that the pain would continue to fade and that she could continue to float and relax. Much to the frustration of the nurses all around, it took the first responder quite some time to get an IV started and then to offer her second statement: "I'm going to assume that your pain is a 10 out of 10. I want you to let me know when the morphine starts working". Sue's response: "I'm at about a 3. Could you talk a little quieter?"

Sue later reported that when the first responders moved her foot back into position, she could feel it but that it felt like a "lump of wood" being moved and didn't hurt. There was no pulse in Sue's foot when she got to the hospital and she went directly into surgery. She reported that she needed almost no pain medication after the surgery because she was able to "go back into that place" with supportive phone calls. Her biggest frustration was that no one at the hospital wanted to hear about hypnosis. "They didn't believe me about the hypnosis. The only thing the doctor or nurses wanted to know was if I wanted more morphine." Only the chaplain was willing to listen to her excitement over her hypnotic experience.

Meanwhile, the hypnosis course continued for the next few days and the "demonstration" with Sue was frequently discussed. Possibly because we had spent the whole morning talking about the power of words, the words spoken by the first responder sounded almost obscene and certainly gave the nurses reason to consider their own language as they interact with patients who are often in a frightened and vulnerable position in the clinic. This case illustrates many of the concepts of hypnotic communication provided in this chapter.

THE FUNDAMENTALS OF HYPNOTIC COMMUNICATION

While there are many aspects to a definition of hypnosis as discussed in Chapter 3, one generally accepted core of the hypnotic experience is its "enhanced capacity for response to suggestion" (Elkins, Barabasz, Council, & Spiegel, 2015). Hypnotic communication utilizes this enhanced receptivity to suggestion to facilitate and guide a patient's therapeutic progress.

Effective hypnotic suggestions operate according to well-known laws and principles set down by master practitioners in the 20th century. These laws and principles operate as guidelines for creating the language and delivery of hypnotic suggestions. The construction of effective hypnotic suggestions must first, however, be built atop a sturdy foundation of a positive therapeutic working alliance and in accordance with the patient's goals. Montgomery, while being interviewed on the definition of hypnosis (Willmarth, 2015), offered that all suggestions were made "...for the patient's benefit". David Reid (2012) wrote, "Hypnotic suggestions, like recommended dining options, should be inviting, desirous, and make sense to the recipient if they are to be accepted and considered" (p. 27). Suggestions can be direct or indirect, questions or statements, passive or authoritarian, and may be embedded in stories and metaphors. There is an appropriate therapeutic application of each of these approaches depending on the patient and situation, but in every case, keeping the benefit of the patient in the forefront of your mind will help avoid unintentional (or intentional) harm.

Yapko (2019) points out that each of us are exposed to hundreds if not thousands of suggestions each day via media, social media, and our own environment. The advantage that therapists may have amid this cacophony of suggestion is that our patients are often seeking us out specifically to receive suggestions that may help them think, feel or behave better than they currently do.

THE LAWS AND PRINCIPLES OF HYPNOTIC SUGGESTION

Coué (1922) observed that people often talk to themselves and that the message was often negative and repeated until it was accepted by the unconscious mind as true, but that these negative "autosuggestions" could be overwritten by constructively worded reversals. Coué offered four "laws" of suggestion: the law of concentrated attention, the law of reversed effort, the law of auxiliary emotion and the law of dominant affect. Godot (2017) gives an excellent summary of these laws, but a brief one will be offered here as well.

The Law of Concentrated Attention

The law of concentrated attention suggests that the more you focus on an idea, the more salient that idea becomes. Think, for example, of the discomfort caused by a shirt's neck tag that disappears from attentional awareness soon after wearing but reappears when you focus upon it once more. This certainly comes into play when discussing self-fulfilling prophecies of both the positive and not-so-positive variety. Coué's (1922) admonitions to repeat "every day, and in every way, I am becoming better and better" is a direct application of this law. So too is the advice taught to most students of hypnosis that key suggestions should be repeated several times for best effect.

The Law of Reversed Effort

The law of reversed effort states that the harder you consciously try to do something, the harder it is to do; this is especially true of physiological effects. Consider the example of attempting to consciously will yourself to sleep: the more that you attempt to force it to happen, the more counterproductive the effort (Hammond, 1990). Experiences that normally operate under the control of unconscious processes cannot be forced and instead must be allowed to unfold (Godot, 2017). There are many acts of physical coordination that operate according to this law: consider how difficult it would be to consciously exert control over every discrete muscle movement involved in walking, and now consider its otherwise apparent effortlessness. Or take learning a musical instrument as an example. Almost anyone who was once a beginning music student has experienced the frustration of trying to master a scale or a piece of music only to find that sometimes by quitting and coming back after a break, they can do what they couldn't do before. Biofeedback is an excellent way to demonstrate this law when individuals are asked to "try hard to relax" and find that the opposite effect is shown on the display screen. Changing the suggestion to "let yourself relax" can have a dramatic impact and encourages the development of passive skills.

The Law of Auxiliary Emotion

The law of auxiliary emotion proposes that the intensity of the accompanying emotions drives the power of a suggestion. The stronger the emotion conjured by the suggestion, the more motivational fuel that that suggestion is imbued with. This is important particularly for those who work with PTSD and other trauma-related disorders, as the emotions attached to traumatic events and phobias are incredibly intense. Anger, rage, and fear of death are powerful emotions that impact both conscious and unconscious functioning. Thus, it is vital for treatment to adjust to these power ratios and consequences. Techniques such as hypnotically assisted systematic desensitization can often help in these situations. When working with a patient who is afraid of heights but hopes to jump from a swimming pool's high dive, for example, you can enhance the power of the suggestion by connecting it to the strongest positive emotions they can expect to feel upon splashing into the water.

The Law of Dominant Affect

The law of dominant affect suggests that stronger emotions always win over weaker emotions. This extends to the idea that the unconscious mind is always more powerful than the conscious mind

(Hammond, 1990; Godot, 2017). Examples of this law in action include the smoker who can give you 10 good logical reasons why they want to quit smoking right before lighting up a cigarette, or the gambler who "follows her gut but not her mind". In some cases, this can also explain why "love is the answer" if, in fact, love is the stronger emotion in the equation. Hypnotic suggestions should therefore be designed with emotional resonance in mind and tailored to the patient's individual preferences. For example:

> "And as soon as you walk through that door, you find yourself in that *place of perfect relaxation*, that *oh-so-beautiful beach* with *sparkling, shimmering* blue water. You feel *wonderfully calm*, and as you begin walking along the water's edge you feel a wave of *peaceful emotions* wash over you."

The Law of Parsimony

Hammond (1990) adds a very important fifth law, the law of parsimony, which suggests that a practitioner should use the simplest and most efficient suggestions that accomplish the therapeutic goal. Less is more, indeed. In the computer coding world, this is called "lean programming". We could not agree more with Hammond's statement that "Esoteric, multiply embedded metaphors and confusing techniques are unnecessary with most patients, are often perceived as condescending, and typically meet the therapist's needs far more than the patients" (Hammond, 1990).

The Principle of Pacing and Leading

Proper hypnotic pacing involves monitoring the patient's breathing, muscle tone, and body movements to determine the optimal rate at which to proceed. A patient whose rate of breathing has not yet slowed from the beginning of the induction may need further deepening, while a face drained of muscular tension, what practitioners call the "hypnotic mask", can serve as a cue that the patient has entered a deep state of hypnosis. Hypnotic leading, meanwhile, is when a suggestion announces a possible experience before it happens, building anticipation in the conscious mind while allowing the subconscious mind adequate time to create the experience. Proper pacing and leading involves observing your patient for clues as to when they are ready to slip deeper into a hypnotic state. For example:

> *"You are sitting in a chair (pacing) ... your feet are on the ground (pacing) ... your hands are on your thighs (pacing) ... and as you listen to the sound of my voice (pacing) ... you realize that your eyes are beginning to get tired, and so you begin to close them (leading) ... relaxing deeper and deeper into the hypnotic state ... "*

The Principle of Positive Language

What do you think of when we tell you, "Don't think of a pink ele-phant"? A pink elephant, most likely. This demonstrates a fundament-al rule of the subconscious mind: it ignores negations. It is therefore an important but informal rule when constructing effective hypnotic language to primarily employ positive language. Rather than directing the client to not think of a negative idea or to not engage in undesirable behavior and thereby drawing their attention to that very thing, it is instead best to direct them toward the antipodal positive idea or behavior. All hypnotic language should be goal-directed. So, if you don't want your patient to think of a pink elephant, "I invite you to picture a pink flamingo."

The Carrot Principle

The carrot principle encourages practitioners to avoid "pushing" patients but instead find ways to motivate positive progress that are client-directed. By concentrating your patient's attention on the appropriate carrot, you encourage more motivation than by "using the stick". People, at least in this one respect, are like strings: changing the direction that they are heading in is best achieved by pulling rather than pushing.

The Principle of Successive Approximations

In addition to principles related to establishing rapport and creating positive expectancy, Hammond (1990) offers the principle of successive approximations, which suggests taking small steps in developing hypnotic phenomena and avoiding the "magical thinking" that patients will achieve instant results with our first suggestions. Suggestions are like acorns. By watering them and nurturing them little by little, your therapeutic suggestions can eventually grow into big, sturdy oak trees.

Principle of Trance Ratification

The principle of trance ratification is an interesting concept that has become less utilized than it once was. Trance ratification encourages the development of positive expectancy by allowing the patient to experience hypnotic phenomena that are essentially "proof" that something powerful is happening. Time distortion, glove anesthesia, and catalepsy are examples of these and are heavily advocated by those promoting the Dave Elman approach to hypnosis (Elman & Elman, 2021). Care must be taken with this approach, however; in some cases, a trance ratification designed to reassure the patient that they are doing well can backfire and cause fear that they are "being controlled". At some level trance ratification is still useful and important but great care should be taken to make sure that it is also therapeutically useful.

CATEGORIES OF HYPNOTIC SUGGESTION

There are four main categories of hypnotic suggestion: direct suggestions, indirect suggestions, permissive suggestions, and metaphors. What follows is a brief description of each category along with representative examples.

Direct Suggestions

Direct suggestions are unambiguously worded suggestions for a given experience or thought to arise. Because they are more exposed to conscious evaluation, direct suggestions work best when resistance is low and the suggestions are amenable to the client (Godot, 2017; Elkins & Olendzki, 2018). Some examples of direct suggestions include:

> *"Your left arm is so light that it feels almost weightless …
> and begins to drift upwards."*
>
> *"Now focus on that spot so intently … that everything else
> fades into the background."*
>
> *"You feel calm and deeply relaxed."*
>
> *"Imagine that you are walking down a staircase … "*

Indirect Suggestions

Indirect suggestions invite the patient to consider an idea without making a claim that a certain type of response is expected or preferred. Categories of indirect suggestion include implications, questions, truisms, and "not knowing".

Implications

Implications, or implied suggestions, do not request specific responses from the patient but instead make it clear that they may arise. Implied suggestions can be useful for advancing the dissociative aspects of a state of hypnosis, from an experience of actively imagining hypnotic suggestions toward an experience of passively noticing suggestions happening (Elkins & Olendzki, 2018). Some examples of implied suggestions include:

> *"When you see the door in front of you, please nod your head."*

> *"Did you open the door handle with your right hand or your left hand?"*

> *"Notice the warmth of the sun against your skin ... "*

Questions

Questions are normal and necessary early in the relationship with a new patient and are often some of the earliest suggestions offered in treatment. This may be the case even before any hypnotic elicitation is attempted and it should be noted that suggestions take place before, during and after the hypnotic intervention. Consider the following questions:

> *"What did your father do to you then?"*

> *"What is your best way of calming yourself?"*

> *"How bad is your pain?"*

> *"What is your current level of comfort?"*

> *"Who can you ask to help you make this change?"*

Each of these questions implies a suggestion that is not all that subtle—some helpful, some not so much.

"Your father did something to you."

"You can calm yourself."

"You have pain and it's bad."

"You have comfort and it comes in varying degrees."

"You can ask for help."

This last question might remind the reader of Motivational Interviewing, a very humanistic, client-centered but directive form of counseling that makes good use of "leading questions". These leading questions can be therapeutically powerful if used for an intentional positive outcome.

When working with a patient who says that they want to quit smoking, the first author often asks the question, "When was your last cigarette? The answer is usually within an hour of them coming to their appointment. By continuing to focus on the *"last* cigarette" theme, the patient eventually realizes that the question was not in fact asking when they had their most recent cigarette. The question was a suggestion: You have had your last cigarette. Note—when asking a patient to take 5 deep breaths, do not refer to the 5th breath as "your last breath"!

Truisms

Truisms are often used to prepare patients to be more receptive to future therapeutic suggestions by getting them into a "yes set", a series of three or more questions designed for unconscious agreement, much the way a good salesman will prepare a customer prior to asking for the sale (Cialdini, 1987). Statements such as "Most people have a favorite food", "It's a nice day, isn't it?" or "Some folks like dogs, some like cats, and some people don't like animals", will generally get agreement even though there is always the possibility that someone will disagree with one or all of the statements. Phrases that start with "Some people ... ", "Most people ... " or "Almost everyone ... " lend themselves to easy truisms, especially if you can match the rest of the sentence to something that has meaning to the client. Some clinicians like to construct truisms out of statements of incontrovertible fact: "You are listening to the sound of my voice", "Your feet are on the ground", and "Your hands are on your lap."

From the standpoint of hypnotic communication and the development of suggestions, many truisms can be developed from carefully listening to the patient. Much of Rogerian therapy was based on this careful listening and rephrasing of a client's statements as a truism which resulted in a collaborative relationship and the feeling of being understood. The skill comes from being able to capture and re-phrase the patient's statements as a truism that they will accept rather than to just repeat their words as an annoying mimic. Ideally, you can repeat the *meaning* of a patient's statement without just repeating their words. "You're frustrated when you can't yet do what you used to be able to do", may summarize a patient's long explanation of physical limits following an auto accident. You may notice the suggestion embedded in that statement. The word "yet" suggests that this is a temporary situation that will change. We do not suggest a formula or schedule for truisms but they may be used throughout the therapeutic relationship to develop and reinforce a positive sense of expectancy and confidence.

Not Knowing

Suggestions can sometimes point out that something about the patient's experience is still unknown. By drawing the patient's attention to a possible idea or experience, these suggestions awaken curiosity and ask if something new might be revealed and learned in the future. For example:

> *"I wonder what it would feel like if your left arm were to become light and weightless ... "*

"You may not know ... how hypnosis is going to benefit you today"

"I don't know what it feels like ... to become so relaxed that you lose all sense of time"

Permissive Suggestions

Permissive suggestions give the patient the chance to make a choice, whether consciously or unconsciously, and may be preferred by some clients who desire greater control. Permissive suggestions can help reduce resistance, according to Elkins & Olendzki (2018), perhaps by "ratifying" a person's experience as trance-like. For example:

> *"As that wave of relaxation flows down past your ankles now ... you will perhaps experience a tingling sensation ... or perhaps a wave of warmth ... or perhaps a different sensation entirely."*

> *"You may notice a change in sensations in your arms and hands as you go deeper into hypnosis ... you may notice a feeling of lightness in your left hand and arm ... or you may experience a feeling of heaviness in your right hand and arm ... or you may find that you experience some combination of the two."*

Too many choices can often confuse the client, so mixing permissive suggestions in among other direct and indirect suggestions may be optimal. The types of suggestions that you decide to use with your patients will depend on the strength of your therapeutic alliance and the patient's goals. In mindful hypnotherapy, more directive suggestions are used early in the hypnotic induction and guide clients to focus their attention and enter the hypnotic state, followed by the use of permissive, indirect suggestions and metaphors later in the hypnotic induction (Elkins & Olendzki, 2018).

Metaphors

The subconscious mind is a symbolic engine powered by the language of metaphor and analogy. As such, it is often appropriate to embed metaphors, or imaginative stories that suggest that one thing is in fact another thing, into your hypnotic sessions with patients. Because the subconscious mind already communicates in images and symbolic language, these metaphors and stories allow for direct imaginative experience and symbolic illustration of positive therapeutic ideas.

The stories that we pass from generation to generation are probably the oldest form of communication and suggestion. These stories shape our understanding and opinions on many topics and help to shape our attitudes and beliefs. The interpretation of a story varies from one individual or culture to another, and the same story may lead people on different paths. The first author likes to share the Legend of the Healing Garden in his hypnosis workshops and classes:

> *"Legend says that for thousands of years, in every land and in every generation, there is someone who becomes known as a great healer. The legend goes on to say that at one time in each of these healer's lives they take a pilgrimage to visit a secret healing garden where they can walk the paths, sit on the benches, and renew and grow their healing powers before returning to spend their lives in the service of others. According to the legend however, over the many years and thousands of visits by gifted healers, the garden itself has taken on healing powers, as if each healer had left a bit of their magic behind as an offering. What we know now, is that anyone who learns about the Garden can go there in their imagination and walk the same paths, sit on the same benches, and enjoy the garden with all their senses while absorbing some of its healing energy. And even if a hundred people learn of the garden and visit on the same day, each*

individual will be alone in the garden to enjoy and receive
the healing energy."

It's always interesting to hear the discussion afterwards as participants share their reactions. Did they see flowers? Although the story mentions a garden, all mention of flowers was stopped after a particularly talented participant started having an allergic reaction. Are the benches made of wood or stone? While stone benches might seem to make sense, since after all they've been there for thousands of years, many participants have non-stone benches in their version of the garden. Some participants say that they saw Jesus on the path because the term "great healer" was used, while others were incredulous at what they felt was a bizarre leap of logic. Interestingly, when this exercise was done during a hypnosis training in Cairo, Egypt, both Muhammad and Jesus made an appearance in the garden when using the Council of Advisors technique described by Hammond (1992) in his Manual for Self-Hypnosis. The most interesting reports, however, come as participants describe how they feel afterwards and the various meanings they attribute to the experience. Because participants are primarily health care providers, there seems to be an even split between those who felt like the point of the exercise was to improve their own health and well-being and those who believed that it was to enhance their ability to help others. Of course, all interpretations are correct!

Milton Erickson was a master at the use of stories and metaphors and many of these are legendary. One of the best overviews of the use of metaphor is Rubin Battino's *Metaphoria* (2005). This book is filled with samples of metaphors by Erickson and many others while discussing the "how to" of building, delivering, and using effective metaphors in a psychotherapeutic setting. Hammond's (1990) Handbook of Hypnotic Suggestions and Metaphors remains a practical reference as well, containing hundreds of well-crafted stories, metaphors and suggestions offered by gifted practitioners.

Metaphors can be subtle or obvious, poetic or simple, but the most effective metaphors come from listening carefully to the language and backstory of your patient. Do they like to fish? Do they enjoy camping? Do they have pets or like animals? Gardens? How do they feel about lakes and oceans? Are they cooks, mechanics or teachers? The answers to any of these questions can help in the design of a metaphor that might resonate with your patient. A patient with a love of the ocean seeking help falling asleep at night may benefit from a metaphor of fish swimming deeper, and deeper, and deeper into the ocean's depths. A patient who loves spending vacations at his lake house may respond especially well to the suggestion of "an early morning fog lifting over crystal clear water revealing ... ", which would be more appealing than a metaphor related to, say, plumbing or soccer, where he would be as lost as a fish swimming in muddy water.

THE SPECIFICITY OF SUGGESTION

Weitzenhoffer (2000) noted that suggestions are not only dependent on what is said and how it is said but also the context in which the suggestion is made. Asking someone within a trance to use their imagination to "Sit down!" can be a loud demand or a gentle offer. However, whether they are imagining a comfortable sofa or the electric chair will make a difference! We should also recognize that people respond to suggestion with or without hypnosis. In a video interview, David Spiegel described hypnosis from the perspective of a telephoto lens. What we see, we see very clearly but the surrounding area, the context, goes away. This allows individuals to respond to a hypnotic suggestion without the critical thinking and evaluation that might take place in a non-hypnotic situation (Willmarth, 2015).

In reviewing the literature on the neurophysiology of hypnosis, Mark Jensen (2011) suggests that " ... different hypnotic suggestions affect activity in different brain areas in ways consistent with the content of those suggestions—hypnosis can be very precise in targeting activity in specific structures ... " (p. 55). He offers that specific suggestions can be crafted to target the somatosensory cortex, the insula, the anterior cingulate cortex, and the prefrontal cortex. This game-changing concept argues that the more we learn about the neurophysiology of hypnosis, the more specific we can make our suggestions. For example, a direct suggestion to imagine the pain fading away and becoming less intense may impact the somato-sensory cortex, while a suggestion to focus on comfort and safety may impact the insula. Jensen (2009, 2011) focuses specifically on the pain matrix in his descriptions but certainly this same principle could be applied to depression, anxiety, and other clinical symptoms that have neurological underpinnings. Both direct suggestions ("your hands are getting warmer") and indirect suggestions ("imagine your hands close to a beautiful campfire") can generate similar results, depending on your patient's abilities.

Direct or Indirect? Passive or Authoritarian?

A wide variety of styles and techniques are popular among the professionals who use hypnosis in their therapeutic efforts. The hypnotic style of choice has shifted enormously in the past 70 years. If you watch movies or demonstrations from the 1950s, suggestions were almost universally direct and delivered in an authoritarian manner, strong and forceful. Milton Erikson was rightly given credit for greatly expanding the possibilities of hypnotic interaction but while he could often present passive, indirect metaphors, he could also be extremely direct and authoritarian if that was what was needed by the patient. Erikson's true genius wasn't in developing inductions and metaphors but in his capacity to understand the patient in the room and to customize an approach that met that patient's needs.

The type of suggestions you choose has a great deal to do with both the patient and the context of the interaction. For instance, when working with a longer-term patient, the first author often weaves suggestions into stories, metaphors, and humor, whereas in a medical emergency or hospital setting, patients often need suggestions that are clear, strong, and direct. During a medical emergency, phrases like "Perhaps you may want to consider ... " should be discarded in favor of more direct, authoritarian approaches such as "Focus on my face, take in a nice breath, breathe out and relax your shoulders ... " First responders who have learned to use truisms such as "The worst is over" and "I'm here to help you now" and make direction suggestions like "I'm going to take care of you" are often remembered years later by patients who needed that reassurance at that time. Meanwhile, comments such as "That looks really bad" or "This is going to hurt a lot" have a better chance of adding to the trauma than of providing relief.

Cultural and generational considerations may also play a role in whether an authoritarian approach would be rejected or accepted. For example, an older patient may tend to hold the doctor in high regard, expect to be told what to do, and would follow those directions with little question. That approach works best when both patient and doctor were trained to accept that relationship. Younger patients (and doctors) have been encouraged to develop a more collaborative relationship or even a relationship where the doctor plays the role of a paid consultant while the patient remains in control and makes most of the decisions. These variations will play a role in how any one client may respond to the hypnotic relationship and help determine which approach may work best for that individual.

The cultural differences in the United States alone make the selection of the "best" approach even more complicated. There are myriad cultures and subcultures from coast to coast and within these various cultures health care professionals may be feared or revered, honored or scorned, trusted or suspected of malicious intent. These conditions are magnified when discussing the topic of hypnosis. Knowledge of cultural and generational beliefs will allow you to start the conversation to develop a working relationship and determine just what suggestions and what style of delivery may have the best chance of success.

Scripts or No Scripts?

There are many strong arguments, both pro and con, regarding the use of scripts in hypnosis. Those who argue against the use of scripts generally speak about the lack of creativity, spontaneity and possibility of utilization when using scripts along with the fact that if the therapist is focused on the script, they are not focused on the patient. We've certainly seen and heard students reading the phrase, "now close your eyes", long after the volunteer's eyes had already closed. Those supporting the use of scripts, meanwhile, point out that some of these scripts have been thoughtfully crafted over days or weeks, carefully considering and embedding suggestions to achieve the greatest effect, developed by individuals with incredibly creative minds and poetic tongues. Studying scripts written by others can also help us avoid the common trap of getting "stuck" on the same induction and suggestions and can spark a more creative approach to communication.

Our resolution to this dichotomy is to agree with both sides. We have no problem with those experienced in hypnosis using or developing scripts. However, the first author avoids using scripts with new students, even though this is the population most eager to have a script. By "thinking on their feet," beginning practitioners learn to observe the client and to stumble with words if necessary until they find their own voice, patter and comfort zone. Along the way the practitioner rediscovers that it is the patient's experience that matters and that even if we stumble over our words or make suggestions that are awkward, the patient will usually fix our mistakes and take what they need from the experience.

Once an individual has a basic comfort with hypnotic elicitation and suggestion, we see no reason not to study the beautifully constructed scripts that are written by those with a gift for language and artistic communication. However, we do not suggest ever "reading" a script during a session. We instead suggest studying many scripts, digesting those parts that appeal, and then making them your own, combined with whatever the moment offers while in session.

CONCLUSION

As mentioned previously, there is nothing automatically "right" or "wrong" with either a passive, indirect suggestion or a direct, authoritarian suggestion. Either could be the most effective approach with a given patient. Moreover, the modifications needed to individualize a script for a patient are just as necessary as the modifications you would make for a patient if you were not using a script. In other words, regardless of the various approaches offered to clinicians, the goal is for all suggestions to be specialized to the needs of each patient. Hypnotic communication is a delicate practice, but what matters most at the end of the day is that proper respect and attention is paid to the individual sitting before you.

CHAPTER 8
REFLECTION QUESTIONS

1. What are the four main categories of hypnotic suggestion?

2. What are three of the laws and principles of effective hypnotic communication?

3. What is the purpose of individualizing hypnotic suggestions for a patient or client?

4. Can you create a hypnotic suggestion that integrates all four categories of suggestion?

REFERENCES

Battino, R. (2005). *Metaphoria: Metaphor and guided metaphor for psychotherapy and healing.* Crown House publishing.

Cialdini, R. B. (1987). *Influence* (Vol. 3). Port Harcourt: A. Michel.

Coué, E. (1922). *Self-mastery through conscious autosuggestion*. George Allen & Unwin Ltd.

Elkins, G. R., & Nicholas Olendzki, P. (2018). *Mindful hypnotherapy: The basics for clinical practice*. Springer Publishing Company.

Elkins, G., Barabasz, A., Council, J., & Speigel, D. (2015.) Advancing research and practice: The Revised APA Division 30 Definition of Hypnosis. *International Journal of Clinical and Experimental Hypnosis*, *63*(1), 1-9. doi:10.1080/00207144.2014.961870

Elman L., & Elman, C. (2021). *Master Class* presented to Saybrook University,

Godot, D. (2017). Formulating hypnotic suggestions, In G. R. Elkins,. (Ed.) *Handbook of medical and psychological hypnosis: Foundations, applications, and professional issues*. Springer Publishing Company.

Hammond, D.C. (1990). *Handbook of hypnotic suggestions and metaphors*. W.W. Norton & Company.

Hammond, D.C. (1992). *Manual for self-hypnosis*. American Society of Clinical Hypnosis.

Jensen, M. P. (2009). Hypnosis for chronic pain management: A new hope. *Pain, 146*(3), 235-237. doi:10.1016/j.pain.2009.06.027

Jensen, M. P. (2011). *Hypnosis for chronic pain management: Therapist guide*. Oxford University Press.

Nash, Michael, et al., actor. *Willmarth Interviews: Defining hypnosis*. Narrated by Eric Willmarth 2015, https://www.youtube.com/watch?v=Rzg7AXE7kB U&t=12s.

Reid, D. B. (2012). *Hypnosis for behavioral health: A guide to expanding your professional practice*. Springer Publishing Company.

Weitzenhoffer, A. M. (2000). *The practice of hypnotism* (2nd ed). John Wiley & Sons Inc.

Willmarth, E., & Willmarth, A. (2011). *Defining hypnosis*. Presentation to the American Psychological Association Annual Convention, Aug. 4-7, 2011.

Yapko, M. D. (2019). *Trancework: An introduction to the practice of clinical hypnosis*. 5th ed. Routledge.

CHAPTER 9
DEEPENING AND INTENSIFICATION
OF THE HYPNOTIC EXPERIENCE

BARBARA McCANN

Chapter Learning Objectives

1. Describe different methods of deepening or intensification of the hypnotic experience.

2. Describe at least two differences between traditional and conversational approaches to deepening and intensification of the hypnotic experience.

3. Provide examples of "seeding" of ideas during deepening and intensification of the hypnotic experience.

Deepening or intensifying of the hypnotic experience (trance) is generally assumed to be necessary to promote optimal therapeutic benefit from clinical hypnosis. Deepening of hypnosis follows the initial induction of the trance and precedes use of the hypnotic experience to provide therapeutic suggestions (Heap & Aravind, 2002). Deepening itself is a suggestion, or series of suggestions, regarding the nature of hypnosis. The explicit suggestion given when deepening begins is that changes in subjective experience have been accomplished through the opening induction, and more marked changes in experience are about to happen as the patient attends to the words of the clinician. In clinical hypnosis the implied suggestion is "You are experiencing hypnosis, but this is only just beginning. You are about to experience even greater changes within you that will enhance your ability to derive something important and useful from this session." Note this implicit suggestion is the bridge between the start of hypnosis (induction) and the therapeutically useful statements, questions, metaphors, and the like that will be offered later.

THE LANGUAGE AND DEEPENING AND INTENSIFICATION

Consider this brief excerpt of a deepening strategy that uses a common counting method to encourage greater intensification of hypnosis:

> *"And with each count you can drift more and more deeply into your hypnosis ... you can go deeper and deeper ... and as you go even deeper, it will help you move closer and closer to realizing your goals ... to experience whatever you want to experience."* (Lynn & Kirsch, 2006, p. 63)

There are several important things to notice in this example. First, words are repeated—more and more, deeper and deeper, closer and closer. Repetition of words and suggestions during hypnosis serves to draw the listener's attention and concentration to key ideas (Hammond, 1990). In this example, the words selected for repetition are those that imply movement and change toward goals and desired experiences. As we shall see later in this chapter, directional movement is a key feature of many deepening techniques. Second, notice the use of the word "as" in the example. This is known as verbal compounding, in the form of "As you X, you can Y." (Yapko, 2019, p. 266), or in the example, "as you go deeper, you move closer". Finally, notice the use of ellipses (...) throughout this brief excerpt. These indicate pauses in speaking on the part of the clinician. These brief, silent moments are important to allow the patient time to think about suggestions and respond to them as they notice and reflect on how they are responding. A common mistake made by many new to the practice of hypnosis and related hypnotic-like therapy techniques such as progressive muscle relaxation, guided imagery, and mindfulness meditation is to rush through the process. Patients need time to process verbal suggestions and experience them.

Traditional Deepening Techniques

Methods of deepening the hypnotic experience are as varied as those of achieving induction, and indeed, techniques for induction may be used instead for deepening and vice versa (Lynn & Kirsch, 2006). There are easily as many techniques for intensifying the hypnotic experience as there are for initial hypnotic inductions. Some common techniques for deepening trance include the stairs (escalator, elevator, downward movement) technique, various counting or countdown methods (e.g., Elkins, 2014; Nash, 1996), the mind's eye closure metaphor (Yapko, 2019), various forms of breathing, progressive relaxation, and even silence (Barber, 1977; Hammond, 1998; Kroger, 2008; Yapko, 2015, 2019). Movement can also form the basis for deepening the hypnotic experience, as when manual compounding or ideomotor phenomena are used.

Counting—up or down—to imply movement into a deeper hypnotic experience is quite common. Consider the following example from Elkins' (2014) work on hypnotic relaxation therapy:

> " ... And it is possible to go into an even deeper hypnotic state ... the deeper the relaxation ... the better the response ... letting go ... and finding that as I count the numbers from 10 to 1 it is possible to become so deeply absorbed in this experience ... the hypnotic state becomes deeper and deeper ... 10 ... Allowing a wave of good relaxation to come to you ... It spreads across your forehead ... across your face ... letting go of all the tension ... drifting deeper ... 9 ... A relaxation that now spreads across your shoulders ... " (Elkins, 2014, p. 73)

Notice this technique combines counting with suggestions for progressive relaxation.

The technique of descending stairs or using downward movement as a deepening strategy often uses a metaphor of descending a staircase and engages the patient in feeling and visualizing, going deeper into hypnosis with each step downward:

> *You now feel pleasantly hypnotized, and comfortable ... and yet it is possible to experience even a greater degree of comfort. You can look around, and notice you are at the top of a grand, luxurious marble staircase ... As you stand at the top of this staircase, you notice the gleaming white marble of the stairs, and you feel a soft, deep carpet beneath you ... You look down and notice your feet are bare, with tufts of carpeting peeking out between your toes ... an incredibly soft and comfortable feeling ... As you reach out and touch the smooth, wooden banister next to you, you notice it is smooth to the touch ... the wood gleaming. You take on step down, first one foot, then the other, sinking deeply into the soft carpet ... and as you do so, you find yourself sinking deeper and deeper into hypnosis ... Your hand glides alongside you, and you feel the silky, polished wood of the banister ... You take another step down, onto the next stair, once again aware of the comforting softness beneath your feet, seeing the stairs descending ahead of you, and aware of a growing sense of peace and comfort inside you. And as you descend onto the third step, you notice something happening, and feeling of inner calm, a sense of deeper and deeper contentment ... And as you continue to step downward, gently slide your hand along the polished wood of the banister ... you go further and further inside yourself, finding a deep feeling of calm and confidence ... of peace ... with each step down, down, you become more and more aware of peace and quiet within you ... inner calmness ... a quiet strength with each deliberate step down ...*

Variations in this technique are limited only by your imagination, and the needs of your patient. The natural progression down a set of stairs lends itself to deepening, and a sense of destination that can signal progression into a metaphorical location for therapeutic suggestions to take place. There are numerous examples of this strategy in clinical practice (e.g., Chaves, 1996; Forester-Miller, 2017; Malekzadeh et al., 2020)

The mind's eye closure technique is particularly useful for helping patients who find themselves bothered by extraneous thoughts and images they may have during hypnosis (Yapko, 2019). In this technique, which pairs naturally with an eye fixation induction (but can be used with any type of induction), patients are told they have an inner eye in their mind that notices distracting thoughts and images even while they are experiencing hypnosis, but this inner eye or "mind's eye" can become tired and need to relax, the eyelid getting heavier until it gradually closes—mirroring the eye fixation induction. The suggestion of the eyelid finally closing is accompanied by the suggestion that any random thoughts and images are finally blocked out, allowing for complete absorption in the hypnotic experience.

Deepening through various forms of breathing strategies and through progressive muscle relaxation are also quite common. In the following example, I provide a partial transcript of a session with a man referred to me because he was worried about his ability to handle pain following dental procedures. This session follows several in which he was taught self-hypnosis to practice relaxation between sessions and amplified his ability to manage discomfort. Given his experience with hypnosis from prior sessions, I used a brief, simple eye-fixation induction and moved quickly into deepening using both breathing strategies and progressive relaxation:

> I invite you to look at a spot on the ceiling, pick a spot to
> look at, and just notice as your stare at the spot, the things
> around you recede into the background, and as you stare at
> the spot you can begin to experience some familiar feelings,

feelings such as the chair supporting you comfortably, your muscles, your limbs getting softer, melting into the chair that is supporting you , and as you continue to stare at the spot, your eyes begin to get a little bit heavy, get heavier ... and you close your eyes and take a deep breath and exhale slowly, and sink further and further into your chair, further into your chair ... that's right ... and it's a comfortable feeling, a good feeling, and you begin to notice as you sink comfortably into where you are reclining right now, you get more and more comfortable, more and more relaxed ... the muscles of your face relax ... the muscles in your forehead, your scalp relax, you get more and more comfortable ... and that heavy, comfortable feeling begins to sink in, making you more and more relaxed. And the noises and sounds around you become less of a distraction as you focus on my voice and go into a nice, quiet, pleasant state of hypnosis. The muscles in your neck relax, in your shoulders ... more and more relaxed ... limp, loose, soft, comfortable, and relaxed. Those feelings of comfort in your muscles, and the heaviness in your muscles continue on down into your arms, your upper arms, your forearm ... your hands, your fingertips even ... and the muscles of your torso and back become soft, comfortable, peaceful and relaxed ... sinking you down deeper and deeper into your chair, deeper still ... and the comfort extends to your abdomen ... even your insides become more relaxed, more comfortable, comfortable and relaxed ... and the muscles in your buttocks, your legs, upper legs, your thighs, your hamstrings ... soft and comfortable and relaxed, melting you right into the chair, so comfortable, so peaceful, and finally the muscles of your lower legs, your shins, your calves, even your feet, become more and more comfortable, more and more relaxed ... and it's a good feeling, this is the initial state of hypnosis where you feel so comfortable ... so relaxed ... so

> *pleasant. And as you feel this sense of pleasantness traveling*
> *throughout the muscles in your body, you can also begin to*
> *notice just how more comfortable you can become ... as you*
> *breathe in and out ... controlled breathing, noticing that you*
> *get more and more deeply comfortable and relaxed, and*
> *peaceful, with every breath you take, every time you exhale.*
> *And as you continue to focus on your breathing, as a means*
> *of deepening your hypnosis even further, isn't interesting*
> *that you can feel more and more comfortable ... right here,*
> *right now ... and with every breath you take, you can*
> *breathe comfort in, and you can breathe any discomfort you*
> *are feeling out. Any discomfort at all. And isn't it interesting*
> *how you can simply focus on relaxation and comfort? And*
> *not pay attention to anything other than feelings of comfort.*

This session continued with suggestions for post-procedural pain management through reduction in pain intensity of any unwanted discomfort following upcoming dental procedures.

Deepening with Seeding of Ideas

Seeding of ideas has been described in the work of Milton Erickson (Haley, 1973; Zeig, 1990) and involves hinting at or activating early on something that will be developed later during therapy or, in his case, hypnosis. Seeding is in many ways like foreshadowing in literature and is closely related to the concept of priming effects in social psychology (Molden, 2014). While the main goal of deepening is to suggest greater depth of hypnosis with the implication of greater hypnotic responding, simultaneously seeding therapeutic ideas that will come up more directly later during the session sets the stage for greater acceptance of those ideas.

The following is an example of a deepening technique I sometimes use with patients who are depressed. Such patients often exhibit an internal, global, and stable attribution style characteristic of the reformulated learned helplessness model (Abramson, Seligman & Teasdale, 1978) and the negative cognitive triad (i.e., negative views of oneself, the world, and the future; Beck, Rush, Shaw, & Emery, 1979). Notice this technique is based on the downward movement strategy previously described, but with some important distinctions. This uses a hiking metaphor, as hiking is an experience common to many who live in the Pacific Northwest of the U.S., where I have my clinical practice. Throughout this deepening strategy, I seed the idea that a superficial (global) look at something can be unimpressive but taking the time to explore and notice the specific components of an experience can be rewarding. This helps set the stage for later use of the session to promote Behavioral Activation as a means of treating depression. This example does not include the induction, which happens before this step. I begin by acknowledging the patient's initial responses to the induction before moving into deepening:

> I can already see (here I describe the physical changes I have
> noticed in the patient during the induction, such as
> softening of the facial muscles, slowed breathing, etc.), just
> how comfortable you can become ... and isn't it wonderful
> how different you can feel today, in this moment? You can
> become even more deeply absorbed, and you can experience
> so much more ... as I invite you to take a journey ... a
> pleasant hike ... deep into an old growth rain forest that you
> could find on the Olympic peninsula, if you went looking for
> it ... (or other suitable location, based on what I know of the
> patient's experiences). It takes time to get there, if we start
> from Seattle—over four hours of driving ... a journey of its
> own, really ... and it is easy to wonder if that long of a drive
> will be worth it. Because from a distance, when you get your
> first glimpses of the rain forest it looks like just a broad,
> never-ending monotonous swath of green trees, all the same
> size and shape ... And it can really make you wonder, why

venture further into it ... why bother to take the time and trouble to get there ... and yet, as you do arrive, and park your car in the paved parking lot and take your first step onto the trail, you notice the softness of the dirt pathway beneath your feet ... and see the trail ahead winding deeper into the forest, beckoning you ... You become aware of the way the light filters through the top-most branches of the enormous trees ... you become more and more absorbed by it ... and notice the differences in the trees themselves ... cedar, spruce, hemlock, and Douglas fir ... and how the sunlight warms the plants in the forest, releasing a pleasant and refreshing scent you notice as you take a deep breath ... The sounds from the trailhead recede as you move further along the trail, taking it all in ... hearing the pleasant stillness as you move deeper into the forest ... and as you move along the trail, you notice more and more of the subtle details ... the enormous ferns springing up from the forest floor ... the downed trees, blanketed in soft lichens and moss ... many different types everywhere you look, even hanging from branches, and yet, so many different shades and textures ... much richer than when seeing the forest from far away ... and deeper still into the forest, next to the trail, you notice the massive roots of an enormous tree, probably hundreds of years old, that has fallen by the trail—the trunk of the tree stretching off into the forest ... and you realize the bright green growth atop the trunk is a series of young trees growing all along this older, fallen one ... a row of bright green, new growth, nourished by the crumbling reddish brown bark beneath it ... you've discovered a nursery log. And so you begin to understand now, that what appeared to be just a solid green mass from a distance, is so varied and intriguing up close ... and as you continue deeper and deeper into the forest, along the trail, you notice other

*delights ... orange and yellow bracket fungus jutting out
from the trunks of trees like shelves ... and as you walk
further along the soft trail, becoming more and more
absorbed in your experience of hypnosis, you become aware
of a lightness ahead, as the forest opens up to reveal a rocky
riverbank ... and a slowly moving river ... then the trail turns
again and the sound of the river recedes ... the trail itself
gently undulating up and down as you become more and
more immersed in the forest ... and then opening up once
again as you are near a small three-sided wooden shelter,
itself covered in moss ... you pass plants with berries—
salmonberry, salal ... and ahead you see the browns of a
cluster of trees ... only to notice them moving slowly as you
draw closer ... a group of Roosevelt elk grazing in the forest
... and your wonder at what other surprises the forest holds
for you deepens, with growing awareness of just how much
there is to see and experience and explore on this journey ...
having a path to follow ... taking you to new sights, sounds ...
and opening up new possibilities ...*

Once this deepening element is complete and I have set the stage for the patient to be able to appreciate the importance of being more specific and less global in seeing the world around them, I may proceed with suggestions to stimulate behavioral activation (Martell et al., 2022) or to generate an understand of how our beliefs shape experience (Beck, 2021).

Indirect Deepening Strategies

Deepening as a distinct step in the hypnosis session is readily identifiable in a session that follows a more traditional approach to hypnosis. Deepening techniques presented thus far often contain very direct statements, as indicated at the beginning of this chapter, that an initial induction has been presented, and now a deepening of the experience will follow. It may be directly suggested that "You are now hypnotized, but you can be even more hypnotized as you continue to listen to my voice." However, a precisely organized session structure is not always used.

More indirect and conversational approaches to hypnosis, as pioneered by Milton Erickson, and often referred to as Ericksonian hypnosis, are less likely to include such readily distinguishable elements of induction and deepening (Short, 2017; Yapko, 2019). Deepening can be suggested indirectly: " ... And you can recognize ... at a very deep level ... that wherever you go ... " (Yapko, 2001, p. 114). In the preceding forest metaphor example, after an explicit suggestion of deeper absorption, I use the word "deeper" often to indirectly reinforce the idea that the patient will experience intensification of hypnosis. Additionally, in a more indirect and conversational approach, the hypnosis session may lack an obvious starting point for the induction, the induction may spill seamlessly into suggestions for hypnosis intensification, and the clinician may converse with the patient during hypnosis.

Suggestions for deepening may take place once a light trance is achieved through the initial induction, as discussed thus far, but may also be given at any point when the clinician observes signs that the trance is getting lighter (Brann, 2012). Consider the following example, in which Michael Yapko checks in with a woman during a hypnosis session, asking her to describe what she has been experiencing:

> ... I'm going to ask you ... to describe for me out loud ... what
> you are aware of at this moment ... And you'll find that you
> can describe to me quite easily ... quite effortlessly ... and
> that even as you describe the experience ... it can deepen
> your involvement ... And so now ... describe for me ... what
> you are aware of ... (Yapko, 2001, p. 116).

In this example, after the woman describes her experiences, Dr. Yapko makes gentle suggestions for re-entry into hypnosis, and deepening of the experience:

> *Okay, alright. Go back inside now (closes her eyes) ... that's right ... and start to reabsorb yourself ... immerse yourself again ... and notice how quickly ... and easily ... you can begin to recapture ... a very deep sense of awareness ...*
> (Yapko, 2001, p. 117).

Notice in this example, there is a suggestion for a very deliberate return to hypnosis ("go back inside now"), followed later by an implicit suggestion of deepening ("a very deep sense of awareness"). There are numerous uses and variations of this strategy. Dr. Stephen Gilligan, a student of Milton Erickson, describes having the patient go in and out of trance during the therapy session, " ... alternating between talking and experiencing trance" (Gilligan, 1987, p. 175), in a process he refers to as fractionation. He believes this method allows for gradual exploration of the hypnotic experience and allows a strong interpersonal connection to develop between patient and therapist (Gilligan, 1987).

Posthypnotic Suggestion and Fractionation

Posthypnotic suggestions can play a key role in facilitating deepening of the hypnotic experience, especially in patients who will be having repeated hypnosis sessions. Posthypnotic suggestions are suggestions given during hypnosis that something will take place—a feeling, thought, or action—once the hypnosis session has concluded. The feeling, thought or action is generally tied to a specific cue but does not have to be. For example, a posthypnotic suggestion during hypnotic relaxation therapy can be given to suggest that desired effects of calm and peacefulness achieved during hypnosis may carry over following re-alerting (Elkins, 2014). In clinical practice, post-hypnotic suggestions are frequently given to suggest that in subsequent therapy sessions, trance will be achieved more quickly (Lynn & Kirsch, 2006; Yapko, 2019). This allows for a quicker transition to therapeutic work during hypnosis and gives patients the opportunity to discover their own skills and abilities.

Fractionation is another strategy for attaining deeper and quicker intensification of hypnosis. While already in hypnosis, the patient is given a posthypnotic suggestion that the next time hypnosis is elicited, they will be able to go into hypnosis quickly and deeply. They are then re-alerted during that same therapy session, and re-hypnotized again. This process can be repeated several times within a given session, as a means of deepening the hypnotic experience Fractionation is thought to be a good technique for use with people with short attention spans (Yapko, 2015, 2019). Drs. Arreed Barabasz and John Watkins (2005) described systematic use of fractionation as follows, following initial induction:

> When I say an odd number, such as 1, let yourself relax more deeply. Go down into a more profound state. However, when I say an even number, such as 2, alert yourself slightly. Let yourself come up a little. But then as soon as I say the next odd number, 3, go down even deeper than before. Go down and down and continue to relax more profoundly until I say the next even number 4. [Continue this way.] Go down on 5. Then up a bit on 6. Down again further on 7. And up, 8. Down, 9. Up, 10. (p. 193)

Once this basic set of instructions has been provided, the authors recommend speaking even numbers lightly then going almost immediately into the next odd number, pronouncing these in a drawn-out fashion. This method continues until a desired level of deepening occurs.

CONCLUSION

Deepening or intensification of the hypnotic experience is often regarded as a prerequisite to satisfactory and therapeutically meaningful hypnotic responses to more elaborate and involved suggestions. However, research on hypnosis has failed to prove this to be the case. The clinical and experimental research on the importance of hypnotic depth, presumably achievable through adequate deepening and intensification by the methods described in this chapter, has been fraught with challenges in conceptualizing and measuring depth. It is unclear whether some methods of deepening or intensification of the hypnotic experience are better than others, based on scientific study of important clinical outcomes. Self-reports of "depth" of hypnosis likely reflect intrapersonal characteristics more than the method of deepening or intensification used. Related constructs such as trance, suggestibility, hypnotizability, and expectancy also present obstacles for definition, conceptualization, and measurement (e.g., Pekala, 2011; Pekala et al., 2010a, 2010b; Terhune & Cardeña, 2010; Wagstaff, 2010). The question "How deep is deep enough and does depth matter?" is difficult to answer.

Fractionation, which was only touched on briefly in this chapter, has also been the subject of study to determine whether clinical assertions that it promotes greater hypnotic responding hold up under scientific scrutiny. In one study of the impact of fractionation on responses to self-hypnosis, no differences in fractionation compared with another deepening strategy (silence) were noted (Hammond et al., 1987). A subsequent study examined whether physiological changes during hypnosis differed depending on whether relaxation or fractionation method was used, finding only differences in peripheral resistance favoring relaxation (Casiglia et al., 2012). Both studies were small, and considerations of sample size and the method of fractionation used may limit the generalizability of the findings. Whether fractionation has the intended clinical effect is subject to debate and requires further study.

Clinically, understanding the use of deepening and intensification of hypnosis following induction, and being comfortable with several different strategies for doing so, are likely to lead to more meaningful sessions for patients. Clinicians new to hypnosis will benefit from studying the methods described in this chapter, tailoring the methods to the needs of the patients, and giving them adequate time to respond to suggestions.

CHAPTER 9
REFLECTION QUESTIONS

1. What are the various techniques of traditional hypnotic deepening and how do they differ from indirect, conversational approach of hypnotic deepening?

2. What are some examples for "seeding" of ideas during a deepening and intensification of hypnotic experience?

3. How are post hypnotic suggestion and fractionation carried out?

REFERENCES

Abramson, L.Y., Seligman, M.E.P., & Teasdale, J.D. (1978). Learned helplessness in humans: Critique and reformulation. *Journal of Abnormal Psychology*, 87(1), 49-74. https://doi.org/10.1037/0021-843X.87.1.49

Barabasz, A., & Watkins, J.G. (2005). *Hypnotherapeutic techniques 2E.* Brunner-Routledge.

Barber, J. (1977). Rapid induction analgesia: A clinical report. *American Journal of Clinical Hypnosis*, 19(3), 138-147. https://doi.org/10.1080/00029157.1977.10403860

Beck, A.T., Rush, A.J., Shaw, B.F., & Emery, G. (1979). *Cognitive therapy of depression.* Guilford.

Brann, L. (2012). Induction and deepening. In L. Brann, J. Owens & A. Williamson (Eds.), *The handbook of contemporary clinical hypnosis: Theory and practice* (pp. 107-122). John Wiley & Sons, Ltd.

Casiglia, E., Tikhonoff, V., Giordano, N., Regaldo, G., Facco, E., Marchetti, P., Schiff, S., Tosello, M.T., Giacomello, M., Rossi, A.M., De Lazzari, F., Palatini, P., & Amodio, P. (2012). Relaxation versus fractionation as hypnotic deepening: Do they differ in physiological changes? *International Journal of Clinical and Experimental Hypnosis, 60*(3), 338-355. https://doi.org/10.1080/00207144. 2012.675297

Chaves, J.F. (1996). Hypnotic strategies for somatoform disorders. In S.J. Lynn, I. Kirsch, & J. W. Rhue (Eds.), *Casebook of clinical hypnosis* (pp. 131-151). American Psychological Association.

Elkins, G. (2014). *Hypnotic relaxation therapy: Principles and applications.* Springer.

Forester-Miller, H. (2017). Self-hypnosis classes to enhance the quality of life of breast cancer patients. *American Journal of Clinical Hypnosis, 60*(1), 18-32. https://doi.org/10.1080/00029157.2017.1316234

Gilligan, S.G. (1987). *Therapeutic trances: The cooperation principle in Ericksonian hypnotherapy.* Brunner/Mazel.

Haley, J. (1973). *Uncommon therapy: The psychiatric techniques of Milton H. Erickson, M.D.* Norton.

Hammond, D.C. (1990). *Handbook of hypnotic suggestions and metaphors.* Norton.

Hammond, D.C. (1998). *Hypnotic induction & suggestion* (revised ed.). American Society of Clinical Hypnosis.

Heap, M., & Aravind, K.K. (2002). *Hartland's medical and dental hypnosis* (4th ed.). Churchill Livingstone.

Lynn, S.J., & Kirsch, I. (2006). *Essentials of clinical hypnosis: An evidence-based approach.* American Psychological Association.

Malekzadeh, M., Mohammadabad, N.H., Kharamin, S., & Haghigi, S. (2020). The effectiveness of group-based cognitive hypnotherapy on the psychological well-being of patients with multiple sclerosis: A randomized clinical trial. *American Journal of Clinical Hypnosis*, *62*(4): 364-379. https://doi.org/ 10.1080/00029157.2019.1709149

Molden, D.C. (2014). Understanding priming effects in social psychology: What is "social priming" and how does it occur? In D.C. Molden (Ed.), *Understanding priming effects in social psychology* (pp. 3-13). Guilford.

Nash, M.R. (1996). A psychoanalytically informed approach in the case of Ellen. In S.J. Lynn, I. Kirsch, & J. W. Rhue (Eds.), *Casebook of clinical hypnosis* (pp. 317-334). American Psychological Association.

Pekala, R.J. (2011). Reply to Wagstaff: "Hypnosis and the relationship between trance, suggestion, expectancy, and depth: Some semantic and conceptual issues." *American Journal of Clinical Hypnosis*, *53*(3), 207-227. https://doi.org/10.1080/00029157.2011.10401758

Pekala, R.J., Kumar, V.K., Maurer, R., Elliott-Carter, N., Moon, E., & Mullen, K. (2010a). Suggestibility, expectancy, trance state effects, and hypnotic depth: I. Implications for understanding hypnotism. *American Journal of Clinical Hypnosis*, *52*(4), 275-290. https://doi.org/10.1080/00029157.2010.10401732

Pekala, R.J., Kumar, V.K., Maurer, R., Elliott-Carter, N., Moon, E., & Mullen, K. (2010b). Suggestibility, expectancy, trance state effects, and hypnotic depth: II. Assessment via the PCI-HAP. *American Journal of Clinical Hypnosis*, *52*(4), 291-318. https://doi.org/10.1080/00029157.2010.10401733

Short, D. (2018). Conversational hypnosis: Conceptual and technical differences relative to traditional hypnosis. *American Journal of Clinical Hypnosis*, *61*(2), 135-139. https://doi.org/10.1080/00029157.2018.1441802

Terhune, D.B., & Cardeña, E. (2010). Methodological and interpretative issues regarding the Phenomenology of Consciousness Inventory—Hypnotic Assessment Procedure: A comment on Pekala et al. (2010a, 2010b). *American Journal of Clinical Hypnosis*, *53*(2), 109-117. https://doi.org/10.1080/00029157.2010.10404333

Wagstaff, G.F. (2010). Hypnosis and the relationship between trance, suggestion, expectancy, and depth: Some semantic and conceptual issues. *American Journal of Clinical Hypnosis*, *53*(1), 47-59. https://doi.org/10.1080/ 00029157.2010.10401746

Yapko, M.D. (2001). *Treating depression with hypnosis: Integrating cognitive-behavioral and strategic approaches.* Brunner-Routledge.

Yapko, M.D. (2015). *Essentials of hypnosis* (2nd ed.). Routledge.

Yapko, M.D. (2019). *Trancework: An introduction to the practice of clinical hypnosis* (5th ed.). Routledge.

Zeig, J.K. (1990). Seeding. In J.K. Zeig & S.G. Gilligan (Eds.), *Brief therapy: Myths, methods, and metaphors* (pp. 221-246). Brunner/Mazel.

CHAPTER 10
HYPNOTIC INDUCTION AND SUGGESTION FOR EGO-STRENGTHENING

LIZ SLONENA

Chapter Learning Objectives

1. Define ego-strengthening and how it can be implemented in clinical practice.

2. Identify four types of ego-strengthening suggestions.

3. Identify four techniques for ego-strengthening in clinical hypnosis.

4. Understand how to use ego-strengthening scripts and individualize them to clients' needs.

The term "ego" has many meanings and holds historical baggage in psychology and modern society. Defining ego and ego strengthening varies depending on the theoretical orientation, ranging from psychoanalytical to third wave cognitive behaviorism. A brief history lesson is needed to understand the origins of ego-strengthening and how it has expanded to the modern-day definition.

From a psychoanalytical perspective, Freud (1961) defined the ego as a coherent organization of mental processes to which consciousness is attached, is the executive of internal and external experience, and is responsible for perception, thought, and action by engaging defense mechanisms. From this perspective, the psychoanalyst is responsible for increasing the internal strength of the ego and enhancing its effectiveness.

DEVELOPMENT OF EGO-STRENGTHENING IN CLINICAL HYPNOSIS

The term "ego-strengthening" became part of the hypnosis vernacular with John Hartland's 1965 "ego-strengthening procedure" script. Heavily influenced by psychoanalytic theory, Hartland believed that the more reliant a patient was on a symptom as a defense, the more difficult and dangerous it would be for a primitive ego to give it up. He urged practitioners to first "strengthen the patient's ability to cope with his difficulties or to encourage him to stand upon his own feet" before direct symptom removal suggestions under hypnosis (Hartland, 1965, p. 89). Hartland's approach to ego-strengthening was authoritarian and direct, mirroring the medical model ethos at that time. According to Hartland, ego-strengthening suggestions are intended to install effective ego control to handle conflicting demands of the id, superego, and reality so that direct symptom removal suggestions are more desirable and effective.

Since Hartland introduced the term, other hypnotic practitioners have expanded the intention of ego-strengthening. For example, Milton Erikson and Ernest Rossi believed that the unconscious has an organic direction towards health, contains the inner resources a person needs for natural internal and external conflict resolution, and that hypnosis can integrate unconscious resources into new conscious responses, behaviors, and beliefs (Erickson & Rossi, 1976). Erickson's guiding principle of *utilization* evolved ego-strengthening to inspire the clinician to use all the patient's verbal and nonverbal cues in an adaptive way for individualizing inductions and suggestions. *Utilization* amplifies therapeutic attunement and encourages clinicians to use ego-strengthening suggestions liberally throughout therapy, not just during formal hypnosis.

Self-efficacy and Quiet Ego:
The Non-Hypnotic Sisters of Ego Strengthening

Outside the field of hypnosis, concepts akin to ego-strengthening can be seen in first wave, second wave, and third wave cognitive-behavioral therapy (CBT). Bandura (1977) and others (Marlatt & Gordon, 1985; DiClemente, 1986) popularized the concept of self-efficacy: the expectation, belief, and confidence of being able to adaptively cope in stressful situations. Individuals with high self-efficacy perceive themselves as being in control whereas people with low self-efficacy perceive themselves as helpless (Bandura, 1997). One of the main goals of CBT is enhancing self-efficacy and relapse prevention so that the client can be their own therapist and use coping skills without the clinician being present. Third wave CBT modalities expand ego-strengthening and self-efficacy concepts with the addition of mindfulness, acceptance, and compassion by visualizing other "selves." For example, Dialectical Behavior Therapy (DBT) presents the concept of "Wise Mind" (Linehan, 1993), Acceptance and Commitment Therapy emphasizes Self-As-Context (the non-judging observer of experience; Hayes, Strosahl, & Wilson, 1999), Internal Family Systems promotes Self-Leadership (Schwartz & Sweezy, 2020), and Compassion-Focused Therapy cultivates a compassionate-being and compassionate-self (Gilbert, 2009).

The most recent development of ego-strengthening involves the "quiet ego" concept for enhancing well-being influenced by positive psychology research, Buddhist philosophy, and humanistic psychology ideals (Bauer & Wayment, 2008). Quiet ego is a self-identity that promotes balance and growth through the reflection and endorsement of 4 values: detached awareness (mindful awareness of self and others without judgment), inclusive identity (interconnection and interde-pendence), perspective-taking (compassion and empathy), and growth (realization of development over time; Bauer & Wayment, 2008; Bauer et al., 2015). The quiet ego can be measured by the Quiet Ego Scale, which higher scores are positively associated with self-esteem, ability to savor positive experiences, life satisfaction, subjective well-being, psychological resilience, and life meaning (Bauer & Wayment, 2015). The qualities of "quiet ego" counters the narcissistic "noisy ego" by balancing the interest of the self and others, cultivating collective growth, encouraging value-consistent goals, and cementing inherent self-worth and inner competence regardless of outcomes (Bauer & Wayment, 2017; Bauer & Wayment, 2018). Quiet ego-strengthening provides a new frontier of compassionate hypnotic suggestions.

An Integrative Definition of Ego-Strengthening

Given the plethora of theoretical approaches and applications of ego-strengthening, we offer an integrative definition that includes hypnosis and non-hypnotic influences. Our definition of ego-strengthening is as follows: Hypnotic suggestions intended to increase confidence, self-efficacy, self-worth, cultivate adaptive coping skills, strengthen personality strengths, maintain emotional stability, enhance resiliency, or amplify self-compassion and wellbeing.

How to Use Ego Strengthening in Clinical Practice

Hypnotic ego-strengthening suggestions enhance the person's capacity to feel empowered, confident, and cope with internal and external challenges in life. The benefits of ego-strengthening suggestions include: 1) improved therapeutic rapport, 2) heightened insight and awareness of strengths and skills, 3) improved self-esteem, self-confidence, self-efficacy, self-mastery, and self-compassion, and 4) enhanced resiliency.

How Ego-Strengthening Improvements Impact Therapeutic Relationships

For any therapeutic intervention to work, especially clinical hypnosis, rapport is needed to build the foundation of a safe sanctuary of healing. The core factors of empathy, warmth, unconditional positive regard, genuineness, congruence, acceptance, and the therapeutic use of self are the pillars for effective ego-strengthening suggestions (McNeal, 2020; Moss, 1999; Rogers, 1957). Research has indicated that hypnosis rapidly enhances therapeutic rapport (Holroyd, 1987; Alladin, 2008; Elkins, 2013) and that attunement in the therapeutic relationship amplifies the capacity for the client to regulate emotions and develop self-compassion (Granit, 2006; Neff & McGehee, 2010; McNeal, 2020). The clinician is the initial source of ego-strengthening via the therapeutic relationship, modeling, and directly highlighting strengths, so that ego-strengthening is eventually self-generated by the client. The clinician can disarm the client's self-criticism and negative beliefs by reinforcing the progress, growth, and uncovering their strengths throughout the sessions together, in and out of hypnosis. Yapko (2019) emphasizes that the strength in ego-strengthening is not in the suggestions themselves, but in the client's power to integrate and use them. The clinician is responsible for empowering the client and emphasizing that they can make a difference in their life in a new way. Suggestions are worthless words until someone is ready to hear them, take them, and use them like gold.

How Ego Strengthening Mobilizes Insight, Strength, and Skills

When ego-strengthening is used during hypnotic phenomenon, there is increased access to the unconscious, retrieving healing imagery, memories, and emotions, with decreased defensiveness and increased receptiveness (Brown & Fromm, 1986; Frederick & McNeal, 1999; McNeal & Frederick, 1994; McNeal 2020). Ego-strengthening also enhances the ability to access inner resources, such as novel problem solving, to create a bridge from insight to actionable change (Erickson & Rossi, 1976; McNeal 2020; McNeal & Frederick, 1993). It is common to mobilize inner strengths by age regression (discussed later in this chapter) to rekindle sources of skills from past success to aid in present struggles, as seen in Shirly McNeal's and Clair Frederick's Meeting Inner Strength and Significant Nurturing Figures scripts (McNeal & Frederick, 1993).

How Ego-Strengthening Bolsters Self-esteem, Self-Efficacy, and Self-Compassion Benefits

Ego-strengthening may bolster the client's self-perception by reinforcing positive emotions, beliefs, and behaviors through conscious and unconscious repetition, and this continued reinforcement may reestablish their self-esteem, self-efficacy, self-mastery, and self-compassion (Carich, 1990). Research has indicated that positive and stable self-esteem may act like a protective buffer against stress, enhancing one's ability to cope and reframe difficult experiences as lessons for growth (Brown, 2010; Stafrace & Evans, 2004; Rutter, 1985). Preliminary research investigating ego-strengthening hypnotherapy may decrease negative self-talk (Vasel et al., 2016), increase self-esteem (Badeleh et al., 2013), and enhance well-being (Na & Elkins, in press).

How ego-strengthening cultivates resiliency

Resilience is defined as the ability to cope with adversity, grief, loss, tragedy, or trauma mentally, emotionally, and behaviorally (de Terte et al., 2014). Viewed as the "psychological immune system," resiliency assists in protecting and rebounding from stressors as a stronger and more resourceful person. Many resiliency interventions involve ego-strengthening including identifying strengths and values that promote coping, accepting what has happened, transforming suffering to meaning, and visualizing actionable steps toward accomplishing goals (Hanson & Hanson, 2018; McNeal, 2020). Hypnotic ego-strengthening can shift the helpless to the hopeful and the powerless to the powerful.

When to Use Ego-strengthening Suggestions in Session Timing

Ego-strengthening suggestions can be used before, during, and after hypnotic interventions. See Table 10-1 for details. The choice and timing of ego-strengthening methods are based on the clinician's thorough understanding of the client, including their history, presenting problem, communication style, and stage of treatment (Frederick & McNeal, 1993). Ego-strengthening disarms the client's hesitation, hopelessness, doubt, amotivation, distress, and anxiety that commonly perpetuates their suffering. The continual use of ego-strengthening suggestions throughout a session, regardless of the client's hypnotic depth, can enhance rapport, positive expectancy, and treatment effects for continued healing. Clinicians can also ask non-hypnotic questions from a "what went right" versus a "what went wrong" perspective that sets expectations for growth. For example, one can set the session agenda by asking "any wins or wisdom you gained this week?" rather than "any problems or concerns this week?" Although a client may come to you expecting you to heal them, ego-strengthening sends the unconscious message that the client is the key to their own freedom.

With depression, it's critical to transform passive helplessness to active hope. Examples include visualizing themselves when they were free from depression and identifying small, actionable steps they can take towards change. In anxiety and phobias, ego-strengthening suggestions can highlight that they are the masters of their minds and body, creating both excitation and relaxation through the power of their breath. With PTSD and traumatic-stress, ego-strengthening themes may emphasize that they are the author of their story, and their trauma narrative can be rewritten so it's no longer the title of their life but a mere chapter. In substance use, eating disorders, and unhelpful habits (nail biting, trichotillomania, etc.), the problematic behaviors can be conceptualized as control and self-soothing strategies with harmful long-term consequences. Ego-strengthening suggestions for these disorders include highlighting their willingness

TABLE 10-1: EGO-STRENGTHENING SUGGESTIONS BEFORE, DURING, AND AFTER HYPNOSIS

	BEFORE HYPNOSIS	DURING HYPNOSIS	AFTER HYPNOSIS
PURPOSE:	Prepare for interventions	Enhance coping skills during procedures and performances	Amplify the longevity of treatment effects
GOAL:	Pre-hypnotic suggestions strengthen willingness to face internal or external difficulties	Installing self-hypnosis suggestions to facilitate their sense of control, comfort, and calm during immediate experiences	Post-hypnotic suggestions to reinforce practice of skills, enhance effects, proliferate positive expectancy for healing
TARGETS:	• Expectancy effects • Facilitates trust • Control & safety • Empowerment • Distress tolerance • Enhance motivation	• Anxiety • Relaxation • Self-efficacy • Adaptive dissociation • Time dilation/compression • Pain relief • Cognitive reframing • Depth of hypnosis	• Coping skill use • Values • Consistency • Willpower • Behavioral activation • Anchoring adaptive states • Self-soothing • Self-regulation
IDEAS FOR USE:	• when client is hesitant to use hypnosis • before OCD/anxiety/ phobia exposures • preparing for trauma reprocessing	• surgeries • dental procedures • chronic pain • diabetes management • sexual functioning • childbirth • anesthesia • during exercise • sports enhancement • performances • working with challenging people/clients	• hypnosis practice • smoking and drug cessation • memory retention & recall • ADHD • healthy habits • completing homework • self-care strategies
EXAMPLE:	In a moment, would you like to experience deep relaxation and see how hypnosis works best for you?	You will know exactly what to do to keep your calm, comfort, and confidence while you exercise/perform/have a great surgery	My voice will go with you, even after your eyes are open, you will find how easy it is to remember everything you accomplished in hypnosis today, making time to use hypnosis, because what you practice grows stronger.

and determination to rediscover helpful ways of self-soothing. Chronic pain and illness commonly struggle with the unpredictability and limitations of their symptoms. Ego-strengthening may target meaningful, consistent, and pleasurable activities clients can do even in symptom flares. In medical hypnosis, it is essential to remind the client that they are not a passive patient but are an active participant and part of the procedure performance. Ego-strengthening suggestions may target how their body and mind are naturally designed towards healing and repair, and that their body knows exactly what to do to have a problem-free procedure. In general, ego-strengthening suggestions are beneficial for remembering what strengths, values, and skills assisted the client through trialing times, thereby enhancing their control, capacity to cope, and mobilizing their power and choice.

CLINICIAN SELF-CARE AND BURNOUT PREVENTION

Ego-strengthening can easily and effortlessly target clinician self-care, prevent burnout, and enhance confidence using hypnosis. It is not uncommon for new practitioners of hypnosis to experience self-doubt, confusion, or even imposter syndrome while learning and implementing hypnosis. These anxieties may resurface even in experienced hypnotherapists when utilizing new techniques or implementing hypnosis with complex clients. Self-hypnosis can be used to soften and soothe anxieties, cultivate confidence, and enhance mindfulness (see Table 10-2). For example, Elkins, Roberts, and Simicich (2018) have recommended mindful self-hypnosis for self-care, using suggestions to enhance mindfulness concepts of present awareness, nonjudgement, acceptance, and self-compassion. Other benefits of practicing self-hypnosis include: 1) experiential learning of ego-strengthening strategies, 2) enhanced confidence and flexibility of techniques, and 3) decreased reliance on scripts.

**TABLE 10-2: SELF-HYPNOSIS EGO-STRENGTHENING SUGGESTIONS
FOR CLINICIANS**

Practicing Self-Hypnosis	Each and every time I practice self-hypnosis, I'm planting the seeds for growth personally and professionally to bloom wherever I'm planted.
Interacting with a challenging client	My source of inner resource guides my words with wisdom, warmth, and welcomes creativity.
Using new techniques	My natural curiosity and creativity are fertilizer to grow calmer and more confident.
Transitioning from work to home	I give myself full permission to rest my body and mind.
Energy and motivation to complete clinical documentation	If I got into graduate school, I am proof that I can do hard things.

FOUR TYPES OF EGO STRENGTHENING SUGGESTIONS

According to Brown and Fromm (1986, p. 194), there are three kinds of ego-strengthening suggestions. We have added a fourth type to better represent the integrative definition of ego-strengthening. The four types of ego-strengthening suggestions are: 1) General ego-strengthening suggestions, 2) Specific ego-strengthening suggestions to rediscover one's strengths and coping strategies, 3) Specific suggestions to rekindle one's sense of self-efficacy and self-mastery for attaining goals, and 4) Suggestions to cultivate self-compassion and quiet ego.

General ego-strengthening suggestions

The epitome of generalized ego-strengthening suggestion is the auto-suggestion, "Every day, in every way, I'm getting better and better" (Coué, 1922a, p. 7,). Hartland's (1965) script relied on direct and general suggestions such as, *"Every day ... you feel more and more independent ... more able to 'stick up for yourself' ... to stand upon your own feet ... to hold your own ... no matter how difficult or trying things may be."* The benefits of general ego-strengthening suggestions are that they are universal, purposefully vague, replicable in clinical trials, and are easy additions to scripts. The limitations of general suggestions are the absence of desired specific outcomes and individualization to the client's concerns and strengths.

Specific Ego-Strengthening Suggestions for Coping Strategies

For more powerful and effective ego-strengthening, it is recommended to use specific suggestions to facilitate the rediscovery of strengths and enhancement of the patient's inner coping strategies. Emerging neurophysiology research indicates that specific suggestions can influence precise perceptual, cognitive, or motor processes and selectively engage relevant brain regions (Landry & Raz, 2017). It is recommended to ask how the client wants to think, feel, and behave and incorporate their exact words, especially metaphors, to use in hypnosis. For example, below is a pre-hypnotic inquiry with a client and in italics would be phrases later used in hypnosis:

Therapist: We have identified that placing boundaries with your parents during the holidays is a goal of yours. But you are hesitant about being assertive because you fear that they will become angry. Tell me how you would like to feel instead?

Client: *In control, calm, and strong.* I don't want to be a *dirty doormat anymore.*

Therapist: And has there been a time before where you were assertive with your parents?

Client: Oh yeah ... I decided to go to college and *major in art instead of biology.* They didn't like my decision, they were furious, but *I knew it was the right decision for me.*

Therapist: I'm noticing your inner strengths of *bravery and creativity* that aided you. Could your strengths be helpful in this situation too?

Client: Hm, *I forgot how brave I was and how important creativity is to me. If I can make that tough decision, then I can make other decisions for myself, too.*

Therapist: That's right, you've always had that bravery and creativity within you. And you've learned new skills since then. What would you do differently if you placed boundaries and your parents became angry at you?

Client: Well, I'd like to *use that broken record technique. I won't crumble to their anger.* I want to be true to my word.

Therapist: Good thinking. And is there someone real or imaginary that you admire that represents calm strength that doesn't crumble under anger?

Client: *Wonder Woman* comes to mind. She's *smart, strong,* and can even *communicate with raging animals to make them calm. Talking to my parents often feels like talking to animals.*

In this example, the clinician is the catalyst for ego-strengthening, illuminating forgotten strengths and skills, probing for problem solving, and encouraging symbols of strength to guide insight to action. In sum, you want to highlight the positive and negate the negative. Pause and ponder: what specific ego-strengthening suggestions would you use with this client?

Specific Ego-Strengthening Suggestions for Self-Efficacy for Achieving Goals

Another type of specific ego-strengthening includes suggestions for bolstering self-efficacy for achieving goals based on the work of Albert Bandura (1982). Self-efficacy is the belief that one can successfully perform a behavior necessary to execute an expected and specific outcome. Bandura (See Table 10-3) specified four ways to enhance self-efficacy: 1) verbal persuasion, 2) emotional arousal, 3) vicarious experience, and 4) performance accomplishments. Each of these aspects can be amplified through hypnotic ego-strengthening suggestions (Elkins, 2013).

Suggestions to Cultivate Self-Compassion and Quiet Ego

Self-compassion is a different construct than self-esteem (Neff, 2011). While self-esteem is an evaluation that is dependent on success and judgement, self-compassion is an attitude that is free from outcome or comparison. Self-compassion involves being kind to ourselves regardless of results, because our inherit worth does not originate from our achievements or accolades from others. Self-compassion and quiet ego-strengthening suggestions are helpful for individuals struggling with self-criticism, perfectionism, and internalized shame (Bauer & Wayment, 2017; Gilbert, 2009; Gilbert, 2010). Suggestions to stimulate self-compassion and quiet ego-strengthening can target self-kindness, common humanity of suffering, and mindful acceptance of inner and outer experiences. Mindful Hypnotherapy and Brief Mindful Hypnosis are evidence-based and manualized approaches that incorporate self-compassion and quiet ego-strengthening suggestions in their scripts (Olendzki et al., 2020; Slonena & Elkins, 2021).

TABLE 10-3: FOUR EXAMPLES OF EGO-STRENGTHENING FOR SELF-EFFICACY

VERBAL PERSUASION Indirect and Direct suggestions	You will be pleasantly surprised in the expected and unexpected ways you are cultivating confidence. Your confidence will be more consistent and more stable with each and every breath you take in. Because just as effortless as it is to breathe… and to hear my words… it's just as easy for your confidence to naturally grow, bloom, and flourish.
EMOTIONAL AROUSAL Anchoring adaptive states Ideomotor signaling	Isn't it interesting that confidence is a muscle that you can strengthen? Go ahead, you can see for yourself. I'd like you to focus your attention on your left hand… and in a few moments, the hand will form into a strong first… easily and effortlessly all by itself… now… and as the first forms, you feel the strength and confidence strengthen… more and more… your confident becomes stronger as the first becomes stronger… and when your confidence is where it needs to be… your unwavering belief in yourself… then the fist can relax… with strong confidence… that's right.
VICARIOUS EXPERIENCE Age progression	As you are sitting comfortably in your chair, you see a TV in front of you, and a remote in your hand… And on this TV you can view that important event that you will do in the near future… as if the future has been recorded with the ideal outcome. When you are ready, you can press "ON" the remote… and you can clearly see the meaningful event unfolding like a movie… and you see yourself as the main character, and you are doing all the things you wish to do in the future with calm, confidence, and strength… Vividly see what you are doing… saying… behaving… and how confidently you are accomplishing your goals with effortless ease… [add additional strengths/skills/ behaviors that will aid goal achievement]
PERFORMANCE ACCOMPLISHMENTS Rating scale pre- and post-hypnosis	Before we go into hypnosis today, I want to check in on your level of relaxation.* From 0 to 10, where 0 represents no relaxation at all, and 10 represents being completely relaxed, where would you rate your current level of relaxation now? … Great, let's see how much of a difference you can make using hypnosis today. *can be any target to increase (confidence, mood, energy, etc.)

FOUR STRATEGIES FOR EGO STRENGTHENING IN CLINICAL HYPNOSIS

Due to the wide variety of ego-strengthening suggestions, I invite you to imagine the techniques existing on a continuum inspired by McNeal

(2020). On one end stands the direct, structured, and authoritative suggestions like Hartland's. In the middle sits guided imagery techniques, where you are a tour guide directing viewpoints while the client chooses where to look in their own imagery. On the other end stands projective/evocative techniques, which can be intentionally unstructured to allow internal resources, skills, or solutions to emerge from the unconscious. Although there are many techniques to cultivate ego-strengthening, the following four strategies will be expanded upon: 1) indirect and direct suggestions, 2) therapeutic metaphors, 3) age regression and progression, and 4) the light within induction.

Indirect and Direct Ego Strengthening Suggestions

Research has indicated that there is no significant difference in effect between using indirect and direct suggestions (Hammond, 1990b). Direct suggestions are clear and have a specific outcome whereas indirect suggestions are ambiguous and offer the client more control and choice in responses. The advantage of direct suggestions is that there is an unambiguous response, whereas the risk is the potential for rejection of the suggestion. Direct suggestions are helpful for highly hypnotizable clients or those with low resistance (Elkins, 2013). Types of indirect suggestions include truisms, questions as suggestions, suggesting multiple responses, using past experiences, and implication of response. Table 10-4 gives examples of using these 5 indirect suggestions for strengthening decision making. The benefit of indirect suggestions includes better responses with clients with trauma, authority issues, and a high need for control, whereas the disadvantage is the suggestions may be so vague that there is no response. It is recommended to use both indirect and direct suggestions and ask for feedback to individualize hypnotic suggestions to the client preferences. For example, I once used the indirect suggestion, "release what no longer serves you," and to my surprise, the client had to pause our hypnosis session to quickly use the bathroom. I have now switched to the more direct suggestion, "release the anxious thoughts that no longer serve you" to avoid any unintended accidents.

Therapeutic Metaphor for Ego Strengthening

Metaphors are suggestions that are communicated twice; once on a conscious, logical, rational, cognitive level and then again on an unconscious, emotional, symbolic, experiential level. Ego-strengthening metaphors can be descriptive guided imagery, idioms and adages, song lyrics, quotes from favorite movies or video games, or formal stories. Keep in mind the Law of Dominant Affect, which states that a stronger emotion overrides a weaker emotion. Because the unconscious operates through associations and communicates best through the language of emotions, experiences, and images, ego-strengthening suggestions are stronger when one uses personally relevant emotional content and imagery (Elkins, 2013). Invite the client to help craft your hypnotic suggestions by listening to their creative language, metaphors, sayings, hobbies, and description of their suffering. For example, a young woman named Sally, a massage therapist who loved swimming in the ocean viewed herself as "broken" because of her childhood sexual trauma. Ego-strengthening metaphors targeting her self-worth included massaging and stretching a tight muscle until it is strong and flexible again, creating a beautiful mosaic from "broken" pieces of glass, and visualizing her serene coral reef at the bottom of the ocean, far away from the tumultuous waves of life. The client eventually declared a new mantra for herself, "I'm not broken, I was bruised. And I am healing every day."

Common metaphoric themes for ego-strengthening include discovering hidden treasure, the hero/heroine's journey, nature and its organic tendency towards growth, the resilience of the Earth or human-made structures, embodying the positive traits of real or imagery role models/religious figures/spirit animals, receiving wisdom from ancestors or mentors in the form of a gift, having a companion or object that represents strength, protection, and wisdom, imaging places that are the epitome of education (libraries) or strength (sports arenas), and being in a personal place that cultivates comfort, ease, and mastery.

TABLE 10-4: EGO-STRENGTHENING SUGGESTIONS FOR PROBLEM SOLVING

With each and every breath, you'll become calmer and more confident making decisions…	Direct
Because being calm and confident is a pleasant sensation… and you can control your breathing any time you wish… and with physical relaxation brings mental relaxation…	Indirect (truism)
And from now on, you can take a breath of air and go beneath the surface of your problems, recognizing them for what they are…	Direct
Isn't it curious that problems are just inconvenient situations…? You can see that being the case, can't you?	Indirect (question)
So… from now on…you can think about your problems in a different way… that what you once thought were problems are merely situations…and you think about yourself differently in this way too…	Direct
I don't know how you will think about yourself differently… but what I do know is that you will see yourself in a new light.	Indirect (implication of response)
And this new light will guide your way to help you become aware of your choices. You can choose every day… every moment… you always have a choice…	Direct
I know you have the choice because you have made many choices to be where you are now… some easier … and some harder than others. Like what you had for breakfast yesterday… or what clothes you put on today… or even when you made the choice to go to therapy… and so many other choices have brought you to where you are now… exactly where you are meant to be…Because your own mental and physical health are important to you. And even with so many options, you chose what was best for you.	Indirect (past experiences)
Regardless of the outcome, you always have the power to choose. You are your own freedom.	Direct
As you absorb these insights and truths of your freedom, your calmness and confidence grows… and you notice expected and unexpected differences when you open your eyes… The differences you see, feel, and know may be gradual or immediate, slow or fast… Perhaps you notice how much easier it is for you to make a decision… Or you make a pro and con list to guide your decision… Maybe you trust yourself deeply and feel your decision is the right one, whatever it may be… knowing that decisions move you forward to where you wish to go.	Indirect (suggesting multiple responses)

Age progression for Ego Strengthening

Age regression and progression are evocative ego-strengthening techniques that intentionally invoke an unconscious search so that the client can rediscover their strengths, skills, or solutions. Age regression can be used to remember and relive times of success and strength. Age progression can be used to imagine future stressors being managed with ease, overcoming uncertainty, visualizing attainment of goals, rekindling hope, and identifying skills and strengths for relapse prevention. Age progression is useful for clients struggling with anticipatory anxiety, whether it is related to academic, artistic, or physical performances, medical procedures, phobias, or social events. These age-related techniques are best used when the clinician is moderately experienced with their client's hypnotic responses because when these projective techniques are intentionally unstructured, the answers may be unpredictable, and there may be a reliance on the unconscious to guide the visualization. When considering age regression, be aware of your client's trauma history to avoid abreactions and spend extra time re-orienting to the present time, date, and current age. The following age-related suggestions can be explored:

> "Remember a time in the past when you felt safe, confident, at your very best"

> "Meeting that strong, younger version of you, what words of wisdom would they give you?"

> "In a moment ... you will meet your future, wiser self who has all the answers to help you overcome this current challenge."

> "What does your wiser-self look like? What are they wearing? Where are they living? How do they hold themselves? What expression is on their face as they look at you?"

"Your future, wiser self has a gift symbolizing their timeless wisdom they want to give you. Open your hands to receive this gift ... What is the gift and what does it mean to you?"

"See yourself through the eyes of your higher, wiser self ... notice the compassion flow to you ... and see that your future self is your present self, always within you."

"Your future, wiser self says goodbye by giving you a hug/handshake/fist bump, and upon that contact, your future self-integrates themselves into your present self."

The Light within Induction

Inspired by Qigong and Brief Mindful Hypnosis approaches, this rapid and activating induction is best used for energizing the client, moving past procrastination, and engaging in action after induction. This induction is also beneficial for active alert hypnosis and self-hypnosis. The clinician models the induction in tandem with the client because of the use of the body. Instructing the induction with the client leverages the neuroscience of mirror neuron activity of observing and engaging in the same behavior, cultivating empathy, rapport, expected social responsiveness, and teaching a new tangible skill of self-hypnosis (Rossi & Rossi, 2011). Lastly, this induction instills a somatic metaphor that a change is self-generated in the body and mind with a single action. This induction is helpful for mobilizing energy before exercising, doing chores, or completing clinical documentation.

Ego Strengthening Induction Transcript

Do you want an easy way to energize yourself and go into hypnotic flow effortlessly? Allow me to show you how and follow along with me. All you have to do is clap your hands [clap] and start rubbing your hands together ... that's right.

[Clinician continues to rub their hands together while talking] Noticing how quickly and easily you are warming your hands up ... And as you feel your hands becoming warmer you'll become more and more focused on this sensation ... and on my voice ... because isn't it interesting that you have the power to change your body and your mind with one action? Quickly, easily, effortlessly ... And now what I want you to do is take a cleansing breathe in through your nose ... hold it briefly ... and as your exhale release your hands down to your sides [release hands] ... and now allow your eyes to close ... great ... as you focus on the sensations in the hands you go even deeper within ... as deep as you wish to go today ... easily drifting into your blissful state so that you can achieve the things you wish to achieve in hypnosis today. Feeling the pleasant warmth and tingling ... radiating with your power. Following the feeling into your blissful hypnotic flow ... That's right. Focusing on that wonderful feeling of hypnosis so that everything else fades into the background more and more. So that any physical or mental tension in your body or mind is released ... now ... And I wonder which of the hands holds the most power ... the left or the right? Or do they equally hold your energy? Feeling the light within you, radiating from the hands up your arms, spreading to the crown of your head ... down to the tips of your toes ... warmly enveloping you with a glow from the inside out ... so that it extends an inch or two outside of your body.

CONCLUSION

Ego-strengthening is an essential technique used in hypnotherapy and non-hypnotic modalities. Since the birth of this term in 1965, ego-strengthening has metamorphosized Hartland's direct and verbatim scripts to include individualization, guided imagery, inner strengths, and age regression/progression to enhance its versatility. Ego-strengthening has been shown to significantly improve well-being in clients with mental and medical conditions, and in some cases, reduction in presenting symptoms. Interventions without ego-strengthening is like having a burger without the bun—sure, you can eat the patty on its own, but it'll lack support, sustenance, and satisfaction.

CHAPTER 10
REFLECTIONS QUESTIONS

1. Why is ego-strengthening an important aspect of clinical practice?

2. What are the four main benefits of ego strengthening?

3. How can ego strengthening suggestions be specified for more individualized outcomes?

4. What are the four strategies for cultivating ego strengthening?

REFERENCES

Alladin, A. (2008). *Cognitive hypnotherapy: An integrated approach to the treatment of emotional disorders.* John Wiley & Sons.

Badeleh, M., Fathi, M., Aghamohammadian, H. R., & Badeleh, M. T. (2013). The effect of group cognitive behavioral hypnotherapy on increasing self-esteem of adolescents. *Journal of Research Development in Nursing and Midwifery, 10*(1), 17-24.

Bandura, A. (1977). Self-efficacy: Toward a unifying theory of behavior change. *Psychological Review, 84,* 191-215.

Bandura, A. (1982). Self-efficacy mechanism in human agency. *American Psychologist, 37*(2), 122.

Bandura, A. (1997). *Self-efficacy: The exercise of control.* New York: W. H. Freeman and Company.

Bauer, J. J., & Wayment, H. A. (2008a). The psychology of the quiet ego. In H. A. Wayment & J. J. Bauer (Eds.), *Transcending self-interest: Psychological explorations of the quiet ego* (pp. 7-19). American Psychological Association.

Bauer, J. J., & Wayment, H. A. (2008b). *Transcending self-interest: Psychological explorations of the quiet ego.* (1st ed.) APA Books.

Bauer, J. J., & Wayment, H. A. (2018). The quiet ego: Motives for self-other balance and growth in relation to well-being. *Journal of Happiness Studies, 19*(3), 881-896.

Bauer, J. J., & Wayment, H.A. (2017). The quiet ego: Concept, measurement, and well-being. In M. D. Robinson & M. Eid (Eds.), *The happy mind: Cognitive contributions to well-being* (pp. 77-94). Springer International Publishing/Springer Nature.

Bauer, J. J., & Sylaska, K., Wayment, H. A. (2015). The quiet ego scale: measuring the compassionate self-identity. *Journal of Happiness Studies, 16*(4), 999-1033.

Brown, D. P., & Fromm, E. (1986). *Hypnotherapy and hypnoanalysis.* Hillsdale, NJ: Lawrence Erlbaum Associates.

Brown, J. D. (2010). High self-esteem buffers negative feedback: Once more with feeling. *Cognition and Emotion, 24*(8), 1389-1404.

Carich, P.A. (1990). Ego strengthening: Encouragement via hypnosis. *Individual Psychology: Journal of Adlerian Theory, Research and Practice, 46*(4), 498-502.

Coué, E. (1922). *Self-Mastery Through Conscious Autosuggestion.* New York, NY: Malkan Publishing Company. [A partial translation of Coué (1922a) by Archibald S. Van Orden.] URL = http://tinyurl.com/gumqlxx

de Terte, I., Stephens, C., & Huddleston, L. (2014). The development of a three-part model of psychological resilience. *Stress and Health, 30*(5), 416-424.

DiClemente, C. C. (1986). Self-efficacy and the addictive behaviors. *Journal of Social and Clinical Psychology, 4*(3), 302-315.

Elkins, G. (2013). *Hypnotic relaxation therapy: Principles and applications.* New York, NY: Springer Publishing Company.

Elkins, G. (2016). *Handbook of medical and psychological hypnosis: Foundations, applications, and professional issues.* New York, NY: Springer Publishing Company.

Elkins, G., Roberts, L. R., & Simicich, L. (2018). Mindful self-hypnosis for self-care: An integrative model and illustrative case example. *American Journal of Clinical Hypnosis, 61*(1), 45-56.

Erickson, M. H., & Rossi, E. L. (1976). Two-level communication and the micro dynamics of trance and suggestion. *American Journal of Clinical Hypnosis, 18,* 153-171.

Frederick, C., & McNeal, S. (1993). From strength to strength: Inner strength with immature ego states. *American Journal of Clinical Hypnosis, 35,* 250-256.

Freud, S. (1961). The ego and the id. In J. Strachey (Ed. and Trans.), The standard edition of the *Complete psychological works of Sigmund Freud* (Vol. 18, pp. 67-143). (Original work)

Gilbert, P. (2009). Introducing compassion focused therapy. *Advances in Psychiatric Treatment, 15,* 199-208.

Gilbert, P. (2010). An introduction to compassion focused therapy in cognitive behavior therapy. *International Journal of Cognitive Therapy, 3*(2), 97-112.

Granit, L. G. (2006). Attachment theory and the relational paradigm. *The California Psychologist, 39,* 16-17.

Guse, T., Wissing, M. P., & Hartman, W. (2006). A prenatal hypnotherapeutic programme to enhance postnatal psychological wellbeing. *Australian Journal of Clinical and Experimental Hypnosis, 34*(1), 27.

Hammond, D. C. (1990a). Formulating hypnotic and posthypnotic suggestions. In D. C. Hammond (Ed.), *Handbook of hypnotic suggestions and metaphors* (pp. 11-44). New York, NY: W. W. Norton.

Hammond, D. C. (Ed.). (1990b). *Handbook of hypnotic suggestions and metaphors.* New York, NY: W. W. Norton & Company.

Hanson, R., & Hanson, F. (2018). *Resilience: How to grow an unshakable core of calm, strength, and happiness.* New York, NY: Harmony Books.

Hartland, J. (1965). The value of "ego strengthening" procedures prior to direct symptom removal under hypnosis. *American Journal of Clinical Hypnosis, 8*(2), 89-93.

Hayes, S., Strosahl, K., & Wilson, K. (1999). *Acceptance and commitment therapy: An experiential approach to behaviour change.* New York: Guildford.

Holroyd, J. (1987). How hypnosis may potentiate psychotherapy. *American Journal of Clinical Hypnosis, 29*(3), 194-200.

Landry, M., & Raz, A. (2017). Neurophysiology of hypnosis. In G. E. Elkins (Ed.), *Handbook of medical and psychological hypnosis* (pp. 19-28). New York, NY: Springer.

Lewis, H. B. (1988). The role of shame in symptom formation. In Clynes M., & Panksepp J. (Eds.) *Emotions and psychopathology* (pp. 95-106). Boston, MA: Springer.

Lewis, K. M., Matsumoto, C., Cardinale, E., Jones, E. L., Gold, A. L., Stringaris, A., ... & Brotman, M. A. (2020). Self-efficacy as a target for neuroscience research on moderators of treatment outcomes in pediatric anxiety. *Journal of Child and Adolescent Psychopharmacology, 30*(4), 205-214.

Linehan, M. M. (1993). *Cognitive-behavior treatment of borderline personality disorder.* New York: Guildford.

Marlatt, G. A., & Gordon, J. R. (Eds.). (1985). *Relapse prevention: Maintenance strategies in the treatment of addictive behaviors.* New York: Guilford press.

McNeal, S. (2020). Hypnotic ego-strengthening: Where we've been and the road ahead. *American Journal of Clinical Hypnosis, 62*(4), 392-408.

Frederick, C., & McNeal, S. (1993). Inner strength and other techniques for ego strengthening. *American Journal of Clinical Hypnosis, 35*(3), 170-176.

Moss, D., & Willmarth, E. (2017). Ego-strengthening. In G. R. Elkins (Ed.), *Handbook of medical and psychological hypnosis: Foundations, applications, and professional issues.* Springer Publishing Company.

Na, H. & Elkins, G. (2022). Hypnotic relaxation therapy to enhance subjective well-being among college students: A pilot study. *International Journal of Clinical and Experimental Hypnosis* (in press).

Neff, K. D. (2011). Self-compassion, self-esteem, and well-being. *Social and Personality Psychology Compass*, *5*(1), 1-12.

Neff, K. D., & McGehee, P. (2010). Self-compassion and psychological resilience among adolescents and young adults. *Self and Identity*, *9*, 225-240.

Olendzki, N., Elkins, G. R., Slonena, E., Hung, J., & Rhodes, J. R. (2020). Mindful hypnotherapy to reduce stress and increase mindfulness: A randomized controlled pilot study. *International Journal of Clinical and Experimental Hypnosis, 68*(2), 151-166.

Rogers, C. R. (1957). The necessary and sufficient conditions of therapeutic personality change. *Journal of Consulting Psychology*, *21*(2), 95-103.

Rossi, E. L., & Rossi, K. L. (2006). The neuroscience of observing consciousness & mirror neurons in therapeutic hypnosis. American Journal of Clinical Hypnosis, *48*(4), 263-278.

Rutter, M. (1985). Resilience in the face of adversity: Protective factors and resistance to psychiatric disorder. *British Journal of Psychiatry*, *147*(6), 598-611.

Schwartz, R. C., & Sweezy, M. (2020). *Internal family system therapy*, Second edition. New York, NY: The Guilford Press.

Slonena, E. E., & Elkins, G. R. (2021). Effects of a brief mindful hypnosis intervention on stress reactivity: A randomized active control study. *International Journal of Clinical and Experimental Hypnosis, 69*(4), 453-467.

Stafrace, S. P., & Evans, B. J. (2004). Self-esteem, hypnosis, and ego-enhancement. *Australian Journal of Clinical and Experimental Hypnosis*, *32*(1), 1-35.

Vasel, M. Y., Farhadi, M., Paidar, M. R. Z., & Chegini, A. A. (2016). The efficacy of hypnotherapy for ego strengthening and negative self-talk in female heads of households. *Sleep and Hypnosis*, *18*(4), 74-81.

Warren, J. I., Stein, J. A., & Grella, C. E. (2007). Role of social support and self-efficacy in treatment outcomes among clients with co-occurring disorders. *Drug and Alcohol Dependence*, *89*(2-3), 267-274.

Yapko, M. (2019) Plenary Addresses: 2019 ASCH Annual Meeting, *American Journal of Clinical Hypnosis*, *61*(4), 426-428.

CHAPTER 11
TEACHING SELF-HYPNOSIS

CATHERINE McCALL

Chapter Learning Objectives

1. Identify appropriate applications for self-hypnosis.

2. Identify self-hypnosis goals that will set the patient up for success.

3. Understand how to collaborate with the patient to design, implement, and revise an effective self-hypnosis practice.

Much of the field of hypnosis focuses on "hetero-hypnosis," that is, the clinical practice of hypnotic therapy that is guided by a therapist. As you may have seen in preceding chapters, experiencing hypnosis under the direct guidance of a clinical hypnotist provides benefit to a myriad of symptoms and goals. However, there are many situations in which it would also be beneficial to experience hypnosis when the therapist cannot be present. This may include such experiences as childbirth, taking an exam, undergoing a medical procedure, giving a speech, or being confronted with a sugary snack while trying to manage weight gain. In these kinds of situations, it would be helpful for one to have the ability to engage in the hypnotic state without the immediate help of the therapist. This practice is known as self-hypnosis, or "auto-hypnosis," and can be effectively taught to patients. Self-hypnosis is simply an extension of hetero-hypnosis in which the patient learns how to initiate and deepen the trance state, utilize suggestions, and exit hypnosis on their own and when needed. This chapter will discuss how to introduce and teach patients to do self-hypnosis, noting techniques that may facilitate specific types of hypnosis, as well as tools to allow patients to quickly enter and exit hypnotic trance as appropriate for the situation.

WHAT IS SELF-HYPNOSIS?

Many patients and therapists consider the practice of clinical hypnosis to be the experience of the patient receiving hypnotic instructions and suggestions from the therapist. This tends to support the notion that hypnosis requires a guide to administer the therapy. However, it is very likely that the hypnotic state is a very natural state of mind and may be experienced by most, if not all people. If you have ever driven somewhere and then realized you had no recollection of the drive, you may have been in a hypnotic state (giving rise to the aptly named term "highway hypnosis"). Likewise, the experiences of daydreaming, as well as highly focused states of working on projects, performing music, or otherwise "being in the zone" of an activity may be considered hypnotic experiences. Even the placebo effect and nocebo effect with medications may be natural extensions of self-suggestions that a treatment will work, or cause side effects, that are separate from the actual effects of the treatment itself (Raz, 2007). Thus, many of us likely already employ self-hypnosis without realizing it.

Some clinicians have also considered whether pathological forms of self-hypnosis may develop, such as "negative self-talk" and other ways in which individuals may provide themselves (usually unintentionally) with suggestions that they are not worthy, or where they blame for bad people, bad outcomes, etc.—often with an unrealistically negative appraisal of themselves and events. Negative self-suggestions may impair performance and create self-fulfilling prophesies in the same way that positive self-suggestions promote better outcomes (Brooks, 2014). Self-hypnosis may thus be a skill that we already employ—for better or for worse—and intentional practice in this realm may simply be a way to harness this natural state of mind for growth and positive change.

Benefits of Self-Hypnosis

There are a variety of reasons to consider teaching patients how to experience self-hypnosis. While hetero-hypnosis may be scripted in such a way to provide benefit in future situations, as in using post-hypnotic suggestions or altering one's mindset about a particular problem, self-hypnosis can be used in the moment when it is needed. Self-hypnosis has been found to be effective for a variety of applications (Eason & Parris, 2018). Self-hypnosis for pain reduction is one example that has been studied extensively in those suffering from chronic pain, acute pain such as during medical procedures, and in childbirth (Elkins et al., 2007; Griffiths, 2014; Grover et al., 2021; Madden et al., 2016; Tan et al., 2015). Self-hypnosis has also been studied for the treatment of anxiety disorders, anxiety related to stressful experiences, and somatic symptoms associated with anxiety (Hammond, 2010). It may be used effectively for other ongoing challenges such as resisting cravings, making healthy lifestyle changes, and obesity management (Bo et al., 2018; Hasan et al., 2014; Pellegrini et al., 2021).

Some types of hypnosis may only be feasible to practice as self-hypnosis, such as those for initiating sleep (Chamine et al., 2018; Otte et al., 2020). Athletes, musicians, and other performers may use self-hypnosis to enter "the zone" of optimal performance during an event, which is unlikely to be conducted during a therapy session (Mattle et al., 2020; Robazza & Bortoli, 1995; Unestahl, 2018). Patients can be taught to utilize techniques to rapidly enter and exit trance for these activities.

Beyond these practical considerations, self-hypnosis can be a powerful tool to expand the effects of hetero-hypnosis by allowing practice outside the therapy session. Practicing between sessions may enable greater progress to be made in a shorter period of time than with traditional hetero-hypnosis alone. Patients can learn to develop a toolbox of hypnotic language and imagery that work best for them, enhancing their engagement and results. Ultimately, learning self-hypnosis provides a means for the patient to gain autonomy, a sense of control, empowerment, and self-efficacy. Some types of patients may even respond better to self-hypnosis than hetero-hypnosis due to having a greater sense of control and trust with self-initiated suggestions (Moss & Magaro, 1989).

Research has also shown that self-hypnosis may have side benefits on objective measures of physiology. Several studies have investigated immune response to self-hypnosis. In one of these studies, college students who practiced self-hypnosis during stressful exam weeks showed a stronger immune response than those who did not learn self-hypnosis (Kiecolt-Glaser et al., 2001). Children who practiced self-hypnosis demonstrated lower rates of respiratory infections, fewer days of illness after contracting infection, and altered cellular and humoral immune responses (Hewson-Bower & Drummond, 2001; Olness et al., 1989). A stress reduction program in self-hypnosis found reduced inflammatory cytokine levels in addition to decreased coping to negative appraisal as well as improved nutritional habits (Schoen & Nowack, 2013). It may be that self-hypnosis exerts its positive impact on immunity by reducing the stress response. This shows that self-hypnosis may be beneficial not only for psychological purposes, but also for physiological sequelae.

WHEN TO CONSIDER TEACHING SELF-HYPNOSIS

Before teaching self-hypnosis to a patient, the following questions should be considered: What are the circumstances in which this individual will be using hypnosis? Has the patient experienced hypnosis before, and found it helpful? Are they familiar with what hypnotic trance feels like? Do they have the time, space, and motivation to practice hypnosis on their own?

Consideration of self-hypnosis may arise naturally in some clinical situations. The patient may come to a therapist specifically with a request to use hypnosis to experience childbirth without anesthesia, or tolerate the anxiety of undergoing medical testing, or become less anxious and more effective as a public speaker. In these situations, self-hypnosis may be a reasonable modality for treatment. In other situations, you may wish to consider teaching self-hypnosis as an extension of hetero-hypnosis to increase its effectiveness; for example, in a patient who wants to quit smoking or adopt healthier eating habits, and finds it difficult to overcome daily cravings.

It is helpful for patients considering self-hypnosis to first have some experience and comfort with clinical hetero-hypnosis. Having familiarity with hypnosis ensures they will be able to recognize what it feels like to be in a trance state. Prior experience also ensures that they will have enough trust in the process and outcome to feel safe and confident practicing it on their own.

When preparing to teach self-hypnosis to a patient, one bridging technique to consider is to record your hetero-hypnosis sessions with the patient and ask them to listen to the recording at home. This establishes a routine that provides continuity of treatment between sessions and offers the opportunity for the patient to experience the trance state in other environments. As the patient becomes familiar with how it feels to be in a hypnotic state in a different environment, they can then begin the transition to self-initiated practice. The principles discussed in the next session can be used when providing guidance for listening to recordings, prior to starting self-guided practice.

PREPARING FOR SELF-HYPNOSIS PRACTICE

As with hetero-hypnosis, there should be a designated space and time for self-hypnosis. Ideally, self-hypnosis should be practiced in a safe, quiet environment in which the patient will not be disturbed. The patient should be encouraged to wear comfortable clothing and be in a pleasant space. Phones and other electronic devices should be put away or turned off to reduce distractions. For some highly hypnotizable patients, it may be helpful for peace of mind to ask a trusted person to be there to ensure the patient is not disturbed, and that the patient returns to their normal baseline state after the self-hypnosis session.

For some types of self-hypnosis, the desired arena of the practice is specific to the goal of therapy. For example, if a patient will use self-hypnosis to relax before falling asleep, the ideal practice environment may be lying down. For an athlete preparing for a gymnastics routine, the optimal environment may be in a gymnasium. The setting should thus be customized to the goals of therapy. As the patient builds skills in self-hypnosis, he or she can start to feel more comfortable using it in a variety of other environments.

It is recommended that the patient set aside 20 to 30 minutes to practice every day, in order to build the habit. Over time, they can start to gain results from hypnosis in shorter periods of time as they learn to more efficiently enter and exit a hypnotic state. The timing of practice should also be customized for the goals of the treatment; for example, a patient wishing to feel more control over meal quantities consumed may practice several minutes of self-hypnosis before each meal. A patient wishing to relax and fall asleep more quickly may practice at bedtime. Longer sessions may be intermixed with shorter sessions to reinforce the practice, depending on the complexity and time frame for the patient's goals.

As noted earlier, self-hypnosis may start with simply listening to the session recording and allowing oneself to experience the steps of hypnosis under the therapist's guidance as they did in the session. Over time, the patient can use this practice to identify that they are in a state of trance while in different environments, and gain comfort with each step in the process. Once they are comfortable and confident in their ability to successfully experience hypnosis from pre-recorded sessions, it is time to begin the self-hypnosis training.

Steps of Teaching Self-Hypnosis

While self-hypnosis is often considered a separate set of skills and tools, a large part of training is simply educating the patient about the explicit steps of hypnosis so that they can reproduce each step themselves. The essential framework is as follows: First, establish specific, realistic goals for self-hypnosis. Then teach the patient about the explicit steps of hypnosis that they have already been experiencing. This includes the induction, intensification, suggestions, and reorienting. You and the patient can adapt these steps to the specific goals of hypnosis. As you collaborate on the script, techniques allowing more rapid hypnotic induction can be introduced, as well as post-hypnotic suggestions to consolidate and prolong positive effects of self-hypnosis. Once you and the patient have practiced the self-hypnosis session together, the patient can then practice going through each step on their own, with the therapist acting only as a coach. This session, as with prior sessions, may be recorded and the patient may then keep this for practice or as a reference. At subsequent sessions, the patient can provide feedback on how the practice went and collaborate on necessary revisions to the script. See Table 11-1 for a summary of these steps. The following sections will provide detail on each component of this process.

GOALS OF SELF-HYPNOSIS

As with any hypnosis therapy, when constructing the suggestions to use for self-hypnosis, it can be helpful to explicitly verbalize the goals of the practice. Try to establish goals that are positive, that will nurture the patient and allow them to grow and succeed in their goals. Positive goals then lead to effective suggestions. For a patient who has a big presentation coming up, the patient might state, "I would like to be less anxious while giving my presentation." A more positive way to state the true goal might be, "I would like to give a dynamic, engaging talk," or even, "I would like to feel comfortable giving presentations." The appraisal of the situation then becomes not to avoid or dampen a negative feeling, but to increase and expand a positive one. For a patient who is anxious about childbirth, the goal might be, "I would like to be fully present to experience the birth of my child and not be focused on the pain" rather than, "I would like to feel no pain." For the patient who wishes to lose weight, encourage statements that emphasize feelings of self-confidence, positive self-esteem, and healthy lifestyle changes rather than statements that may perpetuate low self-worth. For the athlete who wishes to enhance athletic performance, the optimal goal may be, "I want to perform at the top of my ability" for a specific event, rather than, "I want to win the competition." In many cases, this process involves identifying the underlying values and emotions that are desired, and tailoring the goal to them.

It can also be helpful to define goals that are specific to changing behaviors and feelings rather than global traits. The more specific the goal can be, the more easily it may be accomplished. For example, the musician wishing to become a more confident performer may want to think about what it would feel like, how they would act, and what they would do as a confident performer. The goal may then evolve to, "I would like to be as confident in performance as I am in practice, and enjoy sharing my music with others." This provides a springboard for generating the suggestions and imagery to be used in the self-hypnosis practice itself. Large goals may be broken into smaller, more immediate goals that are realistic. When these smaller goals are accomplished with self-hypnosis, this helps build confidence and validates the benefits of this treatment.

EDUCATION REGARDING HYPNOSIS EXPERIENCE

Although individuals who have experienced hypnosis may have familiarity with the overall process, many are not aware that there are explicit steps to entering, deepening, experiencing suggestions, and reorienting from the hypnotic state. You may wish to describe these steps in terms of the specific hypnotic language you have already used with the patient. You may note that over time, the patient may have required less time or have responded to verbal shortcuts or cues to enter a state of suggestibility, because he or she is already familiar with what it feels like to be in hypnosis. This step of educating the patient also serves to "demystify" the process and allows her or him to better understand how to creatively employ these tactics independently. As you are collaborating on the self-hypnosis script, you may wish to perform a simple demonstration with the patient of each step including a brief induction, intensification, some simple suggestions, and then reorienting. The patient can then try it on their own, with you present to prompt them as needed.

Brainstorming suggestions

Hypnotic suggestions are the core of any hypnotic practice. For self-hypnosis, this is an opportunity for patients to collaborate and develop skills of creating suggestions that will work for them. Suggestions can be constructed ahead of the actual hypnosis session to reduce the amount of conscious verbal thought and planning occurring during trance, allowing it to flow more easily in an unconstrained way. When coming up with suggestions, the patient may even record them to play back during hypnosis. Statements may be constructed in the first person ("I/me") or second person ("you") as desired by the patient.

Suggestions can be simple statements that follow naturally from the goals of practice. For example: "I am a confident speaker. I feel excited to speak in front of people" or "I feel comfortable and calm at the dentist's office." Again, positive, affirming statements should be encouraged rather than negative ones. Imagery can also be considered; for example, visualizing oneself having an enjoyable time giving a speech, or excelling at one's sport.

As with goal-setting, suggestions that are specific, positive, and realistic have the best chance of success. Suggestions that the patient will immediately feel no pain, or will defeat their sport opponent, or will fall asleep immediately at bedtime, convey the expectation that hypnosis will perform like a magical command. Unrealistic suggestions also bypass the true goals of the patient to self-actualize how they want to change. Instead, create suggestions that are attuned to how one wants to feel and how one might leverage one's innate strengths and talents. Consider a suggestion to feel warmth, tingling or buzzing sensations instead of pain, or to feel as though time is slowing down when facing a sport opponent, or to feel relaxed and peaceful when one's head touches the pillow. The latter series of suggestions targets the feelings and actions needed to achieve the patient's goals.

As the patient practices with the suggestions, she or he may find that they need to be revised; the goal should be for the patient to develop a sense of what language and imagery might work best for them over time. We will describe additional techniques for suggestions in future sections that may be considered for facilitating specific goals in self-hypnosis.

PRACTICING SELF-HYPNOTIC INDUCTIONS

The induction for a self-hypnosis session should be customized for the situation in which the patient will be experiencing it. One choice is to use a routine relaxation induction. As the patient gains familiarity with hypnosis, the induction can be abbreviated. If the patient feels comfortable with entering and exiting hypnosis, a formal induction can even be replaced by a cue. This will allow the patient to proceed more directly to the hypnotic suggestions. For example: "Take a deep, refreshing breath and then let it go." During trance, you can also provide post-hypnotic suggestions that performing this cue later will enable the patient to quickly and easily enter a hypnotic state.

Inductions for performance hypnosis may, instead of a relaxation induction, use an "awake-alert" induction. An awake-alert induction facilitates a state of readiness and focus for the performative state—athletic competitions, artistic performances, exams, or other activities that require a high level of activity and focus. Awake-alert inductions are often performed with the eyes open, instead of closed, to facilitate greater connection with the task they will be performing. They may also differ from relaxation inductions by emphasizing alertness, physical and/or mental readiness, awareness of the outside environment, and "flow" rather than relaxation and an inward gaze. In this sense, "flow" may be conceptualized as the experience of time passing more slowly, events occurring automatically, a sense of one's body moving easily and effortlessly in response to triggers, and dissociation (Unestahl, 2018). The awake-alert induction may thus be worded to increase energy, strength, and attention to specific actions related to the task.

DEEPENING THE HYPNOTIC STATE

Similarly to hetero-hypnosis, it is helpful to deepen the hypnotic state during self-hypnosis. Optimally, allow 10-20 minutes for this intensification before proceeding to giving suggestions. Deepening the trance state may be accomplished in a number of ways. Some individuals prefer imagining that they are descending a staircase, elevator, or escalator, along with counting the number of steps or floors. With each step or floor, the patient feels themselves going more deeply into a relaxed, focused state. Once they reach the bottom stair or floor, they are deeply calm, relaxed, and focused.

Body-focused imagery and actions are another way to deepen the hypnotic state. This may include breathing slowly and deeply. The patient may be encouraged to first gain awareness of their breathing, starting with the temperature of air entering and leaving the nose, and progressing to the sensation of the rib cage expanding and contracting, and then to the belly rising and falling with the diaphragm. They may be coached to notice relaxation and calmness entering their body with every inhalation, and tension leaving their body with every exhalation. With every breath, they are more deeply calm and relaxed.

Bodily inductions may also include progressive muscle relaxation, in which each major muscle group in the body is tensed and then released, starting with the head and ending with the toes. Each time one releases a muscle contraction, one might say a word facilitating the deepening, for example, "relax." Still other body techniques include focusing on imagining one's feet being grounded to the earth and/or becoming spiritually connected to a higher power.

Others may prefer to use imagery that they are in a real or fictional place that evokes feelings of peace and relaxation. They may imagine that place with all five senses: sight (including colors, shapes, light, the movement of clouds or water, and the presence or absence of other beings), sound, touch (textures, temperature, and sensations of the air, objects, and body position), smell, and taste. Any repetitive cue within the imagery may be used to deepen the hypnotic state; for example, "each time a wave rolls onto the beach, I become more and more relaxed and focused." The more vivid the detail that can be brought forth, the more effective imagery can be to deepen a hypnotic state both during the training session and when the patient is practicing on their own.

It is worth noting that patients may encounter distracting thoughts and feelings during this step, both in the training session and on their own. This may potentially be more distracting when they are practicing in another environment outside of their session with the therapist. Patients may worry about whether the self-hypnosis will work or whether they have time for it, in addition to the numerous thoughts and feelings about the past, present, and future that may clamor for attention in their minds. Strategies for dealing with this may be incorporated into the hypnotic deepening. For example, if imagining a nature scene, they may consider unwanted thoughts or distractions to be leaves falling into their awareness but then blowing or floating away. Likewise, distracting noises in the background can also be incorporated into the hypnotic intensification. For example, the noise of a fan may be imagined as wind through trees or waves on a beach. Background noises may also be used as cues for deepening; for example, the sounds made by traffic going by on the street outside.

The patient in that scenario may tell themselves, "With every passing car, I go deeper and deeper into trance."

It is also important to mention that the experience of self-hypnosis may be different for everyone, and patients may have assumptions about hypnosis from pop culture that are unrealistic. A patient may worry that if they do not feel subjectively as though they are in a trance, that the practice is not effective. It can be helpful to encourage them to allow the process to unfold as it will and trust their inner process and imagination. They may be surprised to experience results even if they do not feel the way they expect. For some patients, you may even wish to identify the experience of self-hypnosis as a daily practice of focused attentiveness, mental imagery, and relaxation.

APPLYING SUGGESTIONS

Once the patient is in the hypnotic state, it is time to focus on the personal suggestions the patient prepared. This can be elaborated on or revised during the session. You may suggest that the patient focus on each statement, visualize it in their mind's eye, and repeat it in their thoughts during the session. They may instead say suggestions aloud or even listen to a recording of their own voice saying suggestions. This is also a good time to expand sensory detail and emotions associated with images, so the patient can easily reproduce them later. Consider using repetition of suggestions with slightly varied language. You may wish to try multiple images to see what is most powerful. Additional techniques can be used as described in the following sections.

Using Symbolic Imagery

There are many ways to harness our natural ability to imagine the world and ourselves. Symbolic imagery is often used during hypnosis to create a conceptual picture of a situation, and then manipulate it.

One application of this technique is to control pain or other sensations in the body. For example, a patient experiencing pain may visualize their entire body as a set of TV monitors, each showing a different body part. The patient may then visualize that each TV monitor has volume dials; and turning down the volume for the body part that is in pain will turn down the pain itself. Another example of imagery used for pain involves using "glove anesthesia," in which an imaginary lead glove is placed over the patient's hand that transfers numbness to any part of the body that it touches. Any part of the body touched by the glove is suggested to tingle or feel cool, then rapidly become numb. Yet another tool for pain might be to visualize the entire body as a glowing figure, with the painful parts becoming dark or even absent.

Symbolic imagery may also be used for other physiologic processes, such as sleep. Participants in one study were asked to imagine a fish swimming deeper and deeper into the water while in a hypnotic state, in addition to hearing suggestions that included words such as "deep," "relax," and "let go." Those who experienced this imagery experienced deeper sleep, as measured by polysomnography, than those who imagined they were on a ship floating on the surface of the sea (Cordi et al., 2014).

Symbolic imagery may also be used to change emotional reactions. For example, one may reduce the size or threatening nature of a feared object by making it smaller, further away, indistinct, or even cartoonish. It may be used to enhance positive emotions by imagining one's bodies being infused with light, gaining energy or power. We can imagine our hearts filling with warmth to increase compassion. We can imagine ourselves being able to fly or having superpowers. These kinds of images can have powerful and positive impact on the way we view ourselves and others. The imagery in self-hypnosis should optimally be generated by the patient, with the therapist helping guide the imagery towards positive change.

Modifying Appraisal

The way that we assess ourselves, others, and situations is a very powerful tool for change. People sometimes adopt patterns of appraisal that are unintentionally negative and harmful. The critical thoughts people may have about themselves, the past, and the future are colored by prior experiences, relationships, and societal beliefs. It is important to understand that these appraisals are often subjective and inaccurate. Hypnotic suggestions can be used to reappraise situations in a way that increases empowerment, confidence, compassion, and empathy. The patient may benefit from a reappraisal of themselves, others, and/or bodily sensations.

An example of self-reappraisal may be someone who feels unable to control their eating with accompanying poor body image and low self-esteem. This patient may present with the stated desire to lose weight, but their true goal may be to feel healthier and more in control of their eating habits. In self-hypnosis, this patient may then wish to visualize themselves as stronger, more determined, fit, and dynamic, with the ability to meet challenges with confidence. They should focus on the feelings they would have in this desired state, the strength and energy they feel, and their ability to overcome cravings. One published study on self-hypnosis for weight loss used these reappraisal techniques in addition to imagery related to being able to face difficulties (for example, climbing a mountain; Bo et al., 2018).

Reappraisal of others may be approached similarly. For example, when focusing on the intentions of the clinical providers during a medical procedure, one's unconscious negative appraisal may be focused on whether the providers will hurt them. The immediate potential threat of short-term pain may cloud the understanding that the procedure is ultimately being performed with intent to help them. The patient may choose to consciously reappraise the situation as one in which they are being cared for by dedicated, well-trained clinicians whose highest priority is to help the patient feel comfortable and improve their health. Imagining being surrounded by love and nurturing attention is a way to promote a more positive appraisal of the clinical environment.

Appraisal of bodily sensations is yet another tool that is very powerful. One study found that simply stating, "I am excited" prior to anxiety-provoking tasks of public speaking, singing, and math problems led to better subjective and objective performance than stating, "I am anxious" or even, "I am calm" (Brooks, 2014). Of note, participants were not explicitly in a hypnotic state when making these statements. The author speculated that simply reappraising anxiety as excitement was more successful than reappraising it as relaxation because anxiety and excitement are "arousal-congruent," that is, they are similar in their bodily experience.

A similar reappraisal technique may be used to transform the experience of pain into a more pleasant experience. For example, participants in a hypnosis study using a cold presser task in which they immersed their hand in very cold water imagined doing this task in their favorite place, in which a context was provided for feeling cold while being relaxed (such as putting their hand into a cool stream). Suggestions for comfort, strength, and confidence were linked to this imagery. Pain intensity and perceived unpleasantness were significantly reduced, as well as the participants' appraisal of how threatening the experience was (Grover et al., 2021).

The key to successful reappraisal is to generate suggestions of an experience that is similar, but more positive, than the negative experience. The positive and negative experiences may be considered "congruent" if they are similar enough to each other. This was demonstrated in the aforementioned examples of reimagining anxiety as excitement, of reimagining cold-induced pain as a refreshing dip in a cool stream, and of reimagining the sterile environment of a medical clinic as a place of healing.

Age regression

In some cases, it may be helpful to return the patient's focus to a time in their past when they felt the way they wish to feel through their hypnotic practice. For example, if the patient is hoping to resist a craving, their attention may focus on a time when they felt satiated, comfortable, and content. They may wish to remember the way that felt in their bodies and emotions. This feeling can be brought back with them to the present time and help them to feel comfortable and content without the object of their cravings. Another example might be, for a patient who would like to optimize their golf performance, to remember a time when they were "in the zone." How did that feel? What kind of mental and physical sensations did they experience in that moment? They can then bring forth that same attention and mental state at will by reproducing the memory in hypnosis.

Age progression

As with age regression, age progression involves moving through time, in this case to the future. Age progression is the act of imagining oneself in a future time during or after having carried out the hypnotic suggestions. This can be a mental rehearsal of the suggestions, or the positive outcome. How do they feel and act? How have their life and/or relationships changed? For example, if the patient wishes to be a more confident public speaker, they may imagine themselves giving a speech that goes well. They may imagine how they speak, inflect, gesture, how they stand or sit, and how they interact with the audience. The patient, while imagining themselves in the future, may also be able to "look back" in time to the choices that were made and the work that was done to get to that point.

Inner advisors

This technique leverages one's innate wisdom during self-hypnosis. While in the trance state, the patient imagines that they are seeking advice from an advisor or panel of advisors. These may be people they know, respect, and trust, or people they have never met but whose wisdom or knowledge they admire. The patient may then imagine sitting together around a table with these advisors, whose job is to help provide counsel to the patient. These advisors can help contemplate decisions, coach one through a challenging task or relationship, or even imbue their most desirable qualities to the patient. Counsel may be in the form of advice, asking important questions or even assigning tasks. Each advisor is, of course, a part of the individual who is in hypnosis, and a manifestation of their inner wisdom. This technique lends itself well to self-hypnosis as it can be performed whenever guidance is needed. As with any practice, the more the patient develops the relationships with these inner advisors, the more useful their counsel will be.

POST-HYPNOTIC SUGGESTIONS

Post-hypnotic suggestions are suggestions made during the hypnosis session for something to occur after one has left the hypnotic state. They can be introduced during the initial training sessions, and practiced during self-hypnosis, to provide continuity of effect and increase confidence in the patient's ability to do self-hypnosis. Post-hypnotic suggestions can be tailored to the content of the self-hypnosis, to help the patient more easily enter hypnosis, and/or to increase the effectiveness of self-hypnosis.

One example of using post-hypnotic suggestions to augment the effectiveness of self-hypnosis might be: "The more you use your deep breathing cue to enter a hypnotic state without the recording, the more effective and long-lasting the suggestions will be." Another example might be: "Entering a relaxed and focused state using your breathing cue will get easier and easier with practice, and you can do this any time you wish to experience this feeling of being relaxed and focused."

Post-hypnotic suggestions can also be linked to a situation when one may benefit from experiencing hypnotic suggestions later on; for example, when offered a cigarette, when feeling anxious before an exam, or when feeling overwhelmed by a to-do list. The post-hypnotic suggestion is often phrased in terms of the situation or trigger that will be encountered, such as: "When I feel [negative feeling], I will [perform an action] and will feel [desired feeling]."

An example of this is the concept of an anchor. An anchor is any stimulus that acts as a reminder of how to quickly and easily return to the hypnotic state, such as a clenched fist, or touching one's index finger to one's thumb (Basker, 1979; Stanton, 1997; Stein, 2011). When the patient is in the trance state, they are first advised to become aware of the positive feelings they are experiencing. They are then instructed to perform the anchor. Then the suggestion is made that whenever they wish to feel exactly as they are feeling now, all they have to do is perform this maneuver and anchor their mind to this experience. For example, "From now on, whenever you feel anxious, all you need to do is clench your fist and anchor your mind to this experience." Additional post-hypnotic suggestions may be made that with practice, the patient will become better and better at using their anchor. An effective anchor can thus facilitate immediate results when needed.

Post-hypnotic suggestions may also be suggested to occur with a trigger that is not explicitly defined in the session. This type of post-hypnotic suggestion implies that the patient may not know exactly when they will use the suggestion, but they will remember and be able to apply it when needed. For example: *This experience of relaxation and comfort will stay with you beyond this session, and will easily return to you when you when you need it."*

Reorienting

As with hetero-hypnosis, once the patient has completed their suggestions while under trance, they will reorient themselves to the current place and time. While doing so, they may wish to return to the imagery or method of deepening, for example the calm and peaceful place they imagined, or the staircase they descended to enter the hypnotic state. If counting was used to deepen the trance, counting in the opposite direction may be used to exit trance. With each step or floor, the patient tells themself to become more awake and alert, perhaps with suggestions to feel refreshed and energized from the experience.

PRACTICE AND REVISION

Once the self-hypnosis script has been developed and practiced during the training session, the patient should then practice it themselves, with the therapist acting only as a coach. The therapist can provide cues or prompts as needed. The session may be recorded for the patient to reference during practice after the session.

At subsequent sessions, the patient can then provide feedback regarding how the practice went. Revision of the script can occur as needed to address any challenges or obstacles reported by the patient. As with the original script, collaboration should be encouraged. The patient will then start to develop a sense for the language and/or imagery that works best for her or him, as well as a sense of when self-hypnosis is effective.

CONCLUSION

Self-hypnosis is a powerful tool that allows us to harness our own skills, creativity, and autonomy for healing and growth. While patients may enter and utilize hypnosis effectively under the guidance of a therapist, many presenting problems will benefit from self-hypnosis practice. This includes experiences when the patient will not have their therapist present, including but not limited to experiences of chronic pain, childbirth, sleep, performances, athletic events, exams, and cravings. In these situations, the patient will benefit from being able to enter a hypnotic state, give themselves suggestions, and reorient themselves without needing to have another person present. Self-hypnosis is likely a state of mind we already utilize unconsciously, for example when daydreaming or performing tasks on "auto-pilot." Many individuals may use it unintentionally to criticize themselves or engage in unhelpful distortions of situations they are in. Self-hypnosis allows the individual to develop and use this skill intentionally for positive change.

Training a patient to do self-hypnosis should occur after the patient has developed some familiarity and comfort with clinical hetero-hypnosis and is ready to extend their practice towards greater autonomy. A helpful transitional practice is to record hetero-hypnosis sessions so the patient can listen to them at home. During this time, you may also teach them the explicit steps of hypnosis and develop a routine that they can comfortably remember and practice at home. Suggestions for self-hypnosis may use language, imagery, reappraisal, age regression or progression, and seeking inner advice. Collaboration with the patient will allow them to learn how to develop techniques and imagery that will work best for them, and provide skills for revising their practice. Ultimately, self-hypnosis allows our patients to take hypnosis out of the therapist's office and out into the world where it is most needed.

CHAPTER 11
REFLECTION QUESTIONS

1. Why is self-hypnosis a beneficial?

2. What is the process for clinicians on teaching self-hypnosis to the patients?

3. What are the methods on implementing successful self-hypnosis—from hypnotic induction, to deepening, to post-hypnotic suggestion?

TABLE 11-1: STEPS OF TEACHING HYPNOSIS

STEP	SUMMARY	CONSIDERATIONS
1	Determine whether self-hypnosis is the right treatment for the patient.	Consider teaching self-hypnosis for outside experiences during which being in a hypnotic state will be beneficial.
2	Ensure familiarity and comfort with hetero-hypnosis.	The patient should be familiar with the feeling of being in a hypnotic state, able to find time and a suitable environment for practice, and feel safe trying hypnosis on their own.
3	Prepare for self-hypnosis.	Encourage the patient to listen to hetero-hypnosis recordings on their own. They should find an appropriately quiet, pleasant, and undisturbed environment for daily practice.
4	Establish goals of treatment.	Be specific, positive, and realistic in the goals of treatment. Focus on feelings and personal attributes to change. Consider starting with more immediate goals and moving to longer term goals to build confidence.
5	Educate the patient about the steps of a hypnotic session.	Teach the patient the steps of induction, deepening, suggestions, and reorienting.
6	Brainstorm a script with the patient.	In collaboration with the patient, develop suggestions and imagery to try during trance. The patient begins to learn how to generate language and imagery that will be personally meaningful and effective.
7	Complete a self-hypnosis session (therapist leading the session).	Go through each step of the self-hypnosis session, further deepening and developing the suggestions and imagery. Consider including cues or anchors for quicker entry to a hypnotic state, and post-hypnotic suggestions to strengthen the effect.
8	Practice the self-hypnosis session (patient leading the session and therapist as coach).	Repeat the entire session, this time with the patient doing it on their own and the therapist acting only as a coach as needed.
9	Revisit the script.	At subsequent visits, the patient will report back on how their practice went. Together, the therapist and patient revise and add to the script needed.

REFERENCES

Basker, M. A. (1979). A hypnobehavioural method of treating agoraphobia by the clenched fist method of Calvert Stein. *Australian Journal of Clinical & Experimental Hypnosis*, *7*, 27-34. https://psycnet.apa.org/record/1980-32838-001

Bo, S., Rahimi, F., Goitre, I., Properzi, B., Ponzo, V., Regaldo, G., Boschetti, S., Fadda, M., Ciccone, G., Abbate Daga, G., Mengozzi, G., Evangelista, A., de Francesco, A., Belcastro, S., & Broglio, F. (2018). Effects of self-conditioning techniques (self-hypnosis) in promoting weight loss in patients with severe obesity: A randomized controlled trial. *Obesity (Silver Spring, Md.)*, *26*(9), 1422-1429. https://doi.org/10.1002/OBY.22262

Brooks, A. W. (2014). Get excited: reappraising pre-performance anxiety as excitement. *Journal of Experimental Psychology*, *143*(3), 1144-1158. https://doi.org/10.1037/A0035325

Chamine, I., Atchley, R., & Oken, B. S. (2018). Hypnosis intervention effects on sleep outcomes: A systematic review. *Journal of Clinical Sleep Medicine*, *14*(2), 271-283. https://doi.org/10.5664/jcsm.6952

Cordi, M. J., Schlarb, A. A., & Rasch, B. (2014). Deepening sleep by hypnotic suggestion. *Sleep*, *37*(6), 1143-1152. https://doi.org/10.5665/sleep.3778

Eason, A. D., & Parris, B. A. (2018). Clinical applications of self-hypnosis: A systematic review and meta-analysis of randomized controlled trials. *Psychology of Consciousness: Theory Research, and Practice*. *6*(3), 262-278. https://doi.org/10.1037/CNS0000173

Elkins, G., Jensen, M. P., & Patterson, D. R. (2007). Hypnotherapy for the management of chronic pain. *International Journal of Clinical and Experimental Hypnosis*, *55*(3), 275-287. https://doi.org/10.1080/00207140701338621

Griffiths, M. (2014). Hypnosis for dental anxiety. *Dental Update*, *41*(1), 78-83. https://doi.org/10.12968/denu.2014.41.1.78

Grover, M. P., Jensen, M. P., Ward, L. C., Ehde, D. M., Mattingley, J. B., Thorn, B. E., Ferreira-Valente, A., & Day, M. A. (2021). An experimental investigation of the effects and mechanisms of mindfulness meditation versus self-hypnosis versus an attention control on cold pressor outcomes. *Mindfulness*, *12*(4), 923-935. https://doi.org/10.1007/S12671-020-01556-7/TABLES/6

Hammond, D. C. (2010). Hypnosis in the treatment of anxiety- and stress-related disorders. *Expert Review of Neurotherapeutics, 10*(2), 263-273. https://doi.org/10.1586/ern.09.140

Hasan, F. M., Zagarins, S. E., Pischke, K. M., Saiyed, S., Bettencourt, A. M., Beal, L., Macys, D., Aurora, S., & McCleary, N. (2014). Hypnotherapy is more effective than nicotine replacement therapy for smoking cessation: results of a randomized controlled trial. *Complementary Therapies in Medicine, 22*(1), 1-8. https://doi.org/10.1016/J.CTIM.2013.12.012

Hewson-Bower, B., & Drummond, P. D. (2001). Psychological treatment for recurrent symptoms of colds and flu in children. *Journal of Psychosomatic Research, 51*(1), 369-377. https://doi.org/10.1016/S0022-3999(01)00212-4

Kiecolt-Glaser, J. K., Marucha, P. T., Atkinson, C., & Glaser, R. (2001). Hypnosis as a modulator of cellular immune dysregulation during acute stress. *Journal of Consulting and Clinical Psychology, 69*(4), 674-682. https://doi.org/10.1037//0022-006X.69.4.674

Madden, K., Middleton, P., Cyna, A. M., Matthewson, M., & Jones, L. (2016). Hypnosis for pain management during labour and childbirth. *Cochrane Database of Systematic Reviews, 2016*(5). https://doi.org/10.1002/14651858.CD009356.pub3

Mattle, S., Birrer, D., & Elfering, A. (2020). Feasibility of hypnosis on performance in air rifle shooting competition. *International Journal of Clinical and Experimental Hypnosis, 68*(4), 521-529. https://doi.org/10.1080/00207144.2020.1799655

Moss, B. F., & Magaro, P. A. (1989). Personality types and hetero- versus auto-hypnosis. *Journal of Personality and Social Psychology, 57*(3), 532-538. https://doi.org/10.1037/0022-3514.57.3.532

Olness, K., Culbert, T., & Uden, D. (1989). Self-regulation of salivary immunoglobulin A by children. *Pediatrics, 83*(1), 66-71. https://doi.org/10.1542/peds.83.1.66

Otte, J. L., Carpenter, J. S., Roberts, L., & Elkins, G. R. (2020). Self-Hypnosis for sleep disturbances in menopausal women. *Journal of Women's Health, 29*(3), 461-463. https://doi.org/10.1089/jwh.2020.8327

Pellegrini, M., Carletto, S., Scumaci, E., Ponzo, V., Ostacoli, L., & Bo, S. (2021). The use of self-help strategies in obesity treatment. A narrative review focused on

hypnosis and mindfulness. *Current Obesity Reports*, *10*(3), 351-364.
https://doi.org/10.1007/s13679-021-00443-z

Raz, A. (2007). Hypnobo: perspectives on hypnosis and placebo. *American Journal of Clinical Hypnosis*, *50*(1), 29-36.
https://doi.org/10.1080/00029157.2007.10401595

Robazza, C., & Bortoli, L. (1995). A case study of improved performance in archery using hypnosis. *Perceptual and Motor Skills*, *81*(3 Pt 2), 1364-1366.
https://doi.org/10.2466/PMS.1995.81.3F.1364

Schoen, M., & Nowack, K. (2013). Reconditioning the stress response with hypnosis CD reduces the inflammatory cytokine IL-6 and influences resilience: A pilot study. *Complementary Therapies in Clinical Practice*, *19*(2), 83-88.
https://doi.org/10.1016/J.CTCP.2012.12.004

Stanton, H. E. (1997). Adorning the clenched fist. *Contemporary Hypnosis*, *14*(3), 189-194. https://doi.org/10.1002/CH.101

Stein, C. (2011). The Clenched Fist Technique as a hypnotic procedure in clinical psychotherapy. *American Journal of Clinical Hypnosis*, *6*(2), 113-119.
https://doi.org/10.1080/00029157.1963.10402330

Tan, G., Rintala, D. H., Jensen, M. P., Fukui, T., Smith, D., & Williams, W. (2015). A randomized controlled trial of hypnosis compared with biofeedback for adults with chronic low back pain. *European Journal of Pain (London, England)*, *19*(2), 271-280. https://doi.org/10.1002/EJP.545

Unestahl, L. E. (2018). Alert, eyes-open sport hypnosis. *American Journal of Clinical Hypnosis*, *61*(2), 159-172. https://doi.org/10.1080/00029157.2018.1491387

CHAPTER 12
STRATEGIES FOR
MANAGING RESISTANCE

AKIRA OTANI

Chapter Learning Objectives

1. Identify four primary reasons that cause client resistance to occur in trance induction.

2. Understand the five strategies to manage client resistance in trance work effectively.

3. Discuss what role power struggle may play in strategies for managing resistance.

Resistance is a ubiquitous phenomenon that is defined in general as "an obstruction that interferes with the work of therapy, something that occurs within the patient and is an impediment to the treatment process" (Blatt & Erlich, 1982, p. 70). The concept has been examined extensively from various theoretical perspectives to elucidate its nature and methods to manage it (*e.g.*, Wachtel, 1982).

Although manifestations of client resistance vary, literature reveals that there are four primary causes: (1) anxiety, (2) confusion about therapeutic tasks, (3) power struggle, and (4) negative expectation and low motivation (Otani, 1989a; Ryland, Johnson, & Bernards, 2021). Uncertainty about therapy process, for example, indicates the first type of resistance, whereas ambiguous homework assignments may characterize the second. The third category of resistance presents itself as power struggle between the therapist and the client (e.g., "Why don't you ... ? — Yes, but ... ") (Berne, 1964). Finally, negative motivation for behavior change, *e.g.*, secondary gains, involuntary treatment, *etc.*, exemplifies the fourth type. Notwithstanding the differences in cause, resistance can hinder both therapeutic process and outcome in therapy. Hypnotherapy is not immune to this predicament.

In this chapter we will examine: (1) factors that trigger resistance in hypnotic work, and (2) effective strategies to manage commonly observed resistance in hypnosis. Each strategy will be illustrated with examples to familiarize the reader with the technique. It is hoped that this chapter will help the reader to better manage client resistance in hypnosis when he or she encounters it.

CAUSES AND FORMS OF RESISTANCE IN HYPNOSIS WORK

What is unique about resistance in hypnotic practice is that *it can occur not only in the treatment phase but also during trance induction.* Although some clinicians attribute induction difficulty to low hypnotizability, studies indicate that this problem is reversible when it is handled properly (Gfeller et al., 1987; Spanos et al., 1987). It is therefore reasonable, and practical, to treat induction troubles as resistance.

The four general causes of client resistance discussed earlier, *i.e.,* anxiety, task confusion, power struggle, and negative expectation and low motivation, apply to trance induction and hypnotherapy as well. Before discussing management strategies, let us start with how each of the four factors affect hypnosis.

Anxiety

It is not uncommon for a client to harbor and sometimes openly express anxiety about being hypnotized. Three sources of anxiety are: (1) losing personal agency and control, (2) divulging secrets, and (3) getting "stuck" in trance (Haley, 1960). Simply put, the client fears becoming "a helpless automaton under the hypnotist's control." Popular Hollywood films and stage hypnosis shows have long exploited the image of a "Svengali-like hypnotist," i.e., a ruthless "villain" who manipulates innocent victims into performing silly, if not antisocial acts "under his or her spell" (Barrett, 2010; Katchen, 1992). The grossly misleading portrayal of the hypnotist has made the public misconceive hypnosis as a form of "mind control" or "brainwashing."

Take, for example, a highly successful film *The Manchurian Candidate* (both the original 1962 version and the 2004 remake). The movies depict a sniper who was hypnotically "programmed" to assassinate a presidential candidate by the hypnotist's posthypnotic cue. A recent Google search has returned 6,720,000 hits under "stage hypnosis videos" (as of 12/02/2021). Most subjects in these internet clips, like in big budget Hollywood movies, are depicted engaging in ridiculous acts (e.g., inability to stand up, pretending to be a famous entertainer, etc.), seemingly without conscious awareness, according to the hypnotist's suggestions. No wonder many clients *misbelieve* that they may end up under the hypnotist control. This anxiety provokes resistance.

The anxiety over divulging secrets is an extension of the hypnotist's "unyielding power" over the client. This issue however has yet an added implication. That is, some clients worry about *spontaneous discovery* of unknown information, e.g., childhood sexual abuse, while in trance. This fear, too, is rooted in the media portrayal of subjects retrieving forgotten memories, such as crime scenes, alien abduction experiences, *etc.*

Research shows that hypnosis can increase production (i.e., hypermnesia), but *not* accuracy, of memory recall. To make the matter more complicated, *the subject's confidence in the accuracy of the retrieved memory heightens* (Erdelyi, 1994; Register & Kihlstrom, 1987). The combination of increased recall and heightened conviction in the recovered memory is a serious issue, both clinically and forensically, and must be dealt with caution to avoid false memory issues.

The third anxiety is being trapped in trance as a helpless "automaton." Aside from re-alerting difficulty, re-alerting *failure* is relatively rare (MacHovec, 1988; Sakata, 1968). Nevertheless, the therapist must make sure of complete and full re-alerting of the client at the end of each session (Kluft, 2012).

Task Confusion

Aside from anxiety, client resistance may emanate from ambiguous, incomplete, or poorly phrased suggestions. They confuse the client. For example, look at the following suggestions designed for eye closure.

> *Your eyelids are heavy, very heavy … they are tired … it is*
> *very difficult to keep the eyes open. Your eyes are very tired.*
> *You cannot keep them open.*

The directives state the heaviness of the eye lids, fatigue in the eyes, difficulty to keep the eyes open; yet they fail to suggest the actual eye closure (*i.e.,* "*The eyes may close any time!*"). Without such explicit direct suggestion, some clients, especially those with high hypnotizability, may not close the eyes because of heightened literal tendency. They are indeed responding to the suggestions by keeping their eyes open! Task confusion creates this behavior and, unfortunately, is interpreted as "resistance" by the therapist.

A more subtle form of task confusion occurs when suggestions contradict the client's observed behavior. It is *pacing failure*. A common example in this category is suggesting to "breath in (or out)" to the client while he or she is breathing out (or in). The mis-timed suggestion feels "out of sync" to the client and creates dissonance with the therapist. When repeated, it obstructs the hypnotic process.

The therapist needs to keep in mind that hypnosis, by definition, is a dialogue with the client. It is not a "monologue" like scripted muscle relaxation that expects the client to unilaterally follow the instructions.

In hypnosis, the therapist carefully observes the client's response to each suggestion and accommodates the subsequent suggestion. Otherwise, the therapist is inadvertently creating client resistance.

Power Struggle

All clinicians at times have experienced power struggles with the client, experiencing trouble securing the client's compliance and cooperation to achieve therapeutic goals. In clinical hypnosis, power struggles happen when the therapist expects the client to respond in the exact ways the suggestions are phrased. In the eye closure example, the therapist awaits the client's eyes closing. When they do not, suggestions are repeated until it (hopefully) happens. Some clients do eventually comply, but others respond to the pressure with psychological reactance. The eyes remain open. The therapist tries harder. This endless negative loop is the root cause of the power struggle.

Why does the interactional power struggle create resistance? An answer to this question is found in what is known as the *ironic process* of mental control in social psychology (Wegner, 1994, 1997). Often referred to as the "white bear problem," the concept refers to a mental process that produces an *opposite effect* of what one intentionally tries (or not) to do. Therefore, trying *not* to think of a white bear ironically makes one thinking of it *more*. Similarly, in the hypnotic eye closure example, the harder the therapist tries to make eye closure happen, the less likely it occurs. Again, this is not true for all clients but for some it is true. It is a case of "reverse psychology" and explains how the therapist-client power struggle leads to resistance (Rohrbaugh & Shoham, 2001).

Negative Expectation and Low Motivation

Finally, resistance to hypnosis can emerge when the client lacks interest in getting better or harbors skepticism about hypnosis. These predicaments are expressed as negative expectation and/or low motivation for being hypnotized (see Benham et al., 2006; Orne, 1966). The client who has potential secondary gain issues and someone who seeks therapy involuntarily (e.g., court ordered, partner requests, school mandates) are well-known cases. In addition, an individual who has certain religious values against hypnosis may exhibit similar negativity.

A unique perspective to account for minimum expectation and motivation is the *lack of readiness* for hypnotic work. According to the transtheoretical model by Prochaska and his colleagues (Prochaska & Norcross, 2001; Prochaska & Prochaska, 1999), the client who is in the *precontemplation stage* of therapy is oblivious to the need for change. As such, the individual regards no intervention, hypnosis or otherwise, is necessary. Lack of motivation and expectancy reflect this disposition. Regardless of the theoretical views, diminished expectation and motivation can seriously hinder hypnotic induction and therapy.

STRATEGIES TO MANAGE
CLIENT RESISTANCE IN HYPNOSIS

We have so far examined the plausible factors that cause resistance in hypnotic work. Let us now discuss specific approaches to manage it. They are five strategies: (1) pre-hypnotic psychoeducation, (2) acceptance, (3) paradoxical encouragement, (4) reframing, and (5) displacement (Otani, 1989b). In each category the reader will learn the theoretical rationale, followed by examples to become familiar with their applications.

Prehypnotic Psychoeducation

Because the image of hypnosis is tainted by many myths and misconceptions, the first step in managing client resistance is to educate the client about what is, and is *not*, hypnosis. Proper understanding about the nature, mechanism, process, and purpose of hypnosis through psychoeducation prior to hypnotic work will significantly lower the client's anxiety (Meyerson, 2014). Prehypnotic psychoeducation also provides a chance for the client to express any concerns about hypnosis, *e.g.*, induction methods, negative effects, *etc.* This process helps raise the client's motivation and strengthen the therapist-client rapport (Barber & Calverley, 1964).

A simple, effective prehypnotic psychoeducation format is the use of "True-False" questions. The **Hypnotic Quiz** (see Appendix 1) lists the typical misapprehensions and concerns surrounding hypnosis mentioned earlier. The items 1 to 4 of the list depict the misguided notions as to how the hypnotized person would behave in trance. The next items 5 through 8 describe the fear of being under the hypnotist's influence. Finally, the items 9 and 10 address mind control and accuracy of hypnotic hypermnesia, respectively. **All correct answers are false.**

In addition to the general myths and misconceptions of hypnosis, the therapist needs to discuss specific concerns relevant to the client, *e.g.*, comfort level using hypnosis, likely impact upon the client, the family, the work, lifestyle, and so forth. In case of possible secondary gains, they need to be addressed openly (see below for details).

The value of prehypnotic psychoeducation cannot be overemphasized in the management of resistance when hypnosis is utilized.

Acceptance

Acceptance is the second strategy to handle client resistance when it emerges in the hypnotic process. Milton Erickson investigated this topic extensively and concluded as follows:

> [Resistance] is part and parcel of [patients'] reason for seeking therapy ... [It] should be respected rather than regarded as an active and deliberate or even unconscious intention to oppose the therapist. Such *resistance should be openly accepted, in fact graciously accepted, since it is a*

vitally important communication of a part of their problems
and often can be used as an opening into their defenses
(Erickson, 1964, p. 8, emphasis added).

Note that Erickson's assertion stands in direct contrast to the traditional view that holds resistance as an "obstruction" or "impediment" to treatment (e.g., Blatt & Erlick, 1982). Instead, he encourages the therapist to *anticipate* and even *utilize* it to facilitate therapeutic process. This positive interpretation of resistance *per se* will likely diminish the client's resistance by facilitating a favorable dynamic in the therapist-client relationship.

Here is an example of acceptance at the beginning of the arm levitation trance induction:

As we begin our work, *you can listen to my voice and let the*
mind and body respond in any way they want. Sometimes
they follow my suggestions and sometimes they may not ...
at least immediately ... or at all. But *that doesn't matter.*
What matters is to *continue wondering what happens and*
be curious about it ... as if you are watching a movie in a
comfortable theater. And *you may notice one of the arms*
feeling a little lighter (Italics are suggestions).

In this illustration, the therapist encourages the client to simply observe the reactions ("*listen to my voice and let the mind and body respond in any way they want*") rather than adhering to specific suggestions. This direction permits the client to feel any response is acceptable ("*Sometimes they follow my suggestions and sometimes they may not*") and leaves little room for resistance. All the client needs to do is simply watch what happens ("*continue wondering what happens and be curious about it*") and this may start an arm movement ("*you may notice one of the arms feeling a little lighter*").

But what if nothing happens? How should the therapist show acceptance if the arm does not show any movement? In this situation, the therapist may say:

It appears neither arm wants to move right now. And *that is absolutely fine.* Your hands and arms know exactly what they want to do. It is their prerogative to move or not move. *Let them continue doing what they choose to do.* In the meantime, *you may keep wondering about what is going on in the mind* ... and *that helps you go deeper into trance* (Italics are suggestions).

The therapist reassures the client that the absence of any arm movement is perfectly acceptable (*"that is absolutely fine"*) because the responses are involuntary (*"Let them continue doing what they choose to do"*). The task of the client is simply to *"keep wondering about what else is going on in the mind"* and *"that helps you go deeper into trance."* The therapist skillfully circumvents resistance by accepting the lack of arm movement.

Acceptance of any response, as illustrated here, is a powerful intervention to bypass client resistance.

Paradoxical Encouragement

The client sometimes manifests resistance by doing opposite of the therapist's directives. It is a form of power struggle. For example, when levitation is suggested, the client's arm may begin *lowering* instead of rising. In a situation like this, *encouraging* the observed behavior to continue proves to be beneficial. Here is an example:

Oh, that is interesting! The arm wants to move down instead of moving up. *That is perfectly fine* (acceptance). *Let it continue moving lower* (paradoxical encouragement) ... and find out where it is going to go. It may be by your side or on the lap. Let the arm decide. Wherever it goes, the arm can *feel more comfortable* ... and *the comfort allows your trance to go deeper* (Italics are suggestions).

In this sequence, the therapist first accepts the client's counter-suggestive response (*"That is perfectly fine"*), then encourages it (*"Let it continue moving lower"*) and, finally, links it to comfort and trance deepening (*"more comfortable ... the comfort allows your trance to go deeper"*). The oppositional behavior is transformed by the paradoxical encouragement and is utilized to enact comfort and deepen trance.

When the therapist openly welcomes and even promotes the contradictory response to the suggestion, the client has little choice but to continue it. It is a *reverse* ironic process that enables "taking the client's (oppositional) wind out of the sail" and applies it to gain cooperation. Jay Haley (1963) explains it this way:

The resistant hypnotic subject ... is encouraged to resist the hypnotist's directions. If he does so, he is following the directions of the hypnotist who is thereby controlling his behavior (Haley, 1963, p. 103).

As he correctly argues, paradoxical encouragement is a way of counter-controlling the client and, in so doing, the therapist avoids power struggle. It is a hypnotic maneuvering of "if you can't beat them, join them."

Reframing

Reframing is a versatile technique that attempts to "change the conceptual and/or emotional setting or viewpoint in relation to which a situation is experienced ... and thereby changes its entire meaning" (Watzlawick et al., 1974, p. 95). It provides a new *context* that allows to view a familiar behavior, situation, or event in a different light. "Social awkwardness" may be reframed, for example, as "inter-personal cautiousness" to suggest a positive quality in social attitude instead of negative meaning. Change in perceived meaning facilitates behavior change.

Reframing suits well in hypnotic resistance management. Here is a real example. A volunteer at a hypnosis workshop was going through a smooth trance induction until he opened his eyes suddenly and said,

"Gee, I'm out of trance. What happened?" How would the reader handle this resistance? The therapist replied to the subject as follows:

> Whoa, you are right. *You jumped out of trance*, didn't you (acceptance). *This proves you are in charge of trance* (reframing). Now that you proved it, *go back comfortably into trance* again (Italics are suggestions).

In this vignette, the facilitator first accepted the volunteer subject's behavior ("*You jumped out of trance*") before swiftly reframing it as a proof of self-control ("*This proves you are in charge of trance*"). He then finally suggested to return to trance ("*go back comfortably into trance*"). As a result of this brief reframing, the man immediately resumed trance, even going deeper than before. The case demonstrates the power of well-timed reframing.

There are other ways to reframe the client's resistance. One strategy is to use the transtheoretical model by Prochaska *et al.* mentioned earlier (Prochaska & Norcross, 2001; Prochaska & Prochaska, 1999). Although the reader is referred to the original sources for details of the theory, it suffices to state that the client's low motivation may be reframed as a lack of readiness for hypnotic work. Here is an example.

> You don't seem to be interested in hypnosis (acceptance). I appreciate that you trust your sixth sense that *you're not ready for it yet. It is not the right time* (reframing). Maybe later but *definitely not now. Let's not push it until you feel ready for it* (paradoxical encouragement) (Italics are suggestions).

As Prochaska *et al.* notes, low motivation is a customary sign associated with the precontemplation stage of change. It is therefore accurate to equate decreased motivation with a lack of readiness ("*you're not ready for it yet. It is not the right time*") for the purpose of reframing. Paradoxical encouragement ("*definitely not now. Let's not push it until you feel ready for it*") is further added to intensify the reframing impact in this illustration.

Finally, client resistance may be reframed as *self-protection.* Ryland et al. (2021) have maintained recently from the polyvagal perspective that resistance is a "protective mechanism to achieve safety" and, as such, the therapist must be "honoring and validating [the client's] in-built [*sic*] protective mechanisms, rather than blaming [the client] for ... resistant behaviors" (Ryland et al., 2021, p. 3). This novel perspective is fully applicable to hypnosis work. Imagine the client who doubts being hypnotizable. In a situation like this, the therapist may start an induction by saying:

> *So, you don't believe you can be hypnotized* (acceptance).
> *That may or may not be true, I don't know.* However, what
> is most important in hypnosis is *your sense of safety. When
> you can't feel safe, the unconscious mind tries to protect
> yourself from going into trance* (reframing). That's very
> reasonable. *My job is to create the sense of safety for you
> and make sure you feel it.* Now can you tell me what will
> help you most? (Italics are suggestions).

The initial two remarks are indirect suggestions to imply the "unhypnotizable" claim is no more than the client's belief (*"You don't believe you can be hypnotized"*) and that the therapist does not necessarily agree with it (*"That may or may not be true, I don't know"*).

Following these suggestions, the therapist emphasizes the client's *"sense of safety"* as the "most important" factor in hypnosis. It is the fear that causes difficulty in trance induction (*"When you can't feel safe, the unconscious mind tries to protect yourself from going into trance"*). This is the first reframing. It shifts the "unhypnotizability" issue to the safety question as to how the client can feel safe in the hypnotic induction process.

The therapist follows this reframing with the second one by declaring the task at hand is to facilitate the client's sense of safety, not to induce trance (*"My job is to create the sense of safety for you and make sure you feel it"*). To consolidate this point, the therapist finally asks the client for advice! This allows the client to focus on how to achieve a sense of safety that leads to hypnotic trance.

Application of reframing is limitless in the practice of hypnosis. It is also good training for the therapist because it requires flexible thinking in viewing client resistance from different angles.

Displacement

Although not many, some clients claim being "unhypnotizable" as we discussed in the previous section. A useful strategy to deal with this resistance is displacement. The term displacement has no psychodynamic relevance but refers to a condition in which trance is permitted to happen only in certain parts or sections of the body (*e.g.,* arms, feet, abdomen, *etc.*). The client can otherwise remain fully aware and alert in this state.

Displacement is utilized in conjunction with the spontaneous hand catalepsy induction. It promotes a quick catalepsy in the client's hand on the spot. The procedure consists of the following five steps.

1. The therapist explains the catalepsy induction and obtains the client's permission to touch a wrist to lift the hand.

2. Let the client choose the hand.

3. Tell the client to *carefully observe the selected hand's movement* while the therapist lifts it slowly by the wrist. In so doing, the therapist controls the touch to be so subtle that the client can only feel his or her own hand.

4. When the client's hand reaches midair, the therapist makes sure of the spontaneous catalepsy.

5. Ratify the hand catalepsy as a sign of trance by remarking *"Isn't that fascinating! The hand has a mind of its own. Let it decide what it will do next."* (Italics are suggestion).

Notice in the trance ratifying remarks, the client's hand is referred to as *"the hand"* and *"it."* This is to suggest dissociation. Once the catalepsy is induced, the therapist may continue conversing with the client or suggest trance deepening.

Displacement using this technique suits well with the doubtful client because the involuntary hand catalepsy creates surprise. This element eradicates the client's doubt and breaks resistance. Spontaneous hand catalepsy is a relatively easy technique to master with practice. The reader interested in the technical details of the induction method is referred to Zeig (1985).

CONCLUSION

We have reviewed in this chapter the major causes of client resistance and several strategies to manage it in the hypnotic context. Anxiety, confusion about therapeutic tasks, power struggle, and negative expectation and low motivation, are the four factors that commonly affect the client in an oppositional manner both in hypnotic induction and treatment. Becoming familiar with them will prepare the therapist to appropriately assess and address resistance when it happens.

We introduced five effective strategies to manage resistance. The therapist always begins hypnotic work by preparing the client to properly understand the nature of hypnosis and dispel harmful myths that generate resistance. Acceptance is a fundamental attitude of the therapist in dealing with client resistance. The therapist openly accepts it, without blaming the client, as a vital part of hypnotic induction and therapy. Sometimes the therapist encourages observed resistance paradoxically and thereby joins the client in the oppositional behavior. Resistance also may be reframed by changing its significance to meet the client's needs. Finally, the therapist can allow the client to experience trance partially, not totally, by way of displacement.

These strategies have been utilized successfully by many clinicians across different theoretical orientations. Nevertheless, their mastery requires time and deliberate practice. Be patient and seek supervision if necessary. Soon the reader will be managing resisting clients skillfully. Good luck!

CHAPTER 12
REFLECTION QUESTIONS

1. What is unique about client resistance in hypnotic practice?

2. What are the five strategies to manage client resistance?

3. What are the four causes of client resistance?

APPENDIX 1
HYPNOSIS QUIZ*

1. Hypnosis is a very deep sleep state ...
    True | False

2. While in trance, the client is rigid and unable to respond in a normal manner ...
    True | False

3. The client must close the eyes to enter trance ...
    True | False

4. The client cannot talk without coming out of trance ...
    True | False

5. It is possible for the client to be "lost" in a trance and never come out of it ...
   True | False

6. When in a trance, the client is helpless and out of control ...
   True | False

7. Clients are under the control of the therapist while in trance and can be made to do things against their will ...
   True | False

8. The client may be forced to reveal secrets in trance ...
   True | False

9. Hypnosis in dangerous because cults use it ...
   True | False

10. Memories recovered in trance are always accurate ...
    True | False

* Adapted from West Virginia University Hypnosis Study Group (2005)

REFERENCES

Barber, T. X., & Calverley, D. S. (1964). Toward a theory of hypnotic behavior: Effects on suggestibility of defining the situation as hypnosis and defining response to suggestions as easy. *Journal of Abnormal and Social Psychology, 68*, 585-592.

Barrett, D. (2010). *Hypnosis and hypnotherapy.* Santa Barbara, CA: Praeger.

Benham, G., Woody, E. Z., Wilson, K. S., & Nash, M. R. (2006). Expect the unexpected: Ability, attitude, and responsiveness to hypnosis. *Journal of Personality and Social Psychology, 91*, 342-350.

Berne, E. (1964). *Games people play: The basic handbook of Transactional Analysis.* New York: Ballantine Books.

Blatt, S., & Erlick, H. S. (1982). Levels of resistance in the psychotherapeutic process. In P. Wachtel (Ed.), (1982), *Resistance: Psychodynamic and behavioral approaches* (pp. 69-91). New York: Plenum.

Erdelyi, M. H. (1994). Hypnotic hypermnesia: The empty set of hypermnesia. *International Journal of Clinical and Experimental Hypnosis, 42*, 379-390.

Erickson, M. H. (1964). A hypnotic technique for resistant patients: The patient, the technique and its rationale and field experiments. *American Journal of Clinical Hypnosis, 7*, 8-32.

Gfeller, J. D., Lynn, S. J., & Pribble, W. E. (1987). Enhancing hypnotic susceptibility: Interpersonal and rapport factors. *Journal of Personality and Social Psychology, 52*, 586.

Haley, J. (1963). *Strategies of psychotherapy*. New York: Harcourt Health Sciences Group.

Haley, J. (1960). The control of fear with hypnosis. *American Journal of Clinical Hypnosis, 2*, 109-115.

Katchen, M. H. (1992). Brainwashing, hypnosis, and the cults. *Australian Journal of Clinical and Experimental Hypnosis, 20*, 79-79.

Kluft, R. P. (2012). Approaches to difficulties in re-alerting subjects from hypnosis. *American Journal of Clinical Hypnosis, 55*, 140-159.

MacHovec, F. (1988). Hypnosis complications, risk factors, and prevention. *American Journal of Clinical Hypnosis, 31*, 40-49.

Meyerson, J. (2014). The myth of hypnosis: The need for remythification. *International Journal of Clinical and Experimental Hypnosis, 62*, 378-393.

Orne, M. T. (1966). Hypnosis, motivation and compliance. *American Journal of Psychiatry, 122*, 721-726.

Otani, A. (1989a). Client resistance in counseling: Its theoretical rationale and taxonomic classification. *Journal of Counseling & Development, 67*, 458-461.

Otani, A. (1989b). Resistance management techniques of Milton H. Erickson, M.D.: An application to nonhypnotic mental health counseling. *Journal of Mental Health Counseling, 11*, 325-334.

Prochaska, J. O., & Norcross, J. C. (2001). Stages of change. *Psychotherapy: Theory, Research, Practice, Training, 38*, 443-448.

Prochaska, J. O., & Prochaska, J. M. (1999). Why don't continents move? Why don't people change? *Journal of Psychotherapy Integration, 9*, 83-102.

Register, P. A., & Kihlstrom, J. F. (1987). Hypnotic effects on hypermnesia. *International Journal of Clinical and Experimental Hypnosis, 35*, 155-170.

Rohrbaugh, M. J., & Shoham, V. (2001). Brief therapy based on interrupting ironic processes: The Palo Alto Model. *Clinical Psychology: Science and Practice, 8*, 66-91.

Ryland, S., Johnson, L. N., & Bernards, J. C. (2021). Honoring protective responses: Reframing resistance in therapy using polyvagal theory. *Contemporary Family Therapy*, 1-9.

Sakata, K. I. (1968). Report on a case of failure to dehypnotize and subsequent reputed aftereffects. *International Journal of Clinical and Experimental Hypnosis, 16*, 221-228.

Spanos, N. P., Cross, W. P., & de Groh, M. M. (1987). Measuring resistance to hypnosis and its relationship to hypnotic susceptibility. *Psychological Reports, 60*, 67-70.

Watzlawick, P., Weakland, J., & Fisch, R. (1974). *Change: Principles of problem formation and resolution.* New York: Norton.

Wegner, D. M. (1994). Ironic processes of mental control. *Psychological review, 101*, 34-52.

Wegner, D. M. (1997). When the antidote is the poison: Ironic mental control processes. *Psychological Science, 8*, 148-150.

West Virginia University Hypnosis Study Group (2005). *The "art" in the science of hypnosis manual.* Morgantown, WV: West Virginia University.

Zeig, J. K. (1985). *Experiencing Erickson: An introduction to the man and his work.* New York: Brunner/Mazel.

CHAPTER 13
PRESENTING CLINICAL HYPNOSIS TO THE PATIENT, MYTHS AND MISCONCEPTIONS, MEMORY AND INFORMED CONSENT

LOUIS DAMIS

Chapter Learning Objectives

1. Describe clinical hypnosis to clients in a welcoming manner that fosters their interest and preparation for hypnosis.

2. Articulate an accurate understanding of the nature of hypnosis and memory.

3. Understand mechanisms of false memory production.

4. Understand the components and importance of Informed Consent for the use of Clinical Hypnosis.

Hypnosis is a naturally occurring lightly altered state of consciousness that we all experience from time to time. It is generally associated with some degree of internally focused attention and decreased attention to less relevant peripheral stimuli. Everyday experiences include becoming absorbed in a book or daydreaming with less awareness of one's immediate surroundings or the passage of time (Scheflin & Shapiro, 1989). Moreover, when clinical hypnosis is elicited in the context of therapy, this state of consciousness is likely associated with greater receptivity to therapeutic suggestions acceptable to the subject.

A prerequisite to the use of clinical hypnosis is the completion of a comprehensive biopsychosocial assessment with particular attention paid to the possibility of early neglect, developmental trauma, and abuse histories. After establishing adequate rapport, mutually agreed-upon treatment goals, and clinically determined relevance of hypnosis, the option of using clinical hypnosis can be presented to the patient. However, adequate education, preparation, and consent for hypnosis are essential to its safe, effective, and ethical application.

The general population abounds with inappropriate beliefs and expectations regarding the nature of clinical hypnosis. Johnson & Hauck assessed the beliefs and opinions about hypnosis held by Minnesota undergraduates; members of a recreational, social club in Arizona; attendees at a women's spiritual conference in Minnesota; and members of a University of Miami Retirees Association. They found that an extremely large portion of respondents regarded hypnosis as a powerful tool for recovering accurate memories as far back as birth and past lives and will give hypnotically refreshed memories more credibility than non-hypnotically refreshed memories (Johnson & Hauck, 1999). Moreover, a great similarity was found among undergraduates sampled in the United States, Australia, Germany, and Iran regarding hypnosis as an altered state of consciousness, that during hypnosis, subjects can remember things that they could not normally remember, that suggestions given during hypnosis can make subjects do things that they would not normally do, and that subjects would tell the truth and cannot lie under hypnosis (Green et al., 2006). As can be seen in the sample of commonly held beliefs about hypnosis, some of them can cause fear and reluctance to participate in clinical hypnosis, some of them can set a foundation for misinterpretation of experiences during hypnosis, including false memories, and some of them support the potential therapeutic benefits of hypnosis. Consequently, it is critical to understand and potentially correct your client's beliefs about hypnosis.

INTRODUCING HYPNOSIS TO YOUR PATIENT

Once the clinician has determined that clinical hypnosis is relevant to treating the individual's target behaviors, it is best first to ask if the individual has had prior experience with hypnosis. If they have had prior experience with hypnosis, clarify if this was positive and beneficial or regarded negatively and unhelpful. Inquire about their experience with hypnosis and determine whether it was provided by a qualified licensed health professional or a lay hypnotist, the goals and methods employed, and the number of sessions. In reviewing this information, it may be obvious why hypnosis was ineffective or unpalatable to the individual, and you can review options to improve the individual's experience and benefit.

If the individual reported a positive experience with the use of hypnosis and some degree of benefit, ask about the prior hypnotherapist's approach and what your patient found helpful. Incorporating aspects of what was positive and helpful previously into your approach to hypnosis will facilitate the client's transition to your use of hypnosis.

If your patient has not had prior experience with hypnosis, ask, "what do you think it would be like to be hypnotized?" If your patient says they have no idea, ask them to guess and remind them that this is not a test. Eliciting their image of hypnosis will provide you with useful information regarding their beliefs and expectations. On occasion, people have very reasonable expectations and a constructive image of hypnosis. However, you will find that individuals harbor media-driven stereotypical and inappropriate beliefs and expectations on many occasions. Correcting these misconceptions is essential to reducing potential apprehensions and misinterpretations of hypnotic experiences.

MYTHS AND MISCONCEPTIONS

Misconceptions about the nature of hypnosis typically include the following (Elkins, 2013; Green, 2003; Lynn et al., 2020; Scheflin & Shapiro, 1989; Spiegel & Spiegel, 2008):

Myth 1: Hypnosis as a sleep or loss of consciousness

James Braid considered hypnosis a kind of nervous sleep and coined the term "hypnosis," derived from the Greek-Roman god of sleep, Hypnos. However, brain activity during hypnosis is similar to non-sleep states of normal consciousness and not characteristic of sleep. Moreover, hypnosis is not associated with loss of conscious awareness, and individuals may question whether they had actually experienced the state of hypnosis because they can remember various aspects of the hypnotic intervention. Consequently, it is helpful to explain to clients that their awareness and memory are expected and useful in addressing their problems.

Myth 2: Some people cannot be hypnotized

Individuals vary in their range of hypnotic capacities. The majority of the population have moderate to high hypnotic capacities and experience useful states of hypnosis. Those few with limited capacities may not find hypnosis as helpful.

Myth 3: Hypnosis as something imposed on the subject

It is common for people to believe that hypnosis is something done to them and that they will be reflexively responsive to whatever is suggested. As noted above, the practitioner guides and coaches the subject's experience facilitating their elicitation of the hypnotic state.

Myth 4: Hypnosis as loss of control

Based on stereotypical media-driven examples of hypnotized individuals, many people anticipate the loss of emotional, behavioral, and verbal control. Descriptions of hypnotic capacities as "susceptibility" also foster a sense of loss of agency when one is in a hypnotic state Rather than speak of hypnotic susceptibility, it is more appropriate and helpful to describe hypnotic capacities as individual "talents" or "hypnotic abilities" (i.e., hypnotizability). Moreover, research has shown that subjects can readily choose not to participate in a hypnotic elicitation and have the ability to return themselves to their fully alert state when desired.

Myth 5: Hypnotist's power over the subject

As noted above, another misconception about the nature of hypnosis is that individuals can be made to do things prescribed by hypnotic suggestions. However, research has shown that individuals will not engage in behaviors counter to their values and morals.

Myth 6: Hypnosis as dangerous and destructive of the will

As hypnosis is a naturally occurring lightly altered state of consciousness that we drift in and out of regularly, the state of hypnosis is quite benign. Some religious ideologies propose that hypnosis renders one open to the intrusion of evil forces and precludes their followers from the use of hypnosis. Whereas this belief may preclude some individuals from participating in hypnotic interventions, it has been this author's experience that it may be beneficial to invite them to activate their spiritual connection and maintain its protective boundary throughout the hypnotic work. Although the state of hypnosis is quite benign, the application of hypnosis by unqualified individuals can result in adverse effects (Gruzelier, 2000).

Myth 7: Hypnosis as a "truth serum"

As noted above and will be discussed further below, hypnosis is not associated with the accuracy of recall or suspension of one's ability to control the information they choose to reveal during or after hypnosis. The hypnotic state does not abolish one's inhibitory controls, and individuals can readily keep information to themselves or intentionally misrepresent their experiences. In the context of adequate rapport and a sound therapeutic relationship, individuals will generally feel safe revealing their experiences during trance.

Myth 8: Hypnosis is therapy or a cure-all

Our current understanding of clinical hypnosis is that it is a state of consciousness wherein one can introduce a wide range of clinical interventions consistent with one's theoretical orientation. The skilled clinician appreciates the characteristics of the hypnotic state and employs interventions tailored to optimally interact with these characteristics, e.g., positive and affirming wording of suggestions. In addition, it is not uncommon for individuals to expect quick fixes from brief hypnotic interventions. In this regard, it is helpful to explain to clients that hypnosis is one component of a comprehensive psychotherapeutic intervention and that benefits will evolve with repeated application.

Myth 9: Hypnotic trance as irreversible

Occasionally, individuals will fear being unable to re-alert. Although it is often the case that individuals would prefer to remain in the pleasant hypnotic state, clients re-alert when directed to and do not get stuck in an unwanted state of trance.

Once you have reviewed and clarified the above misconceptions with your client, it is helpful to orient them to a facilitative approach to their upcoming hypnosis experience. Support the perspective that the hypnotic state emerges from the individual's focusing of attention and that you, the hypnotist, assist in this process by guiding them. Ideally, the hypnotic state is an unfolding of greater internal absorption and the client's awareness of and engagement with responses to therapeutic suggestions. Pre-induction instructions have been found to increase responsiveness to suggestions by providing guidance for reduced critical thought ("Some people find that they respond better ... when they avoid thinking critically. Allow yourself to let go completely ... Don't question what you are being asked to do and experience ... Just go with the flow ... Don't question whether or not it will work ... Let yourself go ... Just go with the flow") as well as increased absorption ("People respond better ... When they are very focused ... Totally absorbed") (Brown et al., 2001, p. 71).

Neurophysiological studies of hypnosis have found that the hypnotic state of consciousness is associated with decreased activity in the Default Mode Network (DMN). Activity in this network is associated with self-referential thinking that occurs when individuals are mentally idle. Examples of self-referential thinking include reflecting on your day's events and speculating on future events. Reductions in DNM activity are associated with quieting of the mind and potential increased responsivity to suggestion (Deeley et al., 2012; Jiang et al., 2017). As many patients experience a welcome sense of quietness and peace during hypnosis, it is helpful to let neophytes know that hypnosis often "quiets the noise of the conscious mind and allows you to take in and learn more effectively from the things you focus on." Describing the experience in this manner helps create positive expectations for trance, in general, and how it will benefit them.

The hypnotic state is also associated with a decoupling of control-related executive functioning and conflict monitoring processes (Egner et al., 2005). Like brainstorming, which involves generating possibilities without evaluative constraints, the hypnotic state of consciousness may allow for more flexible, "thinking out of the box," discovery of solutions. Explaining that the hypnotic state "allows the conscious mind to step aside, although always maintaining control, and allows the creative wisdom of our less conscious mind to facilitate the discovery of new solutions and insights" is also welcoming to clients new to hypnosis.

Sometimes when first learning hypnosis, practitioners feel uncomfortable describing the intervention as hypnosis or as a state of "trance." Speaking to the sociocognitive components of hypnosis, labeling the intervention as "hypnosis" has been associated with significant increases in suggestibility and maintenance of treatment gains at follow-up (Gandhi & Oakley, 2005; Zitman et al., 1992). Moreover, both cognitive-behavioral and trance/dissociation explanations of hypnosis were equally associated with positive changes in attitudes towards hypnosis, greater collaboration, and hypnotizability (Capafons et al., 2005). In addition, the ethical use of hypnosis requires that participants being fully informed.

HYPNOSIS AND MEMORY

Memory is conceptualized as having three components: encoding, retention, and retrieval (Roediger III & Gallo, 2001). Encoding is the first process in memory and involves the original perception and acquisition of information. Retention involves the consolidation and storage of the acquired information, and retrieval is the recollection of stored information. Moreover, memory for events can be influenced by factors occurring before the event that influence encoding, processes operating at the time of retrieval of the event (degree and relevance of cues), and processes occurring after the event that might alter its representation. Furthermore, memory is dependent on both how well it is encoded and the appropriateness and number of retrieval cues provided when information is recalled.

Methods of memory assessment also impact the amount of information recalled as a function of the number of cues provided at retrieval. Free-recall requires subjects to recollect as much information as possible in the absence of any form of cues. Cued-recall involves providing related information or clues associated with the information to be remembered. Recognition involves the provision of multiple-choice options, including one correct item. Retrieval is enhanced by providing cues and is maximized with measures of recognition. However, although the recognition approach can demonstrate the retention of more memory items, the information rendered is limited by the questions asked and may not be of particular value in forensic situations where new leads to solve a crime are sought.

HYPNOTIC HYPERMNESIA

A sizable portion of the population and professionals believe that hypnosis is a useful tool for recovering memories and that memories retrieved during hypnosis are more accurate than those from the normal waking state (Green et al., 2006; Johnson & Hauck, 1999; Yapko, 1994a, 1994b). Hypermnesia refers to an unusually vivid or complete memory or recall of the past. A meta-analytic review of laboratory studies of recall accuracy for nonleading questions after a 1- to 2-day delay favored hypnotized subjects, but this increased recall was also associated with higher levels of inaccurate recall or pseudomemories (Steblay & Bothwell, 1994). However, in his review of the research literature on hypnotic hypermnesia, Erdelyi (1994) identified that hypermnesia was only evidenced on free-recall assessments of high-sense (meaningful stimuli such as poetry). In contrast, hypnotic hypermnesia was not found for studies that employed low-sense (meaningless stimuli like nonsense syllables or word lists) or recognition measures (Erdelyi, 1994). Moreover, he concluded that repeated testing without hypnosis yields as much hypermnesia as hypnosis. Dinges et al. (1992) found that increased recall of pictural stimuli from an initial waking condition baseline to a second recall for subjects in a waking state or hypnosis, found the typical repeated recall hypermnesia effect but that hypnosis did not increase recall. Moreover, they found that subjects high in hypnotizability evidenced increased production of new incorrect recall (Dinges et al., 1992). The hypermnesic effect of repeated recall trials without hypnotic enhancement was also found for incidental learning, (Register & Kihlstrom, 1987) and early memories (Wall & Lieberman, 1976).

In summary, it appears that hypermnesia occurs across repeated recollection trials. Hypnosis may increase the amount of recall but the increase is a mixture of accurate and inaccurate information, and that hypnosis per se does not significantly increase hypermnesia for meaningless stimuli. Moreover, increased retrieval cues and structured format of recognition measures maximize initial recall creating a ceiling effect for subsequent trials and does not allow for the collection of non-inquired information. Consequently, the best way to demonstrate hypermnesia is with free-recall that will also allow for identification of possible leads or clues for other valuable information in forensic investigations.

For studies where hypnotic hypermnesia was demonstrated (Depiano & Salzberg, 1981; Grabowski et al., 1991; Steblay & Bothwell, 1994), several hypotheses about the mechanisms of hypermnesia have been proposed. Prehypnotic attitudes and beliefs can create expectations for individuals that increase their motivation to search for memories and potentially report imagined events or guesses as memories (Lynn et al., 2009). These authors also note that suggestions for hypermnesia during hypnosis create expectations for enhanced memory recall that augment prehypnotic beliefs and create demand characteristics for increased recall. Moreover, aspects of age regression to enhance context reinstatement to foster retrieval are speculated to encourage imagination and fantasizing. Whitehouse et al. found that subjects experiencing hypnosis compared to waking conditions on the second recall of filmed material exhibited significantly greater confidence for responses designated as "guesses" on the prior waking test (Whitehouse et al., 1988). These authors regarded this as a criterion shift, a decrease in the criteria for defining information as a memory for subjects during hypnosis that allows them to report information that otherwise would be withheld. In this respect, the increase in recall during hypnosis is related to a change in report bias rather than greater access to memory. Finally, the state of relaxation often associated with hypnosis may facilitate memory retrieval. In this regard, White et al. noted that "memory gaps are rarely filled by simply trying harder ... [and one of their subjects noted that] under hypnosis, in contrast to the wide-awake state, the [recollections] 'seemed to flow together nicely' ... while he himself remained relatively passive" (White et al., 1940, p. 101). Events that occur after initial recall can also modify memory and impact its subsequent recall. These factors will be discussed below in the context of false memory creation.

FALLIBILITY OF MEMORY

In the 1990s, there was considerable controversy over the validity of recovered memories of childhood abuse. On the one hand, some therapists believed that such abuse was the cause of current presenting problems. On the other hand, others believed that recovered memories were false memories of abuse that never occurred and were the iatrogenic product of misinformed therapies and the use of hypnosis (Brown, 1995). This controversy spurred considerable research on processes associated with the development of false memories.

A review of laboratory studies of the induction of false beliefs and false memories has identified three main methods: imagination inflation, false feedback, and memory implantation (Brewin & Andrews, 2017; Muschalla & Schönborn, 2021). Imagination inflation can occur when subjects vividly imagine words, sentences, and actions, leading to confusion over whether such content was imagined or actually happened. Free and guided imagery combined with journaling has been associated with inducing false memories or beliefs in 20% to 47% of participants (Muschalla & Schönborn, 2021).

Many pseudomemory studies have included strong suggestions that memories from as early as the first day after birth can be recalled in combination with suggestions to try to imagine such events. Malinoski and Lynn found that when participants were instructed to close their eyes, visualize, and focus on their second birthday, a doubtful memory due to infantile amnesia, that 59% reported a birthday memory (Malinoski & Lynn, 1999). "After repeated probes for earlier memories, 78% of subjects reported memories at or prior to 24 months of age, and 33% reported memories within the first 12 months of age" (p. 320). Moreover, the age of the earliest memory during the suggestive interview was correlated with increased levels of compliance, hypnotizability, and interrogative suggestibility.

Bryant and Barnier compared high and low hypnotizable subjects in hypnosis versus nonhypnotized high hypnotizable subjects and administered a suggestion to recall their second birthday (Bryant & Barnier, 1999). These authors found that more highs than lows reported a memory during hypnosis and that after being told that memories that early were not possible, half of the nonhypnotized highs retracted their memory, but none of the hypnotized highs did. Such resistance to disconfirmation of pseudomemories elicited during hypnosis has been noted in other studies (Laurence & Perry, 1983b; Lynn et al., 2009)

False feedback involves attempts to increase beliefs in childhood autobiographical events by misinforming subjects that the event was likely to have happened to them before the age of 10 based on the alleged results of psychological measures they completed. Some of these studies also included imaging potential experiences and answering questions about them. False feedback inductions were found to have size-weighted average percentages of participants developing false beliefs of 35% and false memories of 11.28% (Muschalla & Schönborn, 2021).

Somewhat related to false feedback is misleading information that takes the form of asking a question about a video the subject watched that assumes inaccurate information was part of the original information. For example, asking if the tie the thief was wearing was red or green when the thief was not wearing a tie and finding that the subject later agrees that the thief was wearing a tie. Such misinformation often becomes blended with the original memory and is a notable source of memory contamination. Scoboria et al. found that both hypnosis and misleading questions decreased the accuracy of memory reports and decreased "don't know" responses. Although they noted that the negative effects of hypnosis and misinformation were additive, hypnosis alone was associated with an increase in both accurate and inaccurate memories. In contrast, misinformation was associated only with increased inaccurate memories and significantly more errors (Scoboria et al., 2002). In a subsequent study, Scoboria et al. replicated the finding that misleading questions reduced memory accuracy and "don't know" responses but failed to replicate the negative effect of hypnosis on memory reports (Scoboria et al., 2006).

Source misattribution, confusing the experience of actual events with imagining them or that others suggest them, is one explanation for the misinformation and imagination inflation effects. Ceci et al. (1994) found that for children aged three to six years old, repeated interviewing about events they never experienced and asking them to imagine them resulted in a significant increase in their false assertion of having experienced them (Ceci et al., 1994).

Memory implantation is associated with strong explicit suggestions "to 'implant' a memory of a childhood autobiographical event from scratch by providing explicit 'corroboration' from an authoritative source that the event happened" (Brewin & Andrews, 2017, p. 13). After confirming with participants' parents that the event did not happen, subjects are told that the parent reported that it did (e.g., being lost in a shopping mall or a ride in a hot air balloon). In some studies, subjects were shown doctored photographs that supposedly illustrate their presence at the false event. Subsequently, subjects are encouraged to recall the details of the false event several times. Size-weighted average percentages for such induction attempts were associated with developing false beliefs in 37% of participants and false memories in 26.6% of participants (Muschalla & Schönborn, 2021).

Laurence and Perry selected 27 highly hypnotizable subjects and, during hypnosis, identified a night in the previous week for which they had no specific memories of awakening or dreams occurring (Laurence & Perry, 1983a). They then utilized age regression to take them back to that night and asked if they heard some loud noises that had awakened them. Seventeen of the 27 reported hearing noises, and they were encouraged to describe them in detail. Posthypnotic assessment identified that 13 of the 27 highly hypnotizable subjects accepted the suggestion and stated that the suggested event had actually taken place. Six of those who accepted the suggestion were unequivocal that the event happened and maintained that the noises had actually occurred despite being told they were suggested to them.

As noted above, multiple studies have found hypnotizability associated with increased frequency of memory errors and pseudomemories. However, several studies have found that hypnosis did not increase the likelihood of such memory distortions. Spanos et al. examined the likelihood of subjects experiencing recall of the day after their birth via hypnotic age-regression suggestions and found no difference in these improbable memories for subjects medium to high or low in hypnotizability (Spanos et al., 1999). In fact, participants in the non-hypnotic condition reported significantly more regression memories. Dasse et al. found that highly hypnotizable subjects were more accurate on recall and recognition, hypothesizing that "the trait of hypnotizability may be related to the monitoring and control of memories, something not seen before" (Dasse et al., 2015). This study and others demonstrate that hypnosis is not necessary to create false memories (Bernstein et al., 2009; Garry & Loftus, 1994; Loftus & Hoffman, 1989). Furthermore, low hypnotizability does not protect someone from developing pseudomemories (Orne et al., 1996; Spanos et al., 1999).

Brewin and Andrews (2017) have questioned the criteria by which false memory researchers conclude that memory has occurred. Brewin (1986) proposed that full or complete autobiographical memory was a complex process composed of three types of memory judgment: (1) a belief that the event occurred; (2) a corresponding recollection experience (visual, sensory, affective, perceptual information); (3) confidence in the veracity of the memory experience (Brewer, 1986). Moreover, he reported that a 'full' memory ideally rests on a combination of recollection and confidence. In a comprehensive analysis of pseudomemory induction studies, Brewin and Andrews found that applying more stringent definitions of autobiographical memories resulted in large reductions in evinced full memories, e.g., "in memory implantation studies, some recollective experience for the suggested events is induced on average in 47% of the participants, but only in 15% are these experiences likely to be rated as full memories" (p. 2). They noted that repeated retrieval attempts could be associated with retrieving genuine self-knowledge (hypermnesia) that becomes blended with suggested information. Many studies only induce the belief that a false event occurred rather than create a full memory. Moreover, they concluded that the data they reviewed were "inconsistent with claims that it is easy to create false memories of childhood in others" (p. 19).

In his review of the literature on recovered memories of abuse and false-memory studies, Brown (1995) noted that traumatization is sometimes associated with amnesia, that memories of traumatic experiences may contain accurate and inaccurate information, and that under certain conditions, recovered memories may be total fabrications. He reported that traumatic events resulting in PTSD involve the amygdala-based memory system compared to hippo-campal mediated non-traumatic autobiographical memories, that traumatic events disrupt hippocampal memory processing, and that traumatic memories are frequently partial or fragmented. Brown underscored that memory for central events, or the 'gist' of an event, is much more likely to be retained at the expense of event details and that many of the false-memory studies focus on manipulations of details. Brown also noted that high hypnotizability, not hypnosis, is a risk factor for pseudomemories and that misinformation and post-event suggestions are the primary causes of memory distortions. Moreover, he posited that it is the combination of such misleading information, social pressure, and coercive processes that characterize interrogatory suggestibility that are, the conditions for increased probability of developing pseudomemories or reporting such. Brown concluded that studies positing the ease of autobiographical memory manipulation are based on studies of normal memory in experimental settings and are not generalizable to trauma survivors in psycho-therapy.

In an exhaustive review of memory and hypnosis, Brown et al. (1998) noted that hypnotic hypermnesia makes a unique contribution to recall personally meaningful information; that distortions in memory accuracy and confabulation during hypnotic memory enhancement are increased under conditions of interviewer bias and suggestive interviewing but decreased under conditions of neutral interviewer expectations and revivification combined with free recall interviewing; hypnotic pseudomemory reports are less likely to occur in a social context characterized by neutral interviewer expectations, an egalitarian interview relationship, and free recall, primarily pertaining to personally meaningful information; pseudo-memories that are associated with hypnosis are primarily a function of social and contextual demands of the situation and occur in highly and moderately hypnotizable subjects; hypnotic pseudomemory reports do occur through suggested misinformation; source attribution errors can occur with or without hypnosis; that a mild increase in confidence might occur in some cases most likely attributable to social demands, specific suggestions, and to a lesser extent the level of hypnotizability rather than the use of hypnotic procedures per say; hypnosis does not increase resistance to cross-examination and is generally less effective than usual pretrial preparation in immunization to cross-examination; the use of hypnotic procedures does not appear to constitute a unique risk factor in the development of pseudo-memories; induction and other specific hypnotic procedures do not significantly contribute to hypnotic pseudomemory production; and that it is possible to foster genuine pseudomemories in a small percentage of subjects in studies that have not adequately controlled for experimenter demand characteristics but that these pseudo-memories are relatively unstable in the vast majority of cases and do not appear to constitute a change in the memory representation per se (Brown et al., 1998). Moreover, the conclusions of Brown et al. confirmed those reported by the American Society of Clinical Hypnosis established Task Force on Hypnosis and Memory and reported in their publication of *Clinical Hypnosis and Memory: Guidelines for Clinicians and Forensic Hypnosis* (Hammond et al., 1995).

The research cited above clearly demonstrates that interviewers can create beliefs conducive to the development of false memories, that the use of imagery techniques and suggestion can influence the creation of false beliefs and memories in a minority of subjects, and that misinformation presented following recall can modify subsequent reports of the original memory. Moreover, reviewing recollections, especially in the context of hypnosis, can modestly increase one's confidence in potential pseudomemories. These observations have raised legitimate concerns about using memory retrieval techniques in psychotherapy and have led some authorities to seriously question the validity of recovered memories of abuse (Garry & Loftus, 1994; Lindsay & Read, 1995; Lynn et al., 1997, 2009). Lindsay and Read raise legitimate concerns about self-help and psychotherapeutic approaches that assume current symptom profiles are due to repressed memories of abuse, encourage clients to adopt this model, and engage in suggestive "memory work" techniques. Whereas it is wise not to assume that any presenting problem is an absolute consequence of repressed memories, antagonists to the possibility of veridical recovery of forgotten memories of childhood sexual abuse regard such recoveries as rare, "in our view, research does not support the belief that complete amnesia for recoverable histories of CSA [childhood sexual abuse] is a common occurrence, nor does it support the idea that delayed recollections are necessarily accurate" (Lindsay & Read, 1995, p. 886). Contrary to such opinions, a prospective study of 129 women with documented histories of sexual victimization in childhood interviewed 17 years later found that 38% did not recall the abuse, that younger age at the time of the abuse and molestation by someone they knew were more likely associated with no recall, and that "long periods with no memory of abuse should not be regarded as evidence that the abuse did not occur" (Williams, 1994, p. 1167). Herman & Schatzow found that for a sample of 53 women participating in short-term therapy groups for CSA, 64% did not have full recall of the sexual abuse, that 28% had severe memory deficits for their abuse histories, that those with severe memory deficits had earlier (abuse that occurred in preschool years and ended before adolescence) and more violent abuse histories, and that 74% were able to obtain confirmation of the sexual abuse from another source (Herman & Schatzow, 1987). In addition, Chu et al. reported that a sample of 90 female patients admitted to a psychiatric unit specializing in the treatment of trauma-related disorders were found to have periods of complete amnesia for their histories of physical or sexual abuse, and that corroboration was 93% for physical abuse and 89% for sexual abuse (Chu et al., 1999). These authors also confirmed that earlier age of abuse was associated with a higher degree of amnesia. Most participants reporting complete physical and sexual abuse had their first recollection of abuse while at home alone; only about four were in therapy at the time of recollection, nearly all were alert, and hypnosis was a factor for only one. These authors concluded that their findings "argue against the notion that many or most reports

of childhood abuse are pseudomemories ... [and that] neither psychotherapy nor hypnosis, per se, are treatments that encourage pseudomemories" (Chu et al., 1999, p. 754).

CLINICAL CONSIDERATION FOR WORKING
WITH MEMORY IN HYPNOSIS

Brown (1995) noted that "false beliefs in psychotherapy are very
likely to occur when an *interaction of four primary risk factors* are
present: (1) high hypnotizability; (2) uncertainty about past events;
(3) clear evidence of interrogatory suggestive influence; and (4)
extratherapeutic social influences, for example, peer and family
influence, especially self-help group experiences and available
sociocultural beliefs" (p. 15).

The American Society for Clinical Hypnosis (ASCH Task Force on
Hypnosis and Memory; Hammond et al., 1995) offered recommendations when working with hypnosis and memory with potential abuse
victims (see publication for additional details). The essence of their
considerations, along with this author's recommendations, are listed
below:

1. Prior to hypnosis, evaluate the patient and explore
   his/her expectations about hypnosis and that when there
   are beliefs that abuse may have occurred, evaluate
   potential sources of contamination. Correcting
   prehypnotic misconceptions is the first step in
   decreasing the likelihood of false memory development.

2. Age regression and uncovering techniques in hypnosis
   should only be used by licensed mental health
   professionals practicing within their areas of expertise.
   Moreover, professionals should be familiar with the

literature on hypnosis and memory, have competency in
avoiding leading questions, and training in working with
victims of abuse or trauma.

3. Obtain informed consent prior to the use of hypnosis and
    recognize that uncovering may be contraindicated for
    individuals with extreme emotional lability, tenuous
    control, thought disorder, or some medically impaired
    patients.

4. Evaluate hypnotic responsivity, at least informally.

5. Explain to your patients that *if* they were to have any
    repressed knowledge, repression is a process and not an
    on/off switch that allows such information to come into
    consciousness all at once fully. In this respect, should
    they encounter information that seems new to them, it is
    likely that additional information will come to them as
    they adjust to this new information and that this
    additional information will further clarify the initial
    information that came into their awareness. Moreover,
    such additional information can confirm or disconfirm
    the initial information or leave them uncertain about its
    veracity. These alternatives are preferable to a
    pseudomemory resulting from an immediate assumption
    of veracity or, as I refer to it, premature closure. In
    addition, inform clients that the information presented
    regarding the possibility of repressed memory is not
    meant to indicate that you believe they have a repressed
    memory but that this is information you review with all
    clients prior to using hypnosis.

6. Minimize errors of creating false confidence by creating
    neutral expectations prior to hypnosis and during the
    induction. Neutrality should structure patient

expectations to the effect that further information may or may not be forthcoming and that such information may or may not be accurate. "It shouldn't be suggested that 'everything has been recorded, nothing has been forgotten, and it will now be freely accessible and you can and will clearly remember everything'" (Hammond et al., 1995, p. 37).

7. Patients should be instructed to not interpret questions as suggestions but as inquiries and that if they do not have an answer, this is acceptable.

8. Create a situation of free recall with minimal nonleading questions, simple repetition of patient phrases verbatim, or comments that simply encourage the patient to continue. Do not add information to the patient's report, fill in gaps, make sense of or connect memory fragments, or interpret the information disclosed during hypnosis. Use a posthypnotic suggestion that they will reflect on their experiences in trance today and continue to learn from them in a constructive way and at a pace that is right for them. Follow-up with the client once they have been fully re-alerted and at the beginning of the next session regarding their reactions to the session and whether additional insights came to them since their last session.

9. Document in your progress notes the specific information/descriptions your clients' report verbatim and the comments and suggestions you make. Document enough information that a reader can determine what information came from the client and what information came from you.

10. Keep thorough treatment notes documenting discussions of hypnosis and memory, issues of accuracy of memory, informed consent, the maintenance of neutrality, and the avoidance of offering definite opinions in the absence of corroborating evidence.

11. While maintaining a supportive and empathic stance, assist patients in the nonhypnotized state to critically evaluate material elicited and encourage them to regard material as simply one more source of information that cannot be relied on as superior or more accurate than material already in conscious awareness.

12. It is inappropriate to encourage patients to pursue litigation or confront alleged perpetrators based solely on information retrieved under hypnosis.

INFORMED CONSENT
FOR THE USE OF CLINICAL HYPNOSIS

Many courts of law hold serious, albeit inaccurate, concerns about the reliability and credibility of hypnotically refreshed testimony. These courts maintain that hypnotically refreshed memories are highly influenced by suggestibility, that confabulation can occur, that individuals become unable to distinguish between such confabulations and actual recall, and that they develop unwarranted confidence in the validity of potential confabulations that render cross-examination ineffective (Giannelli, 1995). Federal and individual state jurisdictions differ with regard to the admissibility of hypnotically refreshed memories, with the federal system more likely to judge cases on an individual basis and many state systems adopting a per se rule exclusion preventing the admissibility of information remembered during or after hypnosis (Scheflin & Shapiro, 1989).

Consequently, it is necessary to attain informed consent for the use of clinical hypnosis regarding this possible loss of legal rights to testify.

The goals of informed consent for the use of clinical hypnosis extend beyond documentation of the potential loss of legal rights associated with hypnotically refreshed memories. The informed consent process demonstrates respect for the client's autonomy, decision-making capacity, protects the safety and welfare of the patient, and fosters a collaborative process supporting treatment engagement. Moreover, this critical educational process supports the protection of the client's welfare and decreases the likelihood of pseudomemory development. Furthermore, it encourages critical thinking in determining the potential accuracy of hypnotically refreshed recollections should they occur in the course of treatment.

The components of informed consent include presenting the risks and benefits of a specific form of treatment, alternative treatments, and a statement that the consent is made voluntarily and with an awareness that it can be withdrawn at any time without adverse consequence (Melton et al., 2018). This information needs to be presented in an understandable manner to the patient. In this respect, it is helpful to conceptualize informed consent as a process that may begin with a review of an informed consent document followed by a re-visitation of the information in a subsequent session. The review of the nature of hypnosis and memory and the consent process outlined below is met with client appreciation. Make this process a part of your standard of care, and do not think that because someone has previously participated in hypnosis, they are already aware of the information you provide.

The reader is referred to Appendix A in Hammond et al. (1995) for a sample informed consent document. However, the major points will be included in the recommendations for informed consent described below:

Nature of Memory and Hypnosis

Memory is imperfect under any circumstances. Memory is not a perfect record of all experiences. Some events are not adequately perceived enough to be encoded into memories. Some events are forgotten, and not all prior experiences can be recalled. Memories can change over time.

Memories can be a mixture of accurate and inaccurate information and may include or become blended with information from sources such as books read, movies seen, others' experiences that have been vividly described, such as traumatic experiences reported by self-help or online chat group members.

Memories recalled during hypnosis are, at best, a mixture of accurate and inaccurate information, and hypnosis does not guarantee the accuracy of information recalled.

Memories can be influenced by how questions are asked and by social pressures to agree with the beliefs or reports of others.

Much of memory is reconstructive in that we recall specific details and fill in the gaps with information that may or may not be accurate.

The only way to know that information recalled under hypnosis or other memory enhancement techniques is to obtain independent corroboration.

Should new information come into awareness during hypnosis, it is best to consider it as one source of information to consider along with conscious information already known.

Potential Loss of Legal Rights Associated with Hypnotically Refreshed Testimony

In many states, courts of law have held that a person who has been hypnotized cannot testify about anything remembered during or after the use of hypnosis. Consequently, the use of hypnosis may be associated with the loss of certain legal rights associated with hypnotically refreshed memories.

The only way to fully protect your rights to testify is to forego the use of hypnosis. Moreover, should you have any concerns about your legal rights and the use of hypnosis, it would be in your best interests to review this matter with an attorney knowledgeable about the limitations in your jurisdiction.

Hammond et al. (1995) also recommend a statement releasing the therapist from liability from the patient's voluntary decision to undergo hypnosis and agreement to hold the therapist harmless from any limitations of the patient's ability to testify or the use of the therapist's testimony or records in court based on the competent use of hypnosis.

It is recommended that you place a statement of this information in your Patient-Psychotherapist Service Agreement. Documenting a discussion of this information and an opportunity for your patients to have questions answered in a progress note prior to using clinical hypnosis is also recommended. The time spent addressing the issues reviewed in this chapter will set the stage for the safe and ethical use of clinical hypnosis in psychotherapy, will foster good rapport and client engagement, and your clients will appreciate the education you provide to them.

CONCLUSION

Before introducing clinical hypnosis to a patient, it is important to access the patient's prior experience to hypnosis and correct misconceptions if any is present. Such misconceptions include patients believing that hypnosis would cause them to sleep with a loss of consciousness, that hypnosis is something imposed on the subject with a loss of control even overriding their values and morals, and that everyone can be hypnotized. Other misconceptions include the fact that hypnosis can recall any truths with accuracy, that hypnosis can cure immediately, or that hypnotic trance is irreversible. Afterward, it can be helpful to orient the patient pre-induction by guiding them to reduce critical thoughts, so as to increase responsiveness to suggestion. Moreover, it is crucial to avoid false memory production as hypnosis has been heavily shown by research to increase inaccurate recall of memories especially in meaningful stimuli such as poetry. This is primarily due to three main methods: imagination inflation, false feedback through misinforming subjects, and memory implantation via strong explicit suggestions. Pseudo-memory studies have also found that the risk of hypermnesia increases with increased compliance, hypnotizability, and interrogative suggestibility, in addition to extra-therapeutic social influences that shape sociocultural beliefs. Traumatization also increases one's chances of amnesia, through disrupting hippocampal memory processing and thus causing memory distortions. As a result, ASCH Task Force on Hypnosis and Memory prescribed a list of recommendations for using hypnosis with memory and potential abuse victims to minimize errors and false confidence. Informed consent that presents the risks and benefits of treatment, along with potential loss of legal rights associated with hypnotically refreshed testimony is also necessary. The practices in this chapter set the foundation for safe and ethical use of clinical hypnosis.

CHAPTER 13
REFLECTION QUESTIONS

1. What are the best practices for introducing clinical hypnosis to a patient?

2. What are some common misconceptions that patients can have toward accurate understanding of the nature of hypnosis and memory?

3. What are the mechanisms that account for false memory production?

4. What would a safe and ethical approach be toward working with potential trauma memories?

5. What are the components that are necessary to be introduced in an Informed Consent for the Use of Clinical Hypnosis?

REFERENCES

Bernstein, D. M., Godfrey, R. D., & Loftus, E. F. (2009). False memories: The role of plausibility and autobiographical belief. In *Handbook of imagination and mental simulation* (pp. 89-102). Psychology Press.

Brewer, W. F. (1986). What is autobiographical memory? In D. C. Rubin (Ed.), *Autobiographical Memory* (pp. 25-49). Cambridge University Press. https://doi.org/10.1017/CBO9780511558313.006

Brewin, C. R., & Andrews, B. (2017). Creating memories for false autobiographical events in childhood: A systematic review. *Applied Cognitive Psychology*, *31*(1), 2-23. https://doi.org/10.1002/acp.3220

Brown, D. (1995). Pseudomemories: The standard of science and the standard of care in trauma treatment. *American Journal of Clinical Hypnosis*, *37*(3), 1-24. https://doi.org/10.1080/00029157.1995.10403135

Brown, D., Scheflin, A. W., & Hammond, D. C. (1998). *Memory, trauma treatment, and the law* (pp. xii, 786). W. W. Norton & Company.

Brown, R. J., Antonova, E., Langley, A., & Oakley, D. A. (2001). The effects of absorption and reduced critical thought on suggestibility in a hypnotic context. *Contemporary Hypnosis*, *18*(2), 62-72. https://doi.org/10.1002/ch.220

Bryant, R. A., & Barnier, A. J. (1999). Eliciting autobiographical pseudomemories: The relevance of hypnosis, hypnotizability, and attributions. *International Journal of Clinical and Experimental Hypnosis*, *47*(4), 267-283. https://doi.org/10.1080/00207149908410037

Capafons, A., Cabañas, S., Alarcón, A., Espejo, B., Mendoza, M. E., Chaves, J. F., & Monje, A. (2005). Effects of different types of preparatory information on attitudes toward hypnosis. *Contemporary Hypnosis, 22*(2), 67-76. https://doi.org/10.1002/ch.25

Ceci, S. J., Loftus, E. F., Leichtman, M. D., & Bruck, M. (1994). The possible role of source misattributions in the creation of false beliefs among preschoolers. *International Journal of Clinical and Experimental Hypnosis, 42*(4), 304-320. https://doi.org/10.1080/00207149408409361

Chu, J. A., Frey, L. M., Ganzel, B. L., & Matthews, J. A. (1999). Memories of childhood abuse: Dissociation, amnesia, and corroboration. *American Journal of Psychiatry, 156*(5), 749-755. https://doi.org/10.1176/ajp.156.5.749

Dasse, M. N., Elkins, G. R., & Weaver, C. A. (2015). Hypnotizability, not suggestion, influences false memory development. *International Journal of Clinical and Experimental Hypnosis, 63*(1), 110-128. https://doi.org/10.1080/00207144.2014.961880

Deeley, Q., Oakley, D. A., Toone, B., Giampietro, V., Brammer, M. J., Williams, S. C. R., & Halligan, P. W. (2012). Modulating the default mode network using hypnosis. *International Journal of Clinical and Experimental Hypnosis, 60*(2), 206-228. https://doi.org/10.1080/00207144.2012.648070

Depiano, F. A., & Salzberg, H. C. (1981). Hypnosis as an aid to recall of meaningful information presented under three types of arousal. *International Journal of Clinical and Experimental Hypnosis, 29*(4), 383-400. https://doi.org/10.1080/00207148108409172

Dinges, D. F., Whitehouse, W. G., Orne, E. C., Powell, J. W., Orne, M. T., & Erdelyi, M. H. (1992). Evaluating hypnotic memory enhancement (hypermnesia and reminiscence) using multitrial forced recall. *Journal of Experimental Psychology: Learning, Memory, and Cognition, 18*(5), 1139-1147. https://doi.org/10.1037/0278-7393.18.5.1139

Egner, T., Jamieson, G., & Gruzelier, J. (2005). Hypnosis decouples cognitive control from conflict monitoring processes of the frontal lobe. *NeuroImage, 27*(4), 969-978. https://doi.org/10.1016/j.neuroimage.2005.05.002

Elkins, G. (2013). *Hypnotic Relaxation Therapy: Principles and applications.* Springer Publishing Company.

Erdelyi, M. H. (1994). Hypnotic hypermnesia: The empty set of hypermnesia. *International Journal of Clinical and Experimental Hypnosis, 42*(4), 379-390. https://doi.org/10.1080/00207149408409366

Gandhi, B., & Oakley, D. A. (2005). Does 'hypnosis' by any other name smell as sweet? The efficacy of 'hypnotic' inductions depends on the label 'hypnosis.' *Consciousness and Cognition, 14*(2), 304-315. https://doi.org/10.1016/j.concog.2004.12.004

Garry, M., & Loftus, E. F. (1994). Pseudomemories without hypnosis. *International Journal of Clinical and Experimental Hypnosis, 42*(4), 363-378. https://doi.org/10.1080/00207149408409365

Giannelli, P. C. (1995). The admissibility of hypnotic evidence in U.S. courts. *International Journal of Clinical and Experimental Hypnosis, 43*(2), 212-233. https://doi.org/10.1080/00207149508409962

Grabowski, K. L., Roese, N. J., & Thomas, M. R. (1991). The role of expectancy in hypnotic hypermnesia: A brief communication. *International Journal of Clinical and Experimental Hypnosis, 39*(4), 193-197. https://doi.org/10.1080/00207149108409635

Green, J. P. (2003). Beliefs about hypnosis: Popular beliefs, misconceptions, and the importance of experience. *International Journal of Clinical and Experimental Hypnosis, 51*(4), 369-381. https://doi.org/10.1076/iceh.51.4.369.16408

Green, J. P., Page, R. A., Rasekhy, R., Bernhardt, S. E., & Johnson, L. (2006). Cultural views and attitudes about hypnosis: A survey of college students across four countries. *International Journal of Clinical and Experimental Hypnosis, 54*(3), 263-280. https://doi.org/10.1080/00207140600689439

Gruzelier, J. (2000). Unwanted effects of hypnosis: A review of the evidence and its implications. *Contemporary Hypnosis, 17*(4), 163-193.

Hammond, D. C. et al. (1995). *Clinical hypnosis and memory: Guidelines for clinicians and for forensic hypnosis.* American Society for Clinical Hypnosis.

Herman, J. L., & Schatzow, E. (1987). Recovery and verification of memories of childhood sexual trauma. *Psychoanalytic Psychology, 4*(1), 1-14. https://doi.org/10.1037/h0079126

Jiang, H., White, M. P., Greicius, M. D., Waelde, L. C., & Spiegel, D. (2017). Brain activity and functional connectivity associated with hypnosis. *Cerebral Cortex, 27*(8), 4083-4093. https://doi.org/10.1093/cercor/bhw220

Johnson, M. E., & Hauck, C. (1999). Beliefs and opinions about hypnosis held by the general public: A systematic evaluation. *American Journal of Clinical Hypnosis, 42*(1), 10-20. https://doi.org/10.1080/00029157.1999.10404241

Laurence, J.-R., & Perry, C. (1983b). Hypnotically created memory among highly hypnotizable subjects. *Science, 222*(4623), 523-524. https://doi.org/10.1126/science.6623094

Lindsay, D. S., & Read, J. D. (1995). "Memory work" and recovered memories of childhood sexual abuse: Scientific evidence and public, professional, and personal issues. *Psychology, Public Policy, and Law, 1*(4), 846-908. https://doi.org/10.1037/1076-8971.1.4.846

Loftus, E. F., & Hoffman, H. G. (1989). Misinformation and memory: The creation of new memories. *Journal of Experimental Psychology: General, 118*(1), 100-104. https://doi.org/10.1037/0096-3445.118.1.100

Lynn, S. J., Kirsch, I., Terhune, D. B., & Green, J. P. (2020). Myths and misconceptions about hypnosis and suggestion: Separating fact and fiction. *Applied Cognitive Psychology, 34*(6), 1253-1264. https://doi.org/10.1002/acp.3730

Lynn, S. J., Lock, T. G., Myers, B., & Payne, D. G. (1997). Recalling the unrecallable: Should hypnosis be used to recover memories in psychotherapy? *Current Directions in Psychological Science, 6*(3), 79-83. https://doi.org/10.1111/1467-8721.ep11512662

Lynn, S. J., Matthews, A., & Barnes, S. (2009). Hypnosis and memory: From Bernheim to the present. In *Handbook of imagination and mental simulation* (pp. 103-118). Psychology Press.

Malinoski, P. T., & Lynn, S. J. (1999). The plasticity of early memory reports: Social pressure, hypnotizability, compliance and interrogative suggestibility. *International Journal of Clinical and Experimental Hypnosis, 47*(4), 320-345. https://doi.org/10.1080/00207149908410040

Melton, G. B., Petrila, J., Poythress, N. G., Slobogin, C., Otto, R. K., Mossman, D., & Condie, L. O. (2018). *Psychological evaluations for the courts, Fourth Edition: A handbook for mental health professionals and lawyers.* Guilford Publications.

Muschalla, B., & Schönborn, F. (2021). Induction of false beliefs and false memories in laboratory studies: A systematic review. *Clinical Psychology and Psychotherapy*, *28*(5), 1194-1209. https://doi.org/10.1002/cpp.2567

Orne, E. C., Whitehouse, W. G., Dinges, D. F., & Orne, M. T. (1996). Memory liabilities associated with hypnosis: Does low hypnotizability confer immunity? *International Journal of Clinical and Experimental Hypnosis*, *44*(4), 354-369. https://doi.org/10.1080/00207149608416098

Register, P. A., & Kihlstrom, J. F. (1987). Hypnotic effects on hypermnesia. *International Journal of Clinical and Experimental Hypnosis*, *35*(3), 155-170. https://doi.org/10.1080/00207148708416051

Roediger III, H. L., & Gallo, D. A. (2001). Processes affecting accuracy and distortion in memory: An overview. In M. Eisen, J. Quas, & G. Goodman (Eds.) *Memory and suggestibility in the forensic interview (pp. 3-28)*. Routledge.

Scheflin, A. W., & Shapiro, J. L. (1989). *Trance on trial*. Guilford Press.

Scoboria, A., Mazzoni, G., & Kirsch, I. (2006). Effects of misleading questions and hypnotic memory suggestion on memory reports: A Signal-detection analysis. *International Journal of Clinical and Experimental Hypnosis*, *54*(3), 340-359. https://doi.org/10.1080/00207140600689538

Scoboria, A., Mazzoni, G., Kirsch, I., & Milling, L. (2002). Immediate and persisting effects of misleading questions and hypnosis on memory reports. *Journal of Experimental Psychology: Applied*, *8*, 26-32. https://doi.org/10.1037/1076-898X.8.1.26

Spanos, N. P., Burgess, C. A., Burgess, M. F., Samuels, C., & Blois, W. O. (1999). Creating false memories of infancy with hypnotic and non-hypnotic procedures. *Applied Cognitive Psychology*, *13*(3), 201-218. https://doi.org/10.1002/(SICI)1099-0720(199906)13:3<201::AID-ACP565>3.0.CO;2-X

Spiegel, H., & Spiegel, D. (2008). *Trance and treatment: Clinical uses of hypnosis*. American Psychiatric Pub.

Steblay, N. M., & Bothwell, R. K. (1994). Evidence for hypnotically refreshed testimony. *Law and Human Behavior*, *18*(6), 635-651. https://doi.org/10.1007/BF01499329

Wall, P. D., & Lieberman, L. R. (1976). Effects of task motivation and hypnotic induction on hypermnesia. *American Journal of Clinical Hypnosis*, *18*(4), 250-253. https://doi.org/10.1080/00029157.1976.10403807

White, R. W., Fox, G. F., & Harris, W. W. (1940). Hypnotic hypermnesia for recently learned material. *The Journal of Abnormal and Social Psychology*, *35*(1), 88-103. https://doi.org/10.1037/h0055612

Whitehouse, W. G., Dinges, D. F., Orne, E. C., & Orne, M. T. (1988). Hypnotic hypermnesia: Enhanced memory accessibility or report bias? *Journal of Abnormal Psychology*, *97*(3), 289-295. https://doi.org/10.1037/0021-843X.97.3.289

Williams, L. M. (1994). Recall of childhood trauma: A prospective study of women's memories of child sexual abuse. *Journal of Consulting and Clinical Psychology*, *62*(6), 1167-1176. https://doi.org/10.1037/0022-006X.62.6.1167

Yapko, M. D. (1994a). *Suggestions of abuse*. Simon & Schuster.

Yapko, M. D. (1994b). Suggestibility and repressed memories of abuse: A survey of psychotherapists' beliefs. *American Journal of Clinical Hypnosis*, *36*(3), 163-171. https://doi.org/10.1080/00029157.1994.10403066

Zitman, F. G., van Dyck, R., Spinhoven, P., & Linssen, A. C. G. (1992). Hypnosis and autogenic training in the treatment of tension headaches: A two-phase constructive design study with follow-up. *Journal of Psychosomatic Research*, *36*(3), 219-228. https://doi.org/10.1016/0022-3999(92)90086-H

CHAPTER 14
TREATMENT PLANNING IN
CLINICAL HYPNOSIS

DONALD MOSS AND
ERIC WILMARTH

Chapter Learning Objectives

1. Understand hypnotic dimensions of the patient's decision to seek help and the patient's experience of the first therapeutic encounter.

2. Explain the initial assessment and screening process, to determine the patient's appropriateness and readiness for clinical hypnosis treatment.

3. Explain the value and strategy of coordination with the patient's medical providers.

4. Execute a thorough case assessment to elucidate the information necessary to develop a quality treatment plan.

Planning treatment in clinical hypnosis always involves a balancing between applying the accumulated knowledge in the field and responding to the dynamic interaction with the patient in the present moment. This chapter will outline the knowledge and the craft that should be applied in planning clinical hypnosis, and the communication with patients to obtain their informed consent. The authors also acknowledge that the principle of *utilization* prevails in treatment sessions, and the intended itinerary for a session may shift abruptly, based on what the patient presents in the moment.

PRESENTATION AND COMPLAINTS

Be aware that treatment begins at least with the first entrance of patients into your clinic and often in that earlier moment when they decide to seek help. The patient's first glance at your online presentation on your website or social media sites may give further direction to a change process. Patient expectations are central to the treatment process and each aspect of your physical setting, your staff behavior, and your own welcoming of the patient into your office installs hope and raises expectations or invites discouragement. As Will Rogers pointed out, you never get a second chance to make a first impression (Rogers, 2015).

Be aware of your manner in greeting the patient and be aware of the subliminal messages conveyed by your verbal engagement from the beginning. Most first sessions are devoted formally to assessment and treatment planning, yet this first meeting provides an opportunity that is not-to-be-missed for ego strengthening and other positive suggestive processes. The assessment session is always also a uniquely important treatment session. Suggestion is a fundamental component of hypnosis, but suggestions should be offered long before the first formal induction or trance elicitation. Given the high percentage of patients who do not return for treatment, one of the key goals of the first session is to assure a second session. To accomplish this, some suggestion of hope must be offered.

We may begin by posing some version of the miracle question to the patient, popularized by Steve De Shazer (De Shazer et al., 2021): If you look forward three months and discover that this hypnotic treatment has been successful, what will that look like? How do you imagine life will be different after the sessions have accomplished two or three positive steps in this treatment? It is also critical to listen to the patient's presentation of the problem and consider adopting the patient's language in discussing the problem.

CONDITIONS FOR WHICH HYPNOSIS AND RELATED TECHNIQUES ARE APPROPRIATE

Evidence-Based and Current Outcomes Research

Is the patient presenting with a well-defined disorder such as panic disorder or myofascial pain, for which a variety of effective hypnotic interventions have been developed? Or is the patient describing a more vague and diffuse existential dissatisfaction, without clear diagnosis or evidence-based solutions.

Outcomes research has shown the clinical efficacy of hypnosis with a wide range of medical and mental health disorders, including anxiety, depression, acute and chronic pain, and irritable bowel syndrome. Published protocols, with at least moderate research support, have also been published for habit disorders such as smoking and weight management.

In beginning an overview of therapeutic applications suited for hypnosis, pain management is clearly the area with the strongest history and research support. While reports of hypnosis for pain management go back hundreds of years (Esdaile, 1846), in the past 45 years numerous books have been published specifically on the use of hypnosis for pain management (Hilgard & Hilgard, 1996; Barber, 1996; Schafer, 1996; Eimer & Freeman, 1998; Patterson, 2010; Jensen, 2011; Brugnoli, 2014; and Jensen, 2018, 2019b.) Some authors specifically address pain in the pediatric population (Kuttner, 2010; Anbar, 2021).

Pain can be subdivided into multiple subsets including acute vs. chronic pain, as well as via assessing pain location or cause such as headaches vs. back pain or cancer pain vs. fibromyalgia or procedural pain. For example, Kendrick et al. (2015) reviewed 29 randomized controlled trial studies and found hypnosis decreased acute procedural pain compared to standard care and attention control groups. Adachi et al. (2014) completed a meta-analysis on published studies addressing hypnosis and chronic pain and again found hypnosis treatment to be superior to standard care and other psychological treatments.

Another well supported area for the integration of hypnosis with medical and psychological treatment is that of irritable bowel syndrome (IBS). An estimated 11.2% of the world's adult population suffers from IBS (Lovell & Ford, 2012) with symptoms that range from mildly distressing to severely incapacitating. Palsson (2015), in a summary of his comprehensive review of the literature related to hypnosis and IBS, states:

> Collectively this body of research shows unequivocally that for both adults and children with IBS, hypnosis treatment is highly efficacious in reducing bowel symptoms and can offer lasting and substantial symptom relief for a large proportion of patients who do not respond adequately to usual medical treatment approaches. (Palsson, 2015, p. 134).

Palsson (2006) and Palsson and van Tilburg (2015) also published protocols for using hypnosis with IBS that have been widely accepted and used. Whitehead (2006) also noted that hypnosis appears effective with IBS symptoms even for patients who have been unresponsive to other approaches.

Carolyn Daitch (2007, 2011, 2014, 2018) has long been an advocate for the use of hypnosis with anxiety disorders and suggested that patients suffering from General Anxiety Disorder (GAD) are often ideal hypnosis candidates based on their heightened somatic sensitivity, excellent focused—attention and absorption, and unusual capacity for vivid imagery. According to the Centers for Disease Control and

Preventions (CDC, 2021), the already common condition of anxiety increased markedly between 2020 and 2021 with the appearance of COVID-19, suggesting that almost all treatment planning strategies take the potential impact of anxiety into account either as a primary or secondary factor. Both Alladin (2016) and Daitch (2018) promoted combining hypnosis with cognitive behavioral therapy for the treatment of anxiety. This recommendation was supported empirically by Valentine et al. (2019) in a meta-analysis of hypnotic interventions for anxiety. Patients who were offered hypnosis reported significant reductions in anxiety and those combining hypnosis combined with another treatment had the best results.

The World Health Organization identified depression as the number-one cause of disability globally (Friedrich, 2017; WHO, 2017). According to the National Institute of Mental Health (NIMH, 2019), depression is among the most common mental health disorders in the United States. Fortunately, hypnosis appears to have a positive role to play in the treatment of depression. (Alladin, 2012, 2016; Kirsch & Low, 2013; McCann & Landes 2010; Torem, 2017; Yapko, 2001, 2006, 2009, 2010). An article by Alladin and Alibhai (2007) encouraged the use of hypnosis as an adjunctive addition to an existing treatment, cognitive behavioral therapy (CBT). Their study suggested that while treatment with both CBT and hypnosis resulted in clinical improvement, the best results came with the combination of these approaches. During this time of pandemic, treatment planning should consider both depression and anxiety in developing any treatment plan and hypnosis is well suited to enhance the effectiveness of this treatment. Torem (2017) suggested that treatment planning for depression can use several hypnotic approaches including use of the affect bridge, age-progression, and age-regression, as well as a healthy dose of ego-strengthening.

When there are clear outcomes of research supporting hypnotic treatment for a diagnosed disorder, with well-defined treatment pro-tocols, it can be positive for patient expectations to share that infor-mation. Patients with a higher education level can benefit from reading a clear and straightforward review article. Others will experience more hope when the practitioner simply communicates: "Researchers at Stanford University, Baylor University, and several other research centers have applied hypnosis for your problem, with very strong treatment effects. I am hopeful that you can benefit as well."

When there is very little outcome research for a hypnosis application, but case narratives and anecdotal reports have been published, it is important to communicate an accurate yet hope-enhancing message: "There have been no large clinical trials on hypnosis for your problem, but four therapists in different parts of the country have published case studies with encouraging results in individuals with very similar symptoms. If you would like me to use hypnosis in your care, I am hopeful for a positive result."

CAUTIONS AND CONTRAINDICATIONS

Medical Conditions Masquerading as Psychological Disorders

Each clinical treatment for a diagnosable medical or psychological disorder should begin with a thorough psychosocial and medical history. Is the patient presenting with a long-standing complaint, which has been thoroughly investigated and diagnosed medically? If that is the case, a brief consultation with primary care physicians is appropriate, simply to make physicians aware of the new intervention for their patient and to ensure your through understanding of the medical problems and risks. Brief intermittent communications with the primary care provider of the patient's presenting problem and discussion of the relevant evidence-base can also assure optimal management of the patient's medical condition and strengthen the physician's positive acceptance for hypnotically based treatment.

Be aware that some chronic conditions are managed somewhat delicately, and if hypnosis is effective, medical management might require adjustments. Diabetes for example, is sometimes accompanied by very labile blood glucose fluctuations, exacerbated by stress. When hypnosis and stress management are effective, insulin may need to be reduced, or the patient may experience hypoglycemic episodes. Similarly, when a hypertensive patient's blood pressures are elevated by severe life stress, and hypnotically based treatment significantly moderates the patient's stress response, the anti-hypertensive medication may need titration. Accordingly, the practitioner should monitor the patient's medical symptoms throughout treatment and communicate any change in frequency and severity to the physician.

In some cases, patients present with a new condition with a symptom that has emerged abruptly. If so, we must assure that the patient has already undergone a thorough medical diagnostic evaluation to assure that no life-threatening condition is present. If not, a medical referral is in order. Occasionally, physicians recognize the high level of anxiety and emotional disturbance in a patient and assume without comprehensive evaluation that the symptoms are psychologically driven. Yet, patients with chronic emotional disturbance also are at risk for serious medical illness.

The present authors encountered a new patient complaining of chest pain, which he attributed to stress. He requested hypnosis and stress management to alleviate pain. He had not yet reported the chest pain to his physician. A same-day referral back to the primary care clinic produced a diagnosis of three severe occlusions in the coronary arteries. This illustrates the importance of diagnosis and referral for assessment of presenting symptoms as needed.

OTHER CONSIDERATIONS IN CHOOSING INTERVENTIONS

Regardless of planned intervention techniques, the most important ingredient in successful hypnosis treatment is the therapist-patient relationship, which must be marked by empathy, safety, trust, and understanding. The present chapter authors begin most treatment sessions with a brief exercise in mindful meditation, breathing slowly, setting aside the stress and emotional baggage of the day, and cultivating an openness to the present moment (Moss, 2020). This opening exercise facilitates a better attunement between patient and practitioner, and greater self-awareness and expressiveness on the part of the patient. In addition, it introduces a new life skill for the patient.

Well-Documented Interventions and Informed Consent

Hypnosis is both a science and an art. There are an increasing number of evidence-based protocols for hypnosis treatment of specific disorders, described in peer reviewed research reports and scholarly books (Alladin, 2016; Alladin & Alibhai, 2007; Elkins & Olendzki, 2018; McCann & Landes, 2010; Palsson & van Tilburg, 2015). In addition, several leaders in the field have published the scripts, protocols, and case narratives of master clinicians. For example, in the area of pain, Jensen (2017, 2018, 2019a, 2019b) has published the "Favorite Methods of Master Clinicians" series, presenting best practices in clinical hypnosis of senior clinicians.

Patients presenting in the average clinical setting frequently do not fall into the neat categories of efficacy studies, often presenting with multiple and complex conditions, vague yet distressing conditions, and disorders not yet covered by published randomized controlled trials. In these cases, the practitioner depends on utilizing best practices in hypnotic techniques, applying effective inductions and therapeutic suggestions based on what is known about similar disorders. Alternately, practitioners may isolate elements in the overall symptom presentation that are amenable to hypnotic intervention, such as heightened baseline stress and anxiety accompanying a chronic medical illness. In any case, responsible practitioners document a well-defined baseline in symptom frequency and severity and assess treatment progress intermittently to evaluate whether the approach is producing benefits.

In addition, many patients with complex and chronic symptoms also show a heightened stress response, marked by excessive muscle tension, irregular or rapid breathing, and rapid heart rate. Often a hypnotically enhanced stress management approach will moderate the patient's stress response and reduce the severity of their symptoms (Elkins, 2014).

Once the patient has heard about the likely benefits from hypnosis-based interventions and expresses agreement and "buy-in" for hypnosis, alone or in concert with other therapeutic interventions, a written consent form is recommended. The informed consent *process* begins with this signed consent form and continues beyond the initial session. Every time a new intervention is discussed, every time the therapist assesses and discusses the patient's progress, and every time the therapist examines whether to modify treatment interventions, that too is part of the informed consent process, and should be noted in progress notes.

Seizing the Moment

Healthcare today increasingly emphasizes evidence-based care, clinical applications documented in randomized controlled trials, and standardized treatments. A recent Task Force supported by the major professional organizations in hypnosis elaborated clear standards for assessing efficacy in hypnosis treatment (Kekecs et al., 2021). Yet hypnosis history also shows the power of responding to the moment, utilizing a chance utterance or image expressed by the patient, and utilizing that moment for therapeutic effect. The Ericksonian approach emphasizes that utilizing whatever presents in the moment can be powerfully transformative.

It is critical that the therapist remain fully present to the patient throughout the initial evaluative session, because "utilization" can unfold right in the middle of assessment, with such impact that no further treatment is necessary (Hoyt & Talmon, 2014).

Stepped Care and Integrative Care

Hypnosis is frequently provided in combination with various forms of psychotherapy and behavior therapy, with documented efficacy of their own. Cognitive behavioral therapy, behavior therapy, exposure therapies, dynamic psychotherapy, and mindfulness approaches can all be combined effectively with hypnotic interventions (Alladin, 2016; Elkins & Olendzki, 2018; Green & Lynn, 2018).

In addition, practitioners increasingly integrate hypnotically based interventions with lifestyle interventions, nutritional medicine, and complementary and alternative therapies. McGrady and Moss (2013, 2018) have published guidelines and illustrative case narratives for integrating hypnosis and other mind-body therapies into comprehensive, stepped care treatment for a variety of medical and emotional disorders. Hypnosis combines well with interventions from other disciplines, whether it is acupuncture, functional nutrition, or meditation training.

ILLUSTRATING TREATMENT PLANNING AND CASES

We will close this chapter on treatment planning with two case narratives, illustrating how practitioners assessed two patients and developed treatment programs integrating hypnosis into their overall care.

Case Narrative 1: Planning Hypnosis Treatment for Frances, a 36-Year-Old Male with Irritable Bowel Syndrome (IBS)

Frances was a 36-year-old married sales representative for a financial services software company. Frances experienced the first symptoms of IBS in graduate school and managed the symptoms himself throughout his 20s. The symptoms of diarrhea, gas, bloating, cramping, and pain worsened in his 30s with increasing stress in his sales work and business travel. Increasingly, he delayed necessary work trips, called in sick on days of severe diarrhea, and found any time away from home and office anxiety provoking. He was increasingly vigilant about the locations of rest rooms, and unfamiliar settings were anxiety provoking.

At age 34, Frances sought medical evaluation, and was diagnosed with irritable bowel syndrome (IBS). He met the requirements for an IBS diagnosis following the Rome IV criteria (Hellström & Benno, 2019; Moss, in press). After a poor response to dietary and medication therapies, his physician referred Frances to a behavioral health clinic for evaluation and treatment of irritable bowel syndrome accompanying anxiety disorder and depression.

The behavioral health practitioner reviewed his medical and psychosocial history with Frances and concluded that he had been thoroughly evaluated on the bio-medical side and that he presented a typical behavioral and emotional profile for IBS. IBS has a high co-morbidity with several medical and psychological disorders, including generalized anxiety disorder and depression (Ladabaum et al., 2012). As part of the assessment, Frances completed an anxiety scale called the Beck Anxiety Inventory and a depression test called the Beck Depression Inventory. His score was severe on both questionnaires. He completed the IBS-Severity Scoring System (IBS-SSS) question-naire and scored 260, which is high in the moderate range for this instrument (Francis et al., 1996; Drossman et al., 2011). Finally, the practitioner administered the Elkins Hypnotizability Scale-Clinical Form (EHS-CF), and Frances earned a score of 8, placing him in the high range for hypnotic ability. He was encouraged that he would probably respond well to a hypnotic treatment.

Frances presented himself as open to a mind-body, integrative treatment program. He had read considerably about irritable bowel disorders, attempted several self-help programs, and was excited to work with a clinic team that had treated other patients with bowel disorders. Frances also visited the behavioral health clinic website before his initial visit and was excited to see an inset box about "gut-directed hypnosis" offering hope for bowel disorders. Frances' behavioral therapist suggested a two-pronged approach, including work with a functional medicine specialist, and a program of hypnosis utilizing a protocol developed at the University of North Carolina Digestive Diseases program.

The functional medicine physician conducted blood, urine, and stool samples and diagnosed some food sensitivities. The physician informed Frances that many but not all persons with IBS benefit from reducing foods that are called FODMAPS foods, such as certain vegetables (artichokes, asparagus, beans, cabbage, cauliflower), fruit (apples, apricots, blackberries, cherries, mango, nectarines, pears), and dairy products. Initially, she recommended no dairy, a low or no gluten diet, and gradually increasing the amount of soluble fiber in Frances' diet. She also recommended adding two dietary supplements and a pro-biotic. Frances found that his diarrhea and pain were moderately reduced with the nutritional program, but still troublesome.

The University of North Carolina hypnosis protocol called for two preliminary sessions of education about anxiety management and seven scripted hypnosis sessions focused on bowel symptoms. The therapist explained to Frances that approximately 80% of patients have reported significant improvements in their IBS symptoms in controlled research (Palsson, 2006; Palsson & Van Tilburg, 2015). The therapist also committed that several local men with IBS had benefitted from the UNC protocol. Frances commenced the hypnosis treatment, attended seven scripted sessions, and practiced almost daily with an audio hypnosis recording that supplemented the in-office hypnosis. He reported further reduction of most of his IBS symptoms, to a level that he could more easily manage. He also reported that his anxiety symptoms and his deep discouragement were reduced both by the hypnosis with improvement in his bowel control. His final session included a repeat administration of the Beck scales, and Frances scored in the low moderate range in anxiety and in the mild range in depression. He also showed a large and clinically significant reduction in the IBS-SSS to 155, in the mild range for IBS symptoms.

Case Narrative 2: Planning Hypnosis Treatment for Alice, a 35-Year-Old Female with Multiple Anxiety Disorders

Alice was a pleasant 35-year-old woman referred for psychological evaluation and treatment by her primary care physician for "debilitating anxiety". Alice had been married for 16 years and had three children, daughters aged 16 and 14 and a special-needs son who had died two years previous at the age of 6, after being hit by a stray bullet fired by a hunter over a mile from their home. Alice was initially seen for her appointments via Zoom, because of COVID-19 precautions but also because of acute agoraphobia. Over time she was able to attend therapy sessions in person.

Alice reported that she first sought treatment from her primary care physician because of anxiety following the birth of her son. He was born with multiple medical complications and his extreme medical needs required her to quit her teaching job and care for him full-time. She reported that she also had daily support from a home nursing agency. Her son had multiple near-death events over his first five years of life but appeared to be somewhat more medically stable before his accidental death. Alice was treated with a low dose of a benzodiazepine for several years when her son was younger but discontinued these due to a fear of addiction. She noted a family history involving her father and an older brother with drug and alcohol addiction and she expressed a fear of becoming addicted to her medication. She reported that she had learned to cope much better with her anxiety up until the death of her son.

With the death of her son, Alice explained that she felt rage, guilt, despair, and panic all at the same time. She noted how unfair it was that she and her son had struggled so hard for years to overcome his medical problems, only to have a freak accident take his life. Her guilt centered around her feelings of relief that the burden had been removed. She reported that she could not tell the difference between grief and depression but reported that she couldn't function as a wife nor mother for almost a year. She described her family as incredibly supportive and neither daughter seemed to suffer a drop in school performance or change their social interactions. Alice, however, reported that she became completely housebound, suffering a panic attack at the thought of going outside or of driving. Her husband, an IT consultant who worked from their home, provided all transportation needs for their daughters as well as shopping and other travel needs. Alice noted that COVID-19 "came at the right time" because it allowed her to stay at home even for her doctor's appointments.

In her initial appointment, Alice presented as a pleasant, bright, and motivated woman with some specific goals for treatment. Her summary was simple: "I want my life back". She described a history of being extroverted and active in school and church activities, generally athletic and well liked. Her initial goal was "to be able to leave my house without feeling like I'm going to die." Several trips to the emergency room and follow-up evaluations suggested that she had no underlying medical problems causing her symptoms. Her primary care physician had offered a return to benzodiazepine medication however she rejected this approach.

In the initial stage of treatment planning, it is often helpful to first assess: 1. Issues, 2. Obstacles, and 3. Resources. Some of the issues identified with Alice included an extended history of stress and general anxiety prior to her current panic attacks, the traumatic death of her son, and a family history of substance abuse. The only "obstacle" Alice identified has related to her husband who had become quite "hovering" and overly protective to avoid her suffering anxiety. She noted that her daughters tended to be over-protective of her as well. The "resources" identified included a healthy premorbid state (prior to her son's birth), high motivation, high intelligence and imagination, and good friends "who want me back." Alice was proud of the fact that she had essentially overcome her anxiety without medication prior to her son's death but was frustrated that the skills that she had developed were "completely gone."

Alice was amenable to the suggestion that hypnosis might be helpful and although no formal hypnotizability scale was attempted online, she proved to have a good deal of hypnotic ability. After initial experiences involving safe-place imagery, hypnosis was combined with systematic desensitization to allow her to first imagine and eventually to experience walks outside of her house. This proved to be more complicated since being outside of her house triggered memory of her son's death. Once she was able to accomplish the goal of daily walks outside, hypnosis-assisted systematic desensitization was used to first imagine and then actually drive her car for progressively longer periods of time. This allowed her to begin to attend therapy sessions in person and decrease her dependence on her family. Once she was able to come to the office, cognitive behavioral therapy, hypnosis, and biofeedback were all used to increase her self-regulation skills and decrease the physical impact of anxiety.

While the overall treatment program for Alice addressed issues including grief, anger, depression, shame and anxiety, hypnosis was integrated into the treatment on multiple levels to improve coping and self-regulation skills allowing her to regain the independence she sought. Alice was able to return to part-time work as a substitute teacher and discontinued regularly scheduled therapy appointments, choosing to return on an "as needed" basis.

Treatment planning can also include a provision for treatment assessment. With Alice, little formal psychological testing was done via telehealth, however she did complete a set of Visual Analog Scales which were converted into a 10-point Likert Scale. She initially estimated that both Anxiety and Depression would be a "9" on a 1-10 scale. Follow-up assessment saw these numbers drop to a 3 and 2 respectively. Progress was also measured by her subjective report of improvement as well as her behavior, it this case, her ability to leave home and engage in productive activity. She agreed that, in spite of ongoing grief, she was successful in "getting my life back."

CONCLUSION

In summary, the hypnotic treatment relationship affects therapeutic success, and the patient's first contacts with the provider's website, office staff, and the provider are opportunities to encourage hope and positive treatment expectancy. The initial evaluation should include a thorough medical and psychosocial history, and a screening for possible undiagnosed medical problems, that require immediate medical care. Coordination with medical providers assures a correct and thorough assessment and enhances medical provider support for behavioral and hypnotic interventions. Optimal evidence-based treatment matches the patient's complaint with a hypnotic treatment protocol, which research has shown to be effective for the patient's disorder. When the patient's presenting problems do not match well to available outcome research, the practitioner may select a treatment approach effective for a similar disorder or for some aspect of the patient's clinical condition. For example, many patients' complaints are worse when life stress is high, and a hypnotically enhanced intervention to manage stress may moderate the patient's medical and emotional symptoms.

Finally, it is critical that the practitioner remain attentive to the patient's presentation of images, language, or random comments, even in the initial session, which might be utilized in a patient-centered hypnotic intervention.

Hypnosis is often more effective in combination with CBT or other empirically validated psychotherapy, or in a form of stepped care combining hypnosis with health-enhancing lifestyle change. The two case narratives provide examples showing how the initial assessment can guide treatment planning, culminating in effective care and positive patient outcomes.

CHAPTER 14
REFLECTION QUESTIONS

1. What are the important things to consider for the first meeting with a patient?

2. How does an initial assessment and screening process look like?

3. What are the necessary things to discuss with patient's medical providers before developing a treatment plan?

4. Why is it important for a clinician to pay attention to in the Now moment?

REFERENCES

Adachi, T., Fujino, H., Nakae, A., Mashimo, T., & Sasaki, T. (2014). A meta-analysis of hypnosis for chronic pain problems: Comparison between hypnosis, standard care, and other psychological interventions. *International Journal of Clinical and Experimental Hypnosis, 62*(1), 1-28. doi.10.1080/00207144.2013.841471

Alladin, A. (2012). Cognitive hypnotherapy for major depressive disorder. *American Journal of Clinical Hypnosis, 54*(4), 275-293. doi.org/10.1080/00029157. 2012.654527

Alladin, A. (2016). *Integrative cognitive behavioral therapy for anxiety disorders: An evidence-based approach to enhancing cognitive behavioral therapy with mindfulness and hypnotherapy.* John Wiley & Sons, Ltd.

Alladin, A., & Alibhai, A. (2007). Cognitive hypnotherapy for depression: An empirical investigation. *International Journal of Clinical and Experimental Hypnosis, 55*, 147-166. doi:10.1080/00207140601177897

Anbar, R. D. (2021). *Changing children's lives with hypnosis: A journey to the center.* Rowman & Littlefield

Barber, J. (1996). *Hypnosis and suggestion in the treatment of pain: A clinical guide.* W.W. Norton & Company.

Brugnoli, M. P. (2014). *Clinical hypnosis in pain therapy and palliative care: A handbook of techniques for Improving the patient's physical and psychological well-being.* Charles C. Thomas Publisher, LTD.

Centers for Disease Control and Prevention (2021). Symptoms of anxiety or depressive disorder and use of mental health care among adults during the COVID-19 pandemic-United States, August 2020-February 2021. https://www.cdc.gov/mmwr/volumes/70/wr/mm7013e2.htm

Daitch, C. (2007). *Affect regulation toolbox: Practical and effective hypnotic interventions for the over-reactive client.* W. W. Norton.

Daitch, C. (2011). *Anxiety disorders: The go-to guide for clients and therapists.* W.W. Norton.

Daitch, C. (2014). Hypnotherapeutic treatment for anxiety-related relational discord: A short-term hypnotherapeutic protocol. *American Journal of Clinical Hypnosis, 56*(4), 325-342 doi.org/10.1080/00029157.2013.861341

Daitch, C. (2018). Cognitive behavioral therapy, mindfulness, and hypnosis as treatment methods for generalized anxiety disorder. *American Journal of Clinical Hypnosis, 61*(1), 57-69. doi.org/10.1080/00029157.2018.1458594

De Shazer, S., Doland, Y., Korman, H., Trepper, T., McCollum, E., & Berg, I. K. (2021). *More than miracles: The state of the art of solution focused brief therapy* (classic edition). Routledge.

Drossman, D. A., Chang, L., Bellamy, N., Gallo-Torres, H. E., Lembo, A., Mearin, F., Norton, N. J., & Whorwell, P. (2011). Severity in irritable bowel syndrome: A Rome Foundation Working Team report. *American Journal of Gastroenterology, 106*(10), 1749-1759. doi.10.1038/ajg.2011.201

Eimer, B. N., & Freeman, A. (1998). *Pain management psychotherapy: A practical guide.* John Wiley and Sons.

Elkins, G. (2014). *Hypnotic relaxation therapy: Principles and applications.* Springer Publishing Company.

Elkins, G., & Olendzki, N. (2018). *Mindful hypnotherapy: The basics for clinical practice.* Springer Publishing Company.

Esdaile, J. (1846). *Mesmerism in India and its practical applications in surgery and medicine.* Silas Andrus.

Francis, C. Y., Morris, J., & Whorwell, P. J. (1996). The irritable bowel severity scoring system: A simple method of monitoring irritable bowel syndrome and its progress. *Alimentary Pharmacology and Therapeutics, 11*(2), 395-402. doi:10.1046/j.1365-2036.1997.142318000.x

Friedrich, M. J. (2017). Depression is the leading cause of disability around the world. *Journal of the American Medical Association, 317*(15), 1517.

Green, J., & Lynn, S. J. (2018). *Cognitive-behavioral therapy, mindfulness, and hypnosis for smoking cessation: A scientifically informed intervention.* Wiley-Blackwell.

Hellström, P. M., & Benno, P. (2019). The Rome IV: Irritable bowel syndrome-A functional disorder. *Best Practices in Clinical Gastroenterology*, 40-41, 101634. doi.10.1016/j.bpg.2019.101634

Hilgard E.R. & Hilgard J.R. (1996). *Hypnosis in the relief of pain* (revised edition). Brunner Mazel.

Hoyt, M. F., & Talmon, M. (2014). *Capturing the moment: Singe session therapy and walk-in services.* Crown House Publishing.

Jensen, M. P. (2011). *Hypnosis for chronic pain management: Therapist guide.* Oxford University Press.

Jensen, M. P. (Ed.) (2017). *The art and practice of hypnotic induction: Favorite methods of master clinicians.* Denny Creek Press.

Jensen, M. P. (Ed.) (2018). *Hypnotic techniques for chronic pain management: Favorite methods of master clinicians.* Denny Creek Press.

Jensen, M. P. (Ed.) (2019a). *Handbook of hypnotic techniques, vol. 1: Favorite methods of master clinicians.* Denny Creek Press.

Jensen, M. P. (Ed.) (2019b). *Hypnosis for acute and procedural pain management: Favorite methods of master clinicians.* Denny Creek Press.

Kekecs, Z., Moss, D., Elkins, G., De Benedettis, G., Pallson, O., Shenefelt, P., Terhune, D., Varga, K., & Whorwell, P. (2021). Guidelines for the assessment of efficacy of clinical hypnosis applications. *PsyArXiv.* doi.org/10.31234/osf.io/2cqaw

Kendrick, C., Sliwinski, J., Yu, Y., Johnson, A., Fisher, W., Kekecs, Z., & Elkins, G. (2016) Hypnosis for acute procedural pain: A critical review. *International Journal of*

Clinical and Experimental Hypnosis, 64(1), 75-115.
doi.10.1080/00207144.2015.1099405

Kirsch, I., & Low, C. B. (2013). Suggestion in the treatment of depression. *American Journal of Clinical Hypnosis, 55*(3), 221-229. doi.org/10.1080/00029157.2012. 738613

Kuttner, L. (2010). *A child in pain: What health professionals can do to help.* Crown House Publishing.

Ladabaum, U., Boyd, E., Zhao, W. K., Mannalithara, A., Sharabidze, A., Singh, G., Chung, E., & Levin, T. R. (2012). Diagnosis, comorbidities, and management of irritable bowel syndrome in patients in a large health maintenance organization. *Clinical Gastroenterology and Hepatolology, 10*(1), 37-45. doi:10.1016/j.cgh.2011.08.015

Lovell, R. M., & Ford, A. C., (2012) Global prevalence of and risk factors for irritable bowel syndrome: A meta-analysis. *Clinical Gastroenterology and Hepatology, 10*(7), 712-721. doi:10.1016/j.cgh.2012.02.029

McCann, B. S., & Landes, S. J. (2010) Hypnosis in the treatment of depression: Considerations in research design and methods. *International Journal of Clinical and Experimental Hypnosis, 58*(2), 147-164. https://doi.org/10.1080/ 00207140903523186

McGrady, A., & Moss, D. (2018). *Integrative pathways: Navigating chronic illness with a mind-body-spirit approach.* Springer.

McGrady, A., & Moss, D. (2013). *Pathways to illness, pathways to health.* Springer. doi.10.1007/978-1-4419-1379-1

Moss, D. (2020). The role of mindfulness approaches in integrative medicine. In I. Khazan & D. Moss (Eds.), *Mindfulness, acceptance, and compassion in biofeedback practices* (pp. 19-25). Association for Applied Psychophysiology and Biofeedback.

Moss, D. (in press). Irritable bowel syndrome. In I. Khazan, F. Shaffer, R. Lyle, & D. Moss (Eds.), *Evidence-based practice in biofeedback and neurofeedback* (4th edition). Association for Applied Psychophysiology and Biofeedback.

National Institute of Mental Health (NIMH, 2019). Depression. National Institute of Mental Health. https://www.nimh.nih.gov/health/statistics/major-depression

Palsson, O. S. (2006). Standardized hypnosis treatment for irritable bowel syndrome: The North Carolina protocol. *International Journal of Clinical and Experimental Hypnosis, 54*(1), 51-64. doi:10.1080/00207140500322933

Palsson, O.S. (2015). Hypnosis treatment of gastrointestinal disorders: A comprehensive review of the empirical evidence. *American Journal of Clinical Hypnosis, 58,* 134-158. doi.10.1080/00029157.2015.1039114

Palsson, O. S., & van Tilburg, M. (2015). Hypnosis and guided imagery treatment for gastrointestinal disorders: Experience with scripted protocols developed at the University of North Carolina. *American Journal of Clinical Hypnosis, 58*(1), 5-21. doi:10.1080/00029157.2015.1012705

Patterson, D. R. (2010). *Clinical hypnosis for pain control.* American Psychological Association.

Rogers, W. (2015). Thoughts on the business of life. Forbes.com https://www. forbes.com/quotes/9717

Schafer, D. W. (1996). *Relieving pain: A basic hypnotherapeutic approach.* Jason Aronson Inc.

Torem, M. S. (2017). Depression. In G. R. Elkins (Ed.) *Handbook of medical and psychological hypnosis: Foundations, applications, and professional issues* (pp. 505-521). Springer Publishing Company.

Valentine, K. E., Milling, L. S., Clark, L. J., & Moriarty, C. L. (2019) The efficacy of hypnosis as a treatment for anxiety: A meta-analysis. *International Journal of Clinical and Experimental Hypnosis, 67*(3), 336-363. doi.org/10.1080/00207144.2019.1613863

Whitehead, W.E. (2006). Hypnosis for irritable bowel syndrome: The empirical evidence of therapeutic effects. *International Journal of Clinical and Experimental Hypnosis, 54*(1), 7-20. doi:10.1080/00207140500328708

World Health Organization (2017). *Depression and other common mental disorders: Global health estimates.* WHO Document Production Services. https://apps.who.int/iris/bitstream/handle/10665/254610/WHO-MSD-MER-2017.2-eng.pdf

Yapko, M. (2001). *Treating depression with hypnosis: Integrating cognitive-behavioral and strategic approaches.* Brunner/Routledge.

Yapko, M. (2006). *Hypnosis and treating depression: Applications in clinical practice.* Routledge.

Yapko, M. (2009*). Depression is contagious: How the most common mood disorder is spreading around the world and how to stop it.* Free Press

Yapko, M. (2010). Hypnosis in the treatment of depression: An overdue approach to encouraging skillful mood management. *International Journal of Clinical and Experimental Hypnosis, 58*(2), 137-146. doi:10.1080/00207140903523137

CHAPTER 15
ETHICAL CONSIDERATIONS AND PROFESSIONAL CONDUCT

LAUREN SIMICICH AND GARY ELKINS

Chapter Learning Objectives

1. Describe key concepts and terms that have relevance to the ethical practice of clinical hypnosis.

2. Identify ethical considerations that are unique to the remote delivery of clinical hypnosis services through telehealth.

3. Outline the steps of an effective ethical decision-making model that can be used when confronted with an ethical dilemma in the practice of clinical hypnosis.

Ethics has been defined as "a system of moral principles that serve to control or influence individual/human behavior" (Hornby, Cowie, & Lewis, 1974). In the practice of clinical hypnosis, ethics offers professionals a moral map that can be used to guide decision making as they navigate the sometimes-equivocal terrain of clinical practice. We make intentional space here for discussion of ethical considerations of clinical hypnosis so that we can better understand the landscape of our moral map as clinical hypnosis practitioners. Just as the traveler who studies their map is better suited to skillfully traverse the paths along their journey than the traveler who enters blindly into the forest, practitioners who study ethical practice are better prepared to practice ethically, most especially when muddy waters present. As recognized by Pope and Vasquez (2016), "no one is infallible or immune from engaging in unethical behavior." To be human means to have weaknesses, vulnerabilities, and blind spots, so acknowledging our limitations, we spend time in this way to familiarize ourselves with the map of ethical practice of clinical hypnosis.

Before we bring attention to the similarities across the maps of clinical hypnosis practitioners, we first recognize that clinical hypnosis is practiced by a variety of professionals (e.g., physicians, psychologists, dentists, clinical social workers) across many different settings (e.g., hospitals, academic medical centers, private practice). Recognition of these differences is important because each ethical choice is influenced by context and must be made by taking contextual factors into account. Thus, the unique idiographic factors that comprise each individual's clinical practice environment must be considered, perhaps through entertaining questions such as, "What clinical environment do I find myself in?", "How does this environment impact the way that I practice?", and "What is my function within this patient's care?" Although self-reflective practice can assist in finding answers to these inquiries, each individual professional is not left to flounder in isolation and entertain such questions independently. Indeed, no one is an island. Enter each individual discipline's ethics code.

ETHICS CODES

An ethics code provides professionals with a set of guidelines for making ethical choices in clinical practice; they educate about responsibilities, are a basis for accountability, protect patients, and serve to improve professional practice (Nagy, 2017). The ethics codes of the major professional organizations across healthcare that clinical hypnosis may be practiced (e.g., American Medical Association,

American Psychological Association, American Dental Association, National Association of Social Workers) are structured similarly, consisting of two primary sections: 1) ethical principles and 2) ethical standards. Ethical principles are typically aspirational in nature and provide concepts that can be used to guide ethical decision making. Conversely, ethical standards are enforceable and require absolute compliance; they are the "musts" and "must-nots" of clinical practice.

When the ethics codes of major health provision organizations are compared, differences exist most notably within the standards since they are intended to capture the nuances of each profession. More commonality is found in the ethical principles of each ethics code. We refer to the ethical principles of American Psychological Association (2017) as an example to highlight and surmise these core concepts. Beneficence and Nonmaleficence captures the intent to provide care that maximizes the benefits and minimizes the risks or harm to patients. Fidelity and Responsibility encourages the fulfillment of professional responsibilities and maintenance of civility across all persons. Integrity promotes accuracy, honesty, and truthfulness in clinical practice. Justice supports fairness and the equal treatment of all parties. Respect for People's Rights and Dignity inspires the valuing of each person's autonomy and unique set of values, goals, desires, and experiences.

PROFESSIONALLY ACCREDITED
HYPNOSIS ORGANIZATIONS

In addition to the Ethics Code of the American Psychological Association, leading professionally accredited hypnosis organizations have created ethical codes that provide guidelines specific to hypnosis practices. Some include the American Society of Clinical Hypnosis' Code of Conduct, the Society for Clinical and Experimental Hypnosis' Code of Ethics, and the International Society for Hypnosis' Code of Ethics (American Society of Clinical Hypnosis, 2002; International

Society of Hypnosis, 2002; Society of Clinical and Experimental Hypnosis, 2003). These codes seek to address the unique ethical issues that may arise throughout the practice of clinical hypnosis.

Importantly, unlike many lay organizations, professionally accredited organizations share the perspective that clinical hypnosis should be an extension of a demonstrated competency in a specific health care discipline. As illuminated by Alter (2017), when clinical hypnosis is just one of many skills in a practitioner's repertoire, one is in a better position to safeguard themselves from fulfillment of the adage, "if all you've got is a hammer, then everything looks like a nail." Although both professionals and laypersons alike are capable of unethical behavior as they are both human, those who earn more comprehensive educational and training experiences and strive to adhere to a set of professional guidelines are likely to mitigate the amount of ethical violations they commit (Yapko, 2018).

PROFESSIONAL COMPETENCE

When patients present for services and are seeking help, they are trusting practitioners to deliver services with efficacy and fidelity. For this reason, a perpetual evaluation of professional competence is necessary for ethical practice. Factors that are important to consider in determining whether someone is competent to deliver clinical hypnosis services include an individual's (a) professional education, (b) training, (c) licensure, and (d) supervised experience (Elkins, 2014). Since great variability can exist across these factors, measures have been taken over time to provide greater uniformity in professional education expectations in clinical hypnosis. As identified by Elkins and Hammond (1998), standardization in this way (1) allows for clear identification of the unique qualifications, education, and knowledge of the professional practitioners who utilize clinical hypnosis; (2) provides the public with the opportunity to have dependable metrics regarding the educational background of the hypnosis professionals they consult; (3) assures that new professionals have the requisite knowledge and skills needed to effectively function within a competitive practice environment; and (4) encourages research and scientific inquiry rather than relying only on individual anecdotal experiences.

Specifically, professionally accredited hypnosis organizations offer several standardized training and certification opportunities for clinical hypnosis. The Society for Clinical and Experimental Hypnosis offers several, including (a) Certification in Clinical Hypnosis (CCH), (b) Certification in Academic and Research Applications of Hypnosis (CARH), and (c) Certification by Prior Experience (CPE). Also, the American Society of Clinical Hypnosis has (a) Certification of Clinical Hypnosis and (b) Approved Consultant in Clinical Hypnosis. The highest level of advanced specialty certification in hypnosis is diplomate status, which can be earned through the American Board of a practitioner's unique specialty area (e.g., American Board of Psychological Hypnosis, American Board of Medical Hypnosis, American Board of Hypnosis in Dentistry, American Hypnosis Board for Clinical Social Work). Although certification does not automatically imply professional competence or provide a guarantee that the professional's work will be quality, it does provide reassurances across other domains, such as that the practitioner has undergone advanced professional training, is licensed in their respective state or province, has completed a recognized curriculum in clinical hypnosis including small group practice and individualized instruction, and has had their education and training reviewed by qualified peers (Elkins & Hammond, 1998).

Boundaries of Professional Competence

Evaluation of competence also involves acknowledging the limitations and boundaries of one's professional license and expertise. For the practice of clinical hypnosis, competence is needed in the knowledge, research, and application of hypnosis for the treatment of the specific symptom or disorder presented by the patient. Importantly, if one is not competent to treat a population and/or diagnosis of interest without hypnosis, one should not attempt to treat said population and/or diagnosis with hypnosis (Nagy, 2017). We consider these boundaries and practicing within one's scope of practice as being in direct service of the ethical principle of non-maleficence—to do no harm.

Although a thorough conversation about the topic goes beyond the scope of this chapter, it is worth briefly mentioning that professional competence includes cultural competence (Pope & Vasquez, 2016). Cultural competence is typically characterized as being comprised of three primary components: (a) attitudes/beliefs—an understanding of one's own cultural conditioning that affects personal beliefs, values, and attitudes; (b) knowledge—understanding and knowledge of the worldviews of culturally different individuals and groups; and (c) skills—use of culturally appropriate intervention/communication skills (Sue, 2001). This is an area of professional competence that becomes so important to strengthen as the practice of clinical hypnosis becomes increasingly embraced by diverse peoples across a variety of different clinical practice settings.

When gaps in professional competency are identified, one should seek out continuing education, supervision, and professional development resources, or make an appropriate referral (Etzrodt, 2013). When referral is warranted, in the case of lacking the requisite skills needed to treat a patient, or a host of other reasons, such as noticing that the patient isn't benefiting from services, believing that the patient may be harmed by the treatment, or learning that the patient's safety may be compromised, it is important to conduct the referral process in a way that empowers the patient. It is of note that failing to refer a patient can be harmful as well and would be a prime example of non-feasance; that is, when a professional fails to apply a standard, acceptable practice when action is needed.

Maintenance of Professional Competence

Once competence has been established, it is equally important to maintain competency through continual evaluation of ones' skill set and pursuit of various continuing education opportunities, especially when specific knowledge gaps are identified (Etzrodt, 2013). Continuing education opportunities can include reading books and research journals, attending professional workshops, consulting with colleagues, and seeking mentorship and supervision from other qualified professionals (Elkins, 2014). Maintenance of professional competence also includes ongoing evaluation of one's own mental health and engagement in individual self-care strategies to allow for the delivery of sustainably effective clinical practice across the lifespan (Nagy, 2017).

Competence may also include learning which clinical approaches, strategies, or techniques have demonstrated efficacy and effectiveness as well as which have been shown to be invalid or perhaps even harmful (Pope & Vasquez, 2016). Research within the field of clinical hypnosis provides clinicians with rich opportunities to establish a practice that is rooted in, and guided by, scientific knowledge (Reid, 2012). Staying informed of the current empirical literature allows one to have the most up-to-date knowledge about hypnotic techniques, applications, theoretical perspectives, and clinical interventions (Elkins, 2014). This may be practiced by routinely consulting the leading academic journals within the field of hypnosis, such as the International Journal of Clinical and Experimental Hypnosis, the American Journal for Clinical Hypnosis, and the Contemporary Hypnosis and Integrative Therapy (Elkins, 2014). When research is consumed, we recommend using what Pope & Vasquez (2016) describe as an "active approach", that is, an approach that involves actively seeking out new theory, research, and practices relevant to professional work, actively reading and listening to critics of one's own current beliefs and practices, and actively questioning new claims.

ASSESSMENT

Thorough assessment plays a vital role in ethical clinical hypnosis practice. However even though a well-intentioned practitioner may desire to deliver a hypnosis intervention with immediacy, there is increased potential for harm if an extensive psychological and medical history and a mental status examination are not conducted (Kluft, 2017) as appropriate to the case. Consider the accidental use of a metaphor that inadvertently parallels an aspect of a patient's trauma history and what that might do to the patient's experience. With this in mind, some key areas to consider assessing prior to delivery of an hypnotic intervention include the following: current health status (e.g., illness, chronic pain, history of medical interventions, current medications), current mental health status (i.e., mood disorder, thought disorder, personality disorder), presenting complaints (e.g., anticipatory anxiety, social phobia, nightmares, or some other psychological symptom), history of psychiatric hospitalization, history of child abuse (i.e., physical, sexual, or emotional abuse), major boundary or important trust betrayals (e.g., sex with a former therapist), prior use of hypnosis, and the patient's expectancies or fears about hypnosis (Nagy, 2017). Clinicians may also consider including the assessment of the individual's hypnotizability. After all, as K. S. Bowers aptly stated, "an effect is not a classic suggestion effect [that is, a genuine hypnotic effect] unless it is correlated with hypnotic ability as standardly assessed" (as quoted in Woody & Barnier, 2008). Various hypnotizability scales exist and can function to not only gather information about the patient's hypnotic ability, but also provide a means to introduce and normalize hypnosis to the patient in a relatively nonthreatening way at the onset of a clinical encounter (Woody & Sadler, 2017). In particular, the Elkins Hypnotizability Scale (EHS; Elkins, 2014) is one measure of hypnotizability that is modern, time-efficient, safe, pleasant, and has demonstrated strong psychometric properties (Kekecs et al., 2016).

INFORMED CONSENT

An essential part of ethical hypnotherapy that reflects a respect for patient freedom, autonomy, and dignity is the process of informed consent. Informed consent requires professionals to provide the sufficient information needed by the patient to make an informed decision about whether they should accept the treatment that is offered to them (Pope & Vasquez, 2016). This may include, but is not limited to, information about professional qualifications, information about hypnosis (e.g., what it is and what it is not), description of intended procedures, costs and risks associated with services, anticipated benefits of services, estimated length of services, alternative treatment or service approaches, limits of confidentiality, such as mandatory reporting, nature and extent of the record-keeping, information about fees and billing practices, whom to contact in case of emergency, and patient's right to terminate sessions and any financial obligations if that occurs (Enea & Dafinoiu, 2011).

This exchange of information provides both the patient and clinician an opportunity to ensure that all is adequately understood before proceeding with treatment. Given the essentiality of this mutual understanding, in the relay of this information, it is important to confirm that the patient has the cognitive ability to consent or refuse treatment and understands what is being proposed (Reid, 2012). Relatedly, if the information is provided on a written document, ensure that the patient has the requisite language and reading skills needed to read and comprehend the information on the form (Pope & Vasquez, 2016). It is also wise to pair review of the written document with a discussion of the subject matter.

Informed consent is not just a procedure reserved for the first encounter between patient and clinician; rather, it is an ongoing, evolving process of communication and clarification that verifies that both patient and clinician adequately understand the nature of the relationship and services. As various aspects of the therapeutic relationship evolve over time (e.g., treatment goals, interventions employed), informed consent is re-visited and obtained for whatever part of treatment has changed. It is best practice to document whenever the process of informed consent occurs.

The initial process of informed consent often includes a discussion of confidentiality. Cited as both an ethical standard and legal statute, confidentiality is the practice of keeping information about a patient protected (Pope & Vasquez, 2016). This pertains to both verbal exchanges as well as to written records (Elkins, 2014). The practice of confidentiality requires that a kind of intentionality be brought to each professional responsibility. For example, when consultation is used, only the minimum information necessary to assist the patient is disclosed, or when records are stored, in electronic or paper form, only the allowable entities have access to the documents.

The protection of confidentiality is delicately balanced with its limitations. Practitioners work to maintain privacy while also upholding their professional responsibility to take action and protect others when safety is at risk. For this reason, there are several instances in which many health care professionals are mandated to disclose patient information to external parties, such as when an individual is in danger to themselves or others, when there is abuse or neglect of a child, elder, or person with disability, or when instructed to do so by the legal system. Confidentiality and its limitations are to be reviewed at the onset of the clinical encounter and then re-visited as needed throughout treatment.

How one relates to any aspect of their work will come through in their interactions with patients; the process of informed consent is no exception. Thus, it is important that practitioners view the informed consent process as a useful and meaningful part of the clinical encounter rather than a rote part of treatment that needs to be overcome as quickly as possible so that the intervention can be delivered more readily.

Treatment: Re-Alerting and Use of Recordings

Ethical practice of hypnotherapy requires that patient safety be kept paramount throughout clinical care. This includes leaving enough time to re-alert a patient after hypnosis to ensure that they are fully reoriented and alert (Yapko, 2018). The Howard Alertness Scale (HAS; Howard, 2017) is a helpful tool that can be used to assist in receiving this confirmation.

When recordings are provided to patients, it is best practice to explain the purpose of the recordings, discuss how to use the recordings (e.g., frequency, time of day, location), and address any of the patient's questions (Elkins, 2014). It is also important to remind the patient that the recording is unique to their treatment and thus, should not be shared. We call to mind the principles of beneficence and non-maleficence here. Providing explanation in this way serves to create conditions that put the patient in a position to succeed and maximize the benefits of the intervention. Instructing the individual to prevent from sharing the recording with others serves to limit the harm that could come from distribution of an intervention without idiographic assessment. If recordings are provided to the public, it is important to do so in the most ethical manner possible; the American Society of Clinical Hypnosis has created guidelines for electronic recordings of hypnosis for both public consumption as well as one's own patients that would be helpful to consider.

Record Keeping/Documentation/Billing Practices

Honesty and accuracy in documentation and billing practices is key to the ethical practice of clinical hypnosis. Although the structure and content provided in documentation will vary with the context, setting, and patient variables, the following is some information that may be important to include whenever and wherever a clinical hypnosis intervention is delivered: rationale for using hypnosis with a patient, informed consent obtained, the hypnotic session number and whether it was recorded for the patient's use, symptom that the hypnosis intervention is targeting, the type of induction used and the patient's response to it, length of the hypnotic session, patient's response to the hypnosis intervention, content of the session, re-alerting, and post-hypnotic processing if warranted (Nagy, 2017). It is essential that patient records be stored in a safe and secure location that meets established standards of HIPAA law and is kept confidential; this includes both paper and electronic storage of patient information. It is also wise to verify the requirements, regulations, and guidelines of any insurance providers being used to ensure that one is only billing for the services provided (Yapko, 2018). It is best practice to discuss the aforementioned privacy measures and billing policies/expectations at the initial informed consent discussion.

PATIENT CLINICIAN RELATIONSHIP

Clinicians are in a privileged position of power as patients often enter therapeutic relationship placing trust in the clinician's skills and intentions. Thus, ethical practice of clinical hypnosis requires that boundaries between patient and clinician relationship be acknowledged and respected. These boundaries must be clarified across many planes, such as professional role, time, place, space, gifts, clothing, and physical touch (Wall, 2007). To minimize the potential for boundary crossings, the patient-clinician relationship should be as clearly defined as possible at the onset of care and revisited as necessary throughout the clinical encounter. This may involve discussion of the nature of the intervention, the duration, the cost, communication expectations, evaluation points, and so on especially between sessions (Pope & Vasquez, 2016). Under no circumstances is any sexual involvement with patients acceptable.

Across the duration of one's professional work, practitioners of clinical hypnosis are likely to be met with the possibility of a multiple relationship, that is, a relationship in which an individual participates in two or more relationships or roles with another person (Koocher & Keith-Spiegel, 2016). Such relationships can occur simultaneously or at different times. Gottlieb (1993) offers a helpful model that can be used to assist in evaluating the appropriateness of a potential multiple relationship; each relationship is considered across three dimensions: power differentials (i.e., low, mid-range, high), duration of the relationship (i.e., brief, intermediate, long), and clarity of termination (i.e., specific, uncertain, indefinite).

Professionalism

The ethical practice of clinical hypnosis requires that civility and integrity be upheld across all professional endeavors/activities (e.g., encounters with patients, interactions with colleagues, interfaces with community/public, etc.) across all platforms (e.g., paper ads, social media platforms, email). If the opportunity ever presents to educate others about hypnosis, practitioners are to ground all claims in empirical evidence, present the information in a manner that is truthful and void of falsification, exaggeration, or guarantee of outcomes (Nagy, 2017). This is particularly pertinent to the self-promotion of one's own credentials and services. The verbiage used and information provided in advertisements are to be chosen with respect and care for others, perhaps finding guidance in seeking to uphold the Golden Rule of "do unto others as you would have them do unto you". If the use of testimonials is being considered, perhaps take a moment to reflect on how the power differential inherent to the patient-clinician relationship might impact how a patient responds to this request. We are of the opinion that this creates undue influence and thus, believe that testimonials are to be discouraged. Hypnosis is never to be used for entertainment purposes since doing so risks causing potential harm to the public in addition to perpetuating the very misinformation that often needs to be debunked at the onset of treatment (Elkins, 2014).

Telehealth Delivery of Clinical Hypnosis Intervention

In recent years, various societal changes have presented more and more opportunities to provide clinical hypnosis services remotely via telehealth. Perhaps most notably, the COVID-19 pandemic, for one, has made it such that delivering clinical hypnosis intervention in this way has been adopted by the masses and become somewhat of a new normal. Thus, it is worth highlighting some key ethical considerations unique to this form of service delivery.

Each layer of novelty that is introduced along a practitioner's journey invites opportunity to seek additional training. As for telehealth delivery of clinical hypnosis services, this may mean pursuing continuing education in telehealth generally and then telehealth delivery of clinical hypnosis more specifically. These learnings should include review of the license and jurisdictional rules that pertain to the state that one would like to practice (Desai, Lankford, & Schwartz, 2020). It is equally important for practitioners to gain the necessary proficiencies to successfully navigate the secure telehealth technology platforms and programs that will be used to interact with patients.

Once the necessary competencies are gained, there are several questions to consider before services are initiated, such as how the appropriateness of hypnosis via telehealth for the individual patient and condition of interest will be determined, how patient's privacy and confidentiality will be upheld, what expectations and rules for technology use with patients will be communicated, and how patient crises and safety concerns will be addressed (Wall, 2007). This discussion is by no means comprehensive in nature; instead, it serves as a catalyst for readers to carefully think about the ethical considerations unique to clinical hypnosis practice using telehealth and consult additional resources on the subject. Specifically, the American Society of Clinical Hypnosis offers a helpful set of ethical guidelines specific to remote delivery of clinical hypnosis services (American Society of Clinical Hypnosis, 2020).

ETHICAL DILEMMAS & DECISION-MAKING MODEL

Clinical practice of any kind comes with its fair share of ethical dilemmas, that is, situations where the most ethical way to proceed is complicated and unclear. However helpful ethics codes and legal documents may be, they may not contain "the answer" to some circumstances. In these cases, an ethical decision-making model can assist in determining the best and least harmful course of action. Although there are a variety of ethical-decision making models to choose from, for purposes of this chapter, we will take a closer look at Koocher & Keith-Spiegel's (2016) Nine-Step Ethical Decision-Making Model.

The first step of the model requires clarification that the situation at hand does indeed involve an ethical matter. In doing so, it may be helpful to articulate a problem definition, which may require stating the question, dilemma, or concern as clearly as possible and considering the questions of what the ethical problem is, and why it is a problem. After all, finding the best solution is contingent upon clear understanding of the ethical challenge that presents. Once step one is completed, step two suggests consultation of the already available resources that may offer potential mechanisms for resolution or may facilitate initial formulation of a plan of action. These resources may include, but are not limited to, formal ethical standards, legal standards, and relevant research and theory. This is followed by step three, which prompts taking an intentional pause to consider, to the best of ones' ability, all the variables that might influence the ethical decision-making process. In doing so, one makes explicit acknowledgement of personal factors, such as individual emotions and needs, in an effort to safeguard against these biases having a powerful influence over one's own judgment and final decision/behavior.

Step four suggests consultation with a trusted colleague to acquire a second opinion about the best course of action. It is recommended that the colleague chosen have abilities and expertise relevant to the ethical dilemma in question, and that consultation be conducted with as much objectivity as possible. Step five involves evaluation of the rights, responsibilities, and vulnerabilities of all parties affected by the ethical situation. Clinical choices have the potential to affect not only patient and clinician, but many, so this step provides the opportunity to better understand the potential "ripple effect" that could result from clinical actions.

Inherent to any problem-solving process is generation of alternative solutions so step six invites brainstorming of any and all ways of responding to the ethical dilemma at hand. Endurance is necessary to continue searching for the "best possible response rather than the response that doesn't seem too bad or seems good enough" (Koocher & Keith-Speigel, 2016). Step seven involves thinking through the potential short-term, ongoing, and long-term consequences of each course of action. Evaluation of each decision in this way is likely to benefit from a risk-benefit analysis.

Step eight welcomes review of the potential solutions that were identified and then choosing the best course of action. Once a decision is made, if time permits, pausing once more before taking action to consider the solution selected may be helpful since the simple act of choosing one option and eliminating the others may illuminate the shortcomings of the chosen decision that were previously overlooked. Step nine then calls for implementation of the carefully chosen decision. This "taking action" step of the model includes documenting the process that led up to the decision made, assuming personal responsibility for the consequences, as well as assessing the impact of the decision on all affected parties so that future decision-making processes can be positively informed by the learnings of the present.

CONCLUSION

As a system of moral principles and standards, ethics provides a norm of conduct for practitioners to follow so that people are helped and protected. For this reason, regular study of ethics is a worthwhile endeavor. In this chapter, we discussed some concepts that are key to the ethical practice of clinical hypnosis, such as competence, informed consent, and professionalism, among others. We identified ethical concerns unique to the remote delivery of clinical hypnosis services through telehealth and outlined the steps of an ethical decision-making model to aid whenever ethical dilemmas present in clinical practice. Review of this content highlights both the significant gains that have been made in the field of clinical hypnosis, such as formation of specific ethical guidelines by professionally accredited organizations, as well as some of the gaps that remain, such as the lack of uniformity in training requirements or the inexistence of a singular, comprehensive code of hypnosis ethics. As we look to the future, may the progress made to date be used as inspiration to continue the advancement of clinical hypnosis practice in the direction that is most ethical.

CHAPTER 15
REFLECTION QUESTIONS

1. How can we determine if an individual is professionally competent to deliver clinical hypnosis?

2. How would the delivery of hypnosis via telehealth impact the ethical considerations?

3. What are the steps to handling a case that cannot be resolved directly by ethic codes and legal documents?

REFERENCES

Alter, D. (2017). Certification in hypnosis and specialty boards. In G. R. Elkins (Ed.), *Handbook of medical and psychological hypnosis: Foundations, applications, and professional issues* (pp. 671-677). Springer Publishing Company.

American Psychological Association. (2017). *Ethical principles of psychologists and code of conduct* (2002, amended effective June 1, 2010, and January 1, 2017). https://www.apa.org/ethics/code/

American Society of Clinical Hypnosis. (2002). *American Society of Clinical Hypnosis (ASCH) code of conduct.* (2002, last revised March 2012). https://www.asch. net/aws/ASCH/asset_manager/get_file/609884?ver=2

American Society of Clinical Hypnosis. (2020). *American Society of Clinical Hypnosis (ASCH) ethics for telemedicine and distance education.* (2020, last revised June 2020). https://www.asch.net/aws/ASCH/asset_manager/get_file/614091? ver=1

Desai, A., Lankford, C., & Schwartz, J. (2020). With crisis comes opportunity: building ethical competencies in light of COVID-19. *Ethics & Behavior, 30*(6), 401-413. https://doi:10.1080/10508422.2020.1762603

Elkins, G. R. (2014). *Hypnotic relaxation therapy: Principles and applications.* Springer Publishing Company.

Elkins, G. R., & Hammond, D. C. (1998). Standards of training in clinical hypnosis: preparing professionals for the 21st century. *The American journal of clinical hypnosis, 41*(1), 55-64. https://doi.org/10.1080/00029157.1998.10404185

Enea, V., & Dafinoiu, I. (2011). Ethical principles and standards in the practice of hypnosis. *Romanian Journal of Bioethics, 9*(3), 210-216.

Etzrodt, C. M. (2013). Ethical considerations of therapeutic hypnosis and children. *American Journal of Clinical Hypnosis, 55*(4), 370-377. https://doi.org/10. 1080/ 00029157.2012.746933

Gottlieb, M. C. (1993). Avoiding exploitive dual relationships: A decision-making model. *Psychotherapy: Theory, Research, Practice, Training, 30*(1), 41-48. https://doi.org/10.1037/0033-3204.30.1.41

Hornby, A. S., Cowie, A. P., & Lewis, J. W. (1974). *Oxford advanced learner's dictionary of current English.* London: Oxford University Press.

Howard, H. A. (2017). Promoting safety in hypnosis: A clinical instrument for the assessment of alertness. *American Journal of Clinical Hypnosis, 59*(4), 344-362. https://doi:10.1080/00029157.2016.1203281

International Society of Hypnosis. (2002). *The International Society of Hypnosis (ISH) code of ethics.* (2002, last revised July 2018). https://www.ishhypnosis.org/administration/code-of-ethics/

Kekecs, Z., Bowers, J., Johnson, A., Kendrick, C., & Elkins, G. (2016). The Elkins Hypnotizability Scale: Assessment of reliability and validity. *International Journal of Clinical and Experimental Hypnosis, 64*(3), 285-304. https://doi:10.1080/00207144.2016.1171089

Kluft, R. (2017). Precautions to the use of hypnosis in patient care. In G. R. Elkins (Ed.), *Handbook of medical and psychological hypnosis: Foundations, applications, and professional issues* (p. 651-672). Springer Publishing Company.

Koocher, G. P., & Keith-Spiegel, P. (2016). *Ethics in psychology and the mental health professions* (4th ed.). Oxford University Press.

Nagy, T. F. (2017). Ethics. In G. R. Elkins (Ed.), *Handbook of medical and psychological hypnosis: Foundations, applications, and professional issues* (p. 651-672). Springer Publishing Company.

Pope, K. S., & Vasquez, M. J. (2016). *Ethics in psychotherapy and counseling: A practical guide.* John Wiley & Sons.

Reid, D. B. (2012). *Hypnosis for behavioral health: A guide to expanding your professional practice.* Springer Publishing Company.

Society of Clinical and Experimental Hypnosis. (2003). *Code of ethics.* https://www.sceh.us/code-of-ethics

Sue, D. W. (2001). Multidimensional facets of cultural competence. *The Counseling Psychologist, 29*(6), 790-821. https://doi.org/10.1177/0011000001296002

Wall, T. W. (2007). Ethical considerations with children and hypnosis. In W. C. Wester II & L. I. Sugarman (Eds.), *Therapeutic hypnosis with children and adolescents* (pp. 109-132). Crown House Publishing Limited.

Woody, E. Z., & Barnier, A. J. (2008). Hypnosis scales for the twenty-first century: What do we need and how should we use them? In M. R. Nash & A. J. Barnier (Eds.), *The Oxford handbook of hypnosis: theory, research and practice* (pp. 255-281). Oxford: Oxford University Press.

Woody, E., & Sadler, P. (2017). Hypnotizability. In G. R. Elkins (Ed.), *Handbook of medical and psychological hypnosis: Foundations, applications, and professional issues* (p. 33-41). Springer Publishing Company.

Yapko, M. D. (2018). *Trancework: An introduction to the practice of clinical hypnosis.* Routledge.

CHAPTER 16
INTEGRATING HYPNOSIS
INTO CLINICAL PRACTICE
AND APPLICATIONS

CIARA CHRISTENSEN, AARON FINLEY, AND CONNOR KELLEY

Chapter Learning Objectives

1. List several examples from research which demonstrates how the integration of hypnotic interventions can significantly improve treatment outcomes.

2. Identify 3 examples where hypnotic interventions have been integrated with different therapeutic approaches and can facilitate treatment.

3. Identify and describe the best way to increase a patience confidence.

This chapter provides a brief overview of published research and the evidence of efficacy for the use of hypnosis to treat a of variety of clinical problems. Among other things, it is written to provide information about clinical hypnosis and offer examples of what research supports can be achieved when clinical hypnosis is used. It is also intended to further encourage providers to receive training in hypnosis and consider applying clinical hypnosis into their respective practice setting.

ADDICTION AND RELAPSE PREVENTION

Substance abuse disorders and their associated physical or psycho-logical dependencies are a prevalent and major health issue in countries around the world (Degenhardt et al., 2018). Within the study of substance abuse disorders and addiction there are a variety of per-spectives and models that are in use. McPeake et al. (1991) proposed that it is a basic human motive to attain states of altered consciousness, leading to a propensity to use substances to achieve this goal. Hypnosis has been defined by Division 30 of the APA as, "a state of consciousness involving focused attention and reduced peripheral awareness characterized by an enhanced capacity for response to suggestion" and it is possible that it could serve as an alternative altered state to pursue (Elkins et al., 2015; Kihlstrom, 2018). Prochaska et al., (1992) also proposed a stages of change model to explain substance abuse and addiction. According to their model progression through the stages is dependent on multiple factors, including self-efficacy (Raihan & Cogburn, 2021). Both models contribute to a theoretical basis for the application of hypnosis in the treatment of substance use disorders. In a randomized controlled study comparing a transtheoretical hypnosis and relaxation/stress management intervention to a control group, a multivariate analysis of variance (MANOVA) revealed that the practice of the self-hypnosis audio tapes accounted for 15% of the variance in continued abstinence from substance use after discharge from the study (Pekala et al., 2004). In 2009, Pekala et al., examined the relationship of self-esteem, serenity, and anger/impulsivity to chronic substance abuse. Their findings suggest that targeting negative feelings should be paired with enhancement of positive feelings, and fostering of a connection to a "higher power."

ANXIETY AND STRESS

Anxiety and fear have connotations which can be similar. The primary distinction is that fear relates to a present threat, while anxiety relates to concerns of future threats (Muskin, 2021). Anxiety often presents with behavioral avoidance, increased muscle tension, and often cognitions and ruminations related to worries about future problems. Cognitive Behavioral Therapy (CBT), medication, or coping skills such as meditation or stress management can provide utility in managing the symptoms of anxiety. Hypnosis has received less attention as a treatment modality for anxiety despite several studies which have demonstrated its effectiveness, (Daitch, 2018; Daitch, 2014; Hammond, 2010; Mende, 2009).

A 2019 meta-analysis examined hypnosis as a stand-alone and adjunct to other psychotherapy as a treatment for anxiety (Valentine et al., 2019). Combined, CBT and hypnosis demonstrated larger effect sizes in contrast to hypnosis alone. The effect size of hypnosis on anxiety at the conclusion of the treatment was medium (mean effect size = .79) and at follow up larger effect sizes were reported (mean effect size= .99). Self-hypnosis training and therapist administered treatments showed equal benefit.

Cognitive Hypnotherapy (CH) has also gained attention as a treatment for anxiety (Alladin, 2014, 2016). CH includes induction of relaxation, mind-body connection, suggestions for symptom regulation, and post-hypnotic suggestions to enhance self-efficacy. When the client learns to manage their symptoms, root causes of anxiety can be explored. The client may be asked to identify the meaning and purpose of their anxiety or stress. With the meaning of the root of anxiety in mind, restructuring and acceptance are used to create new and functional associations (Alladin, 2014).

ASTHMA

When broadly reviewing clinical observations, as well as past and present asthma research, studies have compared the effectiveness of treatments with hypnosis and bronchodilators. They have also evaluated the effectiveness of suggestions for relaxation, desensitization, distraction, and increased self-control on different outcome measures (e.g., self-reported symptom reduction, use of pharmacotherapy, health visits, and return to work); results indicate that participants with asthma and with high hypnotizability, improved on pulmonary function and reduced use of inhaled medications for symptom management (Pinnell & Covino, 2000). In a study conducted by Brown (2007), it was demonstrated that integrating the use of hypnosis for asthma reduces symptom frequency and severity, coping with asthma specific fears, managing acute attacks, medication use, and health care visits. Subsequent studies have shown that when patients are taught to use hypnosis for emotion self-regulation (i.e., recognize stress cues/changes in the body, panic and anxiety, and depressive symptoms), they can potentially mitigate an asthma attack, reduce the duration of it, and/or also the perceived severity of it. When compared with patients who solely relied on medication to manage asthma symptoms, the patients who received medication combined with hypnosis showed better overall treatment outcomes and improved quality of life (Pinnell & Covino, 2000; Leher et al., 2002; Huntley et al., 2002; Zobeiri et al., 2009; Brown, 2007; Anbar, 2017; Sutanto et al., 2021).

AUTOIMMUNE DISORDERS

Autoimmune disorders are disorders wherein the body's natural pathogen defense, the immune system, is unable to distinguish self from non-self, prompting the immune system to respond against the self in a protective fashion (Wang et al., 2015). This response causes a variety of symptoms and sequalae, leading to the diversity of disorders identified in literature and practice. While previously considered to be rare, studies have indicated that 3-5% of the population can be considered to have an autoimmune disorder, with autoimmune thyroid disease and type I diabetes being the most common of these (Wang et al., 2015).

Management of autoimmune disorders has traditionally involved the use of powerful immunosuppressant medications to reduce the global immune response and aid in symptom remission. This treatment is effective and considered a "gold standard" of care, but long-term treatment requires continued high-dose use of these medications, leaving room for a variety of complications (Rosenblum et al., 2012). More progressive treatments are currently in development, focusing on tolerance-inducing therapies which serve to manage the immune response by targeting the specific cells involved in the immune response and increasing the immune systems tolerance of them, rather than reducing the immune system's total response (Cauwels & Tavernier, 2020).

Many autoimmune disorders function on a remitting-relapsing course, breaking the treatment of such disorders into two parts; promotion of remission of symptoms, and prevention of relapse. The application of clinical hypnosis in the treatment of autoimmune disorders can be seen in both domains. Moshe Torem, MD, whose research focuses on mind-body integrative medicine, outlines this dual application in a case example of a 25-year-old woman diagnosed with rheumatoid arthritis. Therapy included discussion of the patient's past-experience with remission of symptoms and integrated use of direct, future-focused hypnotic suggestions and imagery, where the patient would return to a state of remission and maintain it. At four weeks follow-up, the patient reported she returned to a remission state and was eager to maintain practice in hopes of maintaining her remission. Follow-ups at three, six, and nine months, showed continued remission (Torem, 2017).

CONVERSION DISORDERS

Conversion disorder (CD) or functional neurological disorder (FND) is described as a neuropsychiatric condition characterized by signs and symptomology which are not due to an underlying medical condition

(DSM-5; American Psychiatric Association, 2013). Prognosis for patients with conversion disorder varies, with some patients having consistent long-term disability and others having spontaneous and total recovery (up to 1/5 of patients; Loriedo & Di Leone, 2017). Trends in the treatment of conversion disorder imply that early and personalized intervention may be a vital contributor to the outcomes of the patient and their overall prognosis (Miller et al., 2020).

An informative case example of a clinical hypnosis in the treatment of conversion disorder is seen in the work of Loriedo and Di Leone (2017). The intervention focused on six factors: 1) a contract defining the short-term nature of the therapeutic relationship; 2) acceptance of this model by both the therapist and patient; 3) acceptance of the risk of failure; 4) incorporation of the conflict etiologically relevant to the presentation; 5) attention to minimal cues, or seemingly unimportant details, and; 6) utilization of the information available to the clinician. The integration of these ultra-brief principles allowed for progressive improvement of the patient's conversion disorder (presenting as paralysis) with significant improvement reported at a three-years follow-up (Loriedo & Di Leone, 2017).

DENTISTRY

Several studies have shown that the use of clinical hypnosis in dentistry can be an effective adjunctive treatment (Dilmahomed & Jovani-Sancho, 2018; Goodman, 2018; Venkiteswaran & Tandon, 2021). Hypnosis appears to help patients reduce dental fears, manage anxiety associated with dental procedures, and can assist with decreased reported severity of pain during dental treatment or surgery (Goodman & Filo, 2017; Montenegro et al., 2017; Rucker, 2018).

Dental anxiety can occur for many reasons including negative experiences, history of trauma, or because of reported heightened sensitivities (e.g., drills, high frequency vibrations). Some research has shown however, anxiety associated with the fear of pain, may be one of the main obstacles in seeking dental treatment (Dilmahomed & Jovani-Sancho, 2018). Clinical hypnosis in dentistry has been used successfully to reduce dental anxiety and associated fears. Data show various hypnosis protocols including hypnotic progressive relaxation (Cozzolino et al. 2020), direct suggestions for pleasant scenery, comfort, reinterpretation of events, deep relaxation, relaxation-based brief inductions (Finkelstein, 2003) and rapid inductions (Barber, 1977; Lang, 2021) can help dental patients manage anxiety or significantly reduce anticipatory procedural anxiety/fears. The use of these protocols has also been shown to offer dental patients additional benefits, including achieving calm, increasing relaxation, acceptance, and lowering blood pressure.

A 2018 review of 15 independent studies (N = 694 patients) demonstrated clinical hypnosis to be beneficial for the management of pain both during and after dental procedures (Dilmahomed & Jovani-Sancho, 2018). The authors divided the selected studies into two categories for review; (1) hypnosis versus no treatment or adjunctive to other treatments and (2) hypnosis versus other treatment. In three studies, the efficacy of hypnosis on pain management was tested by measuring dental pulp stimulation with adjunctive hypnosis to a control group that received no hypnosis. Patients in the hypnosis treatment condition reported experiencing less pain during procedures in contrast to the control condition.

Although hypnosis is seldom used as the only form of anesthetic (Goodman & Filo, 2017), it can be effective as an alternative treatment option when patients report they are allergic to anesthesia or must avoid it (Cozzolino et al. 2020). Selected studies have also documented that when hypnosis is used as an adjunct to local anesthesia and analgesics during dental treatment, it can effectively aid in decreasing the amount of medication used during the procedure and reduce the amount of analgesics post-treatment (Lang, 2021).

DEPRESSION

Depression is the leading cause of global disability, with over 300 million people affected (World Health Organization, 2017). Depression can manifest as both psychological and physiological responses (i.e., sadness, pessimism, low motivation, etc.); or somatic symptoms (i.e., sleep disorders, eating concerns, physical pain such as headaches, etc.; Torem, 2017). Approaches to treating depression with hypnosis have varied.

A 2019 meta-analysis of hypnotic interventions for depression symptoms explored the efficacy and effects of hypnosis treatments on depression. Effect sizes determined in the study demonstrated good evidence that hypnosis can improve depressive symptoms. Hypnosis participants showed greater improvements in depression than 76% of control participants (d = .71). At longest follow-up, the hypnosis participants showed greater improvements in depression than 51% of control participants (d = .52). These effect sizes are on par with other proven treatments for depression such as CBT (Milling et al., 2019).

There are many ways hypnosis can benefit people with depression and facilitate treatment (Yapko, 2010a). Hypnosis can facilitate use of internal resources, enhance coping, provide opportunities for reframing events, orient to positive focus, enhance self-image, foster self-regulation skills, provide perspective on challenges and detachment from one's sense of helplessness and victimhood. The clinician can facilitate hope by instilling expectations for positive change (Yapko, 2010b; Alladin, 2013). A study by Alladin (2010) combined elements of Cognitive Behavioral Therapy (Beck, 2005) with hypnosis to form Cognitive Hypnotherapy (CH) for depression. Patients who received self-hypnosis training aimed at empowering them to use the elements of CH on their own demonstrated reduced symptoms of depression.

EATING DISORDERS

Clinical hypnosis has been studied for the treatment of eating disorders for decades and several studies have shown individuals with disordered eating tend to be highly hypnotizable (Barabasz, 2007; Bachner-Melman, 2016), although individuals diagnosed with bulimia were found to be significantly more hypnotizable than individuals diagnosed with anorexia nervosa (see Torem, 2016 for a comprehensive review).

A 2007 review on the efficacy of clinical hypnosis in the treatment of eating disorders focused on three primary disorders; bulimia nervosa, anorexia nervosa, and obesity. Thirty women, who met criteria for bulimia, were alternately assigned to treatments CBT (n = 15); and CBT plus Hypnosis (CBT+Hyp; n = 15). Hypnotizability was assessed using the Stanford Hypnotic Susceptibility Scale (SHSS:C; Weitzenhoffer & Hilgard, 1962) and subjects who completed treatment had a mean score of 8.27 on the SHSS:C, ($SD = 1.82$). Both the CBT and CBT+Hyp treatment conditions involved eight individual outpatient therapy sessions (60 min) over 7 to 12 weeks. Subjects in the CBT+Hyp condition benefited more than those in the CBT condition alone at posttreatment assessment and at three-months follow-up. Subjects who received CBT+Hyp had statistically significant improvement on all measures including binge frequency, compensatory behavior frequency, and Weekly Behavioral Summary Sheet (WBSS) from pretreatment to three-months follow-up. The author noted that although hypnosis has been documented to be beneficial in the treatment of anorexia nervosa, treatment is complicated and depends on the individual's needs, as well as treatment responses.

A 2016 study examined if appropriateness (e.g., increased sensitivities to cues from their social environment, elevated concerns about personal appearance, and elevated concerns about how others view them) mediates the association between hypnotizability and disordered eating (Bachner-Melman et al., 2016). Fifty participants (age range 15 to 30) were administered Eating Attitudes Test-26 (EAT-26) and the Concern for Appropriateness Scale (CAS). Hypnotizability was assessed using the SHSS:C. Results suggested that EAT-26 scores predicted CAS scores (β = 0.24, p < .001), CAS scores predicted SHSS:C scores (β = 0.38, p < .001), and the mediation model was significant (Sobel Test; R^2 = .24, z = 2.54, p < .01). Participants who met criteria for disordered eating, were more hypnotizable and sensitive to social cues including massages or inner commands/voices about food intake, ideas of thinness, and repetitive autosuggestions about weight regulation. Results supported use of clinical hypnosis as part of an integrative treatment program and demonstrated how hypnotic suggestions can assist with changing internal feedback loops maintaining problematic eating behaviors.

EGO STRENGTHENING

Ego strengthening is a practice of enhancing the patient's confidence and self-efficacy through targeting the "ego", or the construct of the self to which our conscious experience is attached (Moss & Willmarth, 2017; McNeal, 2020). This practice has been present in the field of hypnosis for over 100 years, in forms that include the work of Émil Coué, John Hartland, and others (McNeal, 2020).

The term "ego strengthening" was coined by John Hartland in 1965, though the concept itself was rooted in the work of Émil Coué who would have patients recite positive suggestions repeatedly, such as his well-known phrase "Every day in every way. I am getting better and better." Hartland refined this practice and proposed a step-wise protocol which directed the patient through the practice, including induction, progressive relaxation, deepening of the state through attention to breathing, and an eight-minute sequence of ego-strengthening (Moss & Willmarth, 2017). Studies followed Hartland's proposal, examining the effectiveness of the practice and the mechanisms of change within the intervention. Much of this research concluded that factors such as positive suggestions and imagery, calmness and relaxation, and positive affirmations of self were contributors to the benefits of ego-strengthening; this has informed the progression of current practices (Moss & Willmarth, 2017).

In modern applications, ego-strengthening has paid special attention to the enhancement of self-efficacy and a concept of inner strength. A key example of this focus on self-efficacy is seen in the *Handbook of Hypnotic Suggestions and Metaphors* by D. Corydon Hammond, PhD wherein he provides roughly 50 pages of ego-strengthening scripts and relates the practice to the work of Albert Bandura in its goal of fostering self-efficacy within the patient (Moss & Willmarth, 2017; Hammond, 1990, p. 109). The concept of inner strength has also taken a primary role as the patient is promoted to engage with and pull from their inner strength (McNeal & Frederick, 1993).

FIBROMYALGIA

Fibromyalgia syndrome (FMS) is a syndrome comprised of symptoms including widespread musculoskeletal pain, mechanical pressure sensitivity, increased cold sensitivity, general fatigue and poor sleep, psychological and emotional distress, and cognitive impairment (Kosek et al., 1996; Hurtig et al., 2001; Blumenstiel et al., 2011; Berwick et al., 2021; Arnold et al., 2006; Thieme et al., 2004; Cluaw, 2014; Goebel et al., 2021, Picard, 2013; Yanus, 2007). A consensus for the etiology of FMS has yet to emerge, with some indications that dysfunctional pain processing is associated with central sensitization. Factors which appear to be important to understanding the genesis of FMS include genetics, immune systems and auto-immunity, and hormonal balance (Goebel, 2021; Julien et al., 2005; Mease et al., 2007). Due to a lack of laboratory testing, FMS requires careful clinical differential diagnosis and the diagnostician must rely heavily on the new American College of Rheumatology criteria (Bellato et al., 2012; Wolfe, 2010).

Picard (2013) conducted a study of the effects of hypnosis on fibromyalgia in which "hypnosis interventions were directed toward enhancing patient competence and mastery in managing pain and stress related to disease." In the hypnosis condition, participants were given suggestions related to bodily sensations, breath, connecting to images of places of safety, and deepening the experience of hypnosis. Images and suggestions for analgesic relief and reinterpretation of sensory perceptions of pain were given to direct participants to experience numbness where pain was usually present. Other suggestions targeted reduction in the emotional impact of the experience of pain, increasing stress-management skills in daily living with fibromyalgia, and increased acceptance via new perspectives on participant relationships with disease. Results indicated that the patients who received hypnosis showed significant improvement in sleep quality at six months post treatment as indicated by scores on the medical outcomes study (MOS) sleep scale (p = .01). Catastrophizing associated with increased pain intensity was also reduced at the 6-month follow-ups (p = .01) on the Pain Coping Strategy Questionnaire, as well as improvements related to patient global impression of change at both three (p = .001) and six months post treatment (p = .01).

Other studies suggest using hypnosis and/or guided imagery as an adjunct to other efficacious treatments for FMS such as cognitive behavioral therapy (Thieme et al., 2008; Bernardy, 2011). De Benedittis (2017) studied the impact of hypnosis and standard medical treatment on patient quality of life. Results showed significant improvement in quality of life in the hypnosis group over the standard medical treatment alone group (hypnosis satisfaction 75% vs medical treatment 37%). De Benedittis and Elkins (2017) provide other innovative examples of case studies and a transcript of Rapid Induction Fibromyalgia Relief in the *Handbook of Medical and Psychological Hypnosis.*

HEADACHE

Headaches have a lifelong prevalence of 96%, and are one of the most common medical and neurological complaints (Rizzoli & Mullally, 2018). Several studies have explored the efficacy of hypnosis to treat headaches. One systematic review by Flynn (2018) looked specifically at hypnosis as a treatment for migraines. Flynn found that patients in the hypnosis conditions achieved statistically superior or equivalent treatment effects versus placebo controls in several double-blinded studies.

Ahmadi et al. (2018) compared the effectiveness of stand-alone hypnosis and hypnosis + drug treatments of tension and migraine headaches. Hypnosis was used over 10 weeks with bi-weekly hypnotherapy sessions lasting 30 minutes each. Self-hypnosis was taught to and utilized by the stand-alone hypnosis and hypnosis + drug groups as an addition to the hypnotherapy sessions. Before treatment people in the hypnosis only group experienced 63.3% severe headaches, 36.4% moderate headaches, and no reported mild cases. After treatment with hypnosis, this group reported no severe headache, 54.5% moderate headache, and 45.5% mild headache. Hypnosis outperformed pharmacological treatment for tension headaches. For sufferers of migraine headaches, hypnotherapy and pharmaceutical treatment together showed the greatest benefit, with an 80% reduction in the average compared to that of that treatment groups migraines. Pharmaceutical treatment alone showed a 60% average reduction and stand-alone hypnosis treatment provided a 52% reduction. This indicates that hypnosis as an adjunct to pharmacological treatment can be beneficial and prevent or reduce the need for increased drug dosages.

Tastan et al. (2018) compared three groups: pharmacotherapy, acupuncture, and hypnotherapy. Scores for the hypnotherapy group were comparable to the other groups at the end of one month on the Visual Analog Scale (VAS). At the end of three months however, hypnotherapy began to outperform pharmacotherapy on both the VAS and on the Migraine Disability Assessment. The authors conclude that hypnotherapy can be used as a stand-alone replacement for traditional migraine treatments. Dr. Giuseppe De Benedittis (2017) provides several hypnotic techniques which have been used to treat headache. Example transcripts for hypnotic inductions are included for deep breathing, full body relaxation, comfort, and to notice tension draining from the body.

HYPERTENSION

Hypertension is considered the leading cause of cardiovascular disease and premature death worldwide, bringing to bear the importance of proper and proactive management of the condition (Mills et al., 2020). Traditional management of hypertension typically involves use of an antihypertensive medication, management of diet (with notable emphasis on reduction of sodium intake and proper potassium intake), and physical exercise (Mills et al., 2020). While medication is the first line treatment, it is common for patients to report side effects or simply discontinue taking their medication (Jakubovits & Kekecs, 2017).

A variety of studies have been published analyzing the efficacy of adjunctive hypnotherapy in the treatment of hypertension, including a pilot study published by Raskin and colleagues (1999) wherein a self-hypnosis treatment group showed improved diastolic blood pressure and stability in medication dosage compared to a control and attention-only group. There is also research to suggest an effect of hypnosis on the electrodermal activity and parasympathetic tone of the heart, giving a proposed mechanism for the reduction in hypertension with hypnosis as well as hypnosis' utility in the treatment of other disorders with high levels of sympathetic nervous system involvement (Kekecs et al., 2016). Furthermore, evidence is available for the use of hypnosis in other, non-direct treatment of hypertension through management of risk factors such as obesity, anxiety, and stress (Xu & Cardena, 2007; Cardena et al., 2013; Golden, 2012).

IRRITABLE BOWEL SYNDROME

Irritable Bowel Syndrome (IBS) is a gastrointestinal disorder which alters bowel function. Symptom management and patient care are often approached with a holistic approach (Ahmed & Raza, 2020). Three classifications of IBS are: IBS with diarrhea, IBS with constipation, or Mixed Symptoms (diarrhea and constipation). It is a multifactorial disease resulting from different pathological influences (Chey et al., 2015). Brain-gut interactions and psychosocial status are two of the many factors which contribute to IBS (Chey et al., 2015) with psychological factors influencing the onset and course (Asahina, 2006).

The two evidence-based psychological treatments for IBS are CBT and Gut Directed Hypnotherapy (GDH; Surdea-Blaga, 2016). While the mechanisms for CBT or GDH as treatment of IBS are not clear, somatization and catastrophizing have been proposed as psychological factors which contribute to increased negative patient reported outcomes (van Tilburg, 2013). GDH involves hypnotic suggestion to evoke focused attention and increased receptivity, followed by suggestion for deep relaxation and imagery for gut directed symptom reduction. 71% of 204 participants in a study using GDH to treat IBS reported moderate to very much improved symptoms, with one to five years of lasting effect for 81% of respondents (Gonsalkorale, 2003).

American College of Gastroenterology clinical guidelines recommend hypnotherapy as a gut-directed psychotherapy to improve global IBS symptoms, comparable with CBT or specialized diet (Lacy et al., 2021), though less effective in patients with comorbid mental health conditions. While Lacy et al. makes only a conditional recommendation based on evidence for gut directed psychotherapies

(GDPs) the number needed to treat for GDH and other comparable gut directed psychotherapies (GDP) was listed as four. GDPs share merits such as being low risk with no reported negative outcomes, lasting long-term effects, and not needing to specifically target either of the constipation or diarrhea subtypes of IBS.

MENOPAUSE

Menopause is defined as a permanent cessation of menses resulting from estrogen deficiency (Peacock & Ketvertis, 2021). It is a physiologic transition that can occur naturally (mean age onset 51 years) or can be induced as a result of medical intervention, such as a hysterectomy with or without bilateral oophorectomy (removal of the ovaries) or treatment for breast, uterine, or ovarian cancers (Peacock & Ketvertis, 2021). Approximately 75% of women in the general population report experiencing vasomotor symptoms or "hot flashes" during menopause transition and these symptoms can last on average for 7.4 years (Avis et al., 2015).

Traditional management of hot flashes and other accompanying symptoms have included hormone replacement therapy (HRT). While HRT has been shown to be an effective treatment, there is controversy regarding its use, including increased risk for certain types of cancers, thromboembolism (blood-clot), stroke, and coronary heart disease. Not to mention, in some cases (e.g., treatments of breast cancer), HRT is not an option and reinforces the need for different treatment considerations. Alternatives to HRT include use of selective serotonin reuptake inhibitors (SSRIs), non-pharmaceutical supplementation (Peacock & Ketvertis, 2021) and within the last decade, clinical hypnosis has gained momentum as an evidence-based treatment for hot flashes.

The results of numerous studies investigating the application and efficacy of clinical hypnosis in the treatment of hot flashes in post-menopausal women have been promising (Elkins et al., 2010; Elkins et al., 2013a; Elkins et al., 2013b; Elkins et al., 2014; Elkins, 2017;

Kendrick et al., 2015). In one study, hypnosis intervention led to significant reductions in both subjective hot flash frequency compared to control (74.16% decrease compared to 17.13% decrease at a 12-week follow-up) and hot flash severity compared to control (71.36% decrease compared to 8.32% decrease at a 12-week follow-up; Elkins et al., 2013b). Additional positive findings were reported when hypnotic relaxation therapy was tailored to the client by determining what the client associates with coolness (Elkins et al., 2010). The authors concluded that client report and preference will heavily inform imagery used in hypnotic relaxation, although water is a widely endorsed image associated with coolness. There is currently a self-hypnosis app "Evia" provided by Mindset Health that may be helpful to some patients (for more information on the Evia app see: https://www.mindsethealth.com/hypnotherapy/evia).

OBESITY AND WEIGHT LOSS

To manage sustained weight reduction, treatment commonly involves more than one approach including lifestyle interventions, education as it relates to increasing healthy eating and exercise, as well as goal setting. Self-monitoring and stimulus control are also important facets to treatment and hinge on the individual's ability to engage in the practice of self-regulation (Pellegrini et al., 2021). Clinical hypnosis for obesity and weight reduction generally offers individuals hypnotic suggestions for relaxation, self-control, self-esteem, boosting motivation for change, as well as other food aversion strategies. A number of studies evaluating the efficacy of clinical hypnosis as an adjunct to behavioral approaches for obesity and weight reduction have demonstrated varied, albeit beneficial results (Pellegrini et al., 2021; Ramondo et al., 2021; Milling et al., 2018; Sapp, 2017).

In a 2021 meta-analysis, Ramondo and colleagues reported the more robust line of evidence within the literature which supports adding hypnosis as a treatment accelerant, are studies that compare behavioral/ CBT with CBT plus hypnosis (CBTH). In eight out of nine studies reviewed, which compared CBT vs CBTH, the participants in the CBTH conditions benefited more than participants in the CBT conditions at both posttreatment and follow-ups. In some cases, participants in the CBTH conditions were able to adhere with treatment compliance longer and continued to lose more weight in contrast to participants in the CBT conditions.

Bo et al. (2018) randomly assigned 120 individuals (BMI = 35-50 kg/m^2) to either the intervention (n = 60) or control condition (n = 60). In both conditions participants received individualized diet plans and recommendations for behavioral change and exercise. The hypnosis intervention included three hypnosis sessions which were designed to teach them a rapid induction, self-hypnosis technique. Individuals were instructed to use self-hypnotic suggestions, which were tailored to each person and designed to increase self-control before eating. Both conditions demonstrated weight loss, however individuals who were taught self-hypnosis showed a greater reduction in caloric intake and weight loss.

PAIN

Several published experimental studies evaluating hypnosis for pain relief continue to support the effectiveness of hypnosis as a viable treatment option for reducing pain across multiple pain problems (Thompson et al., 2019; Moss & Willmarth, 2019; Elkins, Jensen & Patterson, 2007; Stewart, 2005). Thompson and colleagues (2019) investigated the effectiveness of hypnosis for reducing pain. In their meta-analysis they reviewed 85 published articles (n = 3,632) which evaluated the effectiveness of hypnosis for pain reduction, as well as potential factors impacting the effectiveness of hypnosis. Results showed that when hypnosis was included, it had a moderate to large analgesic effect for different types of pain problems. Additionally, hypnotic suggestibility and the inclusion of direct suggestions, specifically for analgesia, contributed to the effectiveness of the hypnotic intervention.

In 2019, Moss and Willmarth conducted a comprehensive review of hypnosis in clinical medicine, including anesthesia, pain management, preparation for medical procedures, and dentistry. Consistent with the findings of Thompson et al. (2019), they reported that hypnotic suggestibility contributed to the effectiveness of hypnosis for pain reduction. Patients who received hypnosis combined with other medical interventions benefited more than those who did not, as evidenced by subjective reports of pain and anxiety, used less medications and had better post procedural outcomes.

Brugnoli and colleagues (2018) investigated a long-term intervention (in a palliative care setting) with clinical hypnosis and self-hypnosis as an adjuvant therapy in chronic pain and anxiety versus pharmacological therapy alone. They assigned 50 patients to either the hypnosis group (n = 25) or the control group (n = 25). Patients in the hypnosis condition received hypnotic training across 2 years. Hypnotic training involved weekly classes where patients were taught skills for self-regulation (e.g., manage anxiety) with hypnosis and self-hypnosis. Patients in the control condition only received pharmacotherapy. At two years follow-up, patients who received hypnosis demonstrated significant decrease in pain (as measured by the Visual Analog Scale) and anxiety symptoms (as measured by the Hamilton Anxiety Rating Scale). They also had reduced risk of taking more medication to manage pain, and reported improved sleep, increased energy, hope, and awareness or spirituality as they approach end of life.

POST TRAUMATIC STRESS DISORDER (PTSD)

Post-Traumatic Stress Disorder (PTSD) is a trauma disorder which develops in some people who: have experienced or witnessed a traumatic event such as combat or interpersonal violence; learn of violence or a serious accident having happened to a friend or loved one; or repeated exposure to trauma (APA, 2013). Symptoms typically begin within the first few months of the trauma or can also take time to emerge and can last from six months or longer. Re-experiencing of events, avoidance behaviors, negative alterations of mood and cognitions, and reactivity and elevated arousal are all components of PTSD. Lifetime prevalence rates are 8.7%, with 12-month prevalence of 3.5% in the U.S. and lower rates of 0.5-1.0% in Europe, Asia, Africa and Latin America (APA, 2013).

Combat veterans with PTSD show increased ability to experience hypnosis, making hypnosis a well-suited modality for treatment of PTSD (Eads & Wark, 2015). Abramowitz & Lichtenberg (2010) found using hypnosis for the treatment of PTSD in combat veterans useful because it offers the person a way to separate themselves from their traumatic experience via dissociation. Rotaru and Rusu (2016) conducted a meta-analysis of hypnosis for PTSD treatments and found large effect size (d = 1.17) in the four studies which had post-test measures for comparison. At four weeks after follow-up, effect sizes were also large and stable (d = 1.58).

Another promising hypnosis technique for treatment of PTSD is abreactive ego state therapy (EST). EST allows a person experiencing PTSD to experience an emotional catharsis and therapeutic release. Christensen et al. (2013) investigated the use of EST to treat people suffering from PTSD with a single session of EST which lasted 5-6 hours using a manualized treatment (see Barabasz, Christensen, & Watkins, 2010; Barabasz et al., 2012). Though additional clinician and randomly controlled trials are needed to replicate the findings, abreactive ego state therapy has shown the largest effect in treatment of PTSD (d = 1.99; Rotaru & Rusu, 2016).

Cognitive behavioral interventions have been shown to be effective in treating PTSD when used with hypnosis as an adjunct (Degun-Mather, 2001). Degun Mather provides a case study which found benefits of hypnotherapy for treatment of chronic PTSD with dissociative fugues in a war veteran using a three-stage approach. Stage one used psycho-education and hypnosis with a cognitive behavioral approach. The second stage involved re-processing of trauma via hypnosis through a safe remembering method allowing resolution of negative emotions. The third stage focuses on memory integration and rehabilitation. Sleep disruptions which co-occur as a result of PTSD, may also benefit from cognitive processing therapy (CPT) and hypnosis targeting improved sleep quality. Dr. Arditte Hall et al. (2021) showed people who completed CPT plus hypnosis had a significant improvement in the time it took to fall asleep.

PRE-SURGERY BENEFITS

Individuals preparing for surgical procedures frequently report both increased psychological and physiological distress. Research has shown that for some individuals, unaddressed emotional distress can have negative postoperative consequences on medical procedures (Berliere et al., 2018). In particular, chronic postsurgical pain (CPSP), which can vary depending on the surgery and from one individual to the next, is problematic and can last up to five years (Lee et al., 2019). There are four common predictors linked to CPSP including 1) continued postoperative reports of moderate to high pain intensity over one month, 2) history of more than one surgery, 3) high endorsement of depression and anxiety, and 4) high endorsement of pain catastrophizing (Macintyre et al., 2010). Hypnosis as a clinical intervention, has been shown to effectively help individuals improve coping skills, engage in self-regulation for depression, anxiety, and stress management, and reduce perceptions of pain (Thomson, 2017). Taking into consideration of the predictors frequently associated with CPSP (Lee et al., 2019), as well as unaddressed emotional distress prior to surgery, several studies have effectively demonstrated adding clinical hypnosis is associated with positive treatment outcomes.

In a clinical trial of hypnosis for breast biopsy, 170 patients (mean age 47) were randomly assigned to one of three groups; audio recorded clinical hypnosis intervention with music, music alone, or a control group. While the music condition yielded benefits and aided with reducing anxiety, pain, and stress; patients in the audio recorded hypnosis + music condition, not only decreased levels of reported anxiety, pain, depression, and stress, their ratings remained lower after the biopsy (Sánchez-Jáuregui et al., 2018).

A 2016 review of 29 randomized controlled clinical trials (RCTs) using hypnosis in the treatment of acute, procedural pain further supports evidence which suggests that when hypnosis is included in treatment, patients report decreased pain in contrast to standard care and control groups. To examine the effectiveness of hypnosis in contrast to standard care, 45 measurements were reviewed. Results revealed that the hypnosis condition had significantly lower pain ratings on 28 measurements when compared to the standard care condition. Lower pain ratings were also observed when the hypnosis condition was compared to attention control and hypnosis was significantly more beneficial at reducing pain in contrast to other adjunct pain therapies. Patients appeared to manage pain more effectively in studies with more than one hypnosis session, when hypnosis was used prior to the procedure, and when the hypnotic intervention was less than 30 minutes (Kendrick et al., 2016; also see Moss & Willmarth, 2019; Thomson, 2017).

SKIN DISORDERS

Clinical hypnosis in dermatology has been studied at length and there is continued interest in utilizing it as an adjunctive therapy for the treatment of a variety of skin disorders (Shenefelt, 2017). A 2019 review of 28 studies (1522 patients), which included case reports and clinical trials, evaluated psychological interventions in psoriasis management (Qureshi et al., 2019). When hypnosis was included in the treatment protocols, patients demonstrated positive benefits in psoriasis management. Direct suggestions aimed at relaxation and the use of imagery associated with patients imagining a disease curing glove to treat affected skin areas, were found to be particularly useful in reducing discomfort, skin irritation, and sleep disturbances.

In a clinical study of 27 patients with atopic dermatitis and resistant to topical treatments, direct suggestions in hypnosis aimed at relaxation, relief, lightness and healing, resulted significant improvements (Delaitre et al., 2020). Patients received an average of six hypnosis sessions. Treatment outcomes were assessed using self-assessments and employing the Eczema Area and Severity Index (EASI) which was calculated by the general practitioner who also provided hypnosis treatment. The self-assessment results showed that 14 patients who reported their eczema had improved and 12 patients who reported it had been cured. Eczema Area and Severity Index results revealed significant differences before and after hypnosis treatment (p <0.01) with nine patients producing scores of zero.

In a case report of three adults diagnosed with psychogenic dermatitis (Iglesias, 2005), direct suggestions under hypnosis that focused on relief, enhanced remission of flare-ups and extinguishing neurodermatitis, as well as integrating Ewin's (2002) hypnoanalytic approach to dermatological problems resulted in remission of symptoms. At two-month and one-year follow-ups, each of the cases demonstrated remission of symptoms. Research cleanly demonstrates that integrating clinical hypnosis can successfully help patients improve a variety of skin conditions, help to manage procedural anxiety, as well as assist with reducing harmful habits (skin picking/trichotillomania) and aid with healing (Shenefelt, 2018; Ewin, 2002; Stewart, 2005; Graubard et al., 2021).

SLEEP DIFFICULTIES AND DISTURBANCES

Sleep is important for both physical and cognitive health and functioning (Ohayon et al., 2017; Okun, 2011; Reidy et al., 2016, Rasch & Born, 2013). In 2017, Hinz et al. found that 36% of people ages 18 to 80 reported sleep problems. A 2018 systematic review by Chamine et al. found that in studies that specifically targeted sleep disturbances with hypnosis, 62.5% reported positive findings, 12.5% found mixed results, and 25% reported negative results. This study also explored how the hypnotizability of participants was associated with sleep outcomes. Highly hypnotizable participants appeared to see benefits while lower hypnotizable participants did not (Cordi et al., 2015; Cordi et al., 2014).

Slow wave sleep and slow wave activity have been shown to be beneficial to executive functioning as well as memory consolidation (Wilckens et al., 2018). Slow wave sleep decreases over the lifespan and with the use of pharmacological sleep aids. A 2020 study which examined the impact of hypnosis on slow wave sleep found a significant increase in slow wave sleep compared to a control tape among highly hypnotizable participants (Cordi et al., 2020).

Many sleep disorders have been treated with hypnosis including hypersomnia, sleep apnea, circadian rhythm disorders, somnam-bulism, nightmares, and REM-behavior sleep disorder (Graci & Hardie, 2007). Hypnosis is most amenable to sleep disorders which are not solely biological in nature, but which have a psychological or behavioral component. Hypnosis may be well suited for reducing arousal states such as activation of the sympathetic nervous system (Hammond, 1990). Sexton-Radek and Graci (2008) provide a comprehensive review of hypnosis and cognitive behavioral therapy as a combined approach to the treatment of insomnia, with details about sleep hygiene, stimulus control therapy, sleep restriction strategies, and cognitive therapy (Chapman, 2006).

Behavioral approaches can have advantages over pharmacological interventions due to few if any side effects, ability to remain cog-nitively alert if there is a need to awaken, and the low cost to train someone to utilize behavioral techniques. Hypnosis and relaxation can be used to provide effects which are comparable over the inter-mediate time frame of 4-8 weeks, and even outperform pharmaco-logical treatments in longer term applications of six months to two years (Morin et al., 1994). Cheng et al. (2017) explored hypnosis as a treatment for people experiencing insomnia accompanied by rumination, and found that several domains evaluated by the Pittsburg Sleep Quality index were improved, such as sleep quality, sleep latency, sleep duration, sleep efficiency, sleep disturbances, and daytime dysfunction.

SPORTS PERFORMANCE

Sports Psychology is a proficiency that makes use of psychological knowledge and skills to enhance performance and well-being of athletes as well as the social aspects of the sport organization (APA, 2008). Clinicians may be able to utilize their skillsets in a consultation role, either adjunctively or as a primary form of employment. Hypnosis as a practice may also be useful in the form of a mental training procedure for the enhancement of individual sports performance (Carlstedt, 2017).

A predominant example of the application of clinical hypnosis in sports performance is in the development of the Carlstedt protocol by Dr. Roland Carlstedt. His application of hypnosis to sports performance, as opposed to the relaxation focus of clinical hypnosis, focuses on using hypnotic suggestion to progressively raise levels of activation necessary for engagement in sports-specific tasks, such as moving from the starting line in a 100-meter race (Carlstedt, 2004, 2013, 2017). Inductions are designed with the intention of minimizing negative intrusive thoughts for the athlete, allowing them to experience increased focus, alertness, and mind-body control. It is proposed that once the client has reached a state of mental alertness, active-alert hypnotic suggestions can further increase activation or intensity levels and prime the client for additional physical responses. Video priming may also be used to facilitate mental training about specific technical weaknesses in the athlete's performance (Carlstedt, 2017).

CONCLUSION

This chapter illustrates how hypnosis can be used to treat a variety of clinical problems, through either using hypnosis alone or combined with other treatments. The examples are listed below:

1.   Addiction and relapse prevention—Hypnosis has been shown to help toward the management of substance abuse disorders, through possibly offering an alternative altered state to pursue or by improving factors such as self-efficacy.

2.   Anxiety and stress—Hypnosis combined with CBT has been found to be able to manage symptoms of anxiety, in fact more than hypnosis alone. Cognitive hypnotherapy (CH) is also another useful tool for anxiety and stress management, while being able to identify the root causes of it.

3.   Asthma—Integrating hypnosis for the treatment of asthma has been shown to help toward reducing symptom frequency and severity, through allowing patients to better emotionally self-regulate (stress cues/ changes in body, panic and anxiety, and depressive symptoms).

4.   Autoimmune disorders—Unlike the use of immunosuppressant medications which can leave a variety of complications with continual long-term use, clinical hypnosis has been shown to lead to remission through the use of direct, future-focused hypnotic suggestions and imagery.

5.   Conversion disorders—Clinical hypnosis can be used to treat conversion disorders when it is fairly short-term,

accepted by both clinician and patient, accepted for risk of failure, etiologically relevant, pays attention to minimal cues, and utilizes information that is available to the clinician.

6.   Dentistry—Hypnosis can assist patients to reduce anxiety and fears, as well as pain during dental procedures in addition to creating a calm state, improving relaxation, acceptance, and lowering blood pressure.

7.   Depression—Hypnosis has been shown to improve depression via facilitating the use of internal resources, enhancing coping, providing opportunities for reframing events, orienting to positive focus, enhancing self-image, fostering self-regulation skills, and helping toward detachment from helplessness and victimhood.

8.   Eating disorders—Combining hypnosis with CBT has been shown to be superior to CBT alone, for bulimia nervosa. Participants who are more hypnotizable were also associated with increased sensitivities to social environment and concerns about personal appearance, which makes hypnosis effective toward changing those internal loops that lead to problematic eating behaviors.

9.   Ego strengthening—Positive imagery, calmness and relaxation, and positive affirmations that can be used in hypnotic inductions, can provide ways to improve self-efficacy, inner strength, and confidence, a concept known as ego-strengthening.

10.   Fibromyalgia—When used for the treatment of fibromyalgia, a syndrome that consists of muscle pain,

increased muscle and cold sensitivity, fatigue, poor sleep and emotional distress, hypnosis has been shown to reduce the symptoms by mitigating the experience of pain while improving sleep quality.

11. Headache—Self-hypnosis has been demonstrated to reduce the severity of headaches, in fact, outperforming pharmacological treatments.

12. Hypertension—Hypnosis can also be used to manage hypertension, through increasing parasympathetic tone of the heart affecting electrodermal activity.

13. Irritable bowel syndrome—Gut Directed Hypnotherapy (GDH) can be used to improve symptoms of IBS, as hypnotic suggestions evoke deep relaxation and imagery for gut directed symptom reduction.

14. Menopause—Hypnosis interventions have been found to reduce hot flashes compared to controls, while also attenuating hot flashes frequency.

15. Obesity and weight loss—CBT with hypnosis has been shown to lead to greater adherence to lifestyle interventions compared to CBT alone, which contributes to losing more weight overtime.

16. Pain—Hypnosis offers an analgesic effect, therefore integrating it with other medical interventions has been demonstrated to lead to greater pain reduction than those who did not. Moreover, hypnosis use can help patients better manage pain by improving sleep, increasing energy, hope, awareness, and spirituality.

17. Post-traumatic stress disorder—As hypnosis can help patients separate themselves from traumatic events, it

can be used for the treatment of PTSD, either alone, or adjunct to cognitive behavioral interventions.

18. Pre-surgery—When hypnosis is used before a surgery, it has been shown to decrease pain compared to standard care and control groups.

19. Skin disorders—Hypnosis can be used to reduce skin discomfort, skin irritation, and flare-ups while also helping manage procedural activity and reducing harmful habits that disturb healthy skin (e.g., Skin picking).

20. Sleep difficulties and disturbances—Hypnosis has been shown to outperform pharmacological treatments in the long term for improving sleep quality and duration, while reducing sleep disturbances and daytime dysfunction.

21. Sports performance—Lastly, active-alert hypnotic suggestions can be used to enhance sports performance, through increased focus, alertness, and mind-body control.

CHAPTER 16
REFLECTION QUESTIONS

1. What are some applications of hypnosis in the clinical population?

2. What are some examples where hypnosis is used outside of the clinical population?

3. What is the patient benefit of behavioral intervention in
    comparison to pharmaceutical treatment?

REFERENCES

Abramowitz, E. G., & Lichtenberg, P. (2010). A new hypnotic technique for treating
    combat-related posttraumatic stress disorder: A prospective open study.
    International Journal of Clinical and Experimental Hypnosis, 58(3), 316-328.
    doi:10.1080/00207141003760926

Alladin, A. (2010). Evidence-based hypnotherapy for depression. *International
    Journal of Clinical and Experimental Hypnosis, 58,* 1165–1185.
    doi:10.1080/00207140903523194

Alladin, A. (2013). The power of belief and expectancy in understanding and
    management of depression. *American Journal of Clinical Hypnosis, 55*(3), 249–
    271. https://doi.org/10.1080/00029157.2012.740607

Alladin, A. (2014). The wounded self: New approach to understanding and treating
    anxiety Disorders. *American Journal of Clinical Hypnosis, 56*(4), 368–388.
    https://doi.org/10.1080/00029157.2014.88004

Alladin, A. (2016). Cognitive hypnotherapy for accessing and healing emotional
    injuries for anxiety disorders. *American Journal of Clinical Hypnosis, 59*(1), 24–
    46. https://doi.org/10.1080/00029157.2016.1163662

American Psychiatric Association. (2013). *Diagnostic and statistical manual of
    mental disorders (5th ed.).* Arlington, VA: American Psychiatric Publishing.

American Psychological Association (2008). *Sport psychology.* Retrieved from
    https://www.apa.org/ed/graduate/specialize/sports

Anbar, R. D. (2017). Asthma. In G. Elkins (Ed.) *Handbook of medical and
    psychological hypnosis: Foundations, applications, and professional issues* (pp.
    161-167). New York, NY: Springer.

Ahmadi, A., Jafari, M., Sabzevari, L., Fallah-Tafti, A., & Bidaki, R. (2018). Evaluation of
    the effect of hypnotherapy on the headache. *Sleep and Hypnosis, 20*(2), 114 –
    119. https://doi.org/10.5350/Sleep.Hypn.2017.19.0142

Ahmed, S., & Raza, K. A. (2020). Irritable bowel syndrome: Clinical review. *World Family Medicine Journal/Middle East Journal of Family Medicine*, *18*(9), 106–114. https://doi.org/10.5742/MEWFM.2020.93863

Arditte Hall, K. A., Werner, K. B., Griffin, M. G., & Galovski, T. E. (2021). The effects of cognitive processing therapy + hypnosis on objective sleep quality in women with posttraumatic stress disorder. *Psychological Trauma: Theory, Research, Practice, and Policy*, *13*(6), 652–656. https://doi.org/10.1037/tra0000970

Arnold, L. M., Hudson, J. I., Keck, P. E., Auchenbach, M. B., Javaras, K. N., & Hess, E. V. (2006). Comorbidity of fibromyalgia and psychiatric disorders. *The Journal of Clinical Psychiatry*, *67*(8), 1219–1225. https://doi.org/10.4088/jcp.v67n0807

Asahina, S., Hasegawa, K., & Tsuboi, K. (2006). [Depression in patients of irritable bowel syndrome]. *Nihon Rinsho. Japanese Journal of Clinical Medicine*, *64*(8), 1527–1531.

Avis, N. E., Crawford, S. L., Greendale, G., Bromberger, J. T., Everson-Rose, S. A., Gold, E. B., Hess, R., Joffe, H., Kravitz, H. M., Tepper, P. G., & Thurston, R. C. (2015). Duration of menopausal vasomotor symptoms over the menopause transition. *JAMA Internal Medicine*, *175*(4), 531–539. https://doi.org/10.1001/jamainternmed.2014.8063

Bachner-Melman, R., Lev-Ari, L., Levin, R., & Lichtenberg, P. (2016). Think yourself thin: Concern for appropriateness mediates the link between hypnotizability and disordered eating. *International Journal of Clinical and Experimental Hypnosis, 64*(2), 225-238.

Barabasz, M., (2007). Efficacy of hypnotherapy in the treatment of eating disorders. *International Journal of Clinical and Experimental Hypnosis, 55*(3), 318-335.

Barabasz, A., Christensen, C., & Watkins, J. G. (2010). Ego State Therapy manual: PTSD and ASD (research ed.). Palouse, WA: Authors, distribution restricted.

Barabasz, A., Barabasz, M., & Watkins, J. G. (2012). Single-session manualized Ego State Therapy (EST) for combat stress injury, PTSD, and ASD, Part 2: The procedure. *International Journal of Clinical and Experimental Hypnosis, 60*, 370 – 381.

Barber, J. (1977). Rapid induction analgesia: A clinical report. *American Journal of Clinical Hypnosis, 19*(3), 138-147.

Beck, A. T. (2005). The current state of cognitive therapy: A 40-year retrospective. *Archives of General Psychiatry, 62*(9), 95 –959. https://doi.org/10.1001/archpsyc.62.9.953

Bellato, E., Marini, E., Castoldi, F., Barbasetti, N., Mattei, L., Bonasia, D. E., & Blonna, D. (2012). Fibromyalgia syndrome: Etiology, pathogenesis, diagnosis, and treatment. *Pain Research and Treatment, 2012*, 426130. https://doi.org/10.1155/2012/426130

Berliere, M., Roelants, F., Watremez, C., Docquier, M. A., Piette, N., Lamerant, S., Megevand, V., Van Maanen, A., Piette, P., Gerday, A., & Duhoux, F. P. (2018). The advantages of hypnosis intervention on breast cancer surgery and adjuvant therapy. *Breast, 37*, 114-118.

Bernardy, K., Füber, N., Klose, P., & Häuser, W. (2011). Efficacy of hypnosis/guided imagery in fibromyalgia syndrome – a systematic review and meta-analysis of controlled trials. *BMC Musculoskeletal Disorders, 12*, 133. https://doi.org/10.1186/1471-2474-12-133

Berwick, R. J., Siew, S., Andersson, D. A., Marshall, A., & Goebel, A. (2021). A systematic review into the influence temperature on fibromyalgia pain: Meteorological studies and quantitative sensory testing. *Journal of Pain, 22*(5), 473–486. https://doi.org/10.1016/j.jpain.2020.12.005

Blumenstiel, K., Gerhardt, A., Rolke, R., Bieber, C., Tesarz, J., Friederich, H.-C., Eich, W., & Treede, R.-D. (2011). Quantitative sensory testing profiles in chronic back pain are distinct from those in fibromyalgia. *Clinical Journal of Pain, 27*(8), 682–690. https://doi.org/10.1097/AJP.0b013e3182177654

Bo, S., Rahimi, F., Goitre, I., Properzi, B., Ponzo, V., Regaldo, G., Boschetti, S., Fadda, M., Ciccone, G., Daga, G. A., Mengozzi, G., Evangelista, A., De Francesco, A., Belcastro, S., & Broglio, F. (2018). Effects of self-conditioning techniques (self-hypnosis) in promoting weight loss in patients with severe obesity: A randomized controlled trial. *Obesity, 26*, 1422-1429.

Brown, D. (2007). Evidenced-based hypnotherapy for asthma: A critical review. *International Journal for Clinical and Experimental Hypnosis, 55*(2), 220-249.

Brugnoli, M. P., Pesce, G., Pasin, E., Basile, M. F., Tamburin, S., Polati, E. (2018). The role of clinical hypnosis and self-hypnosis to relief pain and anxiety in severe chronic diseases in palliative care: A 2-year long-term follow-up of treatment in a nonrandomized clinical trial. *Annals of Palliative Medicine. 7*(1),17-31.

Cardeña, E., Svensson, C., & Hejdström, F. (2013). Hypnotic tape intervention
ameliorates stress: A randomized, control study. *International Journal of
Clinical and Experimental Hypnosis, 61*(2), 125–145. https://doi.org/10.1080/
00207144.2013.753820

Carlstedt, R. A. (2004). *Critical moments during competition: A mind-body model of
sport performance when it counts the most* (pp. xv, 264). Psychology Press.

Carlstedt, R. (2013) *Evidence-based applied sport psychology: A practitioner's
manual.* New York: Springer Publishing Company.

Carlstedt, R. (2017). Sports Performance. In G. Elkins (Ed.) *Handbook of medical and
psychological hypnosis: Foundations, applications, and professional issues* (pp.
629-637). New York, NY: Springer Publishing Company.

Cauwels, A., & Tavernier, J. (2020). Tolerizing strategies for the treatment of
autoimmune diseases: From ex vivo to in vivo strategies. *Frontiers in
Immunology, 11*, 674. https://doi.org/10.3389/fimmu.2020.00674

Chamine, I., Atchley, R., & Oken, B. S. (2018). Hypnosis intervention effects on sleep
outcomes: A systematic review. *Journal of Clinical Sleep Medicine, 14*(02), 271 –
283. https://doi.org/10.5664/jcsm.6952

Chapman, R. A. (Ed.). (2006). *The clinical use of hypnosis in cognitive behavior
therapy: A practitioner's casebook.* Springer Publishing.

Cheng, M., Yue, J., Wang, H., Li, L., Zeng, Y., Fang, X., Li, X., & Wen, S. (2017). Clinical
hypnosis in reducing chronic insomnia accompanied by rumination. *Open
Journal of Social Sciences, 5*(9), 296–303. https://doi.org/10.4236/jss.
2017.59020

Chey, W. D., Kurlander, J., & Eswaran, S. (2015). Irritable bowel syndrome: A clinical
review. *JAMA, 313*(9), 949–958. https://doi.org/10.1001/jama.2015.0954

Christensen, C., Barabasz, A., Barabasz, M., (2013). Efficacy of abreactive ego state
therapy for PTSD: Trauma, resolution, depression, and anxiety. *International
Journal of Clinical and Experimental Hypnosis, 61*, 20–37.

Clauw, D. J. (2014). Fibromyalgia: A clinical review. *JAMA, 311*(15), 1547–1555.
https://doi.org/10.1001/jama.2014.3266

Cordi, M. J., Hirsiger, S., Mérillat, S., & Rasch, B. (2015). Improving sleep and cognition by hypnotic suggestion in the elderly. *Neuropsychologia, 69*, 176–182. https://doi.org/10.1016/j.neuropsychologia.2015.02.001

Cordi, M. J., Rossier, L., & Rasch, B. (2020). Hypnotic suggestions given before nighttime sleep extend slow wave sleep as compared to a control text in highly hypnotizable subjects. *International Journal of Clinical and Experimental Hypnosis, 68*(1), 105–129. https://doi.org/10.1080/00207144.2020.1687260

Cordi, M. J., Schlarb, A. A., & Rasch, B. (2014). Deepening sleep by hypnotic suggestion. *Sleep, 37*(6), 1143–1152. https://doi.org/10.5665/sleep.3778

Cozzolino, M., Celia, G., Rossi, K.L., & Rossi, E.L. (2020). Hypnosis as sole anesthesia for dental removal in a patient with multiple chemical sensitivity. *International Journal of Clinical and Experimental Hypnosis, 68*(3), 371-383.

Daitch, C. (2014). Hypnotherapeutic treatment for anxiety-related relational discord: A short-term hypnotherapeutic protocol. *American Journal of Clinical Hypnosis, 56*(4), 325–342. doi:10.1080/00029157.2013.861341

Daitch, C. (2018). Cognitive behavioral therapy, mindfulness, and hypnosis as treatment methods for generalized anxiety disorder. *American Journal of Clinical Hypnosis, 61*(1), 57–69. https://doi.org/10.1080/00029157.2018.1458594

De Benedittis, G. (2017). Hypnosis and Fibromyalgia, In G. Elkins (Ed.) *Handbook of medical and psychological hypnosis: Foundations, applications, and professional issues* (pp, 235-244). Springer Publishing Company.

Degenhardt, L., Charlson, F., Ferrari, A., Santomauro, D., Erskine, H., Mantilla-Herrara, A., Whiteford, H., Leung, J., Naghavi, M., Griswold, M., Rehm, J., Hall, W., Sartorius, B., Scott, J., Vollset, S. E., Knudsen, A. K., Haro, J. M., Patton, G., Kopec, J., … Vos, T. (2018). The global burden of disease attributable to alcohol and drug use in 195 countries and territories, 1990 – 2016: A systematic analysis for the Global Burden of Disease Study 2016. *Lancet Psychiatry, 5*(12), 987–1012. https://doi.org/10.1016/S2215-0366(18)30337-7

Degun-Mather, M. (2001). The value of hypnosis in the treatment of chronic PTSD with dissociative fugues in a war veteran. *Contemporary Hypnosis, 18*(1), 4 – 13. https://doi.org/10.1002/ch.211

Delaitre, L., Denis, J., & Millard, H. (2020). Hypnosis in the treatment of atopic
dermatitis: A clinical study. *International Journal of Clinical and Experimental
Hypnosis, 68*(4), 412-418.

Dilmahomed, H., & Jovani-Sancho, M. (2018). Hypnoanalgesia in dentistry: A
literature review. *American Journal of Clinical Hypnosis, 61*(3), 258-275

Eads, B., & Wark, D. M. (2015). Alert hypnotic inductions: Use in treating combat
post-traumatic stress disorder. *American Journal of Clinical Hypnosis, 58*(2),
159-170. doi:10.1080/00029157.2014.979276

Elkins, G. (2017). *Handbook of medical and psychological hypnosis: Foundations,
applications, and professional issues.* New York, NY: Springer Publishing
Company.

Elkins, G., Barabasz, A. F., Council, J. R., & Spiegel, D. (2015). Advancing research and
practice: The revised APA Division 30 definition of hypnosis. *International
Journal of Clinical and Experimental Hypnosis, 63*(1), 1–9. https://doi.org/10.
1080/00207144. 2014.961870

Elkins, G., Fisher, W. I., Johnson, A. K., Carpenter, J. S., & Keith, T. Z. (2013a). Clinical
hypnosis in the treatment of post-menopausal hot flashes: A randomized
controlled trial. *Menopause, 20*(3), 291-298. https://doi.org/10.1097/
GME.0b013e31826ce3ed

Elkins, G., Jensen, M.P., & Patterson, D.R. (2007). Hypnotherapy for the management
of chronic pain. *International Journal of Clinical and Experimental Hypnosis,
55*(3), 275-287.

Elkins, G., Johnson, A., Fisher, W., Sliwinski, J., & Keith, T. (2013b). A Pilot
investigation of guided self-hypnosis in the treatment of hot flashes among
postmenopausal women. *International Journal of Clinical and Experimental
Hypnosis, 61*(3), 342–350. https://doi.org/10.1080/00207144.2013.784112

Elkins, G., Marcus, J., Bunn, J., Perfect, M., Palamara, L., Stearns, V., & Dove, J. (2010).
Preferences for hypnotic imagery for hot flash reduction: A brief
communication. *International Journal of Clinical and Experimental Hypnosis,
58*(3), 345–349. https://doi.org/10.1080/00207141003761239

Elkins, G., Kendrick, C., & Koep, L. (2014). Hypnotic relaxation therapy for treatment
of hot flashes following prostate cancer surgery: A case study. *International*

Journal of Clinical and Experimental Hypnosis, 62(3), 251–259.
https://doi.org/10.1080/00207144.2014.901051

Ewin, D. (2002). Ideomotor signals: Their value in hypnotherapy. *American Society of Clinical Hypnosis Newsletter, 43*, 6-7.

Finkelstein, S. (2003). Rapid hypnotic inductions and therapeutic suggestions in the dental setting. *International Journal of Clinical and Experimental Hypnosis, 51*(1), 77-85.

Flynn, N. (2018). Systematic review of the effectiveness of hypnosis for the management of headache. *International Journal of Clinical and Experimental Hypnosis, 66*(4), 343 – 352. https://doi.org/10.1080/00207144.2018.1494432

Goebel, A., Krock, E., Gentry, C., Israel, M. R., Jurczak, A., Urbina, C. M., Sandor, K., Vastani, N., Maurer, M., Cuhadar, U., Sensi, S., Nomura, Y., Menezes, J., Baharpoor, A., Brieskorn, L., Sandström, A., Tour, J., Kadetoff, D., Haglund, L., ... Andersson, D. A. (2021). Passive transfer of fibromyalgia symptoms from patients to mice. *Journal of Clinical Investigation, 131*(13), e144201. https://doi.org/10.1172/JCI144201

Goodman, A. (2018). Cases: Clinical hypnosis in dentistry. *American Journal of Clinical Hypnosis, 61*(3), 290-294

Goodman, A. & Filo, G. (2017). Dental applications. In G. Elkins,. (Ed.), *Handbook of medical and psychological hypnosis: Foundations, applications, and professional issues* (pp. 205-211). Springer Publishing.

Golden, W. L. (2012). Cognitive hypnotherapy for anxiety disorders. *American Journal of Clinical Hypnosis, 54*(4), 263–274. doi:10.1080/00029157.2011.650333

Gonsalkorale, W. M., Miller, V., Afzal, A., & Whorwell, P. J. (2003). Long term benefits of hypnotherapy for irritable bowel syndrome. *Gut, 52*(11), 1623–1629. https://doi.org/10.1136/gut.52.11.1623

Graci, G. M., & Hardie, J. C. (2007). Evidenced-based hypnotherapy for the management of sleep disorders. *International Journal of Clinical and Experimental Hypnosis, 55*(3), 288–302. https://doi.org/10.1080/00207140701338662

Graubard, R., Perez-Sanchez, A., & Katta, R. (2021). Stress and skin: An overview of mind body therapies as a treatment strategy in dermatology. *Dermatology:*

Practical and Conceptual, 11(4), e2021091. https://doi.org/10.5826/dpc.1104a91

Hammond, D. C. (2010). Hypnosis in the treatment of anxiety and stress-related disorders. *Expert Review of Neurotherapeutics, 10*(2), 263–273.

Hammond, D. C. (1990). *Handbook of hypnotic suggestions and metaphors.* New York, NY: Norton.

Hinz, A., Glaesmer, H., Brähler, E., Löffler, M., Engel, C., Enzenbach, C., Hegerl, U., & Sander, C. (2017). Sleep quality in the general population: Psychometric properties of the Pittsburgh sleep quality index, derived from a German community sample of 9284 people. *Sleep Medicine, 30*(May), 57–63. doi:10.1016/j.sleep.2016. 03.008

Huntley, A., White, A.R., & Ernst, E. (2002). Relaxation therapies for asthma: A systematic review. *Thorax, 57*, 127-131.

Hurtig, I. M., Raak, R. I., Kendall, S. A., Gerdle, B., & Wahren, L. K. (2001). Quantitative sensory testing in fibromyalgia patients and in healthy subjects: Identification of subgroups. *Clinical Journal of Pain, 17*(4), 316–322. https://doi.org/10. 1097/ 00002508-200112000-00005

Iglesias, A. (2005). Three failures of direct suggestion in psychogenic dermatitis followed by successful intervention. *American Journal of Clinical Hypnosis, 47*(3), 191-198.

Jakubovits, E. & Kekecs, Z. (2017). Treatment of hypertension with hypnosis. In G. Elkins (Ed.) *Handbook of medical and psychological hypnosis: Foundations, applications, and professional* (pp. 273-281). New York, NY: Springer Publishing.

Julien, N., Goffaux, P., Arsenault, P., & Marchand, S. (2005). Widespread pain in fibromyalgia is related to a deficit of endogenous pain inhibition. *Pain, 114*, 295–302.

Kekecs, Z., Szekely, A., & Varga, K. (2016). Alterations in electrodermal activity and cardiac parasympathetic tone during hypnosis. *Psychophysiology, 53*(2), 268 – 277. https://doi.org/10.1111/psyp.12570

Kendrick, C., Johnson, A. K., Sliwinski, J., Patterson, V., Fisher, W. I., Elkins, G. R., & Carpenter, J. S. (2015). Hypnotic relaxation therapy for reduction of hot flashes in postmenopausal women: Examination of cortisol as a potential mediator. *International Journal of Clinical and Experimental Hypnosis, 63*(1), 76–91. https://doi.org/10.1080/00207144.2014.931169

Kendrick, C., Sliwinski, J., Yu, Y., Johnson, A., Fisher, W., Kekecs, Z., & Elkins, G. (2016). Hypnosis for acute procedural pain: A critical review. *International Journal of Clinical and Experimental Hypnosis, 64*(1), 75-115.

Kessler, R. C., Chiu, W. T., Demler, O., & Walters, E. E. (2005). Prevalence, severity, and comorbidity of twelve-month DSM-IV disorders in the national comorbidity survey replication (NCS-R). *Archives of General Psychiatry, 62*(6), 617–627. doi:10.1001/archpsyc.62.6.617

Kihlstrom, J. F. (2018) Hypnosis as an altered state of consciousness. *Journal of Consciousness Studies, 25*(12), 53-72.

Kosek, E., Ekholm, J., & Hansson, P. (1996). Sensory dysfunction in fibromyalgia patients with implications for pathogenic mechanisms. *Pain, 68*(3), 375–383. https://doi.org/10.1016/s0304-3959(96)03188-0

Lacy, B. E., Pimentel, M., Brenner, D. M., Chey, W. D., Keefer, L. A., Long, M. D., & Moshiree, B. (2021). ACG clinical guideline: Management of irritable bowel syndrome. *American Journal of Gastroenterology, 116*(1), 17–44. https://doi.org/10.14309/ajg.0000000000001036

Lang, E. (2021). Rapid hypnosis for medical and dental encounters. *Society for Clinical and Experimental Hypnosis* Webinar Series. Presented (Live) co-sponsored by *The Chicago School of Professional Psychology*, October 29.

Lee, J. K., Zubaidah, J.O., Fadhilah, I. S., Normala, I., & Jensen, M. (2019). Prerecorded hypnotic peri-surgical intervention to alleviate risk of chronic postsurgical pain in total knee replacement: A randomized controlled pilot study. *International Journal of Clinical and Experimental Hypnosis, 67*(2), 217-245.

Leher, P., Feldman, J., Giardino, N., Song, H., & Schmaling, K. (2002). Psychological aspects of asthma. *Journal of Consulting and Clinical Psychology, 70*(3), 691-711.

Loriedo, C., & Di Leone, F. G. (2017). Conversion disorder. In G. Elkins (Ed.) *Handbook of medical and psychological hypnosis: Foundations, applications, and professional issues* (pp. 492-504). New York, NY: Springer.

Macintyre, P. E., Schug, S. A., Scott, D. A., Visser, E. J., & Walker, S. M. (2010). *Acute pain management: Scientific evidence.* Melbourne: Australian and New Zealand College of Anaesthetists

McNeal, S. (2020). Hypnotic ego-strengthening: Where we've been and the road ahead. *American Journal of Clinical Hypnosis, 62*(4), 392–408. https://doi.org/10.1080/00029157.2019.1709151

McNeal, S., & Frederick, C. (1993). Inner strength and other techniques for ego strengthening. *American Journal of Clinical Hypnosis, 35*(3), 170–178. https://doi.org/10.1080/00029157.1993.10403001

McPeake, J. D., Kennedy, B. P., & Gordon, S. M. (1991). Altered states of consciousness therapy: A missing component in alcohol and drug rehabilitation treatment. *Journal of Substance Abuse Treatment, 8*(2), 75–82.

Mease, P., Arnold, L. M., Bennett, R., Boonen, A., Buskila, D., Carville, S., ... Goldenberg, D. (2007). Fibromyalgia syndrome. *Journal of Rheumatology, 34*, 1415–1425.

Mende, M. (2009). Hypnosis: State of the art and perspectives for the twenty-first century. *Contemporary Hypnosis, 26*(3), 179–184. doi:10.1002/ch.383

Miller, L., Archer, R. L., & Kapoor, N. (2020). Conversion disorder: Early diagnosis and personalized therapy plan is the key. *Case Reports in Neurological Medicine*, 2020, e1967581. https://doi.org/10.1155/2020/1967581

Milling, L. S., Gover, M. C., & Moriarty, C. L. (2018). The effectiveness of hypnosis as an intervention for obesity: A meta-analytic review. *Psychology of Consciousness: Theory, Research, and Practice, 5*(1), 29–45.

Milling, L. S., Valentine, K. E., McCarley, H. S., & LoStimolo, L. M. (2019). A meta-analysis of hypnotic interventions for depression symptoms: High hopes for hypnosis? *American Journal of Clinical Hypnosis, 61*(3), 227–243. https://doi.org/10.1080/00029157.2018.1489777

Mills, K. T., Stefanescu, A., & He, J. (2020). The global epidemiology of hypertension. *Nature Reviews Nephrology, 16*(4), 223–237. https://doi.org/10.1038/s41581-019-0244-2

Montenegro, G., Alves, L., Zaninotto, A.L., Pinheiro Falcão, D., & Fernandes Batista de Amorim, R. (2017). Hypnosis as a valuable tool for surgical procedures in the oral and maxillofacial area. *American Journal of Clinical Hypnosis, 59*(4), 414-421.

Morin, C. M., Culbert, J. P., & Schwartz, S. M. (1994). Nonpharmacological interventions for insomnia: A meta-analysis of treatment efficacy. *American Journal of Psychiatry, 151*, 1172 – 1180.

Moss, D., & Willmarth, E. (2017). Ego strengthening approaches in hypnotically assisted psychotherapy. In G. Elkins (Ed.) *Handbook of medical and psychological hypnosis: Foundations, applications, and professional issues* (pp. 535-545). New York, NY: Springer Publishing.

Moss, D., & Willmarth, E. (2019). Hypnosis, anesthesia, pain management, and preparation for medical procedures. *Annals of Palliative Medicine, 8*(4): 498-503.

Muskin, P. R. (Ed.). (2021). *What are anxiety disorders.* Retrieved November 12, 2021, from https://www.psychiatry.org/patients-families/anxiety-disorders/what-are-anxiety-disorders.

Ohayon, M. M., Wickwire, E. M., Hirshkowitz, M., Albert, S. M., Avidan, A., Daly, F. J., ... Vitiello, M. V. (2017). National Sleep Foundation's sleep quality recommendations: First report. *Sleep Health, 3*(1), 6–19. doi:10.1016/j.sleh.2016.11.006

Okun, M. L. (2011). Biological consequences of disturbed sleep: Important mediators of health? In *Japanese Psychological Research.* John Wiley & Sons, Ltd. doi:10.1111/j.1468-5884.2011.00463.x

Peacock, K., & Ketvertis, K. M. (2021). Menopause. In *StatPearls.* StatPearls Publishing. http://www.ncbi.nlm.nih.gov/books/NBK507826/

Pekala, R. J., Kumar, V. K., Maurer, R., Elliott-Carter, N. C., & Moon, E. (2009). Self-esteem and its relationship to serenity and anger/impulsivity in an alcohol and other drug-dependent population: Implications for treatment. *Alcoholism Treatment Quarterly, 27*(1), 94–112. https://doi.org/10.1080/073473208 02587005

Pekala, R. J., Maurer, R., Kumar, V. K., Elliott, N. C., Masten, E., Moon, E., & Salinger, M. (2004). Self-hypnosis relapse prevention training with chronic drug/alcohol users: Effects on self-esteem, affect, and relapse. *American Journal of Clinical Hypnosis, 46*(4), 281–297. https://doi.org/10.1080/00029157.2004. 10403613

Pellegrini, M., Carletto, S., Scumaci, E., Ponzo, V., Ostacoli, L., & Bo, S. (2021). The use of self-help strategies in obesity treatment: A narrative review focused on hypnosis and mindfulness. *Current Obesity Reports, 10*, 351–364.

Picard, P., Jusseaume, C., Boutet, M., Dualé, C., Mulliez, A., & Aublet-Cuvellier, B. (2013). Hypnosis for management of fibromyalgia. *International Journal of Clinical and Experimental Hypnosis, 61*(1), 111–123. https://doi.org/10.1080/00207144.2013.729441

Pinnell, C. M., & Covino, N. (2000). Empirical findings on the use of hypnosis in medicine: A critical review. *International Journal for Clinical and Experimental Hypnosis, 48*(2): 170-194.

Prochaska, J. O., DiClemente, C. C., & Norcross, J. C. (1992). In search of how people change: Applications to addictive behaviors. *American Psychologist, 47*(9), 1102–1114. https://doi.org/10.1037/0003-066X.47.9.1102

Qureshi, A. A., Awosika, O., Baruffi, F., Rengifo-Pardo, M., & Ehrlich, A. (2019). Psychological therapies in management of psoriatic skin disease: A systematic review. *American Journal of Clinical Dermatology, 20*(5), 607-624.

Raihan, N., & Cogburn, M. (2021). Stages of change theory. In *StatPearls*. StatPearls Publishing. http://www.ncbi.nlm.nih.gov/books/NBK556005/

Rasch, B., & Born, J. (2013). About sleep's role in memory. *Physiological Reviews, 93*(2), 681–766. doi:10.1152/physrev.00032.2012

Raskin, R., Raps, C., Luskin, F., Carlson, R., & Cristal, R. (1999). Pilot study of the effect of self-hypnosis on the medical management of essential hypertension. *Stress Medicine, 15*(4), 243–247. https://doi.org/10.1002/(SICI)1099-1700(199910)15:4<243::AID-SMI820>3.0.CO;2-O

Reidy, B. L., Raposa, E. B., Brennan, P. A., Hammen, C. L., Najman, J. M., & Johnson, K. C. (2016). Prospective associations between chronic youth sleep problems and young adult health. *Sleep Health, 2*(1), 69–74. doi:10.1016/j.sleh.2015.11.005

Rizzoli, P., & Mullally, W. J. (2018). Headache. *American Journal of Medicine, 131*(1), 17 – 24. https://doi.org/10.1016/j.amjmed.2017.09.005

Ramondo, N., Gignac, G. E., Pestell, C. F., & Byrne, S. M. (2021). Clinical hypnosis as an adjunct to cognitive behavior therapy: An updated meta-analysis. *International Journal of Clinical and Experimental Hypnosis, 69*(2), 169-202.

Rosenblum, M. D., Gratz, I. K., Paw, J. S., & Abbas, A. K. (2012). Treating human autoimmunity: Current practice and future prospects. *Science Translational Medicine, 4*(125), 125sr1. https://doi.org/10.1126/scitranslmed.3003504

Rotaru, T. S., & Rusu, A. (2016). A meta-analysis for the efficacy of hypnotherapy in alleviating PTSD symptoms. *International Journal of Clinical and Experimental Hypnosis, 64*(1), 116 – 136. https://doi.org/10.1080/00207144.2015.1099406

Rucker, L. (2018). Introducing clinical hypnosis to dentists: Special challenges and strategies. *American Journal of Clinical Hypnosis, 61*(3), 276-289.

Sánchez-Jáuregui, T., Téllez, A., Juárez-García, D., García, C. H., & García, F.E. (2018). Clinical hypnosis and music in breast biopsy: A randomized clinical trial. *American Journal of Clinical Hypnosis, 61*(3), 244-257.

Sapp, M. (2017). Obesity and Weight Loss. In G. Elkins (Ed.), *Handbook of medical and psychological hypnosis: Foundations, applications, and professional issues* (pp. 589-597). New York, NY: Springer PublishingCompany.

Shenefelt, P.D. (2017). Skin disorders. In G. Elkins (Ed.), *Handbook of medical and psychological hypnosis: Foundations, applications, and professional* issues (pp. 409-418). New York, NY: Springer Publishing Company.

Shenefelt, P.D. (2018). Mindfulness-based cognitive hypnotherapy and skin disorders. *American Journal of Clinical Hypnosis, 61*(1), 34-44.

Sport Psychology. (n.d.). Https://Www.Apa.Org. Retrieved December 15, 2021, from https://www.apa.org/ed/graduate/specialize/sportsCarlstedt, R. (2013) *Evidence-based applied sport psychology: a practitioner's manual.* New York: Springer Publishing Company.

Stewart, J. H. (2005). Hypnosis in contemporary medicine. *Mayo Clinic Proceedings, 80*(4), 511-524.

Sexton-Radek, K., & Graci, G. (2008). *Combating sleep disorders.* Praeger.

Surdea-Blaga, T., Baban, A., Nedelcu, L., & Dumitrascu, D. L. (2016). Psychological interventions for irritable bowel syndrome. *Journal of Gastrointestinal and Liver Diseases, 25*(3), 359 – 366. https://doi.org/10.15403/jgld.2014.1121.253.ibs

Sutanto, Y. S. Kalim, H., Handono, K. & Sudiyanto, A. (2021). Effect of hypnotherapy on immune response and standard therapy in psychogenic asthma patients. *Turkish Journal of Immunology, 9*(1), 28-35.

Tastan, K., Ozer Disci, O., & Set, T. (2018). A comparison of the efficacy of acupuncture and hypnotherapy in patients with migraine. *International Journal of Clinical and Experimental Hypnosis, 66*(4), 371–385. https://doi.org/10.1080/00207144.2018.1494444

Thieme, K., Häuser, W., Batra, A., Bernardy, K., Felde, E., Gesmann, M., Illhardt, A., Settan, M., Wörz, R., & Köllner, V. (2008). Psychotherapie bei Patienten mit Fibromyalgiesyndrom [Psychotherapy in patients with fibromyalgia syndrome]. *Schmerz (Berlin, Germany), 22*(3), 295–302. https://doi.org/10.1007/s00482-008-0674-4

Thieme, K., Turk, D. C., & Flor, H. (2004). Comorbid depression and anxiety in fibromyalgia syndrome: Relationship to somatic and psychosocial variables. *Psychosomatic Medicine, 66*(6), 837–844. https://doi.org/10.1097/01.psy.0000146329.63158.40

Thompson, T., Terhune, D.B., Oram, C., Sharangparni, J., Rouf, R., Solmi, M., Veronese, N., & Stubbs, B. (2019). The effectiveness of hypnosis for pain relief: A systematic review and meta-analysis of 85 controlled experimental trials. *Neuroscience & Biobehavioral Reviews, 99*, 298-310.

Torem, M. (2017). Eating Disorders. In Elkins, G. R. (Eds.), *Handbook of medical and psychological hypnosis: Foundations, applications, and professional issues.* Springer Publishing Company, pgs. 589-597.

Torem, M. S. (2017). Autoimmune disorders. In G. Elkins (Ed.), *Handbook of medical and psychological hypnosis: Foundations, applications, and professional Issues* (pp. 169-177), New York, NY: Springer Publishing Company,

Valentine, K. E., Milling, L. S., Clark, L. J., & Moriarty, C. L. (2019). The efficacy of hypnosis as a treatment for anxiety: A meta-analysis. *International Journal of Clinical and Experimental Hypnosis, 67*(3), 336–363. https://doi.org/10.1080/00207144.2019.1613863

van Tilburg, M. A. L., Palsson, O. S., & Whitehead, W. E. (2013). Which psychological factors exacerbate irritable bowel syndrome? Development of a comprehensive model. *Journal of Psychosomatic Research, 74*(6), 486–492. https://doi.org/10.1016/j.jpsychores.2013.03.004

Venkiteswaran, A., & Tandon, S. (2021). Role of hypnosis in dental treatment: A narrative review. *Journal of International Society of Preventive Community Dentistry, 11*(2), 115–124.

Wang, L., Wang, F.-S., & Gershwin, M. E. (2015). Human autoimmune diseases: A comprehensive update. *Journal of Internal Medicine, 278*(4), 369–395. https://doi.org/10.1111/joim.12395

Weitzenhoffer, A., M., & Hilgard, E. R. (1962). *Stanford Hypnotic Susceptibility Scale Form C.* Palo Alto, CA: Consulting Psychologists Press.

Wilckens, K. A., Ferrarelli, F., Walker, M. P., & Buysse, D. J. (2018). Slow-wave activity enhancement to improve cognition. *Trends in Neurosciences, 41*(7), 470–482. doi:10.1016/j.tins.2018.03.003

Wolfe, F. (2010). New American College of Rheumatology criteria for fibromyalgia: A twenty-year journey. *Arthritis Care & Research, 62*(5), 583–584. https://doi.org/10.1002/acr.20156

World Health Organization. (2017). *Depression and other common mental health disorders: Global health estimates.* Geneva, Switzerland

Yapko, M. D. (2010a). Hypnosis and depression. In S. J. Lynn, J. W. Rhue, & I. Kirsch (Eds.), *Handbook of clinical hypnosis* (pp. 391–413). Washington, DC: American Psychological Association.

Yapko, M. D. (2010b). Hypnosis in the treatment of depression: An overdue approach for encouraging skillful mood management. *International Journal of Clinical and Experimental Hypnosis, 58*(2), 137–146. https://doi.org/10.1080/00207140903523137

Xu, Y., & Cardeña, E. (2007). Hypnosis as an adjunct therapy in the management of diabetes. *International Journal of Clinical and Experimental Hypnosis, 56*(1), 63 – 72. https://doi.org/10.1080/00207140701673050

Yunus, M. B. (2007). Fibromyalgia and overlapping disorders: The unifying concept of central sensitivity syndromes. *Seminars in Arthritis and Rheumatism, 36*, 339–356.

Zobeiri, M., Moghimi, A., Attaran, D., Fathi, M., & Ashari, A.A. (2009). Self-hypnosis in attenuation of asthma symptoms severity. *Journal of Applied Sciences, 9*(1), 188-192.

CHAPTER 17
CLINICAL HYPNOSIS TECHNIQUES FOR PAIN MANAGEMENT

DAVID PATTERSON AND JOSHUA RHODES

Chapter Learning Objectives

1. Describe the empirical evidence that supports hypnosis for pain management.

2. Understand the difference between acute and chronic pain.

3. Describe a hypnotic approach to acute pain management.

4. Effectively identify all the factors to consider with the hypnosis model for procedural pain.

Pain management has long been one of the most frequent clinical applications of hypnosis. Going back at least a century and a half, hypnosis has been used to treat virtually every type of pain imaginable. Hypnotic anesthesia was made famous by the British surgeon, James Esdaile, who was reported to have used hypnosis for hundreds of surgeries with no anesthesia (Esdaile, 1957). When ether gas as an anesthetic appeared on the scene, interest in hypnosis for this purpose waned for decades. Nevertheless, hypnosis has been used for pain control and management for decades and continues to be used to this day.

This chapter will first discuss the empirical evidence that supports the use of hypnosis for pain control and management. Often such scientific evidence is important in convincing providers and patients of the viability of any treatment; sadly, with stage hypnosis and the exaggeration of its efficacy, hypnosis has often been relegated to the status of quackery. The burgeoning science that supports hypnosis for pain treatment can often be invoked to offset such skepticism.

This chapter will then briefly review the difference between the use of hypnosis for acute and chronic pain, and the importance of understanding pain etiology. The medical and psychological factors involved in treating both acute pain and chronic will be discussed. Finally, we will discuss hypnotic techniques for both acute and chronic pain, based on the factors that are important in assessing these clinical issues.

EMPIRICAL EVIDENCE

As is the case with almost any new medical or psychological treatment, the first type of evidence in support of hypnosis for treating pain was largely anecdotal. Hundreds of case studies have been published over the last century that provides this type of evidence, and they have demonstrated that hypnosis has been useful for controlling pain from almost every etiology imaginable (Patterson, 2010). As mentioned, Esdaile reported the use of hypnosis successfully with hundreds of surgeries (Esdaile, 1957). More recently, hypnosis has been subjected to more research evaluation with more stringent methodology. The simple quasi-experimental case designs that were the sole support for hypnosis have often been replaced by randomized controlled trials (RCTs) over the more recent decades. In a 2003 review of RCTs, Patterson and Jensen reported that hypnosis was largely successful with both acute and chronic pain etiologies (Patterson & Jensen, 2003). The next level of evidence has been meta-analyses of the controlled trials on hypnosis that have been completed. Montgomery and colleagues (2000) reported that hypnosis is successful in seventy-five percent of participants treated in experimental and clinical studies. Finally, there have been an increasing number of brain activity studies related to pain and hypnosis using such methodology as PET scans, fMRI, and EEG. Hypnosis has been demonstrated to change the actual processing of pain in the brain, at least in experimental situations (Jensen & Patterson, 2014).

ACUTE VERSUS CHRONIC PAIN

It is important in assessment to differentiate whether we are treating patients with acute or chronic pain with hypnosis, as well as any other intervention. Indeed, treatment for these types of pain are on different ends of the spectrum. It is useful to consider the differences between acute and chronic pain in the dimensions of the cause of the pain, duration, sensory qualities and the contribution of physical/biological factors. With acute pain, the nature of the pain is often intense, excruciating and short-lived (Patterson, 2010). Such pain can create the release of stress hormones, delay healing and create long term complications (Bonica, 1990; Martin-Herz et al., 1998). Often with acute pain, the goal is to eliminate pain completely, or at the very least, to minimize it as much as possible. That is why the acute analgesic agents, such as morphine and its derivatives, or techniques such as epidural blocks are often used to keep such pain from ever becoming an issue.

With chronic pain, the duration of the pain is often three to six months, if not longer. Such pain and its associated behaviors often become held in place by complex, multidimensional factors. It is important for both medical and psychological approaches for chronic pain to have an appreciation of the complexity of the etiological factors that are involved. Thus, in treating chronic pain, the goal of treatment is often to do everything other than focus on the pain itself. In a case of chronic pain, it is often a matter of addressing issues such as negative, automatic cognitions, poor sleep, fear of activity, grief, and lack of movement (Jensen & Patterson, 2008).

Factors Influencing Acute Pain

There are essentially two types of acute pain to consider when using hypnosis. One is when the patient is traumatized (e.g., broken bones or injured joints) or going through some type of physiological response (e.g., sickle cell flare ups) where they have intense pain for a limited period of time. In both cases, patients are often frightened or anxious and it is difficult to capture their attention. The principles that are involved with crisis intervention in psychology are often useful in managing acute pain. The clinician is best when confident, reassuring and able to model calmness (Patterson, 2009).

Hypnotic Approaches for Acute Pain

When the patient is in crisis with pain as mentioned above, they are often frightened, and the clinician will likely have trouble capturing their attention. This is often the case with patients who are hospitalized in the emergency room or in the intensive care unit. In such cases, hypnotic inductions should be direct, simple and concrete. Because the patient is challenged with respect to their ability to attend, the therapist should capture their attention quickly and be rapid and succinct with the intervention. Often it is better if the clinician is literally hands-on with the patient given that touch can be important in calming an anxious hospitalized patient (Turner et al., 1998; Forward et al., 2015). To summarize the elements of hypnosis for a patient in crisis and/or acute pain and anxiety:

1. Clinicians should be calm, confident, and optimistic when working with the patient.

2. Hypnotic inductions should be brief, simple and designed to capture the patient's attention quickly.

3. Verbal consent should be obtained by the patient, but a prolonged discussion of this technique will seldom be helpful.

4. The quick induction should be guided by patient feedback, so they are ultimately in control of the process.

A brief approach is described below that is based on a longer script that can be found in Patterson (2010):

> *"I am Dr X. I understand that you are in a lot of pain. We have been using hypnosis here with patients for a number of years. Would you mind if I take a few minutes to use this approach with you? (Informed consent is always important with hypnosis but with crisis situations we often only have the time to ask permission from the patient) I want you to grab my hand, squeeze it hard, and focus all your attention on your hand. I am now going to lift your hand and arm into the air. Just notice that your arm and hand have become light and want to float up in the air (if the hand and arm do not cooperate, then suggest that the hand and arm have become heavy and are sinking into the bed). Now your hand and arm are floating in the air and are going to move down towards the bed slowly. As your arms move downward, notice that you are becoming more relaxed and heavy. I am going to count from one to five. When I reach five and your hand and arm are by your side, you will notice that your eyes have closed and will find that you are deeply, deeply relaxed and comfortable (count to five with suggestions for increased relaxation and comfort. When the arm is by the patient's side, continue with the following language). You are doing very well. Now that you are relaxed, you are going to discover that your inner resources are going allow you to become more comfortable, effortlessly. I don't know how*

your inner resources will serve you, but I do know that you
are going to find yourself deeply comfortable and relaxed."

Note that the clinician is direct, confident and simple in this example. Although this approach is usually successful with the patient, if it is not, you can move to other approaches that may or may not be psychological. In our experience, such quick inductions do not always work, but no harm has been done to the patient if that is the case.

The other type of acute pain is procedural pain. This is likely the most common type of pain that is treated with hypnosis. Procedural pain is most often from medical interventions such as surgery, childbirth, dentistry, burn care and cancer treatment. Although procedural pain is some of the most intense and unpleasant pain imaginable, it is often predictable, so the clinician is able to work with the patient before the pain-generating event occurs. The hypnosis model we recommend for procedural pain is loosely based on progressive relaxation and classical conditioning.

The steps for the induction include the following:

1. Identify the stressor

The stressor is the medical procedure or event such as childbirth. It is a good idea to get some basic information about the procedure such as what it will be, the time and location, and what type of anesthesia will be used.

2. Identify what will occur before the procedure that might elicit anxiety

For a surgery, this might involve going to a care facility on the day of a medical procedure, putting a hospital gown on, and having a line placed in an arm. For dentistry, this might be a matter of the anchoring to the dental chair or the sound of a drill. Preparing a woman for childbirth might be cued to contractions or pelvic sensations.

3. Place the patient in a deep state of relaxation through hypnosis

With this model it is highly recommended to get the patient as relaxed as possible. Most hypnotic inductions involved focusing on breathing and progressive relaxation (done in a much more rapid manner than classic progressive relaxation) and, for this model, the relaxation and deepening should be more emphasized than most other applications of hypnosis.

4. Pair the situations that usually elicit anxiety with comfort and relaxation achieved through hypnosis

For example, patients are given suggestions that when they sit in a dental chair, when they feel labor contractions, or when they put on their gown before surgery, that each one of these cues will elicit a sense of comfort and relaxation. In normal circumstances, such cues will elicit anything from a mild degree of anxiety to a phobic reaction. Rather than fear and anxiety, if this induction is successful, such cues will become post-hypnotic suggestions for relaxation and comfort.

5. The patient is then alerted

As with almost any induction (the induction for acute pain and crisis discussed above being an exception), it is highly advisable that the induction is taped. Currently, most patients have smart phones or similar technology that have a record feature that can be used for this purpose. This induction will almost certainly have far more powerful results if it is recorded and the patient has the opportunity to listen to it several times before the medical procedure.

Dr. Joseph Barber published the Rapid Induction Analgesia in 1977 that follows the model above (Barber, 1977). His article includes a transcript of a very elaborate induction that includes many principles from Milton Erickson's approaches to hypnosis. Although we do not recommend using scripts for the most part, this is one that is particularly effective and powerful. The four or five references to dental care in the script can be substituted for whatever the clinical focus is at hand.

Factors Involved with Chronic Pain

Chronic pain is a complex and multifaceted clinical issue that can seldom be addressed in a single session. In fact, it is the case with both medical and psychological treatments, that chronic pain often can only be managed rather than treated. We often recommended a biopsychosocial conceptualization of chronic pain. The "bio" part of the biopsychosocial model involves such factors as the etiology of the pain, medical techniques that have been used for treatment, and all of the physical factors involved in the patient's presentation. The "psycho" part of this model refers to psychological factors such as how the patient has been coping with their pain, anxiety and depression, or identification of negative thoughts about pain. Identifying automatic dysfunctional thoughts about pain has become a cornerstone of cognitive-behavioral approaches to manage chronic pain. Regarding coping techniques, variables can include whether patients lie in bed and take pain pills, or if they are using more positive techniques such as yoga and supervised exercise. The "social" part of the model refers to the social environment of the patient experiencing chronic pain. It has long been established that solicitous behavior from well-meaning family members often prolongs and exacerbates chronic pain behavior. Further, social and financial disincentives for improvement such as workers compensation often prolong pain behavior (Fordyce, 1976).

Any patient with chronic pain should undergo an extensive evaluation before hypnosis is considered. Hypnosis is often one of the last techniques that should be used for chronic pain. For example, if the social factors discussed above such as workers' compensation or family responses to pain behavior are keeping the pain behavior in place, hypnosis will often be futile. Moreover, patients with chronic pain often have a tendency to somaticize excessively and to experience health anxiety; in such case, addressing the anxiety is far more important than using hypnosis to reduce pain.

Hypnotic Approaches to Chronic Pain.

There are, in broad terms, two different models for treating chronic pain. One model focuses on reducing the pain sensations. With the case of neuropathic pain, unpleasant sensations are largely the product of faulty wiring in the body and are not subject to many factors beyond that. The clinician can often focus on reducing the intensity or unpleasantness of the pain and not be concerned as much with pain behavior or other dimensions of the pain. This approach is because, as discussed above, neuropathic pain is often a product of nerve damage and faulty wiring, and there are no other factors keeping it in place. The steps of the first model include the following:

1. An induction that emphasizes deepening and relaxation.

2. Two to four sessions that focus on a particular suggestion for pain relief (e.g., dimming sensations, age regression or progression, altering negative cognitions about pain, "putting pain in a box").

3. Emphasizing self-hypnosis and free agency in suggestions (e.g., encouraging brief self-hypnosis practice daily).

4. After four sessions, having the patient choose which suggestions are most effective and continuing hypnosis with those suggestions.

5. Making audio tapes of the inductions and instructing the patient to listen to them daily.

Models that focus on reducing pain sensations often involve hypnotic inductions that relax the patient and reduce their cognitive barriers to changes in perception. Thus, most inductions to reduce pain perception will involve extensive relaxation and deepening. Once a patient is relaxed, it is now possible to give them suggestions for reducing pain. For example, we might have the patient picture a dial that can turn down the intensity of their pain.

Another approach is to use hypnotic suggestions for regression or progression. The patient is encouraged to go to a time earlier in their life when they were not in pain, and to be able to use those resources in facing the pain that they are currently experiencing. In hypnotic progression, the patient is encouraged to go into the future and see themselves as functioning well and adaptively. They can then take those resources back to the current time and to use them to help cope with the current neuropathic pain they are experiencing. There are a wide variety of hypnotic suggestions that can aid in the reduction of pain.

The other type of pain to consider is musculoskeletal pain. With musculoskeletal pain, there is often deterioration of joints and ligaments. The second model is based on managing musculoskeletal pain and involves taking a biopsychosocial conceptualization of pain and integrating it with complex hypnotic inductions. This approach involves a thorough assessment of pain and considers factors such as activity levels, sleep, and coping techniques as well as factors that exacerbate or reduce the pain. In this model patients are often encouraged to focus on everything but their pain. Thus, they might be encouraged to increase their activity levels or engage in better coping approaches. Alternatively, there may be instances in which patients are encouraged to focus directly on their pain sensations with mindful techniques.

This second model of hypnosis hopes to address more complex chronic pain presentations. With this approach, clinicians are able to consider the many factors that are involved in chronic pain presentation and ideally, influence as many of them as possible. This model relies on providing a non-linear induction that moves away from direct suggestions. It also creates the context for multiple choices in response to suggestions, as well as multiple layers of suggestions.

To illustrate briefly, a non-linear induction might include elements of the "pacing and leading" induction described by Gilligan (1987). Subjects are given three truisms (statements of what is) followed by a leading suggestion (e.g., You are sitting in a chair, your feet are on the floor, you are breathing in and out, and perhaps you are breathing more slowly). This process lasts roughly 10 minutes and then patients are given multiple choice suggestions for pain management. An example of these multiple-choice suggestions can be found below:

> *"I wonder how you will feel more comfortable today? Perhaps you notice an ability to turn down your pain signals. Or it may be that you have an insatiable desire to follow your physical therapist's suggestions. Or I wonder if you will become so engrossed in playing with your children that you cannot notice anything else. In any case, isn't it interesting that you will find the resources to feel more comfortable much of the day?"*

To elaborate on the approach using hypnosis:

1. Hypnosis is presented in a non-linear approach. "Non-linear" refers to an induction that is neither sequential nor linear. Patients are hopefully able to disengage the critical, logical part of their brain and be more open to suggestion.

2. Hypnotic suggestions are presented in a non-linear fashion and in a manner that the patient is often able to anticipate. For example, suggestions are presented in the context of metaphors, or may address issues independent of pain relief.

3. Patients are presented with multiple choices regarding following suggestions. With specific regard to pain relief, patients may receive multiple choices for how they might reduce their pain.

4. Suggestions are provided based on a biopsychosocial model of chronic pain management. Specifically, multiple suggestions of pain management are provided that not only address pain relief, but also issues such as changing lifestyle, considering alternative approaches to coping, or increasing activity in a safe manner.

5. Tapes are made of each non-linear induction with the expectation that patients will listen to the suggestions on an ongoing basis. With the non-linear emphasis, when patients listen to the induction on tape, they hear different suggestions each time they listen.

CONCLUSION

Hypnosis has long been ignored or underplayed as an approach to pain control or management. It is important to understand the there is an overwhelming body of research that supports its efficacy with the treatment of pain. In addressing pain management with hypnosis, it is important to do a thorough assessment. As is the case with medical approaches, the application of hypnosis to acute pain is often dramatically different than it is with chronic pain. Acute pain control often involves suppression of symptoms and represents hypnosis "at its best". Chronic pain management is almost always complex and involves multiple sessions involving a wide variety of clinical dimensions. Rigorous training in these approaches is of the utmost importance as hypnotic approaches to pain management is best left to professionals that understand the complexity of treating pain.

CHAPTER 17
REFLECTION QUESTIONS

1. How is the treatment of chronic pain different from the treatment of acute pain? In what ways is it more complex?

2. Why is it important that the clinician is direct and confident for the induction toward acute pain management?

3. What are the limitations of hypnosis toward the treatment of chronic pain?

4. What are the different approaches of hypnosis that can be used toward the treatment of chronic pain?

REFERENCES

Barber, J. (1977). Rapid Induction analgesia: A clinical report. *American Journal of Clinical Hypnosis, 19*(3), 138-147.

Bonica, J. J. (Ed.). (1990). *The management of pain* (2nd ed., Vol. 1-2). Lea & Febiger.

Esdaile, J. (1957). *Hypnosis in medicine and surgery*. Julian Press.

Fordyce, W. E. (1976). *Behavioral methods for chronic pain and illness*. Mosby Year Book.

Forward, J. B., Greuter, N. E., Crisall, S. J., & Lester, H. F. (2015). Effect of structured touch and guided imagery for pain and anxiety in elective joint replacement patients - A randomized controlled trial: M-TIJRP. *The Permanente Journal, 19*(4), 18–28.

Gilligan, S. G. (1987). *Therapeutic trances*. Brunner/Mazel.

Jensen, M., & Patterson, D. R. (2008). Hypnosis and the relief of pain and pain disorders. In M. Nash & A. Barnier (Eds.), *The Oxford handbook of hypnosis* (pp. 503-533). Oxford University Press.

Jensen, M., & Patterson, D. R. (2014). Hypnotic approaches for chronic pain management: Clinical implications of recent research findings. *American Psychologist, 69*(2), 166-177.

Martin-Herz, S. P., Patterson, D. R., Ptacek, J. T., Finch, C. P., & Heimback, D. M. (1998, March). *Impact of inpatient pain on long term adjustment in adult burn patients: An update.* Paper presented at the meeting of the American Burn Association, Chicago, IL.

Montgomery, G. H., DuHamel, K. N., & Redd, W. H. (2000). A meta-analysis of hypnotically induced analgesia: How effective is hypnosis? *International Journal of Clinical and Experimental Hypnosis, 48*(2), 138-153

Patterson, D. R. (2009). Acute pain. In A. F. Barabasz, K. Olness, R. Boland, & S. Kahn (Eds.), *Medical hypnosis primer: Clinical and research evidence* (pp. 17-22). Routledge.

Patterson, D. R. (2010). *Clinical hypnosis for pain control.* American Psychological Association.

Patterson, D. R., & Jensen, M. (2003). Hypnosis and clinical pain. *Psychological Bulletin, 129*(4), 495-521.

Turner, J. G., Clark, A. J., Gauthier, D. K., & Williams, M. (1998). The effect of therapeutic touch on pain and anxiety in burn patients. *Journal of Advanced Nursing, 28*(1), 1–20.

CHAPTER 18
HYPNOSIS WITH CHILDREN

KAREN OLNESS AND DANIEL KOHEN

Chapter Learning Objectives

1. Summarize the following:

    a. History of hypnosis with children.

    b. Preparing children and families.

    c. Importance of rapport in workshop training.

    d. Child development considerations in teaching hypnosis.

    e. Emphasis on a child's sense of personal control and self-regulation.

    f. Specific clinical topics including headaches, enuresis, habits, and pain.

2. Describe the value of self-hypnosis training for faculty and learners of child hypnosis practice.

Our thirty-four years of experience in providing child health professionals with the Fundamentals in Pediatric Hypnosis (aka Basic or Introductory) teaches that introductory learning of child hypnosis occurs optimally in the context of a three-day workshop. We strongly suggest that learners initially enroll in a child-focussed three-day workshop and follow that three to four months later with a more general, adult-focussed clinical hypnosis workshop. This approach provides the most effective beginning. Such a three-day, 22- to 24-hour intensive workshop training model offers many advantages, including

- Curricular-based training with focused concentration.

- Exposure to several different, experienced faculty educators (representing developmental-behavioral pediatrics, pediatric psychology, pediatric social work, and pediatric nursing).

- Opportunity for learning via several established educational experiences: didactic presentations, demonstrations (of hypnotic invitations—aka "inductions"—phenomenology, techniques, language), modeling (by faculty, videos, and small group practice sessions with peer colleague learners), and mentor supervision and consultation.

- Freedom from distractions (other coursework, daily work, etc.).

- Planned opportunities for questions, informal learning, networking during breaks, mealtimes.

The detailed content of an Introductory Workshop is reflected in the schedule of a typical Fundamentals in Pediatric Hypnosis Workshop per our National Pediatric Hypnosis Training Institute (NPHTI, see www.nphti.com; Kohen & Olness, 2011b).

Details regarding the function, process, and significance of small groups are found in the discussion.

The curriculum is designed to reach a broad range of child health professionals, and in so doing weaves in child developmental considerations throughout all elements of the Workshop. We have adopted specific criteria which we consider and apply when selecting faculty to develop and present each fundamentals workshop (Kohen, Kaiser, & Olness, 2016). We recommend that hypnosis training organizations or individuals consider these criteria when recruiting new faculty for pediatric hypnosis workshop training. All candidates should:

1. be licensed, highly experienced professionals with at least a Master's degree (in Medicine, Mental Health, Social Work, Nursing etc.),

2. have had extensive clinical work in primary or sub-specialty child health care,

3. have clear passion for clinical hypnosis as reflected in their own extensive and ongoing education and integration of their learning into their practice,

4. have ongoing experience in leadership in the practice & teaching of pediatric hypnosis including, for example, via research, teaching materials, publications,

5. specialized qualities that would provide "value-added" to the overall faculty's expertise (e.g., mid-career or senior status, extensive teaching experience et al),

6. have strong and desirable personal attribute such as:

   a. flexible tactful interpersonal and problem-solving skills

   b. innovative, creative thinking re: teaching, curriculum development

   c. high motivation and positive expectations for success

d. having experience and advocacy for personal self-regulation.

PREPARING THE LEARNER FOR SELF-HYPNOSIS PRACTICE

Throughout workshop training the benefits of self-hypnosis for the learner should be emphasized. During large and small group practices the learner will observe and, hopefully, experience several ways to do self-hypnosis. Learners will vary in their imagery preferences. Some may have excellent visual imagery. Others prefer auditory or kinesthetic or smell/taste imagery. Some imagine in color; others imagine in black and white. Some adults have no visual imagery. Some will easily experience self-hypnosis by imagining a favorite place or scene. Others will prefer to focus on breathing or counting or hearing favorite music.

Some learners will come to the workshop experienced in related skills such as mindfulness meditation, progressive relaxation, autogenic training, yoga, tai chi and/or guided imagery. They are then likely to already have preferred ways to experience self -hypnosis and to recognize the similarities among these practices. As learners recognize the differences among their colleagues, they will be more likely to appreciate the varying preferences among children. It is also important to emphasize to learners that adults generally do not acquire self-hypnosis facility as rapidly as children. They should be willing to commit to daily practice for at least two months in order to develop sufficient skills to benefit from rapid self-hypnosis when needed.

The Importance of Small Group Practice and How It Should Work

In many ways small group practice sessions must be considered the backbone of a fundamentals training program in pediatric clinical hypnosis. A recommended structure of small groups over the course of a three-day, 20- to 22-hour workshop includes:

1. Groups of no more than six participants, preferably mixed by profession when possible. Thus, it is strongly recommended that groups not be constituted as one group of physicians, another of psychologists, another of advance practice nurses, another of social workers, et. but, rather, as interdisciplinary groups in order to promote interdisciplinary peer collaboration. Effort should be made to prevent assignment of office mates, close professional friends, or relatives (spouses, children) to the same group as one another.

2. Throughout the course of the Workshop the members of each group remain together in order to promote comfort in working together during small group sessions. By contrast, the faculty facilitator for each group rotates from group to group. The only exception to that is the first two sessions of the group. We suggest that the same faculty person be the designated facilitator/mentor for each group's first and second sessions. This promotes comfort and also helps prepare the group for a new facilitator for their third and all subsequent sessions.

3. The foregoing structure and following function of the groups should be explained to the attending group of registrants as a PowerPoint presentation preceding the first breakout small group session. After introducing themselves and encouraging the group to introduce themselves briefly to one another, the facilitator of the first small group session should be sure to briefly review the details about the flow of the session.

4. Depending upon the focus of each individual small group practice session, sessions should be scheduled to last from 60-90 minutes. Each session should be preceded by a general group session with a DEMONSTRATION of the hypnotic invitation (induction) that would be practiced in the small group session following immediately thereafter.

5. We have developed a curriculum which focuses upon the skill development experiences provided through the small group practice sessions and augmented by intermittent large group hypnotic experiential exercises integrated within presentations. To do so, we have created seven small group practice sessions. While we are aware that many clinical hypnosis organizations teaching introductory workshops usually have three or four (and, occasionally five) small group sessions during a three day Workshop, we believe that the seven small groups which occupy about 50% of the time of the three days optimize learners' opportunities to learn BOTH how to facilitate a clinical hypnosis experience in a variety of ways AND to personally experience the hypnosis trance as facilitated by the varying clinical colleagues within their small group. Feedback from participants has consistently reinforced that these small groups are the most highly valued of the overall highly appreciated Fundamental Workshops in Pediatric Clinical Hypnosis. The National Pediatric Hypnosis Training Institute website (see references) has information about the curriculum agenda and content specifications for each of the seven small groups.

HISTORY OF HYPNOSIS WITH CHILDREN

This topic should be covered briefly near the beginning of a funda-mentals pediatric hypnosis training workshop. The purpose of including some historical information is not so much to emphasize details but rather to emphasize that hypnosis with children is not new and that it has long been recognized that children learn hypnosis easily.

We recommend that this topic include a brief explanation of the Franklin commission that investigated the "animal magnetism" work of Franz Mesmer. One of the tests devised by the commission was done with a 12-year-old boy. The conclusion of the Franklin commission was that "the imagination is the true cause of the effects attributed to the magnetism" (Tinterow, 1970, p. 114). Prior to the advent of chemical anesthesia an English physician, John Elliotson, described successful surgical operations with children who were in a "mesmeric trance". During the 19th century two French physicians and an English psychotherapist described successful clinical outcomes in children who were taught hypnosis.

The first workshop devoted solely to child hypnosis took place in 1976 sponsored by the Society for Clinical and Experimental Hypnosis. Subsequently the Society for Developmental and Behavioral Pediatrics sponsored an annual workshop on hypnosis with children for 23 years. Since 2010 a new independent organization, NPHTI, has sponsored annual workshops at the fundamental, utilization and advanced levels (nphti.org). Since the COVID-19 pandemic these workshops have been online and have not included fundamentals training. We believe that the 95% of clinicians attending a Fundamentals Workshop are true novices to [formal] hypnosis and the nuances of careful observation and feedback afforded by small group practice. They cannot be reliably experienced or taught via remote participation compared to the intimacy and value of in-person peer learning and support, and in-person mentor supervision.

First efforts to design and implement evidence-based research on child hypnosis took place in the last 30 years of the 20th century.

Compelling clinical reports were reinforced by research studies describing the effectiveness of hypnosis for many pediatric conditions. Future workshops should include reviews of the most current research in order to encourage learners.

Learners should be provided with a bibliography on the history of hypnosis with children. They should also be provided information about professional hypnosis societies including the American Society of Clinical Hypnosis, the Society for Clinical and Experimental Hypnosis and the International Society of Hypnosis.

SPEAKING TO CHILDREN AND FAMILIES ABOUT HYPNOSIS

Fundamental workshops about children and hypnosis should provide guidance on how to explain hypnosis to children and families. This can be provided through didactic presentations and also opportunities for participants to practice speaking with a child or family about hypnosis. Video demonstrations can also be provided.

Children and families often have misconceptions about hypnosis that come from friends, radio, television, comic books and magazines. It is helpful to ask questions about what a child or parent has heard or seen about hypnosis. Most importantly, the child health professional must emphasize that the purpose in teaching hypnosis is to provide the child a useful tool that he/she can control. Practice in using this tool is essential. It is also helpful to make comparisons with mindfulness, mindfulness meditation, relaxation training and guided imagery that may already be familiar to families.

STARTING THE PROCESS—RAPPORT, RAPPORT, RAPPORT

Fundamental to introducing hypnosis to child and adolescent health clinicians is an understanding of what essential ingredients go into the beginning, middle, and **ongoing** process. We have offered an introduction (above) both to the ways and the content we believe are most important in speaking with children and parents about what hypnosis is and what it's not. This understanding is critical from the beginning in order for the patient and family and clinician to recognize, initiate, and create and/or find the hypnosis as it emerges within the clinical encounter.

Unlike what many physicians and other health care clinicians may be taught in medical school or graduate school, there are MANY right ways to do most things, and not just one or two. The problem with a single "right" way, is that *THE* RIGHT way, of course, is that it may simply not work for the next patient or client, or the next. And then it is on us as clinicians to wonder and figure out first how we KNOW that it "didn't work" before then concluding what the "How come?" is, and perhaps more importantly, the "NOW what?!"

What we believe works is from the outset to begin to learn and know WHO this new patient is. To be sure, HOW we do this varies with individual clinicians and styles, and individual patients. That said, however, we can decide and agree that the WHEN and the WHAT are always the same. The WHEN is always "from the beginning" and the "WHAT" always begins with RAPPORT. Nothing is more important than rapport. The clinician could be the smartest clinician on the planet, have the sharpest mind, be up-to-date on all of the literature and research, have the most research grants and a plethora of publications, BUT if they do not invest substantially in refining the skill of developing RAPPORT with their new patient, they have no reason or right to expect the patient to listen, pay attention, or follow directions. We like to say that the 9 essential ingredients in teaching clinicians (and patients) effective clinical hypnosis are RAPPORT—RAPPORT—RAPPORT, HISTORY—HISTORY—HISTORY, and NOTICE—NOTICE—NOTICE. While each of us may have our own bias about HOW we do this, it doesn't seem to matter if it is Rapport—History—Notice—History—Rapport OR some other order. The word "induction" is purposely excluded here because we don't use it much in work with children, however we recognize it is widely used by many researchers and practitioners.

Without a competent and comprehensive history of WHO this child is, in what family they live, and what their problem(s) is/are, AND without REALLY good rapport coupled with careful and extensive noticing (of their behavior, their language, their formulation of ideas) it really doesn't matter how good a "technique" one has or how many different "inductions" (we prefer "invitations" or "initiations") one knows. We don't believe that there is much disagreement with this.

As described earlier in many places above and following, none of these ingredients can or should be "conducted" without the critically essential attention to the significance of developmental considerations. We must recognize and carefully consider the developmental stage and trajectory of the young person (child, adolescent, young adult) as we think about how we talk to and WITH them, how we consider hypnosis and their understanding, how to "do it", how to "be hypnotic" with them, and how to notice and find the hypnosis as it emerges in our encounter(s). All of these considerations vary substantially with age and developmental maturation. In consideration of rapport and history, how we TALK (hypnotically or otherwise) with them and how we BE with children (hypnotically or otherwise) must depend upon our clear understanding of who they are, what family they are in, where they are in their developmental maturation, and what their needs are in a given clinical encounter; not to mention, of course, how we personally understand what hypnosis is and is not, and how we explain it. Whether we call it "rapport" or "joining", there is still a process of beginning, initiating, inviting a child to consider a shift, an "experiment", an opportunity for change. Such learning (novelty!) is part of children's lives and even (or especially) when they have a learning difference or disability, they are usually eager and ready to learn.

Even on the occasion when a child may be referred specifically *for* hypnosis, we believe it is usually (though not always) a mistake to think about "doing" anything formally defined as hypnosis at a first (or perhaps even a second or third visit) until and unless there is a clear readiness as discerned from the rapport, the history, and the nuances of noticing and discovering hypnotic behaviors in the encounter. An exception to this is reflected in the Habit case example below where the child's and parent's readiness were clearly evident early in the initial visit.

Other exceptions to this may be obvious, such as urgent or emergent circumstances where the patient presents in distress and already in a hypnotic state, albeit a negative one, frightened/terrified and narrowly focused on their severe pain, injury, anxiety. Such patients are already "ready"—and experienced, thoughtful, and wise hypnotic approaches are often very welcome and successful adjuncts to other required therapeutic strategies.

CHILD DEVELOPMENT CONSIDERATIONS AND EXAMPLES

Faculty should offer both didactic talks and video examples about the importance of child development and how this relates to hypnosis with children. Small group practice sessions cannot provide realistic guidance about this important topic. Sometimes participants are asked to play the part of a "five-year-old" or "seven-year-old", but this is rarely believable.

Regardless of specialty discipline of a child health professional, e.g., pediatric gastroenterologist, pediatric dentist, pediatric surgeon, it is essential that the person be knowledgeable about how children change over time. If one works with a child over several years, the communication approach must change in order to maintain effective rapport. A four-year-old child is usually very concrete but less so by age nine or ten. The interests of a child also change rapidly over time. Maintenance of rapport with a child depends on being able to adjust to his/her developmental changes and being familiar with their favourite things to do, books, apps, movies, etc.

Children with intellectual disabilities may be functioning at a younger developmental stage than their actual age. The child health professional teaching them self-hypnosis must consider this when planning an approach to these children. Several faculty have made video training tapes that demonstrate how a child does hypnosis differently as he/she ages and changes cognitively. These videos should be shared during fundamental workshops.

Facilitating the Child's Sense of Personal Control and Self-Regulation

Enuresis as an Example

The principle misconception about hypnosis held by the public is that a hypnotist is in control. Efforts to correct this fallacy must be included in all communication with a family and a child about hypnosis. This point should be emphasized in all parts of workshops on hypnosis with children. The child health professional should explain to the child that he/she is like a coach or teacher who can help the child to gain skills. The workshop should include direct and indirect ways to help the child understand that he/she is in control. This can be accomplished via didactic presentations related to specific clinical problems and by videos with children who have practiced hypnosis. The following is an example of information that can be shared during a workshop about the problem of enuresis.

Enuresis is a common childhood problem that often leads a child to feel socially incompetent. Rarely, the cause of enuresis is a problem such as diabetes or urinary tract infection; the child health professional must take care to rule out such causes before proceeding to offer hypnosis training. It is also essential that the child health professional spend time getting to know the child. What is his developmental stage? What are her interests? It is also important to ask the child if he/she has wondered what might be the cause of the problem.

During the first visit the child health professional can make a drawing of the urinary tract, explaining the role of kidneys and demonstrating where urine comes from. The child is encouraged to make a similar drawing and bring it to the second visit. The child health professional also emphasizes that success depends on the child's decision to practice self-hypnosis at home and asks the child what might be a good way to remind himself/herself. It is helpful to speak to parents in the presence of the child and ask them not to remind the child to do the practice. The child health professional can also emphasize that the bladder is a muscle and note that the child has already learned control of many muscles such as those used in walking or throwing a ball or riding a bike. All conversation is directed at letting the child know he/she is in charge.

Videos of a child who has learned self-hypnosis for control of enuresis should be shared during the workshop presentation.

Headaches as an Example

Recurrent and/or chronic headaches are among the most common complaints and concerns in children and adolescents. Up to 10% of children aged 5 to 15 years may experience recurrent headaches (HA), and 17% of U.S. children have frequent or severe HA (Abu-Arefeh & Russell, 1994; Blume, Brockman, & Breuner, 2012). Prevalence in adolescents is as high as 28%. Compared with 13% of adults, almost 20% of children experience migraine HA (International Headache Society, 2013; Split & Neuman, 1999; Kohen, 2017b).

Olness, MacDonald, and Uden (1987) demonstrated that self-hypnosis (SH) and biofeedback were superior to propranolol, a commonly prescribed beta-blocker which, in this study, was no more effective than placebo. Since that time many have shown that training in SH has been an effective therapeutic approach for (self)-management of HAs in children and youth (Eccleston Yorke, Morley, Williams, & Mastroyannopoulou, 2003; Kohen & Olness, 2011; Kohen & Zajac, 2007; Kroner-Herwig, Mohm, & Pothmannm 1998; Larsson & Carlsson, 1996; Masek, 1999; McGrath, 1999).

Beyond saving the cost of over-the-counter or prescription medication, SH also has the advantage of having no adverse effects.

The long-term benefits of SH were demonstrated in our study (Kohen & Zajac, 2007), noting that most patients experienced not only substantial improvement in their discomfort, but also decrease in frequency, duration and intensity of their HAs. As a form of active self-regulation and coping, youths have taught us in their own words (Kohen, 2010) that SH reflects an internally derived and self-reinforcing technique which is self-reinforcing and which they have on their own effectively applied to many other experiences of stress, anxiety, and discomfort in their lives. Detailed description of ingredients of a hypnotic approach to Headaches can be found in several recent publications (Kohen, 2017b, 2018) "So, what am I supposed to DO about these headaches that keep coming?!" (Kohen, 2018).

Case example: Recently a 12-year-old boy (J) was referred for help with anxiety six to eight months' duration; and in the course of the initial visit's rapport and history he said he had also been having headaches for the past year. The anxiety was troublesome, interfering with falling asleep, paying attention in school, and seeming to be causing more arguments with siblings and parents. HAs were increasing from initially "about" weekly to now three or four times a week, often lasting hours, interfering with play, homework, and causing him to sleep in order to get relief. Noise and light exacerbated his headaches and there was a history of migraine in the family. "Usual" medications like aspirin or acetaminophen did not help. He was very clear that he did not "need" either the anxiety or the HAs, and would not "miss them" (!) **when** they were **gone.** (Note: This was purposeful use of expectant, "hypnotic-like" language designed to plant seeds for change when hypnosis was formally introduced at the next visit.) He responded with an eager "YES!" to "Would you like to learn a way to manage these issues?". He said he wanted to first work on HA and then anxiety. With no reference to "doing" hypnosis, I told him a story about a 17-year-old girl who **used to have** terrible migraines. (Kohen, 2017b). After the three to four-minute story, we agreed that at the beginning of the next visit HE could learn what she had learned.

At visit #2, J. was invited to describe various things he enjoyed doing as an introduction to what he could do when learning SH. I told him I would talk about one or more these things and "all you have to do (= it's easy!) is imagine whatever you want what is fun, whether I mention it or not, *because* (of course) it is YOUR self-hypnosis and YOU are the BOSS of it." In response to a simple "Ready?" he said yes, spontaneously closed his eyes, and leaned back in his chair. He was invited to imagine Summertime and swimming in a favorite lake or pool, either alone or with family or friends, with weather and water "just right for you." As imagery of all aspects of swimming was described, he was invited to picture a scale 0-12 as we'd discussed at the initial visit, upon which he had been keeping track of his HAs, with 12 = the worst imaginable HA and 0 = none at all.

He was invited to EITHER notice some 'in between' HA and notice how he reduced it while imagining swimming OR to "just pretend you have one and reduce *that* ... ", the operative principle being HIS choice. Suggestions were offered that with each movement of his arms and/or kick of his legs the level of HA could go down and he could also notice with joyful surprise that there was practically NO anxiety or nervousness or worry at all as he enjoyed swimming *effortlessly.* He was invited to imagine swimming for as long or short as he wanted, *because time is different in this self-hypnosis;* and afterwards he could feel so CALM and so refreshed and so proud because he looked in his mind and saw that the scale was on ZERO!!

After reinforcing positive imagery and relaxation, and the ability to do this at home for himself very easily, he was reminded that "the more you practice the better you get!" and that after re-alerting he should be "sure to bring the good feelings with you when you open your eyes here."

When he re-alerted after this first 'official' SH experience J was practically glowing with pride and joy! He said "It's amazing, I really felt like I was swimming and there were all these beautiful fish swimming next to me and around me ... it was so COOL!!" (I had said nothing about fish!) and then I saw the sun reflections and I saw the scale floating in front of me and it just keep getting lower the closer I got to it ... and it's so funny, I felt like I swam for hours but I'm not even tired!" He had four visits, and over this time his headaches and anxiety decreased steadily and disappeared, with no recurrence at six- and 12-month follow-ups.

Habits as an Example

Many reports have reviewed and described the efficacy of training in self-hypnosis (SH) strategies for the relief and elimination of habit problems (Kohen & Olness, 2011a; Gardner, 1978; Kohen, 1991). These have included learning SH for thumb-sucking, nocturnal enuresis (Kohen & Olness, 2011), tics and Tourette Syndrome (Kohen, 1987, 1995; Lazarus 2010), hair-pulling (Kohen, 1996), habit cough (Anbar & Hall, 2004; Anbar, 2007), and nail-biting (Kohen, 2017a).

In a review of 505 children treated with SH (Kohen et al., 1984), 23 children with habit problems were included. These included tics, habitual sleep-walking, verbal dysfluencies, nail-biting, night-rocking, and thumb-sucking. Eighty-two percent (82%) learned SH easily, and reduced the frequency of their habit by more than 50% or eliminated it completely (48%).

Kohen has recently described an effective hypnotic approach to nail-biting (Kohen, 2017a). A similar methodology of "hands helping hands" is described in the following case report example of a seven-year-old girl with a six-month history of hair-pulling.

Case example: SC (not her real initials) was about seven years old when she was referred by a psychotherapist colleague who told SC's mother "she thought you might be a good fit for my daughter." As rapport unfolded in the initial visit SC was very sweet and deferred to her mother until it was quite clear to the mother that the clinician preferred to hear responses from SC. The onset of hair-pulling was six months earlier and no stress was identified as a trigger to onset, nor was any other family, school, or social event or stimulus identified as a reason for the onset. Picking at her scalp hair and some eyelash pulling (but not removal) increased over Summer, often while watching TV. Restriction of screen time did not alter the frequency, nor did Mom putting SC's hair in a ponytail help. Mom referred to SC as a "scab-picker" and understood quickly when it was explained that "people are **not** their problem" and it would be preferable to talk about how she has "sometimes picked at scabs". Family history revealed that Mother had pulled *her* hair out when she was a young child but "by fifth grade I said 'this is enough' and it stopped". Mother has Anxiety and sees a therapist weekly. SC has three older sisters, none of whom have hair-pulling. Her 12-year-old sister has had anxiety manifest as Selective Mutism and is now improving with psychotherapy.

As SC snuggled with her Mom on the couch, she warmed up easily and, like her Mom, was very friendly and engaging. She often deferred, however, to her Mom, and her sometimes high-pitched squeaky voice made her seem more like four and a half or five years old rather than seven. In developing rapport she was congratulated for her seventh birthday which was two months earlier, and asked "How do you like seven so far?" She said, in a regular seven-year-old voice "It's a lot better than six, six is a much younger number." She happily described her sisters, their ages, their three cats, two dogs, and many fish! She had heard in advance that "You're a fidget doctor that helps people who fidget" and then "I pick my hair, it's a HABIT, A habit is something you do that you can't help." In an immediate re-framing response she was told "Oh, you mean "A habit is something you *didn't know before is something you CAN help …* " Would that be okay?" She nodded, clearly hearing the difference. SC readily showed a 1 inch diameter circular bald area where hair was beginning to grow back on the top back of her scalp. This area was not evident to a casual observer as hair from either side was combed over it. She also showed other areas at the front of her scalp hairline where picking occurs, but they too were visible only when her "bangs" were pushed back. Some thinning of lower lids' eyelashes was evident but none were missing. Upper lids and eyebrows were normal. Both Mom and SC said there was no picking of any other hair or of any other persons' hair, or of pets' hair(s).

SC was asked (with clear re-framing and hypnotic intention but no discussion about it at all) to please show the clinician HOW she "USED TO pick ... and what HAND you *used to use*. AND, before you do that, please show me in SLOW MOTION." A brief modelling of "slow motion walking or running" was done and SC (and Mom of course!) knew about this as she had seen it on TV. As SC proceeded to have her right hand move from her lap toward her face and head she was stopped gently a couple of times with the compliment "That's great, but much, much more SLOWLY please." As she did so she developed a fixed-gaze stare at her hand, her breathing slowed spontaneously, and she was quite still, clear physical concomitants of a spontaneous state of hypnosis. As her hand approached about 2/3 of the way to her scalp she was asked to "STOP ... and just close your eyes." The right hand remained "STOPPED" in a levitated position. The clinician picked up her left hand gently and moved it over to the top of the right hand, while saying "I'm your friend, I'll help you," while gently nudging the right hand **back** to her lap.

She smiled, opening her eyes. When the clinician continued with "GREAT! NOW YOU DO it yourself ... " she did do, moving the right hand up in slow motion, STOPPING at the same place without any prompt verbally or otherwise, and methodically lifting her left hand and slowly moving it to the top of the right hand and gently pushing it down. She was then invited simply and matter-of-factly to "Now, just switch and do the opposite." She knew precisely what this meant, letting the left hand "float" up, stopping 2/3 of the way up, and then having the right hand slowly come over and "help" the left hand return to the lap. As she did so the clinician repeated "That's right, I'll be your friend and help you the same way!" After giving her a "HIGH five" congratulations, the clinician seemed to change the subject, and ask where SC sits in the car while Mom is driving. She said she sometimes is in the back, sometimes in the front. She was asked how Mom (as driver) knows when to go and when not to go. She said there is a RED

LIGHT to STOP or "Yeah, a STOP SIGN". She was then asked to "practice" a few more times, and "THIS time while your eyes are closed see a STOP SIGN or a RED LIGHT in your inside mind and THEN after that hand STOPS, let the helping hand do what it needs to do."

Before the end of this first 90-minute visit SC agreed to practice this method of "creating a NEW pattern" for her hands three times every day for five minutes each time: She chose after breakfast before going to the School Bus, after school before supper, and at bedtime after night-time stories hugs and kisses. Mom agreed to be the timekeeper.

A second visit was two weeks later. SC's Mom reported that after the first visit she (Mom) was optimistic, that both had adhered to the regular practice but that it got boring to do it three times a day so she did it "only twice" but added immediately "It helped a lot and I stopped pulling my hair." Because SC had learned so quickly at the initial visit, I recalled having commented then that I wished I had asked them to video-record that initial visit. They remembered that. When they were asked if we could video-record this second visit, both were quite eager to do so "to help teach other doctors how to help other children. Mom sat and watched and did and said nothing. With the camera running, in response to a simple "Go ahead and show us how you practice" SC did so. This was the "Invitation" (aka "induction"). Intensification (aka "deepening") followed with simple compliments paced to each next step, noting "That's right!" and "Great" when the "helping hand" came over to help the levitated hand return to her lap. At the end she smiled broadly at the "WOW" and additional "High five" followed by couple of stickers, notably saying "SENSATIONAL!"

A follow-up visit was scheduled for a month later. At that visit both reported she remained free of any hair-pulling, had no new problems of any kind, and had continued practicing at bedtime about every other day. Instead of a fourth visit two months later, SC's mother sent an email expressing her gratitude and to report that SC remained "finished" with the hair-pulling habit she "used to have".

CONCLUSION

Workshops on the fundamentals of pediatric hypnosis should be carefully organized with attention to objectives, faculty selection, time allotted to small group practice sessions, training in self-hypnosis for participants and sufficient guidance so participants can immediately apply their learning in clinical work.

CHAPTER 18
REFLECTION QUESTIONS

1. What are the best practices for preparing and training learners in small group pediatric workshops?

2. How would hypnosis to children be different to that of adults?

3. Why are personal control and self-regulation important for hypnosis in children? Give examples of how it is done so.

REFERENCES

Abu-Arafeh, I., & Russell, G. (1994). Prevalence of headache and migraine in school children. *British Medical Journal, 309,* 765-769.

Anbar, R. D. (2007). User friendly hypnosis as an adjunct for treatment of habit cough: A case report. *American Journal of Clinical Hypnosis, 50*(2),171-175.

Anbar, R. D,. & Hall, H. R. (2004). Childhood habit cough treated with self-hypnosis. *Journal of Pediatrics, 144,* 213-217.

Blume, H. K., Brockman, L. N., & Breuner, C. C. (2012). Biofeedback therapy for pediatric headache: Factors associated with response. *Headache 52,* 1377-1386.

Cook, C. R., Blacher, J. (2007). Evidence-based psychosocial treatments for tic disorders. *Clinical Psychology, 14*(3), 252-267.

Curriculum: Fundamentals Workshop in Pediatric Clinical Hypnosis. (2021) National Pediatric Hypnosis Training Institute. Retrieved from www.nphti.com → Training Opportunities → Workshop and Webinar Archives → Fundamentals Workshop-2019 Brochure

Eccleston, C., Yorke, L., Morley, S., William, A. C., & Mastroyannopoulou, K. (2003). Psychological therapies for the management of chronic and recurrent pain in children and adolescents. *Cochrane Database of Systematic Reviews, 1*, 1-46.

Gardner, G. G. (1978). Hypnotherapy in the management of childhood habit disorders. *Journal of Pediatrics, 92,* 834-840.

International Headache Society. (2013). *Headache Classification Committee*

Kohen, D. P. (1987). Relaxation-imagery (self-hypnosis) in Tourette Syndrome: Experience with four children. *American Journal of Clinical Hypnosis. 29*, 227-237.

Kohen, D. P. (1991). Applications of relaxation and mental imagery (self-hypnosis) for habit problems. *Pediatric Annals, 20*(3), 136-144.

Kohen, D. P. (1995). Ericksonian communication and hypnotic strategies in the management of tics and Tourette syndrome in children and adolescents with Tourette syndrome. In S. Lankton & J. Zeig (Eds.) *Difficult contexts for therapy: Ericksonian monographs* (pp. 117-142). New York: Brunner/Mazel.

Kohen, D.P. (1996). Management of trichotillomania with relaxation/mental imagery (self-hypnosis): Experience with five children. *Journal of Developmental and Behavioral Pediatrics, 17*(5), 328-334.

Kohen, D. P., & Zajac, R. (2007). Self-hypnosis training for headaches in children and adolescents. *Journal of Pediatrics, 150*, 635-639.

Kohen, D. P. (2010). Long-term follow-up of self-hypnosis training for recurrent headaches: What the children say. *International Journal of Clinical and Experimental Hypnosis, 58*(4), 417-432.

Kohen, D. P., & Olness, K.N. (2011a). Chapter 10 pp 167-205 in *Hypnosis and hypnotherapy with children* (4th ed). Routledge Publications.

Kohen, D. P. & Olness, K. N. (2011b) Chapter 21 pp 407-421 in *Hypnosis and hypnotherapy with children* (4th ed). Routledge Publications.

Kohen, D. P., & Olness, K. N. (2011c). Chronic daily headache: Helping adolescents help themselves with self- hypnosis. *American Journal of Clinical Hypnosis (Special Issue on Pediatric Hypnosis), 54*(1), 32-46.

Kohen, D. P., Kaiser, P., & Olness, K. N. (2016). State of the art pediatric hypnosis training: Remodelling curriculum and refining faculty development. *American Journal of Clinical Hypnosis, 59*(3), 292-310

Kohen, D. P. (2017a). Nail Biting. In G. R. Elkins (Ed.) *Handbook of medical and psychological hypnosis: Foundations, applications, and professional issues.* (Chapter 34, pp 321-325), Springer Publishing Company.

Kohen, D. P. (2017b). Headaches-Children. In G. R. Elkins (Ed.) *Handbook of medical and psychological hypnosis: Foundations, applications, and professional issues.* (Chapter 27, pp 259-271), Springer Publishing Company.

Kohen, D. P. (2018). So, what am I supposed to DO about these headaches that keep coming?! In M. P. Jensen (Ed.) *Hypnosis for chronic pain: Favorite strategies of master clinicians'* (Chapter 14, pp 276-299), Denny Creek Press.

Kroner-Herwig, B., Mohn, U., & Pothmann, R. (1998). Comparison of biofeedback and relaxation in the treatment of pediatric headache and the influence of parent involvement on outcome. *Applied Psychophysiological Biofeedback, 23*, 143-157.

Larsson, B. & Carlsson, J. A. (1996). School-based, nurse-administered relaxation training for children with chronic tension-type headache. *Journal of Pediatric Psychology. 21*, 603-614.

Lazarus, J. E., & Klein, S. (2010). Non-pharmacological treatment of tics in Tourette Syndrome with videotape training in self-hypnosis. *Journal of Developmental and Behavioral Pediatrics, 31*(6), 498-504.

Masek, B.J. (1999). Commentary: The pediatric migraine connection. *Journal of Pediatric Psychology, 24*, 110.

McGrath, P.J. (1999). Commentary: Recurrent headaches: making what works available to those who need it. *Journal of Pediatric Psychology, 24*, 111-112.

Moore, W. (2017). *The Mesmerist: the society doctor who held Victorian London Spellbound.* London, Weidenfeld and Nicholson.

National Pediatric Hypnosis Training Institute (NPHTI) https://www.nphti.com

Olness, K., & MacDonald, J. (1981). Self-hypnosis and biofeedback in the management of juvenile migraine. *Journal of Developmental and Behavioral Pediatrics, 2*, 168-173.

Olness, K., & MacDonald, J., & Uden, D. L. (1987). Comparison of self-hypnosis and propranolol in the treatment of juvenile classic migraine. *Pediatrics*, *79*(4), 593-597.

Shenefelt, P. D. (2004). Using hypnosis to facilitate resolution of psychogenic excoriations in acne excoriée. *American Journal of Clinical Hypnosis*, *46*(3), 239-245.

Split, W,. & Neuman W. (1999). Epidemiology of migraine among students from randomly selected secondary schools in Lodz. *Headache*, *39*, 494-501.

Tinterow, M.M. (1970). *Foundations of hypnosis: from Mesmer to Freud.* Springfield, IL Charles C. Thomas.

VIDEO RESOURCES

Kuttner, L. (2003). *Making Every Moment Count Documentary* (38 min.) Co-production with The National Film Board of Canada. www.nfb.ca. 1-800-267-7710

Kuttner, L. *"No Fears, No Tears" (29 mins)*. DVD available from http://bookstore.cw.bc.ca email: bookstore@cw.bc.ca US or Canada: 1-800-331-1533 x 3 or Crown House Publishing at http://www.chpus.com

Kuttner, L. *"No Fears, No Tears 13 years later: Children coping with pain" (46 mins)*. DVD available: http://bookstore.cw.bc.ca email: bookstore@cw.bc.ca or, Crown House Publishing at http://www.chpus.com

Sugarman, L.I. (2006). *"Hypnosis in pediatric practice: Imaginative medicine in action."* (70 min.) DVD and booklet. Carmarthen, Wales: Crown House Publishing.

Thomas, J. (2017). Project Director, Primary Consultant: *"You Are The Boss Of Your Brain: Learning How to Manage Pain During Medical Procedures"* (13 min.) produced by Stanford Children's Health and Lucile Packard Children's Hospital. [Video] YouTube. https://www.youtube.com/watch?v=UbK9FFoAcvs

CHAPTER 19
INTEGRATION OF MINDFULNESS AND CLINICAL HYPNOSIS

NICHOLAS OLENDZKI, LIZ SLONENA, AND GARY ELKINS

Chapter Learning Objectives

1. Understand the theoretical similarities and differences between mindfulness and hypnosis.

2. Understand how mindful hypnosis can be used as a primary treatment and adjunctive intervention.

3. Create a strategic plan to deliver Mindful Hypnosis with clients.

4. Learn mindful self-hypnosis for clinician self-care.

Mindfulness is a term with a rich history that makes a single, all-encompassing definition elusive. It has taken on a variety of unique connotations as it has adapted to ancient and modern cultures, differing languages, and a multitude of religious and secular practices. Nevertheless, many modern definitions in the context of mental and physical healthcare tend to coalesce around the following concepts: (1) present-centered awareness, (2) attention or focus on phenomenological experiences, and (3) a mental/emotional stance of non-judgment, open curiosity, or acceptance. It is common for authors to add to this core list to verbally define a term that is quintessentially a nonverbal experience (Germer, 2004). One example definition that incorporates the core concepts discussed would be Kabat-Zinn's (2003), which states " ... mindfulness is: the awareness that emerges through paying attention on purpose, in the present moment, and nonjudgmentally to the unfolding of experience moment by moment" (Kabat-Zinn, 2003).

Mindfulness is often discussed in the context of meditation, and it is important to distinguish between the two. An easy analogy would be to think of mindfulness as "exercise" and meditation as "exercising at the gym". When people go to the gym to exercise, they typically get a concentrated "dose" of exercise over a short period of time. However, when people leave the gym they continue to get exercise when they walk from place-to-place, take the stairs, play tag with their children, or do other physical activities. Similarly, meditation is a concentrated "dose" of mindfulness, but the principles of mindfulness can be intentionally practiced throughout the day. In fact, most mindfulness-based interventions explicitly suggest 'informal' mindfulness into daily activities in order to augment more "formal-ized" meditation practice that has a distinct beginning and end. This distinction between mindfulness and meditation is important for a clinician to understand when implementing Mindful Hypnosis since it neither subsumes or replaces traditional meditation with hypnosis. Clients will get a concentrated dose of mindfulness through a mindful hypnotic induction, and post-hypnotic suggestions can be given to enhance their informal mindfulness practice throughout the rest of the day.

In the context of healthcare, mindfulness is a secular practice which can be of substantial benefit to clients of any faith or cultural background as well as to those who do not practice a faith tradition. Despite its current incarnation as a secular intervention, mindfulness originated in the context of Buddhist beliefs and practices. Buddhist traditions treat mindfulness as just one part of a broader prescription for mental, behavioral, and moral changes that (allegedly) lead to a reduction or cessation of mental and emotional suffering. Over the past decades, healthcare professionals have been actively investigating how a secularized version of mindfulness and meditation can positively impact wellbeing. The results are both significant and promising. For example, mindfulness-based interventions have shown efficacy for stress, anxiety, chronic pain, depression, substance use, borderline personality, and the adverse sequelae of cancer. This list of promising results is by no means exhaustive, but helps to illustrate the broad utility of mindfulness and why a clinician may want to integrate it into their hypnotherapy practice.

The Conceptual and Empirical Basis for Combining Mindfulness and Hypnosis

Stress is a pervasive psychological concern and there is a need for brief and effective treatment interventions (Cohen & Janicki-Deverts, 2007; McLean et al., 2011; Slonena & Elkins, 2021). Meta-analyses investigating mindfulness-based interventions (MBI) have shown significant reductions in stress and improvements in mental and physical health with treatment gains being maintained at long-term follow-up (Grossman et al., 2007; Miller, Fletcher, & Kabat-Zinn, 1995; Bergen-Cico et al., 2013; Chiesa & Serretti, 2009; Solhaug et al., 2019). Although mindfulness interventions are effective for stress reduction in clinical and nonclinical populations, traditional mindfulness treatments are plagued by time burdensomeness and training difficulties for both clients and clinicians (Slonena & Elkins, 2021). For instance, group mindfulness interventions can last 8 weeks, with 2-2.5 hours long sessions, with one hour of homework per day and an all-day silent retreat which may be onerous on clients (Miller et al., 1995). Additionally, emerging research suggests that reducing the number of mindfulness-based stress reduction (MBSR) class hours may not compromise the level of improvement and briefer interventions may lead to greater participation, accessibility, and continued use (Carmody & Baer, 2009; Slonena & Elkins, 2021). In fact, studies indicate that brief, pre-recorded audio mindfulness interventions are efficacious in significantly reducing perceived stress and stress reactivity (Cavanagh et al., 2013; Morledge et al., 2013; Zautra et al., 2012; Zeidan et al. 2010a; Zeidan et al. 2010b; Slonena & Elkins, 2021). Thirdly, mindfulness interventions may be intensive for clinicians to learn and deliver as well. For example, MBSR Teacher Qualification and Certification is estimated to be over $10,000 with multiple workshop requirements (UCSD Center for Mindfulness, 2020), which may not be affordable or practical for some clinicians (Demarzo, Cebolla, & Garcia-Campayo, 2015; Slonena & Elkins, 2021). If a mindfulness intervention could be developed that results in equivalent treatment gains but in a briefer more accessible format, it would be an improvement over traditional mindfulness treatments.

MINDFUL HYPNOSIS:
AN APPROACH FOR ENHANCED
INTERVENTION EFFICIENCY

The intention behind the integration of mindfulness into hypnosis is to enhance the ease, efficiency, and effectiveness of delivering the benefits of mindfulness. Research indicates that hypnosis can be easily combined with CBT, leading to significantly improved treatment gains relative to non-hypnotic CBT (Kirsch et al., 1995; Schoenberger et al., 1997; Ramondo et al., 2021). While hypnosis and mindfulness have different historical roots, philosophical underpinnings, and proposed mechanisms of action, they share central constructs and may be complementary and synergistic in stress-reduction interventions (Alladin, 2014; Elkins, Roberts, & Simicich, 2018; Lynn et al., 2012). Specifically, mindfulness and hypnosis both share suggestions for guided imagery and alterations in attention for an enriched mind-body connection (Elkins & Olendzki, 2018; Otani, 2016; Lifshitz & Raz, 2012; Slonena & Elkins, 2021, Holroyd, 2003). Hypnotic techniques can be applied to catalyze and enhance the delivery of mindfulness skills. Suggestions include relaxation in present-moment awareness without criticism, deepening suggestions for nonjudgement, direct suggestions for acceptance of what cannot be changed or what does need not to be altered, hypnotic imagery of compassion and resilience towards life's difficulties, and even post-hypnotic suggestions enhancing the willingness to practice informal mindfulness by maintaining present-moment awareness (Slonena & Elkins, 2021; Olendzki et al., 2020; Lynn et al., 2010; Yapko, 2010). It is hypothesized that the synthesis of mindfulness and hypnosis principles in a unified intervention may make mindfulness less intimidating while being easier and time efficient to use for stress reduction.

Mindful Hypnosis is defined as a therapeutic intervention that uses hypnotic techniques and direct suggestions to increase mindfulness, achieve specific goals, and reduce stress more quickly (Elkins & Olendzki, 2018; Olendzki et al., 2020; Slonena & Elkins, 2021). It is dialectical in nature, merging radical acceptance and compassionate change towards internal and external experiences. If mindfulness is the medicine for stress relief, then hypnosis would be the pill capsule to easily deliver the medicine into the body and mind in a more digestible way.

Empirical Support for Mindful Hypnotherapy and Brief Mindful Hypnosis

One of the two interventions with empirical support is Mindful Hypnotherapy (MH), which was co-developed and tested using a randomized controlled trial. The sample size was small (48 college students), but the results were both significant and robust (Olendzki et al., 2020). During this study students with high stress completed eight weekly, 1-hour sessions of a standardized protocol. They were also asked to practice daily with short, pre-recorded audio tracks of MH that reinforced the content they were learning during each weekly session. Sessions touched on topics such as present-centered awareness, nonjudgmental awareness, self-hypnosis, and compassion, and by the end of the study researchers observed significant shifts in the way that participants were thinking and feeling. Significant results with large effect sizes were observed for perceived stress and distress, including subscales measuring depression, hopelessness, anxiety, and anger. Unsurprisingly, mindfulness also increased dramatically over the course of the study. Again, these results were based on a relatively small sample and carries all of the appropriate caveats, but the results do pave the way for future research, and show the dramatic and powerful results that MH and other mindful-hypnosis interventions could yield.

Elaborating and expanding the exciting findings by Olendzki et al. (2020), Slonena and Elkins (2021) investigated the impact of Brief Mindful Hypnosis (BMH) on stress reactivity using the Trier Social Stress Test (TSST; Kirschbaum et al., 1993) compared to an active control condition with similar results. The BMH is an audio-based intervention consisting of 3 tracks using modified scripts from the original Olendzki et al. (2020) study focusing on present moment awareness, acceptance and nonjudgmental awareness of thoughts and feelings, and compassion for self and others. The audio-based active control consisted of 3 tracks of cognitive training (Creswell et al., 2014) where complex poems were listened to and analyzed. Fifty-five college-aged participants with elevated stress were randomized to BMH or the CT active-control condition. Participants downloaded the BMH or CT audio-recorded intervention and daily home practice was encouraged. Approximately one week later, participants completed the in-vivo stress-test. BMH produced significant and medium effects in reducing stress-reactivity, weekly stress, and increasing mindfulness, with large increases in immediate relaxation relative to the active-control in approximately 7 days. BHM demonstrated excellent adherence and was rated highly regarding satisfaction, ease of practice, perceived benefit, and likelihood of future use. This study provided support that MH is superior to an active-control for reducing stress-reactivity while increasing mindfulness and relaxation. Modifying MH into online telehealth modalities would be a distinct advantage in times where face-to-face services are not feasible or convenient, such as with busy healthcare providers, rural populations, or during the COVID-19 pandemic.

Future Research of Mindful Hypnosis

With any novel intervention, additional research is needed to establish the effectiveness and efficacy of the treatment. Although there has been clinical and theoretical interest in mindful hypnosis using case studies (Elkins et al., 2018; Yapko, 2010), there are only two randomized empirical studies evaluating Mindful Hypnosis for stress reduction (Olendzki et al., 2020; Slonena & Elkins, 2021). Both studies had similar limitations, with the majority of participants being white, college-aged females, relatively small sample sizes, and a lack of physiological biomarkers (i.e., cortisol, heart rate variability, or ActiWatch actigraphy). Future research endeavors include investigating mindful hypnosis impact on clinical populations, such as insomnia, anxiety, depression, trauma, chronic pain, or substance use. Establishing generalizability to diverse populations, including age, ethnicity, and education, is needed. Another avenue of research is comparing MH to arms of mindfulness without hypnosis to examine whether the hypnotic techniques amplify treatment effects above and beyond traditional mindfulness interventions. Without such investigations, Mindful Hypnosis holds a possibility of being a novel presentation, yet only a recapitulation of existing interventions.

Considerations with Mindful Hypnosis: Abreactions and Contraindicated Populations

Despite the benefits of mindfulness and hypnosis generated by research, neither interventions are 1) panaceas, 2) guaranteed to be blissful experiences, or 3) be beneficial for every client. Abreactions, or intense emotional reactions that may be spontaneous, unconscious, or unintentional reliving of traumatic memories, may occur in both mindfulness and hypnosis. Although Mindful Hypnosis intentionally encourages relaxation and adaptive dissociation to mitigate potential discomfort when mindfully recognizing and compassionately acknowledging thoughts, emotions, and sensations, challenging experiences may emerge. For example, relaxation-induced anxiety is common in individuals with GAD, panic disorder, MDD, and PTSD (Kim & Newman, 2019; Szigethy & Vermetten, 2018). Mindfulness is often viewed as a mental exercise; it can be uncomfortable at first if you have not done a "pull-up" before. Initial relaxation-induced abreactions do not necessarily indicate abortion of mindful hypnosis interventions, but rather careful investigation of why it occurred, discussing treatment preferences, and psychoeducation around desensitization, stress inoculation, and the intention behind mindful acceptance are needed. Clinicians need to be prepared to navigate and stabilize clients when abreactions occur and seek out continued training, supervision, and/or consultation.

At this time, the use of Mindful Hypnosis is contraindicated for the following patient populations: severe mental illness, psychosis, dissociative disorders, and acute suicidal ideation. Individuals with diagnostic indicators or histories of such disorders have contraindications with hypnosis interventions (Kekecs et al., 2016; Walker, 2016). These vulnerable populations may be more prone to faulty reality testing, dissociation, and/or abreactions.

Since consent and buy-in are necessary for any hypnotherapy intervention, another potential rule-out for MH would be if a client objects to using mindfulness or hypnotherapy in general. These objections are generally built on misunderstandings of what mindfulness or hypnotherapy are, and the objections can often be dispelled simply by providing psychoeducation. Examples of misunderstandings that may lead a client to oppose mindful hypnotherapy treatment would be "hypnosis is mind control, and I don't want that" or "mindfulness is the same thing as Buddhism, and Buddhism clashes with my own faith." Although many clients can be reassured that hypnosis is NOT mind control and mindful-hypnotherapy is not a faith-based intervention, a client who remains resolute that they do not want to proceed should not be pressured into treatment.

What Presenting Concerns May Benefit from Mindful Hypnotherapy?

As a primary treatment, Mindful Hypnotherapy was designed for stress management, increasing mindfulness, and enhancing well-being. Since MH is the intentional integration of hypnotherapy and mindfulness, conceptually, it may be beneficial for the concerns that both mindfulness interventions and hypnotherapy have established effectiveness (Elkins & Olendzki, 2018). The 8-session protocol may be generalized to address mood and anxiety disorders, adjustment disorders, insomnia and sleep disturbances, substance use, chronic illness and chronic pain, burnout, and compassion fatigue.

MINDFUL HYPNOSIS AS AN ADJUNCTIVE TREATMENT

Mindful Hypnosis is a useful and easily integrative intervention to enhance your main theoretical approach. Akin to mindfulness skills, MH can be a tool for improving relaxation, well-being, cognitive flexibility, sense of meaning in life, resilience, and distress tolerance. MH can be utilized as a self-compassion and ego-strengthening resource, as well as a burnout and self-soothing skill to be used outside of session. Below are specific avenues of using MH and how it can be integrated in several existing modalities.

Using Brief Mindful Hypnosis as an Adjunctive Treatment

It is well established that homework enhances skill development and is the largest predictor of treatment outcomes (Kazantzis & Lampropoulos, 2002; Nelson, Castonguay, & Barwick, 2007). Importantly, the time spent practicing mindfulness significantly improves the core facets of mindfulness, which in turn leads to symptom reduction and improved well-being (Carmody & Baer, 2008). Clinicians can easily record generalized brief mindful hypnosis tracks and upload them on their website or YouTube for clients to practice with between sessions. The benefits are two-fold; the client can continue their practice outside of session and they can receive effective treatment without a clinician physically present. Furthermore, clinicians can enhance their own practice and hone their skills by writing, recording, and reviewing their Mindful Hypnosis meditations. This can be an excellent practice with a consultant, paying attention to the pace, embodiment of mindfulness principles, and discovering your hypnotic voice.

INTEGRATING MINDFUL HYPNOSIS

Eye-Movement Desensitization and Reprocessing (EMDR) is an empirically validated treatment for post-traumatic stress disorder (PTSD) and has recently expanded to address phobias, grief, substance use, and somatic symptoms (Shapiro, 1995; Zweben, & Yeary, 2006; de Jongh et al., 2019; Tesarz et al., 2019). Intentions to merge hypnosis with EMDR have been largely conceptual, anecdotal, or based on case studies. Phillips (2001) draws parallels between hypnosis and EMDR, suggesting that hypnosis is an ideal intervention to enhance resourcing, ego-strengthening, distress tolerance, and coping skills in EMDR. Other noteworthy parallels between EMDR and hypnosis include intentional alterations in consciousness using visual pendulation (no longer a pocket watch but one's fingers), the use of induction scripts, hypnotic techniques such as age regression and progression, anchoring, guided imagery, ego state work, and direct suggestions to shift emotional, cognitive, and somatic sensations. Because EMDR heavily relies on mindfulness for grounding and holds a philosophy of equanimity that the body and mind know how to organically heal from trauma, integrating Mindful Hypnosis into EMDR is a prosperous marriage.

Mindful Hypnosis can be used during phase 2 (preparation/ resourcing), and before, during, and after trauma reprocessing (phases 4-6), and as an end of session stabilization (phase 7 closure). For example, one can start sessions with a brief mindful hypnosis induction for grounding present moment awareness, then include safe place imagery for deeper relaxation and safety, and have post-hypnotic suggestions for self-compassion, acceptance of thoughts and feelings, and new insights during reprocessing trauma. The client is welcomed to keep their eyes closed and use bilateral stimulation (manually or with the use of buzzers) to reprocess their trauma memories to maintain the mindful hypnotic state and dual awareness. To stabilize the client at the end of session, another brief mindful hypnosis induction is done with suggestions for "the container" exercise if the trauma memory is not yet resolved and/or return to their safe place imagery, with post-hypnotic suggestions for compassion, calm curiosity, and adaptive insights and behaviors to emerge throughout the week. Combining MH with EMDR anecdotally has generated faster reduction of subject units of distress (SUD) to 0 in one session, enhanced mobilization of compassion and self-forgiveness, and decreased talking, "looping," or intellectualizing between sets of bilateral stimulation. Overall, interweaving Mindful Hypnosis with EMDR is an interesting and needed research endeavor.

Integrating Mindful Hypnosis and Third Wave CBT

Third wave cognitive behavior therapies (CBT) are conceptually aligned with Mindful Hypnosis because these interventions use mindfulness and the dialectics of acceptance and behavioral change. Acceptance and Commitment Therapy (ACT; Hayes & Wilson, 1994) and Dialectical Behavior Therapy (DBT; Linehan, 1987) are pivotal treatments that informed the theoretical creation of Mindful Hypnosis. Both ACT and DBT utilize metaphor, guided meditation, and visualization exercises for conveying the treatment principles and therapeutic benefits. We propose that MH can potentiate existing ACT exercises and DBT meditations with skillful use of hypnotic principles. For example, ACT metaphors like "Leaves on a Stream," "Human in the Hole," or "Passengers on the Bus" can be enhanced by using MH inductions, deepeners, and post-hypnotic suggestions to better visualize and hypnotically experience the 6 core ACT concepts to cultivate psychological flexibility. Likewise, MH may amplify DBT meditations in a similar manner while also giving post-hypnotic suggestions for completing homework and diary cards consistently. MH may also supplement delivering ACT via telehealth, as many of the experiential activities are physical in nature (i.e., "tug-of-war" exercise where the client and clinician hold on to a rope). Clinicians can complete the same exercise hypnotically through an induction and visualizing the exercise. While there is currently no empirical research investigating the feasibility or effectiveness of integrating Mindful Hypnosis into existing third wave CBT, it is worthy of future exploration.

BECOMING A MINDFUL HYPNOTHERAPIST

Advanced training in both mindfulness and hypnosis is recommended to fully understand and integrate this treatment effectively. In addition to continuing education, the development of a mindful hypnotherapist is a journey of daily experiential practice. Both mindfulness and hypnosis are experiential phenomena; knowing the research is one leg of the trip while feeling and embodying the shift in consciousness is the other leg of the trip. Because mindfulness and hypnosis have boundless breadth and depth of techniques, it is recommended to strengthen both of your legs through personal practice of mindful self-hypnosis to enhance your understanding and delivery of the intervention. In addition to continuing education, the path of a mindful hypnotherapist is largely based on embodying the 8 core-traits of mindfulness: curiosity, compassion, connection, radical acceptance, non-judgment, non-striving, open awareness, and equanimity (Gunaratana, 2002; Kabat-Zinn & Hahn, 2009). If you have had the opportunity to be in the presence of a meditation teacher, there is a felt sense of these qualities that imbues their thoughts, emotions, actions, and even body posture. How can you cultivate mindful hypnotic presence? Do your clothes allow comfort and ease? Does the tone of your voice convey compassion? Does your clinical environment welcome open awareness? Does your posture, even over telehealth, invoke calm curiosity? As the clinician, you are the teacher, model, and guide for delivering the experience of mindful hypnosis through all the senses.

An easy way to incorporate mindful self-hypnosis is by practicing before you see a client. Betty Erickson was fondly known for going into her own trance before seeing clients to unlock her unconscious for creativity and encourage her clients to unconsciously to go into trance as well. Research has also indicated that therapists who practice mindfulness exhibit enhanced empathy, session presence, and enhanced client outcomes (Ivanovic et al., 2015). Mindful self-hypnosis is also theorized to be an ideal modality for clinician self-care and burnout prevention (Elkins et al., 2018). Below is a simple guide for grounding yourself in mindful self-hypnosis:

1. Use a singing bowl for induction; make it chime for 10 seconds.

2. While you are producing the sound say to yourself, "Now I am entering mindful self-hypnosis." Then stop producing the sound.

3. Close your eyes while you focus on hearing the sound until it is no longer audible.

4. Focus your attention on your breathing for 5 breaths allowing you to go deeper within.

5. Invite a wave of mindful relaxation starting from the crown of your head to your feet.

6. Become grounded in the present moment by visualizing your feet growing roots down into the earth.

7. Visualize yourself as a lotus flower (or any flower) with 8 petals opening and blooming representing the core 8 traits of curiosity, compassion, connection, radical acceptance, non-judgment, non-striving, open awareness, and equanimity.

8. Set a compassionate intention for yourself and your clients. Examples include:

    a. May I connect deeply with my clients today

    b. May my wisdom guide my words

    c. May I see my clients' struggles in a new light

    d. May my compassion flow easily and effortlessly

    e. May I end my sessions on time

9. Open your eyes and stretch back to reorient yourself to the present moment.

Strategic Plan for Working through Clinical Cases using Mindful Hypnosis

Prior to beginning a mindful hypnosis intervention, it is wise to determine the relative benefits, contraindications, and expectations for using hypnosis or mindfulness. These goals can be readily met through completing a thorough clinical intake and appropriate diagnosis. Mindful hypnotherapy is typically well-received by the vast majority of clients, though general contraindications for hypnotherapy will also apply to mindful hypnotherapy, as addressed earlier in this chapter. These contraindications include (but aren't limited to) pre-existing conditions such as schizophrenia, dissociative disorders, acute suicidality, or being involved in a legal case as an eyewitness since there is a legal precedent for calling testimony into question if hypnotherapy is being used as an ongoing treatment. Once it has been determined that mindful hypnotherapy is an appropriate intervention, the remaining sessions may be categorized into three groups:

- Early sessions focus almost exclusively on a client's learning mindfulness *conceptually*, and reinforcing these lessons *experientially* using mindful hypnotherapy inductions in session. Clients should enhance learning through daily home practice between sessions.

- As a client learns initial mindfulness concepts and begins to integrate mindful hypnotherapy into everyday life, middle sessions focus more on reinforcing the client's understanding of mindfulness and deepening their mastery of the concepts at both a cognitive and experiential level.

- Final sessions of mindful hypnotherapy focus on maintaining treatment gains, as the client gains greater autonomy with their ability to practice mindful hypnotherapy and apply mindfulness to new situations as they arise.

Mindful Hypnotherapy presents a scaffold strategy for gradual integration of more complex mindfulness ideals and for compounding their effects over time through experience, reinforcement, and home practice. The process occurs at approximately 8 sessions over the course of 8 weeks focusing on the following topics:

1. Being in the present moment

2. Awareness of the 5 senses nonjudgmentally

3. Awareness and acceptance of thoughts and emotions nonjudgmentally

4. Teaching mindful self-hypnosis

5. Experiencing and understanding compassion

6. Enhancing awareness of one's values, sense of meaning, and equanimity

7. Integration and reflection of mindfulness skills

8. Transition to and development of a long-term practice

Plan for Early Sessions

Early sessions of MH are typically oriented around the themes of *understanding* and *experiencing*. The majority of clients will have either no experience or limited experience with mindfulness or hypnotherapy. Therefore, early sessions will focus on introducing these concepts and allowing a client to experience them directly. If a clinician already has a great deal of experience with introducing mindfulness and hypnosis to clients, they can be guided by their past experience and success in these domains. For clinicians who are relatively new to working clinically with either mindfulness or hypnotherapy (or those looking for inspiration to try a new approach in therapy), consider orienting your sessions as follows. A much more detailed, session-by-session account is laid out in Elkins & Olendzki, N. (2018) *Mindful Hypnotherapy: The Basics for Clinical Practice.*

During the first session(s), define hypnosis and mindfulness in plain terms. Describe how these can be integrated to address the client's presenting concerns, and when the client is ready, guide them through their first mindful hypnotherapy induction. A good place to begin MH practice is to emphasize present-moment awareness since this is one of the most accessible and comprehensible facets of mindfulness. Emphasize the value of daily home-practice with MH recordings and provide the client with recordings to practice with at home. In follow-up sessions, you may begin to build on this foundational concept by introducing the client to the concept of *nonjudgmental* awareness. It is often best to begin teaching this aspect of mindfulness by focusing on a nonjudgmental awareness of physical sensations first. Nonjudgmental awareness is a difficult concept at first, since it runs counter to our instinctual predisposition to change or escape from unpleasant experiences, pursue pleasant experiences, and ignore neutral experiences. Cultivating a curious, open stance toward phenomenological experiences of all kinds is difficult and counterintuitive, but tends to be slightly easier to do with physical experiences than with mental/emotional ones. Once a client has begun to understand and practice nonjudgmental awareness of physical sensations, this skill can then be transferred to being nonjudgmentally aware of thoughts and emotions.

Plan for Mid-Sessions

Mid-sessions of MH are typically oriented around *integration* and *transformation*. Clients who have been diligently adhering to home practice will begin to notice a shift in their default perceptions toward a more mindful outlook, which opens up new possibilities. Clinicians may begin to notice lessening intensity or frequency of symptoms, but also may notice that when symptoms are present, they are less bothersome. If a client habitually treats themselves (or others) with a lack of compassion, this may also be an opportune time to address these issues at a more affective level. Clients can begin to use mindful awareness to accurately discern what they need to thrive, and more easily let go of (or coexist with) unpleasant emotions toward others.

Having absorbed the foundations of mindfulness, therapeutic tasks during the mid-stage of MH usually involve applying what they have learned to their presenting concerns. The client can also enhance their own progress by learning self-hypnosis. Self-hypnosis carries several benefits that enhance treatment gains. For example, it allows an individual to modify pre-recorded MH inductions to be more personally effective for them. In addition, it will help clients integrate brief hypnosis into their day, using the induction methods and suggestions that flexibly address the concerns that arise in their daily life. Amidst the mental and emotional transformation, a client may be able to address deeper and more emotionally laden topics effectively.

Plan for Late Sessions and Termination

Late sessions of MH are oriented around *mastery* and *ownership/ internalization*. Since these sessions are often the prelude to termination, therapeutic focus shifts toward enhancing the client's commitment to continuing to practice and master mindfulness on their own. Later sessions are also a good time to revisit earlier mindfulness concepts or self-hypnotic principles to deepen their understanding of how they function synergistically as a whole. Clients should be encouraged to use MH with greater autonomy and apply MH to emerging challenges in their daily life.

Singing Bowl Induction Script

> *In a moment, you will hear a tone ... and this tone will at*
> *first be clear and eventually become softer until it*

*disappears. You may want to close your eyes so you can
focus even more deeply on the sound. And when the tone
sounds ... you will focus on it so intently ... that everything
else begins to ... fade ... into the background ... easily
focusing on how the tone changes from moment to moment
... attending closely to each nuance of the sound ... with
gentle curiosity ... allow each sensation to pass easily and
effortlessly ... and focusing more and more on the present
moment. When the sound starts to fade, you will find your
mind becoming more and more focused on the fading sound
... as the sound becomes fainter and fainter you will pay
closer and closer attention ... more and more focused ... and
when the tone can no longer be heard, your mind will be as
focused as it is capable of being ... as focused as you allow it
to be. I will stop talking while this tone sounds, so that you
can focus fully on the sound of the [singing
bowl/chime/bell] ... and when I speak again your mind will
be in a deep state of focus ... in mindful hypnosis ... able to
easily respond to each and every suggestion that I give.*

[Wait 5 seconds, then ring the chime so it sustains the
sound for 10 seconds before allowing it to fade. Wait 5
seconds after the tone is no longer perceptible before
continuing the script.]

Deeping suggestions for nonjudgmental awareness of thoughts

*And soon something very interesting is going to happen ... it is
possible to be thinking with one part of your mind ... and yet
with another part of your mind to be **observing** yourself
thinking ... aware of each thought as your mind drifts ...
letting each thought come and go ... gently allowing the
thoughts be just as they are ... The thoughts are like leaves*

*drifting past you in a gentle stream ... each leaf is a thought ...
you can just observe the thoughts drift by without getting
caught up in them ... whether you have thoughts wondering
"am I doing this right?" ... or thoughts about your
responsibilities or what you need to do later ... or thoughts
about previous awkward situations ... or any other thoughts
drifting by ... those thoughts are fine just as they are ... you
can notice them gently ... no criticism, just warmth and
kindness ... their content is unimportant ... they are just
thoughts ... they are not you ... and it is possible for a sense of
kindness to arise within this experience ... criticism is replaced
with kindness ... feeling it like sunshine on your shoulder ... or
perhaps a soft blanket ... warm ... a deep care and openness
as you continue to be aware of each thought ... That sense of
endless kindness and compassion begins **now** ... a sense of
gentleness toward yourself ... softness melting any criticism
or judgements you may have ... and in a moment you will
hear a tone and I will be silent to allow you to observe this
process of warm, mindful thinking ... observing the thoughts
as they come and go like leaves on a stream ... each thought is
a leaf ... coming and going in its own time ... noticing **now**
where your mind goes as I am silent ...* [Ring the
bell/chime/singing bowl, and pause 20 seconds or until the
sound is inaudible] *Good ... and whatever you observed is just
fine ... just continue to rest in a relaxed, mindful state ...
peaceful and serene ... focused on my voice and on what is
happening in the present moment ... Now.*

Re-orienting

*In a few moments it is possible to begin returning to
conscious alertness. Returning to conscious alertness in your
own time and your own pace, in a way that feels right for you
today ... These feelings of peace, kindness, mindfulness, and*

*stability remain with you always ... regardless of any
challenges that come your way ... When that bell sounds, you
will begin to gently return to alertness ... and when the sound
can no longer be heard your eyes will be open. You will be
fully reawakened and rejuvenated, in your normal state of
wakefulness. Ready now? Returning to alertness with the
sound of the chime ...* [Ring Bell/Chime/Singing Bowl]

CONCLUSION

Mindful Hypnosis is a novel intervention integrating hypnosis techniques to deliver mindfulness concepts to attain specific goals and reduce stress. There is a breadth and depth to both mindfulness and hypnosis, philosophically, conceptually, and experientially. To understand and embody MH, continued education in both areas with self-practice is key to delivering this intervention efficiently and effectively. Although the empirical research on MH is still in its infancy, the studies are promising and welcome future examination with clinical trials with clinical populations.

CHAPTER 19
REFLECTION QUESTIONS

1. Why would a clinician want to include mindful hypnosis in their clinical practice?

2. How can mindfulness and hypnosis be combined?

3. What are the best practices for becoming a mindful hypnotherapist?

4. How should mindful hypnotherapy be oriented differently depending on the phase of the intervention?

REFERENCES

Alladin, A. (2014). Mindfulness-Based Hypnosis: Blending science, beliefs, and wisdoms to catalyze healing, *American Journal of Clinical Hypnosis, 56*(3), 285-302. doi:10.1080/00029157.2013.857290

Bergen-Cico, D., Possemato, K., & Cheon, S. (2013). Examining the efficacy of a brief mindfulness-based stress reduction (brief MBSR) program on psychological health. *Journal of American College Health, 61*(6), 348-360.

Carmody, J., & Baer, R. A. (2008). Relationships between mindfulness practice and levels of mindfulness, medical and psychological symptoms and well-being in a mindfulness-based stress reduction program. *Journal of Behavioral Medicine, 31*(1), 23-33.

Carmody, J., & Baer, R. A. (2009). How long does a mindfulness-based stress reduction program need to be? A review of class contact hours and effect sizes for psychological distress. *Journal of Clinical Psychology, 65*(6), 627-638.

Cavanagh, K., Strauss, C., Cicconi, F., Griffiths, N., Wyper, A., & Jones, F. (2013). A randomised controlled trial of a brief online mindfulness-based intervention. *Behaviour Research and Therapy, 51*(9), 573-578.

Chiesa, A., & Serretti, A. (2009). Mindfulness-based stress reduction for stress management in healthy people: a review and meta-analysis. *Journal of Alternative and Complementary Medicine, 15*(5), 593-600.

Cohen, S., Janicki-Deverts, D., & Miller, G. E. (2007). Psychological stress and disease. *JAMA, 298*(14), 1685-1687.

Creswell, J. D., Pacilio, L. E., Lindsay, E. K., & Brown, K. W. (2014). Brief mindfulness meditation training alters psychological and neuroendocrine responses to social evaluative stress. *Psychoneuroendocrinology, 44*, 1-12.

de Jongh, A., Amann, B. L., Hofmann, A., Farrell, D., & Lee, C. W. (2019). The status of EMDR therapy in the treatment of posttraumatic stress disorder 30 years after its introduction. *Journal of EMDR Practice and Research, 13*(4), 261-269.

Demarzo, M. M. P., Cebolla, A., & Garcia-Campayo, J. (2015). The implementation of mindfulness in healthcare systems: A theoretical analysis. *General Hospital Psychiatry, 37*(2), 166-171.

Elkins, G. R., & Olendzki, N. P. (2018). *Mindful hypnotherapy: The basics for clinical practice.* Springer Publishing Company.

Elkins, G. R., Roberts, R. L., & Simicich, L. (2018). Mindful self-hypnosis for self-care: An integrative model and illustrative case example. *American Journal of Clinical Hypnosis, 61*(1), 45-56

Germer, C. (2004). What is mindfulness. *Insight Journal, 22*(3), 24-29.

Grossman, P., Tiefenthaler-Gilmer, U., Raysz, A., & Kesper, U. (2007). Mindfulness training as an intervention for fibromyalgia: Evidence of postintervention and 3-year follow-up benefits in well-being. *Psychotherapy and Psychosomatics, 76*(4), 226-233.

Gunaratana, H. (2002). *Mindfulness in plain English.* Boston: Wisdom Publications.

Hayes, S. C., & Wilson, K. G. (1994). Acceptance and commitment therapy: Altering the verbal support for experiential avoidance. *The Behavior Analyst, 17*(2), 289-303.

Holroyd, J. (2003). The science of meditation and the state of hypnosis. *American Journal of Clinical Hypnosis, 46*(2), 109-128.

Ivanovic, M., Swift, J. K., Callahan, J. L., & Dunn, R. (2015). A multisite pre/post study of mindfulness training for therapists: The impact on session presence and effectiveness. *Journal of Cognitive Psychotherapy, 29*(4), 331-342.

Kabat-Zinn, J. (2003). Mindfulness-based stress reduction (MBSR). *Constructivism in the Human Sciences, 8*(2), 73.

Kabat-Zinn, J., & Hanh, T. N. (2009). *Full catastrophe living: Using the wisdom of your body and mind to face stress, pain, and illness.* Delta.

Kazantzis, N., & Lampropoulos, G. K. (2002). Reflecting on homework in psychotherapy: What can we conclude from research and experience? *Journal of Clinical Psychology, 58*(5), 577-585.

Kekecs, Z., Szekely, A., & Varga, K. (2016). Alterations in electrodermal activity and cardiac parasympathetic tone during hypnosis. *Psychophysiology, 53*(2), 268-277.

Kim, H., & Newman, M. G. (2019). The paradox of relaxation training: Relaxation induced anxiety and mediation effects of negative contrast sensitivity in generalized anxiety disorder and major depressive disorder. *Journal of Affective Disorders, 259,* 271-278.

Kirsch, I., Montgomery, G., & Sapirstein, G. (1995). Hypnosis as an adjunct to cognitive-behavioral psychotherapy: A meta-analysis. *Journal of Consulting and Clinical Psychology, 63*(2), 214-220.

Kirschbaum, C., Pirke, K. M., & Hellhammer, D. H. (1993). The 'Trier Social Stress Test' – a tool for investigating psychobiological stress responses in a laboratory setting. *Neuropsychobiology, 28*(1-2), 76-81.

Lifshitz, M., & Raz, A. (2012). Hypnosis and meditation: Vehicles of attention and suggestion. *Journal of Mind-Body Regulation, 2*(1), 3-11.

Linehan, M. M. (1987). Dialectical behavioral therapy: A cognitive behavioral approach to parasuicide. *Journal of Personality Disorders, 1*(4), 328-333.

Lynn, S., Malaktaris, A., Maxwell, R., Mellinger, D. I., & van der Kloet, D. (2012). Do hypnosis and mindfulness practices inhabit a common domain? Implications for research, clinical practice, and forensic science. *Journal of Mind-Body Regulation, 2*(1), 12-26.

Lynn, S. J., Barnes, S., Deming, A., & Accardi, M. (2010). Hypnosis, rumination, and depression: Catalyzing attention and mindfulness-based treatments. *International Journal of Clinical and Experimental Hypnosis, 58*(2), 202-221.

Malchiodi, C. A. (2020). *Trauma and expressive arts therapy: Brain, body, and imagination in the healing process.* Guilford Publications.

McLean, C. P., Asnaani, A., Litz, B. T., & Hofmann, S. G. (2011). Gender differences in anxiety disorders: Prevalence, course of illness, comorbidity and burden of illness. *Journal of Psychiatric Research, 45*(8), 1027-1035.

Miller, J. J., Fletcher, K., & Kabat-Zinn, J. (1995). Three-year follow-up and clinical implications of a mindfulness meditation-based stress reduction intervention in the treatment of anxiety disorders. *General Hospital Psychiatry, 17*(3), 192-200.

Morledge, T. J., Allexandre, D., Fox, E., Fu, A. Z., Higashi, M. K., Kruzikas, D. T., Pham, S., & Reese, P. R. (2013). Feasibility of an online mindfulness program for stress management: A randomized, controlled trial. *Annals of Behavioral Medicine, 46*(2), 137-148.

Nelson, D. L., Castonguay, L. G., & Barwick, F. (2007). Directions for the integration of homework in practice. In Kazantzis N., L'Abate L. (Eds.) *Handbook of homework assignments in psychotherapy* (pp. 425-444). Boston, MA: Springer.

Olendzki, N., Elkins, G. R., Slonena, E., Hung, J., & Rhodes, J. R. (2020). Mindful hypnotherapy to reduce stress and increase mindfulness: A randomized controlled pilot study. *International Journal of Clinical and Experimental Hypnosis, 68*(2), 151-166. doi:10.1080/00207144.2020.1722028

Otani, A. (2016). Hypnosis and mindfulness: The Twain finally meet. *American Journal of Clinical Hypnosis, 58*(4), 383-398.

Phillips, M. (2001). Potential contributions of hypnosis to ego-strengthening procedures in EMDR. *American Journal of Clinical Hypnosis, 43*(3-4), 247-262.

Ramondo, N., Gignac, G. E., Pestell, C. F., & Byrne, S. M. (2021). Clinical hypnosis as an adjunct to cognitive behavior therapy: An updated meta-analysis. *International Journal of Clinical and Experimental Hypnosis, 69*(2), 169-202.

Schoenberger, N. E., Kirsch, I., Gearan, P., Montgomery, G., & Pastyrnak, S. L. (1997). Hypnotic enhancement of a cognitive behavioral treatment for public speaking anxiety. *Behavior Therapy, 28*(1), 127-140.

Slonena, E. E., & Elkins, G. R. (2021). Effects of a brief mindful hypnosis intervention on stress reactivity: A randomized active control study. *International Journal of Clinical and Experimental Hypnosis, 69*(4), 453-467. doi:10.1080/00207144.2021.1952845

Solhaug, I., de Vibe, M., Friborg, O., Sørlie, T., Tyssen, R., Bjørndal, A., & Rosenvinge, J. H. (2019). Long-term mental health effects of mindfulness training: A 4-year follow-up study. *Mindfulness, 10*(8), 1661-1672.

Shapiro. F. (1995). *Eye movement desensitization and reprocessing: Basic principles, protocols and procedures.* New York: Guilford Press.

Szigethy, E., & Vermetten, E. (2018). Hypnotic interventions for sleep in PTSD. In E. Vermetten, A. Germain, & T. Neylan (Eds.), *Sleep and combat-related post-traumatic stress disorder* (pp. 317-324). New York, NY: Springer.

Tesarz, J., Wicking, M., Bernardy, K., & Seidler, G. H. (2019). EMDR therapy's efficacy in the treatment of pain. *Journal of EMDR Practice and Research, 13*(4), 337-344.

Walker, W. L. (2016). Guidelines for the use of hypnosis: When to use hypnosis and when not to use. *Australian Journal of Clinical and Experimental Hypnosis, 41*(1), 41-53.

Yapko, M. D. (2010). Hypnosis in the treatment of depression: An overdue approach for encouraging skillful mood management. *International Journal of Clinical and Experimental Hypnosis, 58*(2), 137-146.

Zautra, A. J., Davis, M. C., Reich, J. W., Sturgeon, J. A., Arewasikporn, A., & Tennen, H. (2012). Phone-based interventions with automated mindfulness and mastery messages improve the daily functioning for depressed middle-aged community residents. *Journal of Psychotherapy Integration, 22*(3), 206-228.

Zeidan, F., Johnson, S. K., Diamond, B. J., David, Z., & Goolkasian, P. (2010). Mindfulness meditation improves cognition: Evidence of brief mental training. *Consciousness and Cognition, 19*(2), 597-605.

Zeidan, F., Johnson, S. K., Gordon, N. S., & Goolkasian, P. (2010). Effects of brief and sham mindfulness meditation on mood and cardiovascular variables. *Journal of Alternative and Complementary Medicine, 16*(8), 867-873.

Zweben, J., & Yeary, J. (2006). EMDR in the treatment of addiction. *Journal of Chemical Dependency Treatment, 8*(2), 115-127.

CHAPTER 20
OVERVIEW OF HYPNOTIZABILITY ASSESSMENT IN CLINICAL PRACTICE

MING HWEI YEK, MATTIE BIGGS, MORGAN SNYDER, AND GARY ELKINS

Chapter Learning Objectives

1. Define hypnotizability.

2. Describe the rationale for measuring hypnotizability in clinical practice.

3. Identify common hypnotizability measures and the advantages and disadvantages for using each measure.

4. Identify how to provide feedback regarding hypnotizability assessment to clients in clinical practice.

Hypnotizability is defined as "an individual's ability to experience suggested alterations in physiology, sensations, emotions, thoughts, or behavior during hypnosis" (Elkins et al., 2015, p. 383). Hypnotizability is an ability or a trait that remains stable over time (Piccione et al., 1989) and may even be a heritable trait to some degree, with one twin study showing that hypnotizability had a heritability index of .64 (Morgan, 1973). Other types of suggestibility, such as conformity and persuasibility, are not the same as hypnotizability; in fact, there is evidence to suggest that hypnotizability and suggestibility are not related (Tasso et al., 2020; Tasso & Pérez, 2008). Most people are hypnotizable, but there are individual differences in hypnotizability and levels of hypnotizability vary (Woody & Sadler, 2016). Hypnotizability is normally distributed in the population, with most people scoring at a moderate level of hypnotizability (Kekecs et al., 2016).

Hypnotizability can be formally assessed using standardized scales (Woody & Sadler, 2016), which often include a hypnotic induction and suggestions. In the section below, we present several hypnotizability measures that were developed and used in clinical practice. These scales measure hypnotizability by examining how an individual responds to the provided suggestions, which is determined with the use of objective observations and/or the individual's subjective report (Woody & Sadler, 2016).

HYPNOTIZABILITY MEASURES

Several standardized scales have been developed to measure hypnotizability in clinical practice. These scales share several features, including beginning with an induction and measuring behavioral responses to suggestions. These scales also have important differences, such as the number of items, the types of items they include, and the amount of time that it takes to administer each scale. In addition, each scale has advantages and disadvantages, and these will be discussed in the sections below.

Stanford Hypnotic Susceptibility Scale: Form C (SHSS:C)

The Stanford Hypnotic Susceptibility Scale: Form C (SHSS:C; Weitzenhoffer & Hilgard, 1962) was developed to address the limitations of previous versions of this scale, namely the Stanford Hypnotic Susceptibility Scale: Form A and the Stanford Hypnotic Susceptibility Scale: Form B, while maintaining certain characteristics of these previous versions. The SHSS:C includes 12 items that are scored as pass or fail based on behavioral responses to the suggestions. The items include: (1) hand lowering, (2) moving hands apart, (3) mosquito hallucination, (4) taste hallucination, (5) arm rigidity, (6) dream, (7) age regression, (8) arm immobilization, (9) anosmia to ammonia, (10) hallucinated voice, (11) negative visual hallucination, and (12) posthypnotic amnesia. One important feature of the SHSS:C is that it presents items in an order of increasing difficulty. The SHSS:C has shown good internal consistency, with Cronbach's alpha estimated at .85 in previous studies (Hilgard, 1965).

While the SHSS:C is frequently used and was considered the gold standard for measuring hypnotizability, there are significant limitations with this scale. One important limitation is that it takes approximately 60 minutes to administer, which makes it impractical for use in clinical settings. There are also concerns with the pleasantness of the scale, namely the mosquito hallucination and the anosmia to ammonia items, which may be unpleasant for some individuals. Another limitation of the SHSS:C is that items are scored as pass or fail based upon the behavioral responses to the suggestions, and the scale does not consider the subjective or experiential responses to the items.

Hypnotic Induction Profile (HIP)

The Hypnotic Induction Profile (HIP; Spiegel, 1977) was developed for clinical use given that many previous hypnotizability tests were developed for research purposes and not feasible in clinical practice due to their length of administration. The HIP can be administered in 5 to 10 minutes and is scored through observable behaviors (e.g., eye-roll test; Alexander et al., 2021). Using 12 items, the HIP can provide clinicians and researchers qualitative and quantitative data about an individual's hypnotic potential. The 12 items that are used to assess hypnotizability are grouped into larger scores of the Induction Score and the Profile Grade Score. The Induction Score is important in determining the level of hypnotizability of an individual. The Profile Grade Score involves the eye-roll item and ideomotor item (i.e., hand levitation), and can be used to inform the treatment plan when using hypnosis with a clinical patient (Alexander et al., 2021; Spiegel & Spiegel, 2004).

Strengths of the HIP include the short length of administration (i.e., 5 to 10 minutes), which is important for clinical practice, as well as normative data from large samples of clinical patients (Frischholz et al., 2015; Stern et al., 1978). However, the eye-roll test, which has been proposed as a biological indicator of hypnotizability, has been found to poorly correlate ($r = -.17$, Wheeler et al., 1974; $r = .10$, Orne et al., 1979) with the Stanford Hypnotic Susceptibility Scale-Form C (SHSS:C; Weitzenhoffer & Hilgard, 1962). Additionally, the Induction Score has inconsistent correlations with the SHSS:C, ranging from .19 (Orne et al., 1979) to .63 (Frischholz et al., 1980). Lastly, since the eye-roll test independently is not a reliable measure of hypnotizability and the Induction Score does not contain enough items to provide robust information about an individual's hypnotizability, the HIP is limited in its ability to determine a range of hypnotizability (Elkins, 2014; Kihlstrom, 1985).

Stanford Hypnotic Arm Levitation Induction and Test (SHALIT)

The Stanford Hypnotic Arm Levitation Induction and Test (SHALIT; Hilgard et al., 1979) was also developed for clinical use and only takes about 6 minutes to administer. The SHALIT is convenient to administer and score. The scale contains only one item, which is a suggestion for arm levitation. The SHALIT determines an individual's hypnotizability level based on: (1) whether the individual's elbow stays on the table or raises following the suggestions; (2) self-reported depth of hypnosis; and (3) self-reported degree of involuntariness of the arm levitation. The SHALIT has been shown to be a valid measure of hypnotizability, with a correlation of .63 between the SHALIT arm levitation item and the Stanford Hypnotic Susceptibility Scale: Form A. The short time that it takes to administer the scale is beneficial for clinical use, however, psychometrically, the scale is too short and does not measure a full range of hypnotizability. Due to the brevity of the scale and its reliance on primarily motor suggestions, the scale may not be able to identify highly hypnotizable individuals (Hilgard et al., 1979).

Stanford Hypnotic Clinical Scale (SHCS)

The Stanford Hypnotic Clinical Scale (SHCS; Morgan & Hilgard, 1978-1979) is one of the most widely used scales in clinical research (Barnier & McConkey, 2004). It was developed because previous scales, such as the Stanford Hypnotic Susceptibility Scale: Form A (SHSS:A), the Stanford Hypnotic Susceptibility Scale: Form B (SHSS:B), and the Stanford Hypnotic Susceptibility Scale: Form C (SHSS:C) were too long and burdensome for clinical use. The SHCS consists of five items, including moving hands, a dream within hypnosis, age regression, posthypnotic suggestion, and posthypnotic amnesia. The SHCS takes approximately 20 minutes to administer. The scale has been shown to be valid in previous studies and correlates well with the SHSS:C, with a correlation of .72 (Morgan & Hilgard, 1979). One concern regarding the SHCS is the inclusion of the age regression item in the scale. The age regression item may be distressing and may bring up unpleasant memories for some individuals (Cardeña & Terhune, 2009). There are also some psychometric concerns for the SHCS since it is short, including that it may not measure a full range of hypnotizability (Elkins, 2014; Woody & Barnier, 2008).

Elkins Hypnotizability Scale (EHS)

The Elkins Hypnotizability Scale (EHS; Elkins, 2014) was developed to address the limitations of prior hypnotizability measures and to provide a safe, pleasant, and quick assessment of hypnotizability (Elkins, 2014; Kekecs et al., 2016; Kekecs et al., 2021). The standard form of the EHS contains six items including arm heaviness or immobilization; arm levitation; imagery involvement or dissociation; positive hallucination of the smell of a rose; positive hallucination of a block; and posthypnotic amnesia (Elkins, 2014). The EHS scoring system is based on behavioral responses and subjective experiences, using an ordinal scoring system. The hypnotizability score, which ranges from 0 to 12, is obtained by summing the item scores. Total hypnotizability scores of 0 or 1 indicate very low hypnotizability; scores of 2 or 3 indicate low hypnotizability; scores of 4 to 8 indicate middle hypnotizability; scores of 9 or 10 indicate high hypnotizability; and scores of 11 or 12 indicate very high hypnotizability. Development of the EHS strove to have the measure be brief in nature; be perceived as pleasant by the subject; be an adequate test of a range of hypnotizability; and have acceptable reliability and validity (Elkins, 2014; Kekecs et al., 2016). First, the EHS met its goal of being brief in nature; the EHS can be administered and scored in approximately 20 to 30 minutes, which allows for easier administration in clinical settings with limited time from providers (Elkins, 2014; Kekecs et al., 2016). In order to be perceived as a pleasant measure, the EHS utilizes pleasant suggestions, such as being in a flower garden and smelling a rose, rather than aversive suggestions, such as smelling ammonia. Indeed, studies show that the EHS has high perceived pleasantness from subjects (Elkins, 2014; Kekecs et al., 2016). Regarding having an adequate range of hypnotizability, the EHS contains an appropriate number of items to discriminate among levels of hypnotizability (Elkins et al., 2003; Elkins, 2014). Psychometrically, the EHS has high internal consistency, with Cronbach's alpha reported as .85 by Elkins (2014) and .78 by Kekecs and colleagues (2016), strong test-retest reliability (r = .93), and high convergent validity as demonstrated by a strong correlation (r = .91) with the SHSS:C (Elkins et al., 2012). Furthermore, a recent study by Kekecs and colleagues (2021) found the test-retest reliability of the EHS (r = .82) to be higher than the test-retest reliability of the SHSS:C (r = .66), and a difference in the distribution of scores between the SHSS:C and the EHS was also found, with the SHSS:C producing higher average scores than the EHS. An additional strength of the EHS includes the use of ordinal rather than dichotomous scoring for items (Kekecs et al., 2021). Limitations of the EHS include instability of the hypnotizability categories, which has also been found to be true for the SHSS:C. Thus, providers should utilize the numerical scores rather than categorical scores to inform treatment.

In addition to assessing hypnotizability, the EHS can be used as a therapeutic intervention. A recent study by Yek and Elkins (2021) assessed the feasibility of the EHS with 50 college students for stress reduction. The results of the study found low rates of negative effects after EHS administration (5.5% of participants) and a large, significant reduction in stress levels after EHS administration ($d = 0.98, p < .001$). Participants also rated the EHS as a credible therapeutic intervention with significant increases in relaxation ratings during and after EHS administration ($d = 1.61$ and $d = 1.57$, respectively). Furthermore, after 2 weeks of practicing self-hypnosis with the EHS, participants reported significantly decreased perceived stress, psychological distress, anxiety, and depression and significantly increased relaxation. Therefore, results of this feasibility study demonstrate that the EHS can be effectively utilized as a therapeutic measure and has promise for use in clinical practice.

The Elkins Hypnotizability Scale-Clinical Form (EHS-CF) is a clinical version of the EHS (Elkins, 2014; Elkins & Olendzki, 2018). It differs from the EHS as it does not contain the last two items on the EHS, namely the positive hallucination of a block and posthypnotic amnesia. The EHS-CF can be administered in approximately 15 to 20 minutes (Elkins, 2014). Hypnotizability scores on the EHS-CF range from 0 to 9, with scores of 0 to 3 indicating low hypnotizability, scores of 4 to 7 indicating middle hypnotizability, and scores of 8 or 9 indicating high hypnotizability. According to Elkins (2014), the EHS and EHS-CF have been found to be significantly correlated ($r = .962, p < .001$), and the EHS-CF has also demonstrated a strong, significant correlation with the SHSS:C (r = .789, p < .001). Thus, results indicate that the EHS and EHS-CF are arguably the current gold standard for assessing hypnotizability in research and clinical practice.

Hypnotizability In Clinical Practice

According to Woody and Sadler (2016), hypnotizability is central to quality patient care in that it is comparable to individual differences in treatment response, such as individual differences in response to medication or psychotherapy. As mentioned above, hypnotizability is normally distributed in the general population, with the majority of the population categorized as moderately hypnotizable (Kekecs et al., 2016). Furthermore, hypnotizability is stable over time and with the tasks for each individual, such that an individual who is responsive to one difficult suggestion will likely be responsive to another difficult suggestion (Piccione et al., 1989; Woody & Sadler, 2016).

Research has found that the majority of patients, particularly medical or surgical patients, benefit from hypnotic interventions (Montgomery et al., 2002; Schnur et al., 2008). There are several studies that indicate hypnotizability is a moderator of clinical outcomes (Elkins et al., 2011; Flammer & Bongartz, 2003; Friedman & Taub, 1984; Harmon et al., 1990; Liossi et al., 2006; Liossi & Hatira, 2003; Montgomery et al., 2000; Montgomery et al., 2011; Patterson & Jensen, 2003; van Dyck & Spinhoven, 1997). For example, a meta-analysis by Montgomery and colleagues (2011) regarding the effect of hypnotizability on clinical hypnotherapy outcomes found a significant, small-to-medium effect size (r = 0.24; 95% Confidence Interval = -0.28 to 0.75), which suggests that patients with greater hypnotizability may experience greater benefits from hypnotic interventions. These results indicate that assessing for hypnotizability can be of great benefit to providers in identifying clients who will benefit most from hypnotic interventions.

Given that hypnotizability can influence the effects of hypnotherapy on clinical outcomes, assessing for hypnotizability in clinical practice can be helpful for treatment planning and case conceptualization, as well as for normalizing and introducing hypnotherapy to clients (Elkins, 2014; Woody & Sadler, 2016). After using a hypnotizability measure to introduce a client to hypnotherapy, a provider can then utilize the information gathered from the assessment to tailor future hypnotherapy interventions and sessions for the client. Moreover, a hypnotizability measure may be considered a therapeutic intervention itself (see Yek & Elkins, 2021).

Presenting Hypnotizability Assessment to Clients

The EHS and EHS-CF are currently arguably the gold standards of hypnotizability assessment. Since the EHS-CF is shorter than the EHS and does not require the use of any additional materials (i.e., table with white cloth), we argue that the EHS-CF would be most suitable for use in clinical practice. Thus, for the purpose of this chapter, the EHS-CF is the scale of choice when discussing hypnotizability assessment. The EHS-CF is published in *Mindful Hypnotherapy: The Basics for Clinical Practice* (Elkins & Olendzki, 2018). ***The EHS full scale is included at the end of this chapter***.

As mentioned above, hypnotizability assessment can be used to inform treatment plans and can serve as an introduction to hypnotherapy. Prior to assessing a client's hypnotizability, it is important to dispel any myths or misconceptions regarding hypnosis and provide accurate psychoeducation on clinical hypnosis (for more information, please refer to Chapter 12).

In presenting hypnotizability assessment to the client, it is important to explain to the client what hypnotizability is, how it is measured, the utility of measuring hypnotizability, what the client can expect during the assessment, and that the client will be provided feedback after the assessment. It is not uncommon that the discussion of an assessment may exert undue pressure on some clients, which could lead to an effortful engagement in the assessment in order to influence their scores. However, such engagement would often lead to an inaccurate assessment of their genuine hypnotic ability, and it would be important to discuss this with the client as well. An example is as follows:

> "Before we start hypnotherapy, I would like to first measure your ability to be hypnotized. We call this your hypnotic ability, or hypnotizability. We measure hypnotizability by going through a hypnotic induction and giving you hypnotic suggestions. The vast majority of people can be hypnotized, and individuals with various hypnotic abilities can benefit from hypnotherapy. Measuring your hypnotic ability using a hypnotizability scale will be a good chance for you to experience what hypnosis is like, and will provide helpful information for us to figure out how to best use hypnosis for you.

> "To measure your hypnotizability, I will be guiding you through a brief hypnotic induction and give you hypnotic suggestions. This tends to be described by clients as a very relaxing and pleasant experience. After that, I will ask you some questions regarding your experience. I will also give you information at the end regarding your hypnotizability.

> "Please know that there is no 'right' way of undergoing hypnosis. In fact, trying to do it in the 'right' way tends to backfire and make it harder for people to truly experience hypnosis. It also makes it harder for us to measure your true hypnotic ability. The best thing you can do is to approach this with an open and curious mind, and let whatever comes come."

[Ask if the client has any questions and answer them.]

*"Okay, are you ready? You can go ahead and make yourself
comfortable in the chair."*

[Proceed to EHS-CF.]

[After completion of EHS-CF post-hypnotic inquiry, score
the EHS-CF.]

FEEDBACK FOLLOWING HYPNOTIZABILITY ASSESSMENT

It is important to inquire about the client's experience during the EHS-CF prior to presenting the client's score, as this will allow the clinician to provide more individualized feedback to the client. Below, we discuss some things to note while presenting feedback to clients with various levels of hypnotizabilities, followed by an example for each hypnotizability range.

High Hypnotizability Range

Clients who score 8 or 9 on the EHS-CF are in the high hypnotizability range. There is research evidence that people with high hypnotizability receive greater effectiveness from hypnotherapy than individuals in the moderate and low ranges. It would be important to convey this to the client during feedback and build positive expectancies and self-efficacy regarding the use of hypnosis. An example is as below:

*"Great news! You scored 8 on the scale, which places you in
the high hypnotizability range. This means that you have a
high ability to experience hypnosis, even more than the
average person. For example, you mentioned you were able
to smell the rose rather distinctly, which many individuals
are not able to do. We know from research that people with*

high hypnotizability are more likely to have a quicker
response to hypnotherapy, and experience greater positive
effects from hypnotherapy. Your high hypnotic ability will be
very helpful in our work together, and I am confident that
you will benefit from hypnotherapy rather quickly,
especially with self-hypnosis practice."

Middle Hypnotizability Range

Clients who score 4 to 7 are in the middle hypnotizability range. The majority of clients score within this range. It would be important to convey to the client that they would likely benefit from hypnotherapy as with the majority of the population. It would also be important to emphasize that the benefit they reap from hypnotherapy will be greater with more practice. An example is as below:

"You scored 5, which places you in the middle
hypnotizability range. This means that, like the vast
majority of people, you are able to experience hypnosis and
benefit from hypnotherapy. It is great that you were able to
see the garden when we went through the hypnotic
induction just now, because we tend to utilize images during
hypnotherapy. During hypnotherapy, we will use images
that you are familiar with, so you would likely engage even
more with those images when we do hypnotherapy. Your
ability to experience and benefit from hypnosis will become
greater the more you engage in hypnosis practice, so this is
a really good place to start!"

Lower Hypnotizability Range

Clients who score 0 to 3 are in the lower hypnotizability range. Although these clients have lower ability to experience hypnosis than the average person, it does not mean that the client will not benefit from hypnotherapy. The client may require more time practicing hypnotherapy and greater individualization of suggestions in order to reap similar benefits from hypnotherapy compared to people with higher ranges. The clinician may also want to consider using hypnosis as an adjunct therapy. When presenting feedback to clients it would be important not to set up negative expectancies regarding their experience with hypnotherapy, but rather to place more emphasis on how hypnosis can be used to help the client in treatment. An example is below:

"You scored 2, which places you in the low hypnotizability range. This means that you may have a lower ability to experience hypnosis than the average person. However, this does not mean that you will not respond to or benefit from hypnotherapy! The fact that you felt a heaviness in your arm means that you are responding to a hypnotic suggestion. Furthermore, you mentioned feeling relaxed during the hypnotic induction, and that is another way hypnotherapy can be helpful in treating [your presenting problem] too. People in your range tend to benefit more from hypnosis the more you practice it and the more we use suggestions that are tailored especially for you. We can also use hypnosis to enhance the effects of other aspects of our treatment together."

CONCLUSION

In order to be able to inform individual treatment plans, several standardized scales have been developed to measure hypnotizability. Standard Hypnotic Susceptibility Scale: Form C (SHSS:C) was one of the earlier forms that was considered as the gold standard for measuring hypnotizability, however, due it is prolonged length, inclusion of unpleasant items, and lack of experiential assessment, it has been discarded as the standard measure. A shorter form of assessment that has been developed was Hypnotic Induction Profile (HIP), but one of the items, the eye-roll test has been found to be a poor indicator of hypnotizability. Stanford Hypnotic Arm Levitation Induction and Test (SHALIT) was then developed with an even shorter length of time required, but the scale is too short so does not measure the full range of hypnotizability.

Therefore, Stanford Hypnotic Clinical Scale (SHCS) was developed which is one of the widely used forms of hypnotizability assessment. Nevertheless, the scale is still short and may not measure the full range of hypnotizability and items like suggestions for age regression may be distressing for some individuals. Elkins Hypnotizability Scale (EHS) has been developed with more pleasant items, high test-retest reliability, as well as an appropriate number of items to differentiate among different levels of hypnotizability. A shorter form lasting 20 minutes is also available that can be used for clinical purposes, known as Elkins Hypnotizability Scale-Clinical Form (EHS-CF). EHS and EHS-CF are used as the gold standard for hypnotizability assessment in research and clinical practice. Accurate assessment and genuine hypnotic ability of the client are necessary to yield most beneficial treatment results. *The EHS full scale is presented below following the reflection questions and before the references.*

CHAPTER 20
REFLECTIONS QUESTIONS

1. Why is it helpful to measure hypnotizability in clinical practice?

2. How has the development of hypnotizability assessments evolved; leading to contemporary measures such as the EHS?

3. Everyone is hypnotizable and can benefit from

hypnotherapy, what factors including hypnotizability
may be important in hypnotherapy?

ELKINS HYPNOTIZABILITY SCALE
FULL SCALE (EHS)

Gary Elkins Ph.D., ABPP, ABPH

PROTOCOL FOR ADMINISTRATION

Introductory Remarks

[*Note: Ensure that the subject is seated in a comfortable chair with
support for their head, neck and shoulders. A foot-stool may be provided
to allow the subject to elevate their legs, however, if seated in a recliner,
the back of the chair should **not** be reclined. See the "General
Instructions for Administration and Scoring of the EHS for further
information.*]

This is a scale to measure your ability to experience hypnosis and
respond to hypnotic suggestions. It is a standardized scale and
therefore I will be reading from these papers. You may occasionally
hear me writing or hear the sound of things outside this room. You can
pay as much or as little attention to such sounds as you wish. The best
way to determine a person's ability to experience hypnosis is to
complete a hypnotic induction. This will involve focusing your
attention on a spot on the ceiling and suggestions for calmness. After
your eyes close I will give you some hypnotic suggestions. It is
important to ***just respond to what you are feeling and experiencing***.
There is nothing that you have to try to do, just allow yourself to
respond to whatever you experience. Not everyone experiences the
same things and not everyone is equally hypnotizable. At times during

hypnosis I will ask you to verbally describe what you are feeling or experiencing. You will be able to do so without interrupting your experience of hypnosis. As you listen to my words just let whatever happens happen so that we can see how you experience hypnosis and how we can learn to make hypnosis work best for you.

[Note: Place a small table (with a white top) in front of participant before beginning the induction. Ask the participant to extend their arms and bring them down to a relaxed position on the arms of the chair.]

Induction

Now, please roll your eyes upward and focus on a spot on the ceiling. That's right. Now, ***focus on that spot so intently*** ... that everything else begins to fade into the background ... more and more ... Good. Now take a breath of air and hold it for a moment ... hold ... and as you exhale allow your eyes-lids to close normally and naturally ... Good ... Now, allow your body to relax ... Notice a wave relaxation spreading from the top of your head ... down to your feet ... Letting all the tension go ... Head, neck, shoulders ... relax ... arms and legs ... relax ... As you enter a hypnotic state finding a calm ... relaxed feeling. More calm and more at ease ... comfortable and calm ...

Now, as I count from the number ten down to one, with each number that I count ... going into ***an even deeper state of hypnosis***.

[Note: During the deepening suggestions, numbers are counted on the subject's exhalation.]

> ***10*** ... A wave of relaxation spreading across your forehead ... neck ... and shoulders.

> ***9*** ... More relaxed ... your jaw goes slack ... shoulders slump ... and arms become very relaxed.

_8_ ... That wave of relaxation now spreads across your back ...
Your upper back ... and lower back ... deeply relaxed.

_7_ ... A deeper level of hypnosis now as your legs become very
relaxed, letting all the tension go ... feeling more calm ...
feeling more peaceful.

_6_ ... Entering such a deep level of hypnosis **_now_** ... that you
may notice a drifting or floating sensation ... just drifting
... and floating ... deeper and deeper into this hypnotic
state ...

_5_ ... Deeply calm and deeply hypnotized ...

_4_ ... Now allowing that calmness to become **_even more
complete_** ... and entering **_the deepest level of hypnosis_**
...

_3_ ... So deeply hypnotized that you are able to respond to
each suggestion ... and experience each thing that I
suggest ...

_2_ ... Calm and peaceful ... so deeply relaxed ... any tension
that has remained is released ... **_now_** ...

_1_ ... **_All the way there_** ... deeply hypnotized ... calm and
peaceful ...

and it is possible to feel a special sense of calmness ... and you will be
able to experience and respond to each suggestion during hypnosis
today ... Just listen to my voice and let whatever happens happen so
we can see how you experience hypnosis. ...

Arm Heaviness/Immobilization

Now as you remain deeply calm ... you will **_soon_** become aware of a change in sensation in your **_right_** arm and hand ... Soon you will notice that your **_right arm_** will become **_very, very heavy_** ... just as **_heavy as lead_** ... that heavy feeling begins to occur **_now_** ... that arm becomes **_heavier and heavier_** ... and as this occurs it can feel as if the arm were becoming **_less a part of you_** ... **_as you allow it to become as heavy as lead_**.

[*Pause for five seconds.*]

And now that arm will become **even heavier** ... so very heavy that you will find that you **cannot lift this right arm** ... no matter how hard you **try** to raise it ... **it will be too heavy to lift** ... and finding that **you just don't want to lift it**, in fact ... the harder you **try**, the **heavier** the arm and hand will become ... and **now** the arm, the wrist, the hand **and even the fingers** have become **stuck to the chair** ... **They just won't move** ... they are so very heavy.

[*Pause for five seconds.*]

Now ... as this hand and arm remain as **heavy as lead** and too heavy to lift, I want you, **in a moment**, to try to lift them, but **they** will not move ... the arm, the wrist, the hand **and even the fingers are stuck to the chair and too heavy to move**. Go ahead and **try** to lift them, genuinely try, but **they** are just stuck to the chair and they are too heavy.

[*Pause for five seconds.*]

Very good. Now allow your arm to relax, this heavy feeling passes and the right hand and arm rest ... Normal sensation returns ... and as **this** occurs going into an **even deeper level of hypnosis**.

RECORD OBSERVATIONS
1.   Did the arm lift?
2.   Was there obvious effort to lift the hand and arm?
3.   Other observations (Note finger movements etc.)

Arm Levitation

Now as you go into an ***even deeper level of hypnosis*** ... you will ***soon***
become aware of a change in sensation in your ***left*** arm and hand ...
Soon you will notice that your ***left*** arm and hand will become very,
very light ... and weightless ... ***just as light as a feather*** ... that light
feeling begins to occur ... ***now*** ... ***it*** becomes lighter and lighter ... and
as this occurs it can feel as if the arm were becoming ***less a part of***
you ... as you allow it to become so ... ***light and weightless***.

[*Pause for five seconds.*]

And now ... there is a **ribbon** around the left wrist ... and at the other
end of that ribbon are several **balloons** ... red, yellow, green, blue ... all
different colors ... There are quite a few of them ... **four or five**
balloons ... and these balloons are lighter than air and **they begin to**
float upward ... ... and as they do ... the left hand begins to **float**
upward ... Just notice the balloons are tugging ... pulling ... lifting the
wrist **up** ... **up** ... **up** ... **it just drifts and floats up** ... feeling lighter and
lighter ... Floating up **higher and higher** ... Just allowing the **arm** to
float up ... **all by itself** ... just as high as **it** wants to go ... Floating up
now ... higher and higher.

[*Pause for 5 seconds for the response to occur.* WAIT UNTIL
LEVITATION STOPS.]

Very good. Now this feeling passes and your hand and arm begin to drift downward to its comfortable resting position ... (Wait for the arm to begin to lower, additional suggestions for normal sensations and arm lowering may be given) The balloons are gone ... Normal sensation returns to your arm and hand and as this occurs **going into an even deeper level of hypnosis**. (If the arm remains lifted, instruct the participant to lower the arm to the chair.)

RECORD OBSERVATIONS
1. Did hand or arm lift?
2. Was there obvious effort to raise the arm and hand?
3. Did the elbow raise from the arm of the chair?
4. Other observations

Imagery Involvement/Dissociation

And now something **_very interesting_** is going to happen ... It is possible to **_hear my voice with one part of your mind_** ... and with another part of your mind ... to find that **_you will feel as if you are in a different place_** ... Soon you will find that you can feel as if you are **_no longer in this room_** and **_instead_** you will experience **_being in a beautiful flower garden_** ... And when this occurs, you will be able to see everything there ... You will experience every sight ... sound, smell ... and feeling in this garden ... When this occurs you will find that ... you feel as if you are no longer in (state present place) and instead you will, experience being in a flower garden experiencing everything **_there_** ...

Now, as you hear my voice, at the same time seeing before you a gate that leads into the flower garden ... Seeing the gate now ... and as I **_count from one to four_** you will find that you are walking through that gate and into the flower garden ... more than just imagining it ... soon ***you will be in a flower garden*** ... walking through the garden.

One ... Going through the gate now ...

Two ... As you go into the garden you can see the flowers that are there ...

Three ... able to continue to hear my voice as you are there ... experiencing every sight, sound, smell and feeling in this ***flower garden*** ...

Four ... ***now*** you are there ... you are ***in a flower garden*** ...

[*Pause for 5 seconds and then proceed.*]

Good. It is a warm day ... and yet you can feel a gentle cool breeze in the air ... It is very pleasant ... Feeling safe, secure and relaxed ... Before you is a path. As you walk down this path notice that there are flowers all along the path. The grass is very green and there are many beautiful flowers. Now, notice the colors of the flowers ... whether you see red, yellow or any other colors.

There ... ***There*** is a very beautiful red ***rose*** ... You can see this rose ... Now, stopping there for a moment ... go close enough to ***smell the wonderful sweet aroma*** of this beautiful rose ... The aroma of the rose becomes stronger now ... it is a pleasant smell ... now take a breath and ... ***Just smell the rose*** ... and notice how ***strong*** the smell is ...

[*Pause for five seconds.*]

Now ... as you are ***there*** ... you can describe what you are experiencing without interrupting your experience of hypnosis. Please describe what you are experiencing.

[If the subject does not respond the first question; prompt with ... "YOU CAN ANSWER VERBALLY ... " Record responses to each question.]

Where are you?	
What do you see around you?	
Do you see the rose?	
Do you smell the rose?	
Other comments:	

Very good ... Now, soon returning back to this room at (state present place) and the present time ... as you remain **_deeply hypnotized_** ... Now walking back through that gate and returning to the present time and back to (state present place) ... You are now here deeply hypnotized and comfortably experiencing hypnosis ...

Positive Hallucination

And now ... going into an **_even deeper state of hypnosis_** ... In fact, **_going very deeply hypnotized and very deeply calm_** ... Good ...

Now, in a few moments I will ask you to open your eyes as you continue to remain in a deep state of hypnosis ... When you open your eyes **_you will see a small blue block on the table in front of you_** ... A little square block ... **_The kind of block that a child might play with_** ... The block is **_bright blue_** ...

In order for you to be able to **_see the block_** on the table it may be helpful to first **_see it in your mind_** before you open your eyes ... A little **_blue_** block ... sitting on the table ... The kind of block a child might play with ... Just really see it in your mind ... and, in a moment, when you open your eyes **_you will see the block on the table_**.

[pause for five seconds]

All right ... now, as I count from one to three, I will ask you to open your eyes ... You will remain deeply hypnotized and you will see ***a small blue block on the table in front of you***.

Some people see the block right away, while others see more of a ***blue color***, ... ***a shape or shadow at first***.

One ... beginning to open your eyes

Two ... eyelids opening

Three ... eyes open ***now*** ...

Now, look at the table in front of you ... Just continue looking ... and notice what you see on the table ... just really looking ... and noticing ... whatever you see there ...

[Note responses to each question.]

What do you see on the table? (Inquire as needed: Do you see the block?)	
If the subject does not report seeing the block, inquire further	
If no description of a block, inquire as needed to determine if there is any perception of a color, shape or shadow etc.: **Do you see anything on the table? Do you see any color, shape or shadow of a block?** (Note detail of any evidence of a positive hallucination such as a color, shape or shadow etc.)	

[*Note: If no perception of a block is reported, then add, "*NOT EVERYONE SEES SOMETHING ON THE TABLE." *and proceed as below.*]

Very good ... Now allow your eyelids to close and go _**into an even deeper state of hypnosis**_ ... relaxing deeply and feeling calm and relaxed ...

Post-Hypnotic Amnesia

Now, while remaining in a deep state of hypnosis ... you can hear my voice and all of the suggestions that I give to you. In a few moments I will suggest that you return to conscious alertness. However, when you return to alertness you will find that ... _**you are not able to recall any of the things that happened**_ ... during the hypnosis session today ...

You have been _**so deeply absorbed**_ in experiencing hypnosis that you will have a great deal of difficulty in recalling any of the suggestions I gave you and the things you experienced ... In fact, the harder you _**try**_ the more difficult it will be to recall these things ... It will be much easier to just forget ... you will not be able to recall anything about the hypnosis session today ... It will seem like there is a wall between you and the memory ... Just allow this to occur ... so that the wall is there _**now**_ ... and you will find that you just _**don't want to remember at all**_. _**You will not be able to recall anything that happened during hypnosis**_ today until you hear me say these words,

"NOW YOU CAN RECALL EVERYTHING."

**Then the wall will lift** and then you will be able to recall all of your experiences ... Now, as I count from one to ten you will return to alertness ...

Alerting

All right, returning to conscious alertness now. [*Note: Increase volume of voice as counting.*]

> 1, 2, 3 beginning to return to conscious alertness.
>
> 4, 5 more alert and eyes beginning to open.
>
> 6, 7 eyelids opening and returning to alertness.
>
> 8, 9 ... alert and refreshed.
>
> And 10 ... fully alert.

Do you feel alert? ... Good. [*Note, assure that the subject reports alertness before proceeding with the Post-Hypnotic Scoring Inquiry.*]

POST HYPNOTIC SCORING INQUIRY

Post Hypnotic Amnesia Scoring Inquiry

I want to ask you a few questions about your experience. Please tell me what you can recall about what happened during our session today. What do you remember?

[*Record the subject's responses. Ask, "ANYTHING ELSE?" until the subject reaches an impasse.*]

ITEM	DETAIL
☐ Arm Heaviness	
☐ Arm Levitation	
☐ Dissociation/Imagery	
☐ Positive Hallucination	
☐ Post-Hypnotic Amnesia	
AMNESIA ITEM SCORING	
0	if the subject recalls more than 1 item
1	if the subject recalls 1 item or less

Now listen carefully to what I am going to say next. "***Now you can recall everything.***"

What do you recall now? [*Record responses.*]

☐ Arm Heaviness	☐ Arm Levitation	☐ Dissociation / Imagery
☐ Positive Hallucination	☐ Suggestion for Post Hypnotic Amnesia	

[*Note: The rose/olfactory hallucination is included as part of the Dissociation/Imagery and is NOT a separate item for post-hypnotic amnesia scoring.*]

Arm Heaviness/Immobilization Scoring Inquiry

Earlier I suggested to you that your right arm and hand would feel
heavy and then I suggested that they would be too heavy to lift. I want
to find out what your experience was.

ITEM	DETAIL
When I suggested that your right arm and hand would feel heavy; did you feel a sense of heaviness in your right arm and hand? Did they feel heavier? (Determine if subject experienced <u>any</u> feeling of heaviness.)	☐ Yes ☐ No
(If the hand/arm did <u>not</u> lift, ask) *Did you try to lift your hand and arm?* Determine if there was effort to lift the hand and arm. *Were they too heavy to lift? Did they feel stuck to the chair?*	☐ Yes ☐ No
Did the subject's hand and arm remain immobile and "stuck" to the chair? Review previous observations to determine if the subject's hand and arm remained on the chair with just minimal, temporary movements. Inquire as needed to determine if arm immobilization occurred. (*Note: small finger movements or <u>temporary</u> slight movements often occur with <u>successful</u> arm immobilization. Arm immobilization refers to an inability to lift the hand and arm.*)	☐ Yes ☐ No
ARM HEAVINESS ITEM SCORING	
0 if no heaviness	
1 if the subject reports feeling a subjective sense of heaviness	
2 Beyond slight movements, the hand and arm did not lift. Arm immobilization occurred.	

Arm Levitation Scoring Inquiry

Earlier, I asked you to experience a very light and weightless feeling in your left arm and that the arm would lift all by itself.

INQUIRY
Did your arm feel lighter? Even if your arm did not lift, did it feel lighter?
(If the arm lifted, ask) ***Did it float up <u>all by itself</u> without any willful effort on your part?*** (Inquire as needed to clarify the subject's experience. Determine if the subject experienced a sense of involuntary lifting. ***Could you feel it floating up all by itself or did you feel like you were lifting it? Did it feel like the balloons were pulling it up?***)

ARM LIGHTNESS ITEM SCORING	
0	Score 0 if the answer to the first question is no whether or not the arm lifted. Score 0 if no subjective description of lightness.
1	Score 1 if the answer to the first question is yes, but the arm <u>did not lift out of its resting position</u>. (Score 1 if a <u>subjective sense of lightness is reported</u> and the hand did not lift.)
2	Score 2 if the answer to the second question is yes, and the arm did lift out of its resting position. (Score 2 if a subjective experience of lightness is described and there is some movement of the hand from the chair <u>with</u> a subjective description of an involuntary movement.)
3	Score 3 if the answer to the second question is yes and the elbow lifted. (Score 3 if a subjective experience of lightness is described and there is a movement of the hand of one inch or more with a subjective description of an involuntary movement and the elbow lifts.)

Imagery Involvement/Dissociation Scoring Inquiry

Also, earlier, I asked you to experience going for a walk in a flower garden.

INQUIRY
1. *Were you able to experience what I suggested or were you just listening to my voice?* (If no imagery or only vague imagery is reported, state *"Some people do not experience clear imagery."*)
2. *Did you <u>imagine being in the flower garden</u>? Was the image clear? Could you really imagine being in a flower garden?* (Determine if the subject was able to imagine being in a garden. Determine if the image was clear or only vague (i.e. colors etc. but no specific imagery of the flower garden.) Review the previous observations and the subject's verbal responses to the questions presented during the item. Determine if the subject's response to the questions: "Where are you? What do you see around you?' indicate that the subject may have experienced dissociation (i.e. felt that they were actually in the garden).
3. If the subject's responses suggested possible dissociation, ask: *Did you feel that, in a sense, you were no longer in this room and instead you were actually in a flower garden, experiencing everything there?* (Determine if the subject experienced an alteration in perception in which they felt that they were no longer in the room and instead experienced being in a flower garden. Continue inquiry as necessary to distinguish between questions 2 and 3, i.e. "Did it feel like you were actually experiencing (<u>*insert subject's report of sensations*</u>) while you were <u>in the garden</u> or that you were here and imagining it?")

MENTAL IMAGERY / DISSOCIATION SCORING INQUIRY	
0	If the answer to the first question is no (no imagery or only vague imagery)
1	If the answer to the second question is yes (clear imagery but no dissociation)
2	If the answer to the third question is yes (clear imagery and dissociation)

Rose Olfactory Hallucination Scoring Inquiry

Now, I also suggested to you that you could smell a rose.

INQUIRY	
Did you smell the aroma of a rose? Did you actually smell it?	
0	If the answer is no. *Did not actually smell the rose?* (even if it was imagined)
1	If the answer is yes. *Smell was faint.*
2	If the answer is yes. *Smell was distinct.*
Establish the subjective rating of the intensity of the aroma. Check the subject's rating of the aroma: ***How strong was the aroma? Please rate it as none, faint, or distinct.***	
☐ None ☐ Faint ☐ Distinct	

Positive Hallucination Scoring Inquiry

Also, earlier, I asked you to experience seeing a small block on the table in front of you.

INQUIRY
Did you see anything on the table? (Note: if response is "nothing" repeat that **"Some people do not see anything."**)
(If the subject reports <u>any</u> perception, inquire further) **Please describe what you saw. Did you see the block? Please describe it. Did you see anything on the table? If yes, please describe what you saw. Where was it?**

POSITIVE HALLUCINATION SCORING	
0	If the subject answers negative to perception.
1	If there is any hallucinated perception. Scoring is lenient (i.e. score one, if the subject reports perception color, shape, shadow etc.) Note if the subject reports a vague perception of any hallucination.
2	If the subject reports a clear perception of a block. The block is described with detail of color and shape. The block was clearly hallucinated.

NOTE DETAIL:

EHS SCORING SUMMARY

Examiner: _____   **Date:** _____

ITEM	CRITERIA	SCORE
Arm Heaviness / Immobilization	No heaviness	0
	Subjective report of heaviness	1
	Heaviness. Immobilization occurred.	2
Arm Levitation	No weightlessness.	0
	Subjective report of lightness.	1
	Subjective report of lightness and effortless arm levitation.	2
	Effortless elbow lift.	3
Imagery Involvement / Dissociation	No experience — Just listening.	0
	Experienced clear imagery, but no dissociation.	1
	Experienced clear imagery, and dissociation.	2
Rose Olfactory Hallucination	No experience.	0
	Reports mild or moderate smell.	1
	Reports strong smell.	2
Amnesia	Recalls more than 1 item	0
	Recalls 1 item or fewer	1
Positive Hallucination	Negative report.	0
	Describes vague hallucination only.	1
	Reports clear hallucination of a block.	2
TOTAL		

0 – 3	Low
4 – 7	Middle
8 – 11	High
12	Very High

REFERENCES

Alexander, J. E., Stimpson, K. H., Kittle, J., & Spiegel, D. (2021). The Hypnotic Induction Profile (HIP) in clinical practice and research. *International Journal of Clinical and Experimental Hypnosis, 69*(1), 72-82. https://doi.org/10.1080/00207144.2021.1836646

Barnier, A. J., & McConkey, K. M. (2004). Defining and identifying the highly hypnotizable person. In M. Heap, R. Brown, & D. Oakley (Eds.), *The highly hypnotizable person: Theoretical, experimental and clinical issues* (pp. 30-60). New York, NY: Brunner Routledge.

Cardeña, E., & Terhune, D. B. (2009). A note of caution on the Waterloo-Stanford Group Scale of Hypnotic Susceptibility: A brief communication. *International Journal of Clinical and Experimental Hypnosis, 57*(2), 222-226. https://doi.org/10.1080/00207140802665484

Elkins, G. R. (2014). *Hypnotic relaxation therapy: Principles and applications.* Springer Publishing Company.

Elkins, G. R., Barabasz, A. F., Council, J. R., & Spiegel, D. (2015). Advancing research and practice: The revised APA Division 30 definition of hypnosis. *American Journal of Clinical and Experimental Hypnosis, 57*(4), 378-385. https://doi.org/10.1080/00029157.2015.1011465

Elkins, G. R., Marcus, J., & Rascoe, T. (2003). *Development of a new scale to measure hypnotizability in clinical research.* Paper presented at the 44th Annual Meeting of the American Society of Clinical Hypnosis. Arlington, VA.

Elkins, G., Fisher, W., & Johnson, A. (2012). P02.30. Assessment of hypnotizability in clinical research: Development, reliability, and validation of the Elkins Hypnotizability Scale. *BMC Complementary and Alternative Medicine, 12*(Suppl 1), P86. https://doi.org/10.1186/1472-6882-12-S1-P86

Elkins, G., Fisher, W., Johnson, A., Marcus, J., Dove, J., Perfect, M., & Keith, T. (2011). Moderating effect of hypnotizability on hypnosis for hot flashes in breast cancer survivors. *Contemporary Hypnosis & Integrative Therapy, 28*(3), 187-195.

Elkins, G. R., & Olendzki, N. (2018). *Mindful Hypnotherapy: The basics for clinical practice.* Springer Publishing Company.

Flammer, E., & Bongartz, W. (2003). On the efficacy of hypnosis: A meta-analytic study. *Contemporary Hypnosis, 20*(4), 179-197. https://doi.org/10.1002/ch.277

Friedman, H., & Taub, H. A. (1984). Brief psychological training procedures in migraine treatment. *American Journal of Clinical Hypnosis, 26*(3), 187-200. https://doi.org/10.1080/00029157.1984.10404162

Frischholz, E. J., Tryon, W. W., Fisher, S., Maruffi, B. L., Vellios, A. T., & Spiegel, H. (1980). The relationship between the Hypnotic Induction Profile and the Stanford Hypnotic Susceptibility Scale, Form C: A replication. *American Journal of Clinical Hypnosis, 22*(4), 185-196. https://doi.org/10.1080/00029157.1980.10403227

Frischholz, E. J., Tryon, W. W., Spiegel, H., & Fisher, S. (2015). The relationship between the Hypnotic Induction Profile and the Stanford Hypnotic Susceptibility Scale, Form C: Revisited. *American Journal of Clinical Hypnosis, 57*(2), 129-136. https://doi.org/10.1080/00029157.2015.967069

Harmon, T. M., Hynan, M. T., & Tyre, T. E. (1990). Improved obstetric outcomes using hypnotic analgesia and skill mastery combined with childbirth education. *Journal of Consulting and Clinical Psychology, 58*(5), 525-530. https://doi.org/10.1037//0022-006x.58.5.525

Hilgard, E. R. (1965). *Hypnotic susceptibility.* Harcourt, Brace & World.

Hilgard, E. R., Crawford, H. J., & Wert, A. (1979). The Stanford Hypnotic Arm Levitation Induction and Test (SHALIT): A six-minute hypnotic induction and measurement scale. *International Journal of Clinical and Experimental Hypnosis, 27*(2), 111-124. https://doi.org/10.1080/00207147908407551

Kekecs, Z., Bowers, J., Johnson, A., Kendrick, C., & Elkins, G. (2016). The Elkins Hypnotizability Scale: Assessment of reliability and validity. *International Journal of Clinical and Experimental Hypnosis, 64*(3), 285-304. https://doi.org/10.1080/00207144.2016.1171089

Kekecs, Z., Roberts, L., Na, H., Yek, M. H., Slonena, E. E., Racelis, E., Voor, T. A., Johansson, R., Rizzo, P., Csikos, E., Vizkievicz, V., & Elkins, G. (2021). Test-retest reliability of the Stanford Hypnotic Susceptibility Scale, Form C and the Elkins Hypnotizability Scale. *International Journal of Clinical and Experimental Hypnosis, 69*(1), 142-161. https://doi.org/10.1080/00207144.2021.1834858

Kihlstrom, J. F. (1985). Hypnosis. *Annual Review of Psychology, 36*, 385-418.
https://doi.org/10.1146/annurev.ps.36.020185.002125

Liossi, C., & Hatira, P. (2003). Clinical hypnosis in the alleviation of procedure-
related pain in pediatric oncology patients. *International Journal of Clinical and
Experimental Hypnosis, 51*(1), 4-28.
https://doi.org/10.1076/iceh.51.1.4.14064

Liossi, C., White, P., & Hatira, P. (2006). Randomized clinical trial of local anesthetic
versus a combination of local anesthetic with self-hypnosis in the management
of pediatric procedure-related pain. *Health Psychology, 25*(3), 307-315.
https://doi.org/10.1037/0278-6133.25.3.307

Montgomery, G. H., David, D., Winkel, G., Silverstein, J. H., & Bovbjerg, D. H. (2002).
The effectiveness of adjunctive hypnosis with surgical patients: A meta-
analysis. *Anesthesia and Analgesia, 94*(6), 1639-1645.
https://doi.org/10.1097/00000539-200206000-00052

Montgomery, G. H., DuHamel, K. N., & Redd, W. H. (2000). A meta-analysis of
hypnotically induced analgesia: How effective is hypnosis? *International
Journal of Clinical and Experimental Hypnosis, 48*(2), 138-153.
https://doi.org/10.1080/00207140008410045

Montgomery, G. H., Schnur, J. B., & David, D. (2011). The impact of hypnotic
suggestibility in clinical care settings. *International Journal of Clinical and
Experimental Hypnosis, 59*(3), 294-309.
https://doi.org/10.1080/00207144.2011.570656

Morgan, A. H. (1973). The heritability of hypnotic susceptibility in twins. *Journal of
Abnormal Psychology, 82*(1), 55-61. https://doi.org/10.1037/h0034854

Morgan, A. H., & Hilgard, J. R. (1978-1979). The Stanford hypnotic clinical scale for
adults. *The American Journal of Clinical Hypnosis, 21*(2-3), 134-147.
https://doi.org/10.1080/00029157.1978.10403968

Orne, M. T., Hilgard, E. R., Spiegel, H., Spiegel, D., Crawford, H. J., Evans, F. J., Orne, E.
C., & Frischholz, E. J. (1979). The relation between the Hypnotic Induction
Profile and the Stanford Hypnotic Susceptibility Scales, forms A and C.
International Journal of Clinical and Experimental Hypnosis, 27(2), 85-102.
https://doi.org/10.1080/00207147908407549

Patterson, D. R., & Jensen, M. P. (2003). Hypnosis and clinical pain. *Psychological Bulletin, 129*(4), 495-521. https://doi.org/10.1037/0033-2909.129.4.495

Piccione, C., Hilgard, E. R., Zimbardo, P. G. (1989). On the degree of stability of measured hypnotizability over a 25-year period. *Journal of Personality and Social Psychology, 56*(2), 289-295. https://doi.org/10.1037/0022-3514.56.2.289

Schnur, J. B., Kafer, I., Marcus, C., & Montgomery, G. H. (2008). Hypnosis to manage distress related to medical procedures: A meta-analysis. *Contemporary Hypnosis, 25*(304), 114-128. https://doi.org/10.1002/ch.364

Spiegel, H. (1977). The hypnotic induction profile (HIP): A review of its development. *Annals of the New York Academy of Sciences, 296*, 129-142. https://doi.org/10.1111/j.1749-6632.1977.tb38167.x

Spiegel, H., & Spiegel, D. (2004). *Trance and treatment: Clinical uses of hypnosis* (2nd ed.). American Psychiatric Publishing, Inc.

Stern, D. B., Spiegel, H., & Nee, J. C. (1978). The Hypnotic Induction Profile: Normative observations, reliability and validity. *American Journal of Clinical Hypnosis, 21*(2-3), 109-133. https://doi.org/10.1080/00029157.1978.10403967

Tasso, A. F., & Pérez, N. A. (2008). Parsing everyday suggestibility: What does it tell us about hypnosis? In M.R. Nash & A.J. Barnier (Eds.), *The Oxford handbook of hypnosis: Theory, research, and practice* (pp. 283-309). Oxford: Oxford University Press.

Tasso, A. F., Pérez, N. A., Moore, M., Griffo, R., & Nash, M. R. (2020). Hypnotic responsiveness and nonhypnotic suggestibility: Disparate, similar, or the same? *International Journal of Clinical and Experimental Hypnosis, 68*(1), 38-67. https://doi.org/10.1080/00207144.2020.1685330

van Dyck, R., & Spinhoven, P. (1997). Does preference for type of treatment matter? A study of exposure in vivo with or without hypnosis in the treatment of panic disorder with agoraphobia. *Behavior Modification, 21*(2), 172-186. https://doi.org/10.1177/01454455970212003

Weitzenhoffer, A. M., & Hilgard, E. R. (1962). *Stanford Hypnotic Susceptibility, Form C.* Palo Alto, CA: Consulting Psychologists Press.

Wheeler, L., Reis, H. T., Wolff, E., Grupsmith, E., & Mordkoff, A. M. (1974). Eye-roll and hypnotic susceptibility. *International Journal of Clinical and Experimental Hypnosis, 22*(4), 327-334. https://doi.org/10.1080/00207147408413012

Woody, E. Z., & Barnier, A. J. (2008). Hypnosis scales for the twenty-first century: What do we need and how should we use them? In M.R. Nash & A.J. Barnier (Eds.), *The oxford handbook of hypnosis: Theory, research, and practice* (pp. 255-281). Oxford: Oxford University Press.

Woody, E., & Sadler, P. (2016). Hypnotizability. In G. R. Elkins (Ed.), *Handbook of medical and psychological hypnosis: Foundations, applications, and professional issues* (pp. 35-41). New York, NY: Springer Publishing Company.

Yek, M. H., & Elkins, G. R. (2021). Therapeutic use of the Elkins Hypnotizability Scale: A feasibility study. *International Journal of Clinical and Experimental Hypnosis, 69*(1), 124-141. https://doi.org/10.1080/00207144.2021.1831390

CHAPTER 21
CERTIFICATION IN CLINICAL HYPNOSIS AND ACADEMIC/RESEARCH HYPNOSIS

SAMUEL STORK AND GARY ELKINS

Chapter Learning Objectives

1. Recognize the importance of clinical hypnosis certification programs.

2. Understand requirements for the hypnosis certification programs offered by SCEH and ASCH.

Certification in clinical or academic/research hypnosis via professionally recognized organizations is an important step for any clinician or researcher that seeks to incorporate hypnosis into their work (Alter, 2016). There are a number of certification programs, however the Society for Clinical and Experimental Hypnosis and the American Society for Clinical Hypnosis are most widely recognized among health care practitioners and researchers. The Society for Clinical and Experimental Hypnosis and the American Society for Clinical Hypnosis not only require that one completes scientifically informed hypnosis training with uniform educational standards, but also a core clinical, academic, and experiential foundations in healthcare practice or research (Alter, 2016). Thus, certification in clinical hypnosis via a recognized and accredited organization helps to identify training, experience, and professional licensure in area of practice.

Of course, certification in clinical or academic/research hypnosis via a professional organization does not automatically guarantee competence. It does, however, indicate several important qualities: the individual is a healthcare or academic professional, has undergone advanced training in their profession, has completed a recognized curriculum in clinical hypnosis including individualized instruction, and has had their education and training reviewed by well-qualified experts. Additionally, certification in clinical or academic/research hypnosis via a professionally legitimate organization signifies that an individual is knowledgeable about the ethical use of clinical hypnosis and is prepared for a competitive practice environment. This allows the public to have dependable expectations regarding the educational and training background of the professionals they consult (Elkins & Hammond, 1998).

CERTIFICATION PROGRAMS OFFERED BY AMERICAN SOCIETY FOR CLINICAL HYPNOSIS
and
THE SOCIETY FOR CLINICAL AND EXPERIMENTAL HYPNOSIS

The American Society of Clinical Hypnosis (ASCH) and the Society for Clinical and Experimental Hypnosis (SCEH) are both examples of professional organizations that offer certification in clinical hypnosis programs. The application requirements for the certification programs offered via ASCH and SCEH are outlined below.

ASCH Certification in Clinical Hypnosis

ASCH Certification in Clinical Hypnosis is a certification track for practicing health care professionals who are licensed or certified in their state or province to provide medical, dental, or psychotherapeutic services (American Society of Clinical Hypnosis [ASCH, n.d.]). The application requirements for ASCH Certification of Clinical Hypnosis include:

1. Licensure or Certification at the independent practice level in the state/province in which one practices.

2. A master's degree or higher in a health care discipline considered appropriate by ASCH (i.e., medicine, psychology, dentistry).

3. Membership in a professional society consistent with one's degree.

4. Completion of Level 1 and Level 2 ASCH sponsored or approved Clinical Workshop training.

5. Minimum of 20 hours of individualized training/consultation with an ASCH Approved Consultant.

6. Minimum of two years of independent practice utilizing clinical hypnosis (i.e., two years from the completion of the Level 1 course).

7. Two letters of endorsement, including one from the Approved Consultant providing the applicant's individualized training, and the other from a professional colleague who can comment on the applicant's character, professional ethics, and use of hypnosis.

8. Attestation to accept the ASCH Code of Conduct

Importantly, certification through ASCH must be renewed every three years. In order to renew an ASCH Certification, one must have completed at least 20 hours of ASCH-approved hypnosis training within the last three years.

SCEH Certification Programs

SCEH offers three certification programs: Certification in Clinical Hypnosis (CCH), Certification in Academic and Research Applications of Hypnosis (CARH), and Certification by Prior Experience (CPE; Society for Clinical and Experimental Hypnosis [SCEH], n.d.). Details of each SCEH certification program will be outlined below.

SCEH Certification in Clinical Hypnosis (CCH)

SCEH CCH is a certification track for practicing health care professionals. The application requirements for SCEH CCH include:

1. Documentation of being licensed or certified at the independent clinical practice level in a health care profession recognized by SCEH in the state/province in which one practices. Recognized health care professions include physicians, dentists, doctoral level psychologists, social workers who have been awarded a Master's or doctoral degree in social work by a university accredited by the Council on Social Work Education, doctoral level speech pathologists, chiropractors and those with a Master's degree in nursing, psychology, counseling, or marital/family therapy, doctoral level practitioners of Traditional Chinese Medicine who are accredited by the Accreditation Commission for Acupuncture and Oriental Medicine (ACAOM), or other fields recommended by the Credentials and Membership Chair and approved by the Executive Committee.

2. Documentation of having received an eligible degree from a university or college accredited by its appropriate regional accrediting body.

3. A minimum of two years of experience using clinical hypnosis subsequent to the completion of the first attended approved workshop.

4. A signed agreement to abide by the SCEH Code of Ethics.

5. Documentation of workshop/education training provided by SCEH, ISH, ASCH, or a recognized affiliate completed within the past five years. All training must be informed by contemporary clinical and experimental hypnosis research and practice. Training requirements include a total of 70 hours of attendance at workshop, scientific programs, and case consultations on hypnosis as outlined below.

   a. 12.5 hours of Basic level hypnosis workshop training guided by the Standards of Training in Clinical Hypnosis.

   b. 12.5 hours of Intermediate level hypnosis workshop training.

   c. 31 hours of Advanced level workshop training and/or Case Consultation (this can include an individualized consultation workshop). Any Case Consultation hours must take place either with an American Board of Hypnosis Diplomate or an individual certified by SCEH or ASCH and must be documented by a letter from the consultant.

   d. 3 hours of ethics training in a clinical hypnosis workshop or webinar. (The Ethics modules in the basic hypnosis and intermediate hypnosis training satisfy this requirement).

   e. 11 hours clinical/experimental hypnosis research training. This requirement may be fulfilled by attendance at the SCEH Annual Scientific Program or a SCEH workshop on Clinical/Experimental Hypnosis

Research or a combination of the two for a total of 11 hours of clinical/experimental hypnosis research training.

f. Attendance at one or more SCEH annual meetings or regional workshops in the three years prior to certification. *Note: Diplomate status in the American Board of Clinical Hypnosis fulfills the workshop/education training requirements for certification.*

SCEH CCH requires renewal every three years and should include documentation verification of at least 20 hours of SCEH approved continuing education in clinical hypnosis (workshops or scientific meetings at SCEH, ISH, ASCH or affiliate). Additionally, the 20 hours of CE credit must include two hours of ethics training (SCEH regularly offers ethics webinars to provide training satisfying the certification and re-certification requirements).

SCEH Certification in Academic and Research Applications of Hypnosis (CARH)

SCEH Certification in Academic and Research Applications of Hypnosis (CARH) is designed for those who are engaged in teaching or research on hypnosis. CARH endorses the individual's acquiring of sufficient training to utilize hypnosis in academic teaching as well as research. However, CARH does not endorse that the individual has completed preparations to conduct clinical hypnosis in clinical practice. Instead, the application requirements for SCEH CARH include:

1. A master's or doctoral level degree from a regionally accredited University or College.

2. A total of 70 hours of attendance at workshop, scientific programs, and case consultations on hypnosis.

a. 12.5 hours of Basic level workshop training.

b. 12.5 hours of Intermediate level training.

c. 31 hours of Advanced training through workshops, academic coursework, or case consultation (academic coursework must be documented by official transcript).

d. 3-hour ethics workshop. Of note, the ethics modules included in SCEH's basic and intermediate hypnosis trainings satisfy this requirement.

e. Documentation of 11-hours of clinical and experimental hypnosis research training in a workshop or academic course (may include Institutional Review Board training). This requirement may be fulfilled by attendance at the SCEH Annual Scientific Program or a SCEH workshop on Clinical/Experimental Hypnosis Research or a combination of the two for a total of 11 hours of clinical/experimental hypnosis research training.

f. Attendance at one or more SCEH annual meetings or regional workshops in the three years prior to certification.

3. A signed agreement to abide by the SCEH Code of Ethics.

SCEH CARH requires renewal every three years and should include documentation verifying least 20 hours of SCEH approved continuing education in hypnosis and documentation of either teaching or conducting research on hypnosis.

SCEH Certification by Prior Experience (CPE)

Individuals who have an established career record of 10 or more years of clinical practice or academic/research applications of hypnosis may apply for Certification by Prior Experience (CPE). The requirements for SCEH CPE include:

1. A Curriculum Vitae narrating professional experience and training.

2. Evidence of 40 hours of CE activities in hypnosis in the previous five years.

3. Two letters by professional colleagues describing the applicant's past training and practice in hypnosis.

Once certified, individuals who have qualified for CPE will follow the same renewal process and fees as the other SCEH certifications.

CONCLUSION

This chapter highlights importance of standards of training in clinical hypnosis and certification programs. Requirements such as adequate certifications as well as minimum hours of individualized training/consultation are beneficial to professionals seeking training in clinical hypnosis as well as for the public to identify provides with recognized training. Professionals, patients, clients, third-party payers, managed care programs, hospitals, and academic institutions are able to effectively identify health care providers and academic professional/researchers that have completed a recognized curriculum in clinical hypnosis.

CHAPTER 21
REFLECTION QUESTIONS

1. Does certification ensure an individual's abilities are effective?

2. What are some of the differences in qualification regarding the *ASCH* and *SCEH* certification programs?

3. What are some limitations of certification in clinical hypnosis programs?

REFERENCES

Alter, D. (2016). Certification in Hypnosis and Specialty Boards. In G. R. Elkins (Ed.), *Handbook of medical and psychological hypnosis: Foundations, applications, and professional issues* (pp. 673-678). New York: NY, Springer Publishing Company.

American Society of Clinical Hypnosis. (n.d.) Retrieved January 15, 2022, from https://www.asch.net/aws/ASCH/pt/sp/certification-program

Elkins, G. R., & Hammond, D. C. (1998). Standards of training in clinical hypnosis: Preparing professionals for the 21st century. *American Journal of Clinical Hypnosis, 41*(1), 55-64.

Society for Clinical and Experimental Hypnosis. (n.d.). Retrieved January 15, 2022, from https://www.sceh.us/certification

ABOUT THE EDITOR

Gary Elkins, Ph.D., ABPP, ABPH is a Professor of Psychology and Neuroscience at Baylor University, and Director of the Mind-Body Medicine Research Laboratory, where he leads a team of doctoral and post-doctoral researchers focusing on hypnosis and mind-body interventions. Dr. Elkins is the Editor-in-Chief of the *International Journal of Clinical and Experimental Hypnosis*. He has over 100 publications in the areas of hypnosis and mind-body medicine, which includes the *Handbook of Medical and Psychological Hypnosis: Foundations, Applications, and Professional Issues*; and *Mindful Hypnotherapy: The Basics for Clinical Practice*. He has served on numerous NIH scientific review groups. In recognition of his research, he has received major awards: the Society of Behavioral Medicine (2012, Complementary and Integrative Medicine Investigator Research Award), and the American Board of Psychological Hypnosis (2008 Morton Prince Award for Professional Achievement to Psychological Hypnosis, and the 2022 Distinguished Contributions to Scientific Hypnosis from the American Psychological Association-Division 30 Society for Psychological Hypnosis. He is board certified by the American Board of Professional Psychology (ABPP) and the American Board of Psychological Hypnosis (ABPH). He is a Past-President of the Society for Clinical and Experimental Hypnosis; and the American Society of Clinical Hypnosis as well as co-author of the landmark publication, *Standards of Training in Clinical Hypnosis*. In addition to a tenured Professor of Psychology and Neuroscience at Baylor University, he is an Adjunct Professor at Texas A&M University College of Medicine, and a Medical Associate with Baylor Scott and White Hillcrest Medical Center. His research has been continually funded by the National Institutes of Health for over 20 years with funding exceeding $10 million for clinical hypnosis research. Dr. Elkins is an internationally recognized speaker on hypnosis on topics such as clinical hypnosis, mindful hypnotherapy, hypnosis research, smoking cessation, women's health and hypnosis, sleep, and posttraumatic growth. and is a consultant to the **Boulder Crest Foundation**. Dr. Elkins has two self-hypnosis apps from **Mindset Health**: *Evia* (self-hypnosis for hot flashes and sleep) and *Finito* (self-hypnosis app for smoking cessation) mindsethealth.com.

Made in the USA
Middletown, DE
02 December 2024

65869702R00289